Few push such ultimates. This compass, say,
Will help you cross the ridge in a straight line —
No matter how you twist among the trees…
— Ann Stanford

Pushing Ultimates:
Fundamentals of Authentic Self-Knowledge

Diagrams on page 326 are from *Mind Tools: The Five Levels of Mathematical Reality*, by Rudy Rucker, published by Houghton Mifflin, 1987;
Diagram and Shri Yantra on page 328 are from *The Tao of Symbols: How to Transcend the Limits of Our Symbolism*, by James N. Powell, published by Quill, 1982

ISBN-13: 978-0-9773733-9-0
ISBN-10: 0-9773733-9-8

Library of Congress Control Number: 2005909020

Manufactured in the United States of America
by Tri-State Litho
71-81 Tenbroeck Ave.
Kingston, NY 12401

Cover painting *"Primal Geometry"* by Lew Paz

PlumBell Publishing
P.O. Box 640
Eureka, CA 95502

PUSHING ULTIMATES

Fundamentals of
Authentic Self-knowledge

LEW PAZ

PlumBell Publishing

Contents

Preface

*I have been criticized for being a wayfarer, as though this made me
the less worthy. Let no one hold it against me if I defend myself
against said allegations. The journeys I have made up until now
have been very useful to me, because no man's master grows in his
own house, nor has anyone found his teacher behind his stove.*
— Paracelsus

Be not ignorant of any thing in a great matter or a small.
— Ecclesiasticus 5:15

With months of Thoreauvian solitude ahead of me and little
interaction with civilization over the distant mountain, I sit
at my table in the partially rebuilt loft of a huge barn, near
the large opening of an incomplete wall, thirty-five feet above a
rushing river frothing with melting batches of spring snow. I pause,
as echoes of varied journeys weave meaningful patterns in my mind.
Nearby is my frayed suitcase containing years of collected notes
written on whatever was available at the moment, matchbooks, nap-
kins, even pieces of torn cardboard. On a nearby table is a computer.
I shall use this avenue of knowledge unhesitantly, along with dozens
of essential books I have collected along the way. May this pen's calculated scritch and scratch, caught within the amorphous magnetism
of your perception, interlock our humanity in deeper currents of
awareness.

This book will attempt to condense the vast offerings of humanity's banquet of significant teachings to what the attainment of
substantial self-knowledge requires, without, I hope, becoming either overly simplistic or abstruse. Thus, I will take only what needs

to be taken from pertinent fields of study, leaving behind what is unnecessary to this aim. Hoping to illuminate the plight of individual awakening within the fog and turmoil of the human predicament, I begin like the Eskimo whittler of ivory who has no idea what his final creation will be, but just begins carving until the figure within reveals itself. Though I respect the way of the scholar, this will be more of a free flowing seeking out of truth, one subject connecting with another in a mosaic of thought. Look upon this reading as similar to strolling along a wending creek, where you come upon a small patch of wildflowers in deep shade. A bit further you find another patch in direct sunlight—same kind of flowers, yet because of difference in light and setting you discover something about them you would not have noticed of those in the shadows. Thus I will touch on a subject to a certain extent, and further on perhaps touch on it again from another angle. What may seem repetitive I hope will be understood as actually a matter of varying perspective.

The reader might take what I have written so far to imply this book shall reveal profound new insights into what our existential-spiritual situation is all about, and the individual's place in it all. Well, that depends on how far the reader has come on the quest for spiritual awareness when he or she picks this book up. Let's face it, despite volumes elucidating ways and means to bring about spiritual enlightenment, despite New Age popularization of yoga and multitudinous books espousing popular no-strain self-development teachings, only a small percent of those who find interest in the concept of in-depth self-knowledge will pursue it to a significant life changing degree. Though this writing may not present final answers to ultimate questions for everyone, perhaps it may at least illuminate what is sufficient for the needs of some, contributing to that certain alchemical formula suitable for their journey. It all depends on so many uniquely individual attributes that make a person's receptiveness coincide with the moment he/she opens this book: metabolism, mood, intelligence, attitude, openness, upbringing, education, bias, and more. But the essential ingredient for comprehension is the unquenchable desire to understand, to fully grasp everything you are capable of concerning who and what you are and your individual place within the immense cosmic surge of existence. After all, what other pursuit is there which holds such well rooted meaning for a human being than to "know thyself," fully, completely, whatever the cost?

As we begin our approach of the depths, please note that I consider the deepest knowledges within these pages to be mere glimpses into the core of things that give life meaning. Yet as C. S. Lewis wrote:

> *A glimpse is not a vision. But to a man on a mountain road by night, a glimpse of the next three feet of road may matter more than a vision of the horizon.*[1]

To conclude, my obligation to put pen to paper is clarified by the following three passages:

> *It is the duty of one who goes his own way to inform society of what he finds on his voyage of discovery, be it cooling water for the thirsty or the sandy wastes of unfruitful error. The one helps, the other warns. Not the criticism of individual contemporaries will decide the truth or falsity of his discoveries, but future generations.*[2]
> —C .G. Jung

> *Here we are together*
> *in this place like Noah's ark.*[3]
> —May Sarton

> *We are all in the same boat in a stormy sea,*
> *and owe each other a terrible loyalty.*[4]
> —G. K. Chesterton

Thus, dear reader, permit me voyage into the sanctuary of your mind.

1 – The Perennial Quest

It is important for psychological maturation (individuation)
that the Ego not hold the compass and give direction to a person's life.
It is important that the compass holder be this deeper Self.
— C. Michael Smith

According to Western civilization's complex, sometimes arbitrary, sometimes precise history of astronomical and astrological calculations, this 21st century falls within the threshold of the Aquarian Aeon, an age which confronts us with challenges and complexities demanding a consciousness committed to and prepared for transcendent truths now dawning on the spiritual horizon. Though the broadest segments of the emerging "New Age" movement have not manifested the authenticity of depth their prophets have proclaimed, a certain foundational cultural shift is certainly occurring with the rise of psychological and spiritual systems of self-growth. And yet, though such widespread activity relating to inner development can help dissipate the spiritual cancer of materialism, the Aquarian cycle requires so much more, demanding a commitment from concerned individuals to challenge their existence by stepping forward to seek a more daring and spiritually fruitful life, rather than comforting themselves with ideas easily gleaned from varied religious belief systems, with no attempt at experiential validation.

Yes, traditionally embedded religious and philosophical belief systems help people get through life with less anxiety, stress, uncertainty, giving them a sense of guidance and hope—so, what's wrong with that? What's wrong is most of these belief systems maintain a barrier of bias constructed to shun any truth that may demand essential changes. Once such a bias becomes operational it taints and distorts all meaningful teachings. Thus all too often, the appearance of coping, of a lessening of stress, is a false mask built of self-deception. The individual who will be able to actually cope with the cultural complexities of this millennium, to the extent of being free of belief systems based on half-truths, falsehoods, and acculturated conventions, must be flexible, adaptable, and above all intrepid in the face of bewilderment which greater truths in the quest for self-knowledge can bring about. The most important task a person can undertake during the course of this third millennium A.D., is to strive to be aware <u>as</u> <u>far</u> <u>as</u> <u>possible</u> of the full truth concerning our actual existential/spiritual situation. This is a fundamental tenet of the emerging Aquarian paradigm, and though it covers many different approaches, there is an underlying affinity which basically has to do with an individual's endeavor to seek his/her own unique truth as a human being within the awesome surge of evolution. As Sartre put it, speaking for every human: *"Truth is my possibility awaiting me, and I am the being through which the truth will come from within into the world."*[1]

At birth, each of us enters upon an ever expanding endlessly branching labyrinth of chance and possibility. The choices we make will create the quality of meaning of our entire existence. Authentic commitment to this quest calls for a spontaneously adaptable and open mind ready to discard any generally accepted religious or political belief, or spiritual fad, if newly attained knowledge and experience verifies it to fall short of a more encompassing truth. To live otherwise, to avoid seeing reality as clearly as possible for what it is, physically, psychologically, and spiritually, is to live ensconced in an all too human ambit of unrecognized self-deceit.

The concepts of self-knowledge and transcendence have become much reiterated clichés, so let me clarify what "authentic self-knowledge" means within the pages of this book. The word authentic is defined in Webster's dictionary as: *"valid,"* *"true in substance."* Thus, to render valid one's life as true in substance is what existential-spiritual authentication is all about. This is no easy task, since the majority of human beings, whether they be ultra-rich or living in dire poverty, atheist or staunchly religious, are ensconced in an accumulation of distorted opinions and acculturated beliefs, and thus base their lives upon false premises from which very few can ever free themselves. Sadly, the way the world is, by the time humans become adults, few are mentally or socially in a position to commit themselves to the endeavor of awakening. In fact the majority are not even dimly aware of the need for such an undertaking. Though a growing segment of the population is becoming involved to various degrees in New Age pursuits of spiritual growth, that segment still entails only a small percentage of the entire population—and within that segment itself, those involved to a degree which ignites authentic self-knowledge comprise an even smaller percentage.

From the works of numerous scholars of varied fields, it is clear that a vast proportion of the population is alienated from authentic self-awareness.[2] This alienation has been described as a psychological/spiritual stultification of the evolution of consciousness, brought about by mass subservience toward external socially oriented goals, which disregard knowledge of human spiritual essence. As the great Hindu sage Sri Aurobindo maintained, authentic knowledge begins when we probe beyond appearances, beyond ossified traditional belief systems and sterile scientism. The quality of knowledge this book is concerned with is, as the scholar Henri Corbin wrote, *"knowledge that changes and transforms the knowing subject."* Do the spiritual endeavors encompassed within the New Age movement possess such quality of knowledge? To a certain degree, yes. Actually, what is called the New Age movement is not really new. Such popularized fervency concerning spiritual growth, entailing mysticism, religious quackery, occult and paranormal explorations, creating a bewildering brew of both madness and valid pursuit of truth, from dredged up superstitions to genuine awakening, has been periodically rampant from as far back as the Hellenistic period of Greece, recurring predominantly within the first decade of every new century throughout Western civilization. Anyone appraising the New Age movement must recognize it as a manifestation of ancient longings, repressed irrational tendencies, and the transformation of limited religious concepts.

Even though he was a materialist and insufficiently aware of the deeper truths beneath the surface of things, Carl Sagan was a very insightful fellow and in touch with the social current during his last years, when he wrote,

I worry that, especially as the Millennium edges nearer, pseudo-science and superstition will seem year by year more tempting, the siren song of unreason more sonorous and attractive... When we agonize about our diminished cosmic place and purpose, and when fanaticism is bubbling up around us, it is then that habits of thought familiar from ages past reach for the controls.[3]

Well, the Millennium has come about, and what we call the New Age Movement has a certain stench of such unreason within its ambit of activity. The Heaven's Gate suicide incident was only a glimpse into extreme elements of distorted paranormal beliefs and mystical fanaticism at large across the globe. Myriad traveling fairs crisscross America, offering their patrons superficial tarot and astrology readings, phony aura photography, mystical crystals and glass pyramids for healing and gaining psychic power. To the person setting forth into the cosmic-terrestrial obstacle course in pursuit of self-knowledge, the ability to separate truth from falsehood within the array of such manifestations is vital.

A parallel stream of unreason can be seen in the resurgence of a militant Christian fundamentalism, which distorts the teachings of the Prince of Peace to condone warlike tendencies. Such "Crusader" mentality is spread through religious/political organizations by way of the spoutings of dozens of megalomaniac televangelists who fill auditoriums with thousands—some so deranged they have claimed God cast Hurricane Katrina upon New Orleans because there were too many abortion clinics! Such events are definite indicators of threshold-of-the-millennium turmoil within the traditional religious ambit. Just as the sophomoric simplification of the concepts of karma and reincarnation within the New Age milieu distorts essential spiritual truths of the East, an unbalanced Christian fundamentalism subject to political manipulation leads millions of faithful astray from the very essence of what the authentic mytho-spiritual truth of Christ means to the soul's journey.

There are of course prominent persons of both New Age and traditional religious persuasion whose lectures and writings give meaningful guidance to many who are in need, but all too often such popular figures see themselves as being chosen by higher powers, angels, spirits, even God, to bring faith and healing to the multitudes. The syndrome of psychological inflation these authors and gurus often succumb to reveals a lack of authentic self-knowledge, which can be remedied only by cultivating a harsh self-criticism, requiring introspective alertness to any delusional self-imagery that enhances the ego. As the great Christian-Gnostic sage C. G. Jung put it,

*It is better indeed to discover behind one's lofty ideals, narrow fanatical convictions, all the more cherished for that, and behind one's heroic pretensions nothing but crude egotism, infantile greed and complacency. This calls for a process of deep self-examination and self-disgust, painful, yet an unavoidable stage.*4

There is a widespread assumption within the New Age movement that equates the quest for self-knowledge with the Buddhist search for enlightenment. But this so-called "search for enlightenment" has had a tendency to bring about the cultivation of an external image of spiritual serenity rather than authentic in-depth development, inducing egoic games in those supposedly striving to transcend the ego. We need only read insightful biographies by ex-followers of famous gurus, sorcerers, Zen masters, in addition to works of investigative journalism concerning ashrams, cults, etc., to reveal the histrionics of lies and back-biting during struggles for power and control surrounding various New Age figures of East and West. Within various movements, devotees naively kowtow to pseudo gurus while pursuing the acquisition of status which comes with being involved in inner-circle activities. Such "prestige climbing" is far more prevalent than genuine pursuit of spiritual growth. This syndrome is not confined to ashrams and communes, but occurs within all groups where egoic impulses and the delusion of "enlightenment" overcome authentic spirituality. Spiritual leaders among us imbued with true inner integrity are the exception. As Phillip Wheelwright put it, *"There is no more ironic illusion than to suppose that one has escaped from illusion."*5 Authors of dozens of books have attempted to expose the misguidance the seeker may become entangled with along this precarious way, but they are usually of the atheistic Skeptical Inquirer sort, very helpful at spotting the phonies but lacking in the psychological/spiritual awareness such a task requires.

The inability to see hubris behind the façade of certain "higher consciousness" personalities is a major failing of the New Age human potential movement, equal to the inability of many Christians to see the anti-Christ spirit in the war mongering teachings of some of their charismatic leaders. When people abandon necessary skepticism and astute reasoning, they become susceptible to any teachings persuading them they are awakening. This creates a movement of self-deceit, not self-knowledge. *"Gnothi se auton"= "Know thyself,"* originally inscribed on Apollo's Oracle of Delphi Temple, was often quoted by Socrates, but even more significant was his exclamation concerning what this knowing requires: *"Give attention to the soul."*₆ Thus, when we speak of authentic self-knowledge, we imply a knowledge of high expansive quality. The Sufi mystic Hakim Sanâi said, *"Knowledge that does not take you beyond yourself is worse than ignorance."* The "thyself" Socrates spoke of is similar to what Jung meant when he spoke of the Self, which is not to be confused with the persona/ego sphere of "me, myself, and I." The Self implied in these pages is the deeper essence dimension of our being.

True self-knowledge has certain affinities with what is known in the history of religious ideas as "gnosis" — a belief system somewhat obscure, which goes back to ancient Egyptian teachings with branchings into Hellenistic Rome. Though the term has been tainted by various religious interpretations, gnosis essentially means that amid the terrifying radiance of existence one seeks attainment of a unique awareness of spiritual essence, which renders the seeker's existence authentic in substance. Such awareness entails a harmonious merging of significant knowledge of the depths of consciousness with worldly experience. This merging brings about an extensive comprehension of the human predicament encompassing both good and evil.

The ancient Roman sage Cicero considered the quest for substantial self-knowledge to be the most difficult task a person could undertake. Where does one begin? There is no definite starting place or step to take. It is different for each individual. Some who are reading these words perhaps began some time ago, others may have just become aware of a desire to learn, to explore, to know more, in order to find the deepest, most meaningful truths to live by. After delving awhile in this direction, you are apt to come across various methods of expanding your awareness through the knowledge of alchemy, including tales and other expositions of the medieval alchemist, who was thought on the popular level to be involved with trying to turn base metals into gold. More than likely there were those of materialistic inclination who spent their lives in this pursuit. But the genuine inner oriented alchemist was actually an investigator of nature's bounty, studying, mixing, cooking, and on certain occasions ingesting various ingredients of herbs, fungi, plants, to discover deeper insight into his or her very soul, using occult and magical symbols as a code to record meaningful discoveries. It could be said the true alchemist of medieval Western civilization was an intriguing fusion of witch, shaman, philosopher, scientist, magician, with certain attributes of the monk.

From what is known, it seems alchemy, like many significant arts, crafts, and scientific endeavors, cannot be pinpointed as to place of origin. Also, a lot depends on how one defines alchemy. Some write of certain ancient rites and rituals of transformation within megalithic Celtic culture dating 3200 BC, some of ancient Egypt, involving experiments with the mummification process. In China alchemical writings dating to the eighth century BC have been found. Archaic portions of the Vedas touch on the subject of alchemy. The Greek God Hermes presided over alchemical activity. In fact, in the Odyssey, Hermes teaches Odysseus about the magic use of a plant called *"mōly,"* which clearly demonstrates the Greeks were aware of the alchemical use of plants and herbs. But there were many goddesses predating Hermes who were in some way related to alchemical activities. For thousands of years prior to the first Egyptian dynasty, within matriarchal cultures the cooking fire was a sacred central place in the tribal setting. Certainly the tribal priestess-shamaness (alchemist) with her cauldron of spiritually nourishing ingredients came forth from such a configuration of primal cultural activity.

In a medieval manuscript by the alchemist Basil Valentine, there is an illustration which shows three serpents, each with a heart shaped tail, spinning in a counter-clockwise spiral. The three serpents in alchemy represent the triumvirate of salt, sulfur and mercury. Salt symbolizes the solid physical world of the body, sulfur symbolizes transformation to a more subtle spirit or intellect, and mercury symbolizes the volatility or changefulness within the soul.

In his book, *The Cosmic Serpent,*₇ Jeremy Narby clarifies how the serpent as transcendent symbol of divine potential is found in cultures over the entire earth. Serpents and spirals carved or painted at ancient ceremonial sites are universal mytho-religious symbols representing the potential revelation of hidden knowledge. The Mahabharata clarifies that the spiral symbolizes the swirling maelstrom of which all creation partakes. Consider the sea horse's spiral curve of a tail, or the human embryo in its earliest stages, the curl of mollusk shells, a swirling galaxy of a billion burning suns, an oceanic whirlpool, the churn of a tornado, the twist and twine of climbing vines, the horns of a great ram, or the double helix dance of DNA. Various fields of research clarify the recurring symbol of the serpent is often found curling around an ancient object in a spiraling movement. With the medical caduceus, as with the sacred staffs of ancient high priests, two serpents are entwined, representing the play of dualities. Certain scholars have elucidated how the Aztec god Quetzalcoatl can be related to twin winged serpents. Ancient pre-patriarchal Egypt worshipped Ua Zit, the winged cobra goddess, who was the creator of all life. Winged serpents and dragons are found in alchemical text and ancient hieroglyphic writings concerning sacred rituals. Wings are primal symbols for transcendence, and the serpentine spiral is the esoteric symbol of hierarchical degrees of consciousness.

Patriarchal Judaic mythology distorted the serpentine symbol to represent only the negative aspect of "forbidden" knowledge. An alchemical-Gnostic interpretation of the serpent in the Garden of Eden would be to perceive the serpent as representing Kundalini, the awakening of consciousness, with Adam eating the apple as the first use of nature's bounty in a shamanistic act to ignite self-knowledge, awakening from the long instinctual sleep within the womb of the Great Mother. In this rendition, Eve does not spring from Adam's rib, but from his soul or anima, spurring on his inborn impulse to probe the farthest limits of possibilities.[8] The seeker must learn to take from established religions what is worthy and useful, leaving behind that which can become an unnecessary weight and divergence from genuine inner truths. To do this effectively, one must be acutely discerning, a requirement that will be stressed many times during the course of this book.

If the serpent was such a revered symbol during millennia of matriarchal domination, how and why was the fruit of awakening turned so completely upside down by ancient Judaic authorities into a baneful forbidden offering from a deceitful malefactor? The answer is complex, and we shall delve into it more thoroughly later on. Let me just say here that Judaism was significantly influenced by the mytho-religious imagery of ancient Egypt, circa 1300 BC, where the sun god RA had to fight the serpent of darkness, Apep, in order for the day to arise from the night. Such powerful Egyptian mytho-religious imagery, merging in the Hebrew psyche with streams of Iranian dualism, strongly influenced patriarchal authorities to convert what were harmonized chthonic forces into opposing powers, suitable for evolving Judaic concepts. Though the ancient patriarchs of Judaic tradition created the myth of forbidden knowledge as an extension of past oral legends rooted in the well-founded fear of evil actually lurking within the shadows of greater knowledge, they manipulated these legends to instill unquestioning obedience.

An image often emerging when we think of the alchemist, is a figure high up in some secluded castle tower, or well built cottage in the wilderness, sprinkling various substances into a simmering retort. I personally am fond of the image of an intensely involved Merlin, a magician figure in close association with the archetype of the "wise old man," stirring his simmering brew. This is similar to the medieval witch stirring the intriguing ingredients of her huge cauldron, the strange brew swirling a vortical hypnotic pattern. Actually, the witch was an alchemist. In fact, there were women who were highly respected alchemists, such as the priestess whose ceremonial name was "Isis," and another who went by the name "Cleopatra," who wrote alchemical formulas such as found in the text of her work *The Chrysopoeia*. They used code names to prevent being persecuted. During those medieval centuries, individual involvement in the pursuit of deep self-knowledge would arouse the suspicion of both superstitious neighbors and church authorities, whose power was unrestrained. The Inquisition was capable of burning at the stake anyone accused of dabbling in witchcraft and magic, and the fear produced by this supposedly God sanctioned organization caused certain works of alchemy to be cloaked to mimic involvement with metallurgy and chemistry.

Alchemy should never be looked upon as just an interesting phenomenon of medieval superstition. Through the work of Jung, we now recognize that for the Westernized psyche there is a soteriological element to alchemy, which merges with an individual's endeavor of spiritual-psychological transformation. This process was known to alchemists as the *mysterium magnum* = The Work. There are also significant relationships of alchemical transformation with the quest for the Holy Grail, as well as the Philosopher's Stone. It is quite clear the mind can be perceived as the simmering retort, with the ancient alchemist projecting his/her inner intensity into its fiery activity, most likely igniting visions and carefully deciphered hallucinations in the process, perhaps with the occasional help of ingesting some of the brew, which might have contained psychedelic plants or fungi—thus mind as retort.

Both philosophical idealism and modern science hold that human perception is basically mental—all external phenomena are essentially productions of your mind. While it is certainly true what you see is an emergent image of electro-chemical information derived from the brain's complex process of interpreting light photons, this need not be confined to a physicalist perspective = all and everything is an epiphenomenon of physical processes. Despite claims of obsessively confident materialists based on empirical research extensively revealing the intricate instrumentality of the brain/perception process, the fundamental nature of conscious imagery remains an enigma. But it is quite clear, as the alchemist knew in his own way, and as shamans and yogis know in their unique ways, the electrochemistry of the brain-consciousness process can be a conduit for the self-cultivated expansion of human awareness. Such is how the alchemical process of self-exploration begins, gradually refining our ingredients as we move from the crude cauldron of conventional consciousness, to the stage involving the retort of individuation, to the crucible of spiritual awakening. Then, as the primal energies of the ego begin to refine and cohere into a specific configuration tailored to the individual involved, the process flows into the alembic of meditative disciplines for final distillation. Such an undertaking is hardly a common activity. In the pages of an ancient alchemical text are the words, "*Aurum nostrum non est aurum vulgi*" – "*Our gold is not the common gold.*"9

Though many alchemists of stature left no writings verifying their magical endeavors, there have been individuals of historical significance whose works have come down to us in tangible form. In the first century BC, the multi-talented Bolos of Mendes was an expert concerning precious stones and fine cloth, plus ancient Egyptian methods of coloring metals, which were exoteric activities creatively related to his esoteric alchemical delvings. He wrote copiously on many subjects, and is looked upon by some as the father of modern physics. There was Maria the Jewess, circa first to third century AD, who is regarded as a significant figure in alchemical lore, and the invention of certain alembic methods of the alchemical process are attributed to her. Her influence may have been known to the Essene community of spiritual seekers of which Jesus may have been a member. Such are the intriguing facts and speculations concerning the history of alchemy. And, of course, there is the famous Paracelsus (1493-1541), who experimented with chemical compounds, plants, herbs and fungi, attempting to discover healing medicines and, quite possibly, brews to explore consciousness. Paracelsus was in pursuit of the Philosopher's Stone, a Medieval European symbol for the experience of ultimate wisdom. From a Jungian approach this stone represents the true inner self, the center and totality of the psyche.

The colorful turbulent history and vast prehistory of the human race, is itself a story of a greater terrestrial alchemy, of earth as cauldron for the evolving of human spiritual consciousness. This has nothing to do with the reductive New Age idea of "Earth as spiritual school," with conscious evolution following a divinely ordained linear curriculum for everyone on the planet. As we shall make clear, any concept of a preordained cosmically planned program set forth by a divine being, is but another delusional belief having no affinity with the actual bewildering harsh and wild novelty, the astonishing continual genesis, of both terrestrial and spiritual evolution. Of course, the discarding of the delusion of a divinely oriented plan does not rule out the possible intervention of divine guidance — especially in relationship to the courageous cultivation of individual endeavors committed to spiritual awakening, which alchemical exploration entails.

Over the last two millennia, those rare persons of Western civilization involved in the quest to discover their essential truth within the mystery of things, have usually taken one of two basic approaches. The first is that of the sorcerer, the witch, the shaman, the magician, the alchemist, all figures found in the history of every culture, both primitive and civilized, who were delvers into alternate dimensions of consciousness, daring the realms of the irrational, the risk of madness, by use of plant and fungi, ritual, chant, magic formula, and, except for the shaman and the medicine-man, were for the most part outside the pale of their social setting. The other approach is that of the sage, the philosopher, the priest, the theologian — important members of their socio-political setting who ap-

proached the unknown areas of the mind through rational speculation, intuition, occasional mystical insight, and the acquisition of
learned knowledge. The person of the 21st century genuinely involved in the quest for truth must be capable of merging the above
two approaches, refining the techniques of the first group and adding a Dionysian element of daring to the second, with the whole
process assisted by a third significant ingredient—yoga and meditation disciplines from the East. This brew of disciplines is what the
alchemy of awakening to one's true spiritual essence requires.

A crucial aspect of the holistic alchemical endeavor to explore
the deeper realms of being, is what is known in the yoga practices of
Hinduism and Buddhism as "jnana" = the vanquishing of "avidya,"
or ignorance of both oneself and the world. Though in ancient India
there were traditional ways and means to follow, such vanquishing
of ignorance within modern society, which is hardly accomplished
by formal education, occurs according to the unique circumstances
of individual challenges inspiring self-knowledge. Such an endeavor
involves striving to discover the most comprehensive and reliable
account of the "why and wherefore" of human existence. This demands eclectic discernment of the quality of sources from which any
significant knowledge is gleaned, and thorough Socratic weighing
and measuring of such knowledge against all worthy opposing criticism, keeping only that which can withstand and successfully
counter such criticism. Ironically, this entails knowing where Socratic methodology fails.

An important requirement of such comprehensive alchemy is
to learn exactly what ingredients are needed for the seeker's individual psychological and spiritual brew, with which he/she can
work to awaken to truth and cultivate a greater *"radius of comprehension."* "Radius of comprehension" is a term I respectfully adapt from
the work of Gina Cerminara,[10] which has incisive affinities to E. F.
Schumacher idea of *"adequatio,"*[11] and what the philosopher Martin
Heidegger refers to as *"ableness to stand in the truth."* "Radius of comprehension" extends outward and inward from a person's ego-center
to various degrees, depending on the extent of their self-knowledge
and knowledge of the world. The spiritual quality and psychological
stability of the person attaining a more expansive "radius of comprehension" of existence depends on the fidelity of their commitment to truth, to the quest. Kenneth T. Gallagher speaks of *"fidelity*

toward presence"[12] as free-flowing, flexible commitment to consistent opening toward the significant unknown.

What we will essentially be dealing with in this book definitely has the potential of extending the reader's spiritual radius of comprehension. That implies not only scope of knowledge but priority of what an individual strives to comprehend. It is far more important to substantially comprehend that which ignites spiritual awakening than to have expertise in any other subject you can think of, from auto mechanics to politics, animal husbandry to economics. Pursuing a degree in any field of endeavor has no detrimental effect on a person's inner potential as long as spiritual knowledge has priority. But substantial comprehension of significant subject matter is mandatory to the seeker of truth.

It is here I feel the need to pause in concern for any reader with an overwrought religious sensitivity who is beginning to fear he/she may be treading into realms perhaps leading to unsavory occult experimentations. Let me set your mind at ease. If this work had been studied by Dr. Jekyll, he would never have fallen into the clutches of Mr. Hyde, although he would surely have come to know that demonic aspect of himself quite well. Dr. Jekyll, lacking the balanced centering of yogic discipline and shamanic preparation, yet foolishly delving into the primal aspects of his inner self, triggered a schizophrenic possession and was helpless before the unhindered power of his lower impulses.

There is no forbidden knowledge, nothing is taboo in the pursuit of authentic existence — there is only misuse of knowledge. Esoteric spiritual knowledge has never been hidden and is not related to what is popularly conceived as occult knowledge. Esoteric knowledge just happens to lie beyond the normal range of intelligence, and differs from exoteric knowledge in that what is revealed depends on the quality of spiritual development of the person who comes upon it. Traditional Christian religion interprets the Bible in an exoteric pseudo-spiritual way as factual historical narrative, whereas a spiritually awakened person is able to distinguish between the wheat of the esoteric message and the chaff of literalism.

And so, to approach the mastering of psychological-spiritual-alchemical skills, the first element to be dealt with should be what is not only the most intimate and significant aspect of our entire existence, but also that which most people mistakenly believe they already know thoroughly. What would that be? Your very own mind.

Most people are quite confident they know their own mind as well as they know their own personality, for their everyday thoughts, dreams, hopes, desires, likes, dislikes, their entire subjective worldview, is what they take to be "mind." But this is actually only the ego sphere of embodied mind. There is vastly more. You are much more than you believe yourself to be. Yet the ego sphere of consciousness is the potential cauldron in which the brew of self-knowledge must begin to roil and boil, producing the transcendent steam of higher consciousness. The opening lines of the Buddha's Dhammapada state, *"Our life is shaped by our mind. We become what we think."*[13]

2 – Psychological Perspectives

Men must endure their going hence
even as their coming hither.
Ripeness is all.
--Shakespeare
King Lear

Every culture on earth has its stream of spiritual and esoteric teachings from which anyone can eclectically select a system of physical and mental ways and means to spur self-discovery. One of the most significant is yoga. There are numerous schools of yoga, and enough books explaining them to fill a bus, so I will highlight only essentials. The most popular in the West over the past thirty years is called Hatha yoga, which is meant to prepare the physiological system to activate intense psychic energies. Of course, such energies may never be tapped. Even after decades of Hatha yoga, which is all too often concentrated on physical fitness, occasionally involving gymnastic contortionism, genuine inner growth may not occur. Since it is easy to reap physical and egoic vitality with no real commitment to pursuing the higher forms of yoga, most practitioners are satisfied at this basic level. A few merge Hatha with other forms, such as Jana yoga, which is what you are involved in right now—the endeavor to learn and gain through reading and research, as much knowledge as possible concerning the vast complexities of psychic-spiritual life as a whole, including higher mystic levels of consciousness. Karma yoga focuses on everyday actions, making sure you do everything with as much attention and awareness, compassion and truthfulness, as possible. Bhakti yoga consists of practices that directly express your yearning for and devotion to higher spiritual development and your idea of "God." Raja yoga involves ever deeper meditation. Authentic expansion of conscious-

24

ness requires the harmonizing of all the above forms of yoga into an integral life discipline. The consistent sincerely committed activation of such discipline leads to a kind of awakening—for the ordinary individual's everyday ego consciousness is a level of sleep when compared to activated consciousness.

Awakening requires a process of individuation entailing genuine introspection which exposes a person's negativities and opens his/her inner being to the potential of spiritual growth. Such "self-centered" venturing which breaks the ties of conformism is always condescended to by the collective, which fears genuine individuality—thus defensive jokes about foolish yogis contemplating their navels. But the seeker learns to ignore the "sour grapes" scorn of the mass-minded person. The Sufi mystic Ibn al-Farid stated, *"I was a prophet sent to myself from Myself, and it is myself, by my own signs, who was guided to Myself."* Al-Farid's statement seems to be narcissistic self-absorbed babble to those who cannot distinguish between the mystical intuitive quality of listening to a deeper inner guidance and the egoic hype of the self-achiever's external success. For the "myself" of the ego/persona to awaken to the "Myself" of greater Essence-Being, has nothing to do with self-glorified displays of personality flamboyance, fame, prestige. In fact, getting rid of the craving for such recognition is part of the process of authentic individuation. Of course, renunciation of egotistic desires and impulses does not mean one need become an ascetic cut off from all involvement with the world. If spiritual growth maintains priority, a person can pursue a meaningful career with a sense of integrity and inner strength resistant to all the side-tracking temptations. This has little to do with activating the "power of positive thinking" formula, which is based on a socialized orientation. Like most worthwhile systems which strive for development of psychic totality, genuine individuation is truly challenging, demanding the courage to look clearly at your shortcomings, self-deceits, vanities, sometimes even to the point of enduring the pain of psychological-spiritual crisis. But becoming sincerely committed to the pursuit of self-knowledge creates the strength you will need to endure and overcome whatever crisis might occur.

Patanjali, thought to have lived somewhere between 100 BC to 200 AD, is looked upon as the most renowned expositor of yoga. In his ancient writings, which organized a thousand years of yogic teaching, the emphasis is on disciplines such as meditation and pranayama (breathing), and he hardly mentions the need for an extensive system of physical development. Gradually, over the centuries, more movements (asanas) were added so that those committed to months of deep unmoving meditation could remain physically flexible, thus keeping inner vital energies flowing evenly throughout the body. Somewhere around 1900, due to over a century of English colonization of India, certain aspects of Western gymnastics merged with the teaching of asanas. Now we have Americanized New Age "hot yoga" videos to keep the body fit and beautiful, pep up the ego-mind, create an image of awakening and forget about deeper elements of self-discovery. This can be seen in yoga magazines catering to the affluent, containing ads for ashrams as opulent and exclusive as any jet set resort, as well as ads for the most "in look" attire to wear while performing yoga asanas. There have been Oprah episodes about yoga which were like Tupperware parties, lots of fun, but with no idea why Siddhartha became a wandering ascetic or Bodhidharma spent nine years in a cave. Fashionable Westernized forms of yoga distort essential elements of Eastern teachings. Anyone with substantial potential to use yoga as a means for spiritual development would know that being "yoga chic" is not only unnecessary but detrimental to true individuation.

For the beginning seeker, working one's way through the phonies, the naïve, and the mimics of wisdom within the New Age movement, is an obstacle course in a class by itself. In his work, *Jung and the New Age*, David Tacey writes,

> *The New Age basically awards "spiritual blessing" to trends and attitudes that are already existent in Western culture: consumerism, hedonism, materialism, and narcissism. The New Age does not offer a critique of society, but simply mythologises and mystifies the things that already preoccupy us.*[1]

Hatha yoga does not require any belief, religious or otherwise, and the powers it may bring can be used strictly to enhance egoic pursuits. Of the millions who practice yoga, only a rare few probe the deeper realms of consciousness such disciplines prepare them for. Popularization of anything to do with human development is more of a sign of dilution and dispersion of intensity than true cultural integration.

The practice of higher order yoga for the sake of individuation opens one to the eternal within. The level of spiritual awakening flows on a gradient, with the quality of transcendence depending upon the breadth and scope of self-knowledge. Cultivation of one's spiritual potential transforms coarser psychic energies to finer, which then resonate "upward," degree by refined degree, within the spectrum of consciousness. In esoteric teachings of Buddhism, Hinduism, Islam, this metaphoric "vertical" progression moves by way of Kundalini energies traversing the serpentine staff of the chakras. Chakras are energy spheres located along the spinal column, formulating at the base and passing through the center of the esoteric cross of the heart chakra and upward toward the crown chakra of spiritual awakening. An eclectic blend of the forms of yoga mentioned earlier can refine chakra energies and induce this upward flow, stimulating one's potential to awaken. A strenuous physical regimen is unnecessary. Zen monks practice zazen and never partake of contortionist yoga movements. About twenty basic yoga asanas will keep the spine pliant enough for chakra energy flow. These, harmonized with quality dieting, will keep one in sufficient physical condition. The highest aim of yoga, as well as zazen, has always been to completely still the egoic mind so that one's inner essence opens to the silence of the infinite and eternal.

In the realm of esoteric yoga there are higher demands to which the ego must be willing to give way. It is not that the ego is to be annihilated, because a strong confidence and self esteem is necessary to undertake the extensive mental disciplines authentic self-knowledge requires. But the ego must grasp its place as a tiny fragment of a greater Self. One method of realizing this is to find an isolated place during a magnificent star-strewn night, lie spread eagle on your back, gaze up at the brilliant stars and look for the tiniest sparkle of a star you can detect. When satisfied you have found the most distant star observable, hold it in sight and contemplate the fact that way out there, in the farthest depths of space, that tiny sparkle is a blazing sun, and from that far out in space our own sun would be no more than a tiny twinkle, and, if you went farther and farther, the twinkle of our sun would fade into the immense all-engulfing darkness, to vanish like a subatomic particle, our entire solar system as insignificant as a grain of sand on an immense beach. From the cosmic perspective you are a less than microscopic creature among six billion others scrambling their way across the earth, all finding various ways to deny their actual situation, blessed and cursed by the random quirk of forces, powers, energies, which all merge in the brief bewildering flash of ego conscious existence. And the ego's relationship to the "inner cosmic" dimensions of our unconscious mind is no less bewildering — yet, if approached rightly, it can be a salvational venture.

The wily Greek-Armenian sage Georges Gurdjieff said, "*As a slave longs for freedom, the seeker must long for awakening.*" Undeniably, authentic awakening can be attained. Just as the ancient alchemists sprinkled herbs and plants and other substances into their retorts, we can add various knowledges such as yoga discipline, shamanic exploration, and Western processes of psychological development, to the retort of our mind, creating a brew capable of unfolding our inner potentials. And, as one of the great books of India, the Rig Veda, clarifies, in some numinous enigmatic way, which has been known esoterically for centuries, one individual's solitary struggle to awaken contributes to the awakening of others. A spiritual seeker's stance, though at times seemingly alienated from society, (as Bodhidharma in his cave), may eventually resonate throughout the social ambit. Such spiritual resonance can permeate mass consciousness, at times purely on a psychic wavelength, manifesting as an idea ripe for the zeitgeist. This interactive effect between the "I" of the individual seeker and the "Thou" of the collective is critical for human cultural existence.

If humanity's potential to awaken spiritually is left uncultivated, and siphoned off by the collective for only external expansion through political-social orientation and technological advancement, it can become the unconscious instrument of our destruction. Humanity now stands at a critical juncture. The first decades of this millennium promise to be the most dire and decisive era ever known to humanity. With the chemical, biological, and nuclear weapons now available, and the capitalistic pursuit of profit given priority over environment across the globe, any halfway intelligent person should know such a warning is based on more than mere opinion. The dire straights we are moving toward on the level of terrestrial existence is a manifestation of humanity's spiritual stultification, mired in obsolete religious and political systems of belief. If you consider such admonition to be but hot air rhetoric, remember, Cassandra's prophecies of doom were true, but the multitudes would not believe her. Either we remain enwrapped in acculturated patterns such as arrogant ethnocentrism, reductive religious anthropomorphism, patriotism that creates nationalistic selfishness, pernicious globalization, and thus through these combined failings destroy civilization, or a sufficient number of us will "turn, turn, turn," drinking deep of the Perian Spring of knowledge, making full commitment to live and act according to the broadest scope of understanding possible for humans to achieve.

To understand is to reveal. To reveal, our situation must be approached in a way that may occasionally seem condescendingly judgmental. Judgment of others concerning the human predicament is always a morally precarious undertaking, requiring clear psychological perception and well honed experience of the world at large. When it comes to the quest for spiritual awareness, only the very discerning eye can separate shallowness from depth, superficial image from authenticity. In ancient text going back some three thousand years, words that can be found in various religious teachings across the earth, state, "*Do not judge unless you are fully prepared to be judged.*" I believe that's fair. Thus when I speak of the hypnotized masses, the common mentality of the majority, the blind collective, the sleeping multitudes, which encompass every class, king and peasant, rich and poor, liberal and conservative, most of whom have little if any authentic self-knowledge in which genuine awakening can take root, I do not do so with condescending scorn or overwhelming disgust. As Brecht said, "*My fellow men have a foul smell in their sweat, but then again, so do I.*"

There are sparks of truth and compassionate consciousness flickering with various degrees of intensity within every individual on earth, and a culture must be brought about willing and able to amplify and intensify those sparks, igniting a fire in the collective soul of humanity. Do such hopeful intentions concerning human culture seem but romantic utopianism? I can understand such a response. Nevertheless, what is possible as to endeavors necessary for the spiritual and social enhancement of human existence should not be casually shrugged off. I know of other things I would prefer to be doing than spending the next year or so like a monkish scribe laying out things I believe of import for my fellow earthlings. But each of us having the ability to contribute to the spiritual-social enhancement of culture must do what we can.

I do not expect this work will overly disturb the mesmerized majority within a nation like the United States. Social mesmerization is a numbing of the potential to attain and comprehend significant knowledge. Such mass numbness is a notorious American character-istic, brought about in a variety of ways—not only mass entertain-ment and consumerism catering to the ego's infantile search for con-stant gratification, but alcohol and drug dependency. There are over 100,000 deaths every year due to alcoholism, and those account for only a small percent who habitually drink to alleviate stress, worry, despair, anguish. And we are all aware of the abuse of prescription drugs oversweeping the nation, not to mention street drugs such as heroin and cocaine. But the supreme addiction an overwhelming majority of the population succumbs to in order to alleviate stress and escape any deeper reflections concerning human existence, is the hypnotic opiate of consumerism. Americans not only cram their homes with unnecessary possessions, but have to rent storage facili-ties to hold all the excess their houses have no room for. Such con-sumerism is rooted in a disease which has been called "affluenza," which is the title of a book by authors DeGraff, Wann and Naylor.[2] Americans have an attraction to shopping similar to a heroin addict observing several spoonfuls of heroin. Such widespread alcoholism, drug dependence, and rampant consumerism, are surface manifesta-tions of a deeper plague of self-ignorance, of spiritual blight, of psy-chological imbalance. So, where do we begin to find solutions? The only solution is for each individual to begin to acknowledge the ad-dictions, cravings, desires, vain ambitions, that inundate his/her own personal sphere of ego-consciousness, and thus begin the proc-ess of self-transformation.

Ego consciousness is all that you believe you are, all that you believe you know of the world. Yet the egoic sphere includes another psychological dimension—the ambit in potentia, harboring the pos-sibility of activating the process of psychic expansion, which requires dispersion of certain ego structures and belief systems. Such disper-sion is necessary to free oneself from the bonds of acculturation. For ego is conditioned by socially engrained information and opinions which have shaped our view of who we are, our goals, our very idea and image of self. There is no egoless person, though there are spiri-tually purified persons whose egos become translucent conduits of transcendent consciousness. Though self-knowledge, or what is re-ferred to as "enlightenment," doesn't require ego annihilation, it does demand expansive perception and annihilation of delusions and il-lusions concerning the persona-ego sphere of being, which, if occurring intensively and suddenly, can ignite the experience known as "ego death" and spiritual rebirth. To be able to perceive your own ego from a more objective perspective, you have to become familiar with areas and abilities of your mind ordinary consciousness is only partially aware of, and even areas it is completely unaware of, entailing subconscious depths and transpersonal states of consciousness.

Self-observation is a foundational aspect of self-knowledge. You learn to periodically pause to take note of what you are thinking about, the quality of your thoughts, catching yourself involved in useless fantasies, daydreams, futile longings, petty vindictive urges, sexual imagery, etc. At first, attempting to keep your mind purified of such meaningless meandering, you will be amazed at how helpless you are to change the direction and quality of most of your thinking. But this helplessness will gradually be overcome. The mental discipline of periodically saying "stop," and observing your thoughts, can develop into an enriching practice to help you gain a significant degree of mental control. To bring about a change from habitual energy-wasting thought activity to constructive directed consciousness is an essential element of the process of spiritual awakening.

Attaining a genuine state of "self-objective" centering that involves keeping vigilant watch over that which you identify subjectively as "I" and "me," is not an easy task. You have become the "I," the "me" you think of yourself as, through the long and gradual process of acculturated development, from infancy to this very moment. Acculturation is so thorough it works as though it were an innate attribute of our psycho-physiological condition. Scholarly research from varied fields maintains acculturated influence upon our perception and attitude is present in every experience we have.

We are so intimately familiar with our ego-personality, we feel quite at home as to who and what we are, whether prince or pauper, CEO or taxi driver. Because of this "at homeness," most of us feel harmonized and balanced, believing our occasional envies, jealousies, petty frustrations, greeds, prejudices, selfishness, are just normal and acceptable aspects of being human, though at the same time we acknowledge such traits shouldn't be given complete license. The majority assume that to get along in the world, they need not know any more than they learned from kindergarten through college, with Sunday school services on the side. Individuals who dwell complacently within such collective confidence are in a situation similar to goldfish believing their fishbowl is the whole world. Though it may seem it would not take much to shatter such an illusion, the fishbowl of acculturation is made out of bullet proof glass. We must thoroughly consider our at-homeness, and realize we must become amphibians, climbing out of the fishbowl and checking out our psychic closets, cellars, and attics, not just the sunshiny living room we've been gazing at for years, safe within our bowl, calling it the "known world."

A foundational element of self-knowledge is to thoroughly know your positive and negative psychological traits. The positive traits are those which help you keep a grateful commitment to the quest, despite hardship, fear, or collective pressure. The negative is anything which may sway you away from commitment. Negative traits can be subtle and hard to detect, because they are often seen in a positive light by the collective — vanity perceived as justified self-esteem, selfishness as prudence, lust for prestige as healthy ambition, greed as necessary self-assertiveness. If the ego has excessive and unbalanced self-esteem, relying too much on persona vanities, once it taps into meta-psychic energies it can become vulnerable to Faustian impulses, scorning and abusing the weaknesses in others. Paradoxically, the ego must be strong enough to let itself be weakened as it disperses engrained delusions, regaining and renewing its strength once stabilized at a more expansive level of consciousness.

As all great sages and profound contemplators of the human predicament acknowledge, the vast degree of imploded egoism among the multitudes is the primary impediment to humanity's further cultural evolution. Thus it is clear from centuries of genuine spiritual teachings, the narcissistic ego must be rendered sufficiently passive in order to activate the unfolding of deeper realms of mind. It is our own self image which imprisons us within a limited conceptual grid. We have become willingly trapped, like a chick seeking to remain warm and secure by refusing to peck out of its egg. We can look upon our acculturated world view as a gilded egg we are "at home" within, feeling no need to even begin pecking. The element necessary to do the pecking is a facet of this very ego-mind which entraps us. To be able to stop the mind's meaningless actions ignited by ignorance, vanity, selfishness, and worthless desires, we must activate willful intention. Overcoming the power of acculturated influences that subliminally manipulate us requires a stern and disciplined commitment to conquer common habits of conformism and socially programmed needs. In this way we can rid ourselves of banal desires and activities, converting excess energy we gain from plugging this meaningless drainage into exercises of self-reflection, meditation, and eclectic meaningful research.

The awareness of bias, conscious and unconscious to varying degrees, is a very important element of perceiving where truth abides in any situation. There are various classifications of different types of bias, but for the purposes of this book we shall deal with "confirmation bias" and "oversight bias." Confirmation bias is the mind's tendency to confirm only data that enhances one's opinions, and oversight bias is the conscious and subconscious avoidance of information adverse to those opinions. Such bias is a kind of self-defensive lying to oneself, functioning as an instrument of self-distraction to avoid consciously considering any criticism intimated to have the power to undermine one's ideology or belief system. Bias is prejudice rooted in subjective psychodynamics which shape perception and cognition, derailing intelligent discernment. It is an engrained attitude of the enclosed mind. An open minded person is consistently prepared to willingly revise his/her version of reality, if doing so brings it in line with a more substantial truth of how things really are. In order to grow one must be ready to jettison even cherished beliefs along the way—though most beliefs needing to be tossed aside for one's soul to expand will eventually be seen as not having been worth cherishing in the first place.

People can attain enough knowledge from the shallow springs of our media-drenched society to mistakenly perceive themselves as sufficiently knowledgeable concerning existence, without having even once contemplated knowledge of significant depth. Those of higher education succumb to an even more amplified confidence in their opinions because they have become "professionals." Though there are brilliant men and women docents within the "halls of ivy," far too many university and college teaching positions are filled by shallow persons who are all too common beneath their cultivated image of being substantially knowledgeable. Higher formal education has only a slight corresponding relationship to the cultivation of genuine self-knowledge and spiritual awareness.

Recognizing this vast tendency toward biased self-delusion among people of every class, philosophers and sages speak of the majority of their fellow beings as the ignorant masses. This is not condescending scorn. The majority of people ARE ignorant of knowledges of great import. As the writings of Heidegger quite thoroughly elucidate, the multitudes, including people from every walk of life, perennially lose the substance of their spiritual growth by becoming unquestioningly entranced with the externalities of the egoic arena of societal existence. Gurdjieff referred to this mass trance as a "cultural hypnotic spell." The person of valid self-knowledge breaks this spell, transcending the common predicament—thus the alchemist's "our gold is not the common gold."

The hustle-bustle pursuit of status and prestige, over-zealous identification with patriotism, and unquestioning kowtowing to religious belief, are potent psychological addictions which fortify the "cultural trance." The problem is, while bolstering superficial self-esteem, such addictions actually cause the potential for self-knowledge to diminish. The conventional mind of the multitudes, be it of lower, middle or upper class, remains occupied with "roof brain" ego-chatter, rehashing the same secure opinions on politics, religion and personal prejudices of all kinds, year after year, as their potential for awakening slowly dies. But don't misunderstand. I am not attempting to detract from the enthralling and vastly varied drama of tragedy and triumph, agony and ecstasy, joy and sorrow, happiness and horror, of the universal human experience. I can truly say, after over fifty years of mean streets and dusty road-travel, nothing human is alien to me. I myself have lived in big cities and small towns over half the earth, have experienced all the drugs, worked at every kind of labor there is, succeeded in my own business, spent years in the military, had the iron barred doors of prison slammed behind me, hovered on the edge of death more than once, attended colleges and universities, and helped many in need just as I have been helped. I find beauty in all cultures, in the heroic and loving hearts of their common folk. I am comfortable in and adaptable to any environment on earth, whatever country, culture, town or city I might find myself in. I strive to perceive the numinous behind the ignorance and folly of any person I deal with. And yet, I face the plain fact that if people are not giving top priority to the quest for truth and self-knowledge, they will not rise above a certain collective condition of mental limitation, never consciously partaking of the spiritual essence of existence. Because of this, they are vulnerable to the many negative forces that can sway the mind, miring the human race in the quicksand of political discord which entangles billions in an unending succession of wars and economic hardship. The overcoming of this perennial condition is a significant aspect of what the quest is all about.

The word quest is intimately related to the word questioning. Michael Novak has written:

> *There is nothing in me that I cannot question. Every form that the drive to question assumes is subject to questioning ...Raising a question' is not only a matter of uttering an interrogative sentence, but more often a matter of attentive experience, alertness, noticing: having an open and hungering attitude toward experience. Questions often take the form of directing attention in a new way, of allowing fresh elements of experience into consciousness, of permitting the preconscious play of affects and images to subvert our ordinary, conventional, conscious sense of reality.*3

According to Hans-Georg Gadamer, "*Questions always bring out the undetermined possibilities of a thing ... Questioning opens up possibilities of meaning...*"4 Heidegger speaks of significant questioning as daring to venture, to give oneself over to an inner unfolding. Nietzsche equates such questioning with digging into the pit of one's being.

Every individual's existence consists of constantly changing possibilities of awakening, but most of them are overlooked. Once one enters the arena of the quest, there exists a kind of feedback loop where each opportunity for awakening, if perceived and acted upon, stimulates ever more enriching possibilities. Knowledge begets exploration, exploration begets expansion of self-awareness, which begets further possibilities of exploration, imbuing the individual's day to day existence with constant potential for more expansive awakening. But such possibilities only become actualized if the knowledge being accumulated is of a meaningful quality, otherwise it becomes no more than the gathering of intellectual data resulting in little in-depth self-discovery. The quest cultivates an intelligence of which the intellect is just one avenue of enrichment.

The quest does not demand that one become a Himalayan hermit, or a big city recluse. As the seeker gathers knowledge and perceives the sad plight of humanity, discerning actions within the social arena that may be taken to help alleviate pain of poverty and injustice, he/she should by all means pursue such activity if it can flow parallel to the inner quest—and it usually can. Social activism can be an enriching experience if it doesn't become an evasion of inner discipline, or an escape from existential angst, or a game of egoic image enhancement, but is an extension of one's spiritual growth. Spiritual sages such as Gandhi, Sri Aurobindo, Jesus, who were involved in clashes with established political authority, gave their spiritual life top priority, and their political activism was an extension of their inner awareness. Above all, the true sage's involvement in any activity of a political nature is imbued with a selfless quality. Though true selflessness is rare, every so often through the media we witness people of every culture and class involving themselves in high risk situations in order to help alleviate the pain and suffering of complete strangers. Such selfless acts outshine what many "enlightened" New Age gurus, and most televangelists, have contributed to the betterment of the human condition. One need only visit Mother Teresa's "Home for the Dying and Destitute" in Calcutta, and watch the nurses and volunteers, to grasp what selfless giving is about. Such selfless giving, whether temporary, during a certain stage of growth, or for an entire lifetime, can never be detrimental to one's spiritual enrichment.

The quest for realization of wholeness of being is a uniquely individual thing, and though there are guidelines one can pick and choose from, there is no set pattern, no regimented step-by-step plan for everyone to follow. As Nietzsche stated, *"There is in the world one road where no one may go, except thou: ask not whither it leads, but go forward."* How far a person's consciousness may evolve over a period of years depends on intriguing variables of possibilities. But the quest does demand definite actions which create a tangible lifestyle for constantly awakening dormant spiritual potentials. This entails a persevering effort to comprehend knowledge you thought you never could understand, or felt you had no reason to learn. Know this, the potentialities and truths of the quest for spiritual awakening and all it implies, have been totally substantiated from a thousand year stream of accumulated knowledge and over a century of scientific discovery. You do have a very important reason to ponder and learn about the ultimate meanings of existence. Hopefully, if you do not yet grasp this, you will when you come to the last page of this book.

3 – Hui Chen Tzu

It is the singular person, inexplicably drawn
from familiar comforts toward a nebulous goal,
lured often enough to death – it is he, or she,
whose peregrinations can never be thoroughly
understood, who is worth watching.
—Evan S. Connell

A sense of the mystical is the sower of all true science.
— Albert Einstein

There are those—shamans, yogis, Siddhas, and psychic-spiritual explorers of every kind—who know little about the subjects in which a highly educated person is versed, yet are experienced with higher levels of consciousness and alternate realities the average scholar or scientist would be bewildered by. Still, in this age, scientific insight is a valuable aspect of self-knowledge, and it is advantageous to merge such knowledge with that of the more mystically inclined explorers. One should cultivate an interest in the basic aspects of quantum physics, anthropology, evolution, astronomy, cosmology, mysticism, theology, religion, philosophy, various schools of psychology, mythology, and when exuberant curiosity is ignited, expand wherever a subject may lead. The accumulation of such knowledges merges into a unified comprehension according to the intention and dedication of the individual involved. Of course, such cerebral endeavor should be balanced with substantial worldly experience. A person can be highly cultured, know the classics, speak several languages, quote from literature, art, science, and various schools of philosophical inquiry, yet be a shallow fool as to the deeper more significant experience of existence. If knowledge becomes no more than an intellectual acquirement, its deeper potential is lost.

Eclectic gleaning of significant knowledges does not call for years of formal schooling and specified research. Others have done that for us, and bless them for it. Scholars have sacrificed decades researching and writing volumes concerning every field of study mentioned above, and more, making it possible for a person to spend a limited amount of time attentively reading significant works of any subject in order to get a fair grasp of it. For instance, mythology. Several months spending a few hours a day reading the works of Joseph Campbell, Mercea Eliade, Edith Hamilton, Thomas Bulfinch, James Hillman, and significant sections of Jung's work, is sufficient to awaken anyone to how mythology fits into the evolution of human consciousness, and its place in shaping the philosophical and religious belief systems most humans base their lives upon. Each and every field of pertinent knowledge can be approached in this manner. This differs from formal curricula in that you follow your curiosity, delving into the subject matter that coincides with your own individual pattern of growth.

The pursuit of significant knowledge is an ever branching, deepening process that can last a lifetime, and should. As the years pass, a distilling and refining hones it down to a few specific works. This is what the process of in-depth self-education is all about. Millions of people with Ph.D.'s acquired from eight to twelve years confined to the halls of ivy, sadly verify that formal schooling in the United States rarely points one in the direction of authentic self-knowledge. As Librarian of Congress James H. Billington stated in U.S. News and World Report,

> My concern is that the academic enterprise in America is incessantly preoccupied with giving definitive answers to trivial questions instead of tentative answers to important ones.[1]

Deeper knowledge of existence can only be accumulated through extensive individual exploration. Having been an astute student at several community colleges and a couple of universities, and having spent sunup to sunset days doing freelance research at a half-a-dozen more institutions of higher learning, I am aware that a person can discover more about every field of knowledge browsing the shelves of any well stocked library than they can pondering ninety percent of the textbooks and lessons presented in most classrooms. Mark Twain said, "*I never let my schooling interfere with my education.*"2 Of course, a person can set his or her sights on a college degree, pursue it diligently, and not necessarily bypass the deeper truths of life. But many of our most intelligent poets, writers, philosophers, psychologists, scientists, though highly educated people, were dissatisfied with the regimentation of class work and learned to pursue more meaningful knowledge in a free flowing personal way, outside the walls of academia.

A lifestyle of aesthetically oriented "refined poverty," unstressed and easy going, free from the eight hour a day work routine, social obligations, static schoolroom curricula, creates the best conditions for the committed seeker. Such was the core of the original bohemian, beatnik, hippie lifestyles, all founded on the urge to step aside from the conforming crowds in pursuit of answers to ultimate questions. This was not what the media perceived of such movements, which was a biased defensive socialized perception focusing on drugs, sex, slothfulness. Of course, once popularized, such negative traits did seep into these movements. But their worth abides in the fact that they came about as an attempt to creatively compensate for the time-confined mental automation modern society perpetuates.

Why is it our nation's school system has not produced the cultural effects and the leaders of worthy intelligence that are so greatly needed? Though there were undoubtedly altruistic elements involved in the founding principles, public schools open to everyone were basically put into operation not as a benevolent gesture to spread knowledge, but as a system to inculcate patriotism, national values, and fill the professional job gaps in our social structure, keeping the economic network running as smoothly as possible. That is why it was made compulsory. As Cornelis Verhoeven has written,

> *We are dealing now with general education as a form of knowledge, and that is one thing it is not. It is the exact opposite, not because it is incomplete but because it is artificially tailored...General education is based not on real interest but at best on a sort of hobbylike quasi-interest which is not concerned with things as such but rather with the social advantages that knowledge seems to bring with it...It creates and preserves mediocrity. It does not demand that contact with things, the piercing of*

*man's self-righteous subjectivity which is precisely the beginning of knowledge.*3

. For centuries hundreds of our colleges and universities have been pouring graduates into society, and the world of commerce and status seeking has swallowed all without any significant evidence that "formal" education produces substantially knowledgeable men and women, let alone those with any inkling of genuine wisdom. 99.99% of our politicians, corporate executives, world leaders — those who hold important positions in the realms of power — are college and university educated. It is clear they have not only accomplished nothing of significance as to a broad scope of genuine cultural enhancement, they have actually fostered an extensive stream of corruption and incompetence that now flows throughout the entire economic/political structure. Evidently, even those possessing a "higher education" have a lot of blank areas within their well-schooled minds. Much of this was brought about through specialization within career ambits during prime years of mental development. Most politicians and CEO's are not any more culturally cognizant of literature, art, psychology, philosophy, than your average working man. Though the process of years of structured schooling may clear a person of the charge of blatant ignorance, it certainly fails when it comes to a cultivated "radius of comprehension." Our education system is not exactly functioning to produce well rounded intelligence and holistic awareness of the world. In the long run, the system of schooling we have established for the advancement of society fails. Political and corporate leaders make world shaping decisions lacking the sound knowledge and wisdom required for such responsibility. Yes, of course, there are formally educated people in many professions — doctors, teachers, what have you, (even a few politicians) — who are people of genuine integrity and perform their expertise to the benefit of their fellow humans. But they accomplish this despite the shortcomings of formal education, not because of the way the system operates.

A person of holistic self-cultivated awareness has a radius of comprehension that partakes of the most profound and significant knowledges, whereas a person with a high IQ, though extensively informed, usually has serious shortcomings in the deeper and more meaningful areas of psychological and spiritual development. Consider the fact that most of the Nazi doctors during the Second World

War who performed horrible experiments on human beings, gradu-
ated from the best medical schools. After 1945, during the War
Crimes Trials, they were given the standard IQ tests used throughout the United States. Some of them had IQ's verging on the level of
genius. If a Nazi torturer can pass such tests with the flying colors of
genius, what does that imply about our concept of intelligence?
What does that imply about the entire educational system which
shapes the intelligence of all those within it? The implications are
somewhat frightening. Of course, since 1945 standard IQ tests have
gone through significant overhauling. And yet, even the most up-
dated versions are incapable of revealing a person's actual mental
capabilities and moral depth. Over the past few decades the fallacy
of psychometric testing systems has been clarified in significant
ways. It is now being realized that high test scores depend upon a
person being mentally adapted to the information Western society
deems as necessary for progress in social, economic, political and
technological endeavors. Moral values are less than secondary; spiritual awareness, existential understanding, and the concept of self-
knowledge are not even considered. From my own experience with
members of MENSA, most people with an IQ over 130 have little
personal involvement with ultimate questions of human existence,
or any significant awareness of higher states of consciousness, and
are as entrenched in common vanities, desires, habits, as any ordinary person. A television mini-documentary about the "Smartest
Man in the World,"[4] who's IQ is beyond the 200 range, clearly revealed how ridiculous the title is. It was blatantly clear he completely lacked any psychological depth, let alone spiritual transcendence of ordinary egoic vanities and ambitions. You can watch the
contestants on the TV show, Jeopardy, and other similar shows, and
it is remarkable how informed they are about many facts and subjects; but any truly perceptive person can see that most of them definitely lack spiritual awareness and depth-of-life experience.

In their book, Descartes' Dream,[5] Davis and Hersch thoroughly
demonstrate how essentially meaningless the concept of IQ is, showing that though IQ testing is exact, consisting of number and linear
gradation, intelligence itself is elusive, amorphous, uncapturable in
its relationship to time, place, predicament. There is an important
difference between a person with an expansive holistic consciousness and one with a high IQ who is gifted at gleaning and retaining
much socially oriented knowledge. When you think about it, you can

understand why great spiritual teachers like Christ and Buddha, great thinkers like Plato and Socrates, and even great writers like Shakespeare, all agreed the true path to wisdom is learning to "know thyself," which involves not only knowing about your weaknesses and strengths, likes and dislikes, but in facing the darkest aspects of yourself in order to explore your own mind, in all its depth and scope, as thoroughly as you are capable. This eventually means becoming aware of the soul realm of existence and what your individual responsibility is to the inner quest. The concept of self-knowledge is only a signpost, an abstract indication of the mysterious significance of your own unique existence, which only you may finally grasp. As the Zen master Sosan warned us, the finger pointing at the moon is not to be confused with the moon itself.

Since the essential quality of a person's life and awareness depends on the depth and scope of his/her comprehension of the human existential-spiritual condition, wouldn't anyone who truly cares pursue knowledge which brings about the most all encompassing comprehension? It is this self-chosen existential commitment that separates the seeker from both the aseptic erudition of the intellectual and the somnambulistic multitudes. The methodology of such a pursuit of can take a variety of forms. For some, drugs of a psychedelic quality become an aspect of their pilgrimage, which they learn to use with utmost care. Though certain plants and fungi have potential to awaken a person to deeper elements of the quest, all too many young people today begin using mind altering psychedelics with no idea of the depths and forces they may delve into. Totally unprepared for experience of archetypal dimensions, many are permanently impaired. On the streets of every large city we can find tattered homeless teenagers and mentally disoriented adults who validate the misuse of mind altering drugs. Others, though not mentally unhinged, burn their spiritual potential up by careless and continuous indulgence. Only self-knowledge sought with disciplined eclectic attentiveness creates the psychological stability needed to even begin exploring with psychedelic substances. And yet, because paradox, perplexity, and intriguing contradiction underlie the flurry and stratagems of human reality, even among the tattered homeless and mentally wounded users of drugs, there are those who have more insight into our cosmic-spiritual situation than most college professors, priests, or world leaders.

The path of self-knowledge is undertaken as a way to arrive at authentic "gnosis tes hodu" = knowledge of God—in other words, insight into the very soul of things. It is getting in touch with, as Phillip Wheelwright put it, "*the intimation of a something more, a beyond the horizon, which belongs to the very nature of consciousness.*"₆ This calls for an urgent desire to rise out of ignorance toward truth, to reach a state of consciousness uniting one with the source of all creation, which accumulated knowledge verifies is an actual possibility, and the most meaningful goal of human existence. The circumstances which ignite this impulse to know, to grow, to be aware, are as varied as the individuals involved. The only vehicle available is your own mind, and as we shall clarify, the mind encompasses enigmatic and wondrous territories. Beyond our ordinary grasp of the world dwell hellish demonic depths and overwhelmingly glorious heights of archetypal "beings," which we sometimes sense within us through dreams, bestial urges and sublime intimations.

Such inner realms have been acknowledged in Western civilization for centuries, but were forcefully confined and reduced to an orthodox religious orientation. In the West during the era known the Renaissance, 1400 - 1750, perspectives regarding the mind began to broaden. Around 1515 Johann Weyer began to look at mental disease as a treatable condition. In the 1600's Quakers created sanctuaries for the mentally ill, striving to heal them with care and compassion. Somewhere around 1792, in Paris, Doctor Philippe Pinel was given charge of a hellish asylum for the insane. He set the patients free of their chains and stopped beatings and other cruelties. He began treatments involving care, concern, and a careful study of responses. His reputation spread. In 1875 William James founded the first psychology laboratory in the United States, at Harvard. Fifteen years later, around 1890, the work of Freud appeared and awareness of the mind's irrational depths once again made its way into a larger sphere of cultural consciousness. Psychology opened windows, letting a fresh breeze of awareness join accumulating winds of the scientific revolution, including the world shaking contributions of Darwin and Einstein. Psychology revealed how our daily conscious level of mind, believed to be an ambit of logic and reason, is all too vulnerable to subconscious irrational influences which begin to shape the personality from childhood on, holding sway over our adult attitudes and perception of the world. During the 20th century a variety of schools of psychology came forth, each having its own approach.

The influence of materialism and secularism upon psychology created a split orientation, one side perceiving any "spiritual" aspects of a troubled mentality strictly from a physicalist perspective, the other side, branching from Jung, realizing that, essentially, most psychological problems have a spiritual basis.

During the last fifty years the use of drugs has become predominant in treating with dramatic effect an array of mental illnesses which were once deemed hopeless. But the "quick cure" use of drugs has got completely out of hand. In all too many cases, the drugged patient is not cured, but rather chemically adjusted to function "normally." Other approaches are coming about which can go hand in hand with the use of psychiatric drugs, eventually even replacing them. These "other methods" — revisions of "old school" ideas and therapeutic techniques merged with New Age insights — are reaching into areas where they are effective in helping people free themselves of negative psychological entanglements, or open creative potentials they would not have experienced without the help of deeper self-probings. Such methods can become avenues to spiritual growth and genuine self-knowledge. The Jungian school of psychology has been a significant avenue in this endeavor. And there are alternative approaches gleaned from other cultures, such as shamanistic "soul retrieval" processes. From the East, Indian psychology, which has a metaphysical base entailing yoga and meditation, is adding its knowledge to the endeavors of healing and enhancing the mind.

The psychological structure of the egoic mind is analogous to the architecture of a building. If the foundation is off kilter when a building is being constructed, it will turn out to be a crooked structure, off balance and out of harmony — it may even collapse. Thus the pursuit of self-knowledge requires us to initiate a thorough introspective exploration of our psychological condition to gain insight into the forces that have shaped us. Such effort is like breaking chains the past has wrapped around our minds, confining us to false perceptions and distorted conceptions of what life is all about. We can rid ourselves of such negative influences while keeping all positive elements of our heritage intact.

How do we go about this weeding of distorted influences that have shaped us since birth, and throughout formative years as a child, teenager, young adult? The key is the acceptance of the strug-gle to live an existence on the planet earth as free of as many illusions and delusions as possible. To truly know yourself is to struggle to overcome psychological weaknesses and develop inner strength through knowledge and understanding, to learn to grapple with what you've been taught to believe about life, God, politics, love, art, and much more—and keep on struggling till you know what is true and what is based on inadequate knowledge and distortions of tradition and custom. Such introspective wrestling induces the cultivation of a discerning and balanced skepticism about the world and the institutions of our fellow earthlings, without pessimism or nihilism interfering. Philosophically and psychologically, a nihilistic perception of existence is as off kilter as "power of positive thinking" mind-pablum.

As the struggle deepens it produces the alchemical fire which ignites spiritual awakening. One should not avoid in-depth self-exploration because of fear of possible emotional upheaval, for most people do not realize how highly adaptable the mind is to external and internal intensities. When the harshness of in-depth self-insight begins, and the struggle is underway, things open up, dormant strengths come forth, inspiring the further cultivation of an individual's radius of comprehension, which entails enthusiastic striving toward acute awareness of essence. This process is benefited by the harmonious development of both mind and body. Such was the original impulse behind the cultivation of ancient yoga disciplines. Physical health creates a dependable source of energy, strength and stability, thus the occasional psychic wounds inner exploration may bring about will heal much sooner. Though care of the body is very important, care of the mind takes precedence. Essentially, the mind needs even more nourishment than the body. A person would have a more authentic existence living as a spiritually aware quadriplegic than a physically fit athlete of ordinary "jock" mentality. Significant spiritually oriented knowledge is to your mind what eating high quality substantially nourishing food is to your body. Self-satisfied complacency and unrecognized ignorance starve the mind.

Chuang Tzu, said: "To be truly ignorant, be content with your own knowledge of things." Yet most people are all too content with their common habitual knowledge of things. They do not believe they need to know any more about their mind or the human situation than what they have learned through the acculturated channels of school, media, church. They prefer "chicken soup for the soul" rather than the zesty Gypsy goulash authentic spiritual endeavor serves up.

The majority of human beings never really understand what genuine self-knowledge is. When he spoke of both the feverish mob shouting for his crucifixion and the arrogant smugness of the Roman ruling class, Jesus said, *"They know not what they do."*[7] If a person does not really know what he is doing, then he does not really know himself. He has no idea what *"Know Thyself"* means. Despite this, the majority of people with little self-knowledge or knowledge of the world, when asked, will claim to know themselves quite thoroughly. This is a delusion of the common ego. The science of cognitive psychology has verified that once people find comfort and security within a certain life orientation, they steadfastly refuse to see any flaws in their situation. It's a proven fact human beings will deceive themselves in order to avoid seeing anything adverse to the settled pattern their life has conformed to. Do you grasp that? People can convince themselves a falsehood is a truth if it supports their way of life and system of belief. This is very entrenched when it comes to religious, ethnic and political beliefs. Such self-deception can also be found among many within the New Age movement, who are prone to consider themselves far more "awakened" than they actually are. When it comes to the syndrome of self-deception, people who would never tell a lie sometimes live an even greater lie.

As a simple example of the ubiquitous syndrome of self-deception, we need only observe Jehovah Witness or Mormon youth knocking on our doors. Though they have little experience of life and no depth of knowledge, they are fully confident of holding the truth concerning human existence, God, salvation, and are here to save you. Still, such youths have the excuse of innocent naiveté, whereas those adult televangelists reeking of similar yet even more engrained self-deceptive confidence, have no excuse at all. This self-deception is rampant within religious fundamentalist sects, cults, organizations, and can be observed in zealous political movements, decidedly in conservatives of far right persuasion as well as left-wing anarchists. Would you really want to live a life founded upon conceptual falsehoods and delusions, even if you were successful and quite satisfied? If so, you might as well close this book and go your way. Far too many live such complacent self-satisfied lives. It is very easy to gradually deceive yourself if facing greater truths seems unnecessary or too much of a burden. As William Barrett succinctly put it, *"The modern world has wonderfully multiplied all devices of self-evasion."*[8]

People enwrapped in an illusory system of belief are very confident in their opinions of what the world is all about. But mere opinions, even eloquently stated, do not guarantee truth. The ancient goddess Aletheia, from which the Greek word for truth came, made it clear to her devotees they must heed the distinction between statements by those whose words were mere opinion and those whose words were rooted in truth substantiated by breadth and scope of knowledge and experience. Those who seek to base their lives on truth must seek out its dwelling places, dredging it up from every aspect of life where it is in question. Truth does not make reality secure or comfortable, despite the marshmallow spoutings of New Age lecturers, Christian televangelists, and the majority of Western born gurus wrapped in Eastern garb. The truth will set you free, yes, but in the process the truth of our existential-spiritual situation is quite likely to beget mind churning wonder, bewilderment, even occasional panic. As Henri Tracol maintained, which I paraphrase, the full gale force of disorientation must overwhelm a person to shock him/her from self-confined ignorance and prejudices. Gurdjieff was well aware of the necessity of psychic shock to awaken the common mind. To live oriented to truth requires both occasional ego rupturing shock and constant patient inquiry.

The Chinese sages would call a person who has sincerely dedicated many years to dredging for nuggets of truth: "Hui Chen Tzu" = one who has become conscious of truth. Unfortunately, in these days where the intelligentsia has been produced by a system of schooling permeated by the influence of materialism, secularism, relativism, and determinism, a sterile skepticism has come about that scorns all faith in the reality of revealed or ultimate truth. In such a cultural atmosphere, a state such as Hui Chen Tzu is usually smugly dismissed as a relic of a past age or another superstitious concept born of the New Age conspiracy. Well, I am not here to persuade overzealous skeptics, for they dwell in a self-created mire. As for the above 'isms, they stand like sand castles on the beach as the tide of the 21st century rises.

The task of discovering essential meanings concerning the significant aspects of our lives is far from just a simple exposing of falsehood and thus revealing of truth, for existence is rife with contradiction. It is said that for a statement to qualify to be a truth, there must be universal validation of its meaning and substance. Yet if we limit such verification to the inflexible logic of empirical methods of science, we limit our comprehension of the enigmatic immensity of existence. Consider the various ways empirical science has attempted to explain the phenomenon of love—psychologically, neurologically, biologically, genetically—dealing with it as if love could be confined to a Petri dish. Any approach using empirical methodology is out of its league and subject to insidious distortion in its attempts to define love. The truth of genuine love is universally validated within the heart of human beings every moment across the entire planet. As to higher qualities of spiritual love and mystical truth, these too have universal validation within the sphere of human existence. For example, Heidegger spoke of truth existing in the art of Van Gogh,[9] referring not to the realism of objects portrayed, but to a visceral intuitive revelation that unfolds in the heart of the attentive individual viewing the works of such artistic genius. Though validated within the heart of such an aesthetically attuned observer, this quality of truth is beyond rational definition or scientific analysis. Yet we can say one reason Van Gogh's art radiates truth is that his creative intention entailed self-crucifixion. As D. H. Lawrence expressed it,

> *The vision on the canvas is a third thing, utterly intangible and inexplicable, the offspring of the sunflower itself and van Gogh himself. The vision on the canvas is forever incommensurable with the canvas, or the paint, or van Gogh as a human organism. You cannot weigh or measure or even describe the vision on the canvas. It exists to tell the truth...*
>
> *It is a revelation of the perfected relation, at a certain moment, between a man and a sunflower. It is neither man-in-the-mirror nor flower-in-the-mirror, neither is it above, below, or across anything. It is between everything, in the fourth dimension. And this perfected relation between man and his circumambient universe is life itself.*[10]

Those who claim there are no truths, or that all truths are illusions, are usually of the same intellectual ilk as those who subscribe to moral relativism, which holds that truth has a relative quality to it, being dependent on time and place within a variety of cultural contexts. Moral relativism is often erroneously connected to Einstein's "Theory of Relativity," which is a blatant distortion of concepts. Moral relativism has to do with ethics and morality, whereas the

"Theory of Relativity" has to do with laws of physics entailing the speed of light, motion, perspective. Actually, the title "Theory of Relativity" was not Einstein's first choice, for he initially thought of it as the "Theory of Invariance" after hearing a reference by Min-kowski to "Invariant Postulates." Invariance refers to something fixed, stable, no matter what is changing in the surrounding environment. Einstein's Theory of Relativity has to do with the speed of light not only being invariably the same from any stance and by any measurement, but absolute in that no phenomena can move faster. To attempt the use of relativity to bolster moral relativism's disregard for the incisive stability of universal truths, is a misrepresentation. Einstein, responding to the distortion of his theories, said,

> *The meaning of relativity has been widely misunderstood. Philosophers play with the word, like a child with a doll. It does not mean that everything in life is relative.*[11]

Truth is inherently invariant. Thus it relates to the coherent theory of ideas, yet without being confined to empirical validation in all circumstances. Though the truth of a certain event, or fact, or concept, can be perceived differently from varied directions, its core remains constant. Perceptions of a situation may be variant, but truth comes from understanding the entire situation, encompassing all perspectives, meticulously evaluating each. From any point of consideration, from a thousand different points, what is true is true and can never be anything else but true. Water is wet wherever it is found. Fire is hot. It is similar with universal moral values, though not always as distinctly defined as wet and dry, or hot and cold. That universal moral truths can be subverted within certain cultural ambits due to ignorance or undeveloped collective conscience, does not imply invalidation but rather aberration.

We could say truth is a primary invariant of the human psychological/spiritual matrix. From a more esoteric perspective, the human concept of truth is universally invariant because it is rooted in satya meta-frequencies which resonate throughout all quotidian reality, branching in streams and rivulets that are nourished by mystical vision, intuitive apprehension, well honed intimation, and impeccably applied logic. Despite the vast entanglements scholars get themselves into concerning the subject of truth, which fill library shelves in every university, truth will reveal its clarifying power to those who are attuned to its Sophianic depths. This is a vital aspect of the essential quest this book deals with. As Edward Bulwer-Lytton put it: *"For the accomplishment of whatever is great and lofty, the clear perception of truth is the first requisite."*[12] And, according to Kafka, *"Truth is perhaps life itself."*[13]

Existentially significant universal moral truths — such as no one, under any circumstances, has the right to ever unjustifiably harm others — despite cultural aberrations, are validated by their universal acknowledgement among the vast and diverse multitudes of the planet, and are expounded upon in every religion — as in the Christian *"Do unto others as you would have them do unto you."* Again, there is no cultural or moral relativism to be considered here. Though the multi-modality of truth encompasses variation of perspective, intrinsic values such as just and unjust, right and wrong, true and false, do not change in fundamental meaning despite the flow of history and the shifting of cultural perception. Only distortions claiming to be truth change, having been revealed as untruth. Only moral standards constructed of limited particular cultural beliefs and not from a universal radius of comprehension change. Anything in one culture or another once believed to be true or right and later proven to be false or wrong, was never universally true or right in the first place. For example, human sacrifice, or cannibalism, was once a highly valued rite in various ancient societies, but is looked upon now as an activity founded on primitive lack of an empathic humanitarian sense of justice. This has little to do with relativism of perspective, whether moral, cultural or historical, and much to do with the evolution of consciousness and incorporation of evolved spiritual values into the human cultural ambit. Mortimer Adler, who demonstrated justice as a supreme human value, stated:

> One can want too much liberty and too much equality — more than it is good for us to have in relation to our fellow men, and more than we have any right to. Not so with justice. No society can be too just; no individual can act more justly than is good for him or for his fellow men.[14]

Any culture, primitive or modern, that sanctions the abuse and mistreatment of human beings is under the influence of a conceptual distortion stemming from under-developed consciousness. Substantial research suggests that the human sense of empathic concern and the concept of justice came forth from the interaction of primal intuition with an evolving spiritual comprehension of the human predicament. For thousands of years this empathic sense of justice has been expansively enhanced by apprehension and acknowledgement of a higher compassion by way of religious orientation and collective cultivation of humanitarian moral values. Though the human race has failed to live up to its consciousness of justice, we are still evolving. In a thousand years we may be looked back upon as a semi-civilized people plagued with injustice, war and tyranny, who could not spiritually comprehend and thus live in authentic accord with the essential wisdoms of our religious beliefs.

The vastly varied nuances of each individual's acculturated comprehension of reality calls for the committed responsibility of each sincerely striving seeker to clean out his/her own subjective back yard in order to live according to clearly establishedc universal truths. This process is assisted by the accumulation of significant knowledge which expands radius of comprehension, and simultaneously depth and scope of perception. Consider: a professional mountain climber will see a mountain as a series of challenging footholds and crevices, etc; a geographer's perception will tend to focus on strata, rock formation, exposed veins of minerals, etc; an artist will be oriented toward color, light and shadows, that express the mountain's beauty and haunting majesty; a mystically inclined person may see the mountain symbolically, as a great goddess he/she will merge with upon reaching the summit. A person versed in all four viewpoints—knowledgeable in climbing technology, geology, art, and mysticism—would have the most holistic view of the mountain, thus a more expansive radius of comprehension.

It takes courage to face the ultimate truths of life in all their wondrous and terrible complexity, head-on—especially facing one's self. Questioning your belief systems to validate whether or not they are built on sufficient truth, will intensely test your mental and emotional endurance. Such testing will change your life. Of course, and I will stress this many times, once their lives are on a seemingly stable track, the majority of people do not care to change. Recent cognitive research reveals it takes an immense amount of reliable information to cause the average person to change his/her set attitudes, but very little, even questionable information to justify the impulse to avoid change. If you are intent upon discovering the essence of who you are and what the essential meaning of your life on earth is, you must be prepared to endure the periodic stress of psychological challenge that significant changes in your life will bring about. Just as with a mountain climber struggling toward the peak, there will be psychological obstacles, such as the desire to give up and return to the comfort and security of base camp. But if sincere and determined, the majority of social, psychological and spiritual obstacles you confront can be overcome. A surprising and intriguing fact is, the more you commit to follow the quest for self-knowledge, inner courage comes forth as required. You gain psychological strength just by choosing to grow, because the human organism craves growth, and the mind when deeply stimulated rewards itself for any activity that motivates it in this direction.

Sincere committed inquiry into the deeper dimensions of our being, if determinedly pursued, will eventually penetrate the numinous essence sphere of life, the "God"-soul realm. This can also, along the way, bring about a crisis confrontation with evil. Existential inquiry, if delved into with one's whole self, evolves from the level of an intellectual psychological/philosophical probe into a veritable spiritual endeavor. To blend intellectual philosophical pursuit with Jana yoga disciplines, plus, if need be, the courage of alchemical shamanistic experimentation, can only lead to penetration of the "smoking mirror," into the archetypal cauldron where the gods dance. Without this daring surrender, this crossing of the borders between reason and the irrational, no one, no one at all, can sound the true depths of his/her being. In these depths we may risk our very minds and lives. Yet it is necessary. As Jesus said, *"Those who shall not risk their lives shall lose them."* They shall lose the potential for a truly meaningful life of soul awareness, of challenge. No matter what a person's social status, or faith and commitment to religious activities, he/she is as if half alive in comparison to a truly spiritually awakened person attentively treading the razor's edge.

Though there are hardships and dangers which most likely will confront those who commit their lives to the quest, from the mulch of such experience comes forth rewards of both existential and numinous quality outweighing all pain, risk and trouble. When we diligently pursue the exploration of ultimate questions, each day becomes vibrant with discovery. We need not ask if the end of such a quest makes the struggle worthwhile. The quest makes the HERE AND NOW worthwhile. And when the end comes, it will occur in the NOW.

4 – Considering Evolution

We are as yet below the level of existence
to which it is possible to rise.
— William Barrett

Let us go up!
Like two acrobats
Our faces petrified
In the faint smile of effort
Let us go up farther
With the physical possession of our arms
And the measureless muscles
In the convulsive calm of ascension.
— Vinicius de Morais

During years living a semi-nomad existence, while browsing through the aisles of the local library in whatever town I happened to be, I would often pause in the children's section to peruse the colorfully illustrated books on physics, relativity, chemistry, geometry, and other subjects. I discovered children's books frequently clarified things so simply that insights into complex subjects came forth which wouldn't have had I confined myself to the works of scholars and professionals. It isn't a stretch to say the most basic, seemingly simple aspects of our lives, in one way or another connect with the most complex and profound. "Basic" and "simple" need not imply a lack of complexity. Just studying the basic attributes of the human body — its anatomy and physiology — reveals how it so magnificently functions from the level of microscopic splendor to the ultrasensitivity of the flesh, verifying the amazing intricacies of our physical nature. With our eyes, tongue, ears, nose, and skin, we are able to see, taste, hear, smell, and feel, along a broad spectrum, from harsh to mild, foul to fair, coarse to fine, pleasure to pain. Take for instance our ability to smell a remarkable variety of aromas. The phenomenon we call aroma is an interactive relationship between certain sensory attributes and molecules in the surrounding air, which in turn are made up of atoms, which in turn are made up of phantomlike subatomic particles. A certain formulation of molecules, for instance emanating from a pie baking in the oven, permeate the air throughout a house like a miniscule flurry of snowflakes engulfing the space about you, thus contacting the olfactory epithelial cells in your nose. These cells in turn stimulate certain nerve and brain centers, creating the sensation of smell, which evolved as a necessary aspect of our primal survival. What exactly happens in that moment of brain stimulation, when sensation ignites conscious recognition of what we call a specific smell, still eludes empirical investigation. This demonstrates the simple act of smelling is actually an amazing complexification of varied qualities of matter in action. Yet it is only one aspect of myriad elements of energy swirling about us and merging with the physiological-psychological activities of our being. Eating, hearing, breathing, seeing, are just as complex and remarkable. And these "basic" elements are just a hint of the tremendous fervency of forces, from the aroma of a pie, to cosmic gravitation, to solar flares, in which we are immersed, by which we are permeated, and with which we are imbued. We are each like a whirlwind of solar, biological, quantum energy frequencies encapsulated in physical form.

An appreciative comprehension of the astonishing ways and means of how our sensual nature came about and functions, is an essential ingredient of self-knowledge. The existence of humanity is embedded in the remarkable process of terrestrial evolution, which Teilhard de Chardin, Sri Aurobindo, Gurdjieff, and other sages and thinkers have elucidated to be a wondrous current within the greater river of cosmic-spiritual evolution. We are dealing with tremendous and marvelous complexity involving immense stretches of time few people can really grasp, encompassing awesome catastrophic events as well as microscopic yet extremely potent mutations of genes, creating an illimitable array of shape, size, coloring, of constantly changing life forms ever busy adapting, branching throughout the processes of evolution on earth. From this immense brew did the primate species come forth that would become hominid, thus eventually Homo sapiens, thus you and I. I shall not spend too many words exposing the lunacy of those desperate folk who deny evolution with such schemata as "scientific creationism," which attempts to reduce the magnificence of natural evolution to a six day magic trick, exhausting the "Great Magician" to the extent that He had to rest on the seventh day. The works of many others have accomplished that exposé thoroughly.

Materialistic science, though exceedingly limited when it comes to the inner spiritual dimensions of existence, does have an empirically verifiable comprehension of cosmic-terrestrial evolution, whereas the "scientific" creationist is out of touch altogether. Sane intelligent analysis of geological strata, stress field foliation, mineral recrystalization, plate margins, fossil records, and varied other methods of research, leaves absolutely no room to doubt evolution is the wondrous extensive process encompassing all life forms science claims it to be. Even devoutly religious Lord Kelvin, in 1854, prior to Darwin, just by attentive consideration of rock, strata, and other geological formations, concluded that the earth had to be at least 20 million years old. Over eighty years ago Ernest Rutherford began the process of radioactive dating of rock and pitchblend, speculating the age of the earth to be over 700 millions years. Over the past twenty years, dozens of state-of-the-art scientific dating methods have revealed the earth to be at least four and a half billion years of age. Yet nearly 50% of the population of the United States refuse to acknowledge evolution, clinging to their rigid religious belief in biblical genesis occurring 6000 to 10,000 years ago. That various Christian sects even claim prehistoric fossils are cunning tricks put there by Satan to fool us only validates the desperate state of such defensive self-deception.

Of course, great paradigm shifts usually take one to three centuries to be fully integrated, as dissolving obsolete paradigms die out. Yet, to deny the evidence for evolution science has accumulated over the last hundred and fifty years, proving the earth to be billions of years old, is to deny the entire scientific paradigm—which includes not only the fields of geology, paleontology, cosmology, biology, oceanography, anthropology, but by implication, history and all technological advancement. To deny what science has validated about evolution is like denying what the field of aerodynamics has validated about the physics of flight, or claiming airplane design hasn't improved since the Wright brothers. To deny we evolved from proto-hominid creatures is to claim modern humans have no ancestral relationship to those early precursors of homo-sapiens that came out of Africa, or Neanderthal and Cro-Magnon, who lived in similar conditions to the Australian Aborigines, the Bushmen of Africa, the Amazon Indians, the New Zealand head hunters. Millions of Christians believe Adam and Eve, supposedly the first human beings, after being evicted from Eden, lived a lifestyle similar to that of an 18th century peasant farmer! The creationist's denial of the evidence proving the actual reality of evolution is the denial of truth in order to defend an anachronistic religious concept. Such a defense is rooted in fear, and is very similar in mode of thought to the anti-Semite and white supremacist's denial of the Holocaust. All are clear examples of deeply entrenched confirmation/oversight bias.

A method to move beyond the distortion of such willful ignorance in order to reveal truth, is put forth lucidly by Michael Shermer in an article from Skeptic magazine, "Proving the Holocaust: the Refutation of Revisionism and the Restoration of History." Shermer writes:

> *Within all these fallacies of thinking about both evolution and the Holocaust, there is an assumption by the creationists and the revisionists that if they can just find one tiny crack in the structure the entire edifice will come tumbling down. This is the fundamental flaw in their reasoning. The Holocaust was not a single event. The Holocaust was 10,000 events in 10,000 places, and is proved by 10,000 bits of data that converge to one conclusion... A less cumbersome phrase might be called CONVERGENCE OF EVIDENCE. Evolution, for example, is proved by the convergence of evidence from geology, paleontology, botany, zoology, herpetology, entomology, biogeography, anatomy, physiology, and comparative anatomy. No one piece of evidence from these diverse fields says 'evolution' on it. A fossil is a snapshot. But a fossil in a geological bed, with other fossils of the same and different species, compared to species in lower strata and upper strata, contrasted to similar modern organisms, juxtaposed with species in other parts of the world, past and present, and so on, turn that snapshot into a motion picture. Each set of inductions from each field jumps together to a grand conclusion – evolution.*[1]

The philosopher of science Phillip Wheelwright also speaks of "proof of convergent evidence" as inductions drawn from various facts and events which, building on one another, finally create a clear perception of truth within the ambit of what is being considered. The convergence of scientific evidence from a broad scope of varied fields undermines and vanquishes all the claims of scientific creationism. However, Michael Shermer, being a physicalist, does not apply this same process to evidence undermining materialism.

Though empirical methodology can be depended upon to an extensive degree, scientific materialists who perceive the process of evolution as just blind movement of matter, have their own limited bias. The convergence of evidence from para-psychology, depth psychology, Jungian psychology, transpersonal psychology, history of mysticism, psychedelic research, anthropological investigation, and quantum physics, overthrows a strictly materialistic concept of reality, especially concerning human consciousness and the spiritual essence of our being.

Despite the fact that no one knows just how the origin of life came about, we do know terrestrial evolution is the process through which life on the planet Earth—the mulch of our animal being, thus egoic consciousness—has proceeded. There are a variety of ways to describe the immense journey of our physical and mental evolving. Dozens of books and videos have told the story of how, over billions of years of seething growth involving varied life forms, the blossom of ego-consciousness arose from the ferment of primate instinctual existence. This has been approached by professionals such as the Leakey's, Loren Eiseley, Donald Johnson, Carl Sagan, from the scientific ambit, and others such as Sri Aurobindo, Eric Neumann, Ken Wilber, and Pierre Teilhard de Chardin, elucidating the process from a spiritual perspective. To get at the truth as far as humanly possible, the eclectic use of both perspectives is necessary.

Concerning the origin of life, of bacterial spread and the immense diversified primal spawning of oceanic life, of the first creatures coming out of the sea and the first hominid coming forth from primate ancestors, of the gradual expansive unfolding of consciousness, the knowledge science has accumulated and organized over the past 150 years can give us a fair glimpse into the wondrously complex fruitfulness of it all. However, the usual popular narrative of upwardly inclined linear evolution, from amphibian creatures to ape, to caveman, to guy in business suit, is exceedingly reductive.

Darwin opened the collective consciousness to greater horizons concerning how life evolved, but he, like all early explorers, did not have the complete picture. In actuality, mammalian-hominid evolution is more like one offshoot spurt amid a hugely explosive ultracomplex process of novelty, mutation, and shotgun scattered expansion of varied life forms, with no end in sight till the sun burns out.

Before speaking further of great eras and epochs of evolution, we should consider just what millions and billions of years mean, since most people, when hearing such numbers, have no comprehension of the mind boggling immensity being discussed. As K. C. Cole points her insightful book, *First You Build a Cloud,*[2] once we begin speaking of hundreds of millions, and billions, it all becomes a blur, and 60 million seems no different than one billion. So read the following attentively. If you began counting twenty-four hours a day nonstop, it would take you approximately twelve days to count to one million. At the same rate of counting, it would take you over forty years to count to one billion. It takes a thousand millions to equal one billion.

We know the age of this planet is somewhere around 4.5 billion years, and recent discoveries have established deep sea biological activity dating to 3.85 billion years, when the earth was landless, covered entirely by the wild turbulent ocean, in which, fathoms down, frothing molten lava from volcanic eruptions burgeoned into the tenebrous depths. During hundreds of millions of years, as varied primal forces accumulated within the immense fervent silence of cauldronic interaction, something occurred. Simple single-cell life appeared, and hundreds of millions of years more brought forth more complex organisms with cells that possessed nuclei and organelles. Following hundreds of millions of more years of bacterial-cellular brewing, fomenting billions of algae formations, eventually, over seething aeons, this vast alchemical frothing produced plant life, and, somewhere between plant and animal, sea anemones thrived and began to compete for food. Complexity expanded, forms mutated, variation bloomed, amplified, novelty went berserk. Thus began the incipient activity of most creatures on the planet—to devour and be devoured. Some uncanny instinctual survival response within the complexification of DNA inspired designs for bizarre appendages of destructive weaponry and defense. Approximately 540 million years ago, during what paleontologists call the "Cambrian explosion," which lasted over a period of about twelve million years, an epidemic growth of razor teeth, claws, spikes, armor, spread through the oceanic realm, and the great perennial terpsichorean buzz and flurry of predator and prey flourished. Jaws, claws, teeth and tentacles, grew in size and begot an astonishing variety of frightful forms. Somewhere in this rapacious primeval broth, the first faint inklings of the sensory components of our physical and instinctual impulses began to form, evolving up through amphibian horseshoe-crab-like creatures who, 370 million years ago, first crawled forth onto land to lay eggs in sand safe from the multitudes of sea prowling predators. Even now, not only in the sea depths but in those quiet and beautiful tide pools we see along the coastline, the process of eating and being eaten, hunting and being hunted, continues. Even the seemingly serene starfish is constantly involved in slow motion predation. Tiny delicate flower like jellyfish flowing gently by prowl the tide pools for prey. If there be any element of a supreme creator's intentions in such an array coming forth in those primal depths, it would be of a frightening sort indeed. Paradoxically, nature has also given us gentle deer, honeybees, chipmunks, butterflies and bunny rabbits. We have room to breathe easily. We have space to be at peace.

With the first signs of microbial activity going back over three and a half billion years, we know nature, in its vast, patient, alchemical strivings, was in no special hurry for that strange amphibian to crawl out of the sea and suck in those first breaths of terrestrial air. Shall we call that creature Adam? After all, we would not be here had it not made that pivotal clawing gesture to drag itself onto some primeval beach. Millions of years following this, another creature, most likely still with amphibian abilities, wandered farther inland, searching, hunting, precipitating the electro-chemical interplay between reptilian spinal column bulb and the most basic elements of what hundreds of millions of years later was to become the brain of early primates.

Despite its abundant procreativeness, nature is excessively self-destructive, unconcerned with the multi-varied forms of life which "she" has spewed forth like a million Jackson Pollock's on methamphetamine. Science has been able to verify five major extinctions, and many minor ones. What science calls the Permian Extinction, a horrendous catastrophe, (possibly the result of a huge asteroid impact), occurred somewhere around 225 million years ago, obliterating ninety percent of the species then living. Even in the ocean only five percent of the creatures survived. Yet, the tenacity of this force we call life was never even bruised, and from the great lizard/dog-like creatures—Synapsids and others—survivors arose, and another vast diversity of bizarre creatures small and great, including dinosaurs, would roam unhindered for the next 140 million years or so, until an asteroid from the depths of outer space struck the earth 65 million years ago. This last mass extinction wiped out an overwhelming percentage of all living plants and animals. Again, if we speculate as to any intelligent creator God behind such zoological variety and the cataclysmic destruction of the creatures "It" created, what is currently being called "Intelligent Design" should more fittingly be called something like "Epileptic Design," or "Delirium Design," or, in an artistic vein, "Drunken Dali Design"—that is, if one is desperate for some simplified explanation for such paradoxical display of stupendous fecundity followed by immense life-destroying carnage. Apart from all theological speculation, "life" has consistently proven again and again, despite such devastation, to be a basically mysterious and amazingly resilient process with no essential goal, just open-ended random profusion instinctually exploring for designs which produce survival benefits.

How life could, in its smallest units (bacteria, protozoa, etc.), have spontaneously come forth from a "lifeless" primal chemical soup, is a question we may never be able to answer. Whether attempting to establish an answer that depends on a creator-God, Intelligent Design, or a physicalist schema, no one has any idea of the origin of life on earth. There is not even any established scientific definition of life. Self-replication is its most unique quality, and can only be artificially mimicked by certain lifeless computerized processes. Have you ever looked at a dead animal lying in the street, a dog or a cat—a creature that was spry, alert, leaping, running, with an attentive sparkle in its eyes that no longer exists in the corpse? Look upon the branch of a tree that has broken off and lies brown and dry, while those still on the tree are blossoming with the vibrancy of life. What is this exquisite sparkle of attentiveness, this springtime blossom vibrancy, which so starkly separates that which is imbued with life from the dead dull corpse and the broken dried branch? We do not really know, and yet here we are, alive within an immensity of surrounding living forms.

To consider a deeper perspective than mere scientific-intellectual rumination, listen to a description of life by a patient of Stanislav Grof undergoing psychedelic opening:

> *A great howling light...an arc-light of billions of volts...a roaring of a thousand suns...blazed with a radiance primordial, with an intensity that was absolute... This roaring was life itself. It shrieked and pulsed through everything living... I was connected with it as if by an immense shuddering optical fiber of not only light, but energy... It was not awesome, but awe itself...life alive.*

The science of organic chemistry has revealed the composition, properties, and processes of substances of which all life forms are made, and the transformations they undergo. From a purely scientific perspective, as humans, along with every living creature on earth, we are basically electrochemical beings imbued with the essential attribute of light, which, as Bohm clarified, is the *"fundamental activity in which existence has its ground."* Thus the primal substance of the "great howling light," of "life alive," was there within the cosmic fury of the Big Bang, pulsing and shrieking, ubiquitous in the turbulent sea covering the newborn earth. Volumes of scientific research indicate that extreme temperature changes and billions of lightning strikes over hundreds of millions of years, causing mucho electro-chemical activity within the primal oceanic broth, may possibly have stimulated a natural genesis of single cell forms capable of absorbing life force. We could speculate that such tremendous planetary brewing brought about an energy resonance magnetizing meta-consciousness frequencies from other "higher-deeper" dimensions, pulling them into the electro-chemical frothing of the primal sea, adding the first diminutive spark of instinctual consciousness permeating life forms. But whatever the source, this unintentional manifestation of life magnetized to the primal alchemical brew seems to fit the random "just happened to happen" novelty nature abundantly expresses. Thus even those most spiritually oriented can't just casually toss aside the possibility that life was generated on earth from the random electro-chemical-quantum play of things. But it is a possibility that does not rule out the enigmatic numinous orientation of the "great howling light" which is "life itself."

The numinous orientation I speak of has no relationship to creationism, Intelligent Design, the Anthropic Principle, or any religious or theosophical combination of these theories which interpret just happened to happen occurrences in nature as purposely designed activities. Yet, considering convergence of both empirical and non-empirical documentation, only an inflexible rationalism refuses to consider the possibility that the play of immense, complex, and mysterious forces, combining against all odds to kindle the seed of life on earth, just may have a spiritual component to it. This need not imply that any spiritual energies imbued in the immense surge of natural phenomena are intentionally concerned with the ultra-novelty of its essential designing activity. When something happens amid the seething cosmic-terrestrial complexification of processes, it happens—that's it. Supernovas explode, black holes appear, meteors fall, volcanoes erupt, cookies crumble, etcetera ad infinitum. Pause. This is not a declaration supporting a theory of mindless expansion of life. From a certain valid perspective, everything is mind. We are attempting to look at our situation without knee-jerk recourse to any established theories or beliefs, whether scientific or religious.

Over millions of years following the last vast extinction, another great diversity of creatures arose, including the first small mammals, and eventually, over millions more years of fervent ultra-creative ever-adapting evolving, the first primate. Primate creatures can be traced by reliable fossil dating going back 55 million years, and recent statistical dating claims even 80 million. During those primal epochs a hundred species of primates roamed over half the planet. It is certainly clear the unique branching of one species from a hundred, which differentiated hominid evolution from primate ancestry, was a process of timeless aeons of intriguing complexity few today even attempt to comprehend. Simple religious explanations are so much easier to live with. But substantial amounts of clear-cut evidence cannot be ignored. Denying evolution is a distinct sign of a closed mind.

Following millions of years of survival adaptations, change and mutation, a species of what is now thought to have been a hybrid bipedal-arboreal primate gradually came down from the trees, extending time spent on the ground to expand territorial needs. Eventually, through a haunting quirk in the mutational play of biological alchemy, creatures we call proto-hominids came forth, roaming the primeval unnamed lands now known as Africa. The branching-off stages of proto-humans from our ape-like ancestry is speculated to have occurred seven to ten million years ago, though some evidence may soon push it farther back. As of 2001, the remains of a bipedal hominid dating back six million years was discovered in northern Kenya. This hominid, called "Millennium Man" by the popular press, is known to scientists as Orroran Man. Whatever the name, it predates by three million years one of the most famous finds of the last two decades, known as Lucy. And just months following Orroran Man, in the Sahel desert of Chad, another skull was found dating back to possibly seven million years. It is known as Sahel anthropus.

Though they had a developed instinctual consciousness, those very first hominids who roamed the earth over three million years ago existed prior to attaining the mental ability to conceive an idea, or cohesive self-aware thought, or the urge to express themselves through a creative medium, myth, art, ritual, craft. Just when and why did such creative cultural manifestations so exceedingly transcending the activities of all other animals on earth, come forth? We do not know, but scientists have found well crafted spears dating back to 400,000 years ago. A hundred and thirty-five thousand years ago, Neanderthal people buried their kind with ceremony that indicates special care and concern for ritual, which implies symbolic thought We have found 50,000 year old bones of prehistoric eagles on which Cro-Magnon people made etchings indicating the changes of the moon. There is evidence that primal humans would crawl for hours through deep natural tunnels just to find a cave isolated enough to perform sacred ceremonies. Are such things not astonishing? You out there who comfortably attend church every Sunday — how far would you crawl through such dark caverns to make ceremonies of worship for your God?

The entire perception of our primitive "caveman" ancestors' cognitive abilities has been exceedingly limited. We now know homo sapiens existed in intelligently developed cultural settings much earlier than was previously thought. In February 2005, remains qualifying as "modern" homo sapiens dating back 195,000 years were found in Ethiopia. It is probable they had crafts and buried their dead with ritualistic care. What marvelous biodegradable things did they make which we shall never find? We know for sure 40,000 years ago extensive artistic creativity among our ancestors was in full swing across the globe. Surely elements of self-awareness and speech must have coincided with creative activities such as tool and weapon making, crafts, and primitive art.

Can we compare the minds of primitives living this very day in primal environments with those of our ancestors who lived as far back as a quarter of a million years ago? This is an intriguing question. We have early documentary films of white explorers confronting New Guinea aborigines in the early 1900's, who had no idea "civilization" or the white man existed, yet, though at first hesitant, they exhibited an extremely childlike openness and curious friendliness toward the strange pale foreigners. And these were head hunters who made warfare a sacred ritual. Yet within a few years some were going to school and speaking English. Can we compare their cultural situation with the thick browed Neanderthal, who roamed the earth 250,000 years ago, or to the more advanced Cro-Magnon, who was still hunting and gathering 50,000 years ago? Why not? We now know Neanderthal was not the "dumb" caveman depicted by cartoons over the past century, and Cro-Magnon is indistinguishable from modern humans as far as brain features and basic mental capabilities are concerned—they just had no awareness of the world beyond their tribal territory. They would most likely have adapted as easily to the modern world as many primitive people have done over the past 200 years.

Our human ancestors most definitely lived in what Heidegger called "preconceptual intimacy" with the world—neither purely instinctual animals, nor thinking, reasoning, self-aware humans. Within that primal world environment such hominids were undeniably involved in innovative grow-or-die activity demanding perceptual attunement to the surrounding environment, thus the activation of crude fight-or-flight "thoughts" about killing and the chance of being killed. The intense survival mode of those early hominids added a certain creative capability for confronting and mastering their immediate environment, not only allowing them to focus on what was dangerous, what there was to eat, where to sleep safely, who were friends and who were foe, as other animals did, but igniting a growing knowingness, a faint intuitiveness, an inkling of a certain separateness as to their interplay with the surrounding "otherness" of unnamed natural phenomena. In the immense multi-diverse novelty of evolution's mutational surge, this knowingness-feedback would have meant no more than pollywogs turning into frogs, or certain land creatures turning eventually into birds, if something exquisitely unique had not happened, which we can partially describe from a scientific perspective as the amplification of neural activity occurring within the lower hominid brain, resonating through the more recently evolved "higher" portions of the brain, creating the numinous alchemy of incipient egoic consciousness—thus brief and faint but remarkable states of "I/me" awareness. From this mental mulch inklings of abstract thought began to sprout. Despite this budding tremor of self-awareness, our ancient hominid's main attentiveness was still primarily oriented to fulfilling the simplest survival needs, which was all the five senses had evolved to accomplish. That first trembling of self-aware consciousness within the hominid mind was like a ripening bud, opening at an exquisitely slow pace, waiting some distant Spring.

Though we have come a long way, we are not disconnected from our most ancient past. Our basic senses still function in that same primal survival mode. Physiologically, the "brain stem" portion of our brain is nearly identical to the entire brain of primal amphibian/reptilian creatures. In fact, this lower portion of our brain is sometimes called the "reptilian brain." We began in the depths of the sea. The womb is an alembic of sea liquid. At a certain stage in prenatal development, the human embryo has webbed fingers and toes, and a tail, thus illustrating an intimate bond to that primal creature which came forth from the rapacious sea world of multi-diversified crawling, swimming, and stationary creatures, all armored with shell, with ripping teeth and tearing claw, with fleshy spears and poison tentacles, living only to eat and be eaten. We are even more closely related to our primate ancestors—98% of our genetic makeup is the same.

As will be clarified, the further evolving of human consciousness cannot be left to nature's instinct for survival. Self-evolving of consciousness relies on higher mental faculties which have developed over the past fifteen thousand years, involving the growing impulse to comprehend the vaster complexities of the world and the deeper nature of reality. But as culture itself has become slowly stifled by ossifying traditions and conventions, further development is an individual responsibility. This is recognized by our significant sages, who stress that we must strive to transcend evolution's blood drenched narrative of rapacious competition, which manifests in "modern" humans in the form of "look out for number one" egotistical rivalry, bringing about both conflicts between individuals and mass confrontations called war. The pursuit of economic domination of one corporation over another, or one nation over another, is also a manifestation of our primal predatory nature seeping into the cultural ambit. As we begin to investigate the depths of our mind, we come to understand how the influence of our animal impulses upon our desires, dreams, relationships, our entire emotional response to the world, can become all too subtly predominant. In order to become fully what we are as spiritual beings, we must accept our animal nature, yet not be helplessly manipulated by its instinctual coerciveness. We must learn to recognize and consciously suppress negative egoic traits: selfishness, greed, envy, racism, unnecessary fear, which are all rooted in survival impulses. This should be accomplished not with Calvinist disgust or Puritanical repression, or any quality of condescension toward our natural tendencies, but with conscious disciplines to refine and transform chthonic energies for transcendent spiritual purposes. Any activity of intentional discipline performed to induce or enhance one's radius of comprehension transcends the merely instinctual and behavioristic factors of existence. Such discipline need not dampen our Dionysian spirit. As Nietzsche, who despised repressive morality, yet also scorned unhindered passions, stated, *"The man who has conquered his passions enters into the possession of the most fecund region, like the colonist who has become master of woodland and marsh."* Nietzsche was a lover of nature's wonders, thus his "mastering" does not imply domination of an ecologically destructive sort, but a harmonized relationship.

Our proto-hominid past is steeped in the unknown, our narrative riddled with variables, gaps, guesswork. We must realize, on the scale of possibly ten million years of hominid existence, what we call civilization is no more than a 10,000 year spurt of technological ingenuity and innovative manipulation of our environment. This modern society we are so adjusted to, with its myriad of technological conveniences, is largely a manifestation of the last one hundred and fifty years—an incredibly brief episode in the flow of things. And here we are, with our world in a quandary, which will be looked back upon in a thousand years (if anyone is around) as an era of extreme abuse of the gifts of our planetary environment and deranged misuse of the brilliant accomplishments of technology. But whatever our historical-social situation, the seeker must step aside from the current political-economic turmoil and explore the greater expanses of our predicament, encompassing the beginnings and continuing narrative of our species, as well as the subjects that will be dealt with in the coming chapters. Why? Well, you either have an inner magnetism to seek, to question, to explore, to know, or you remain within the sphere of willful ignorance and somnambulistic complacency with the masses. The choice is yours. Leave off or continue.

It should be clear that the planet-engulfing process of evolution is a verified actuality which only a fool would deny. We are mammals immersed within a fantastically extensive four billion year evolutionary surge, encompassing the first pulsing of primal bacteria up through burgeoning and branching of multi-varied life forms, including the entire primate family, to the first hominid, to us. And of this entire incredibly complex process, the most astounding phenomenon manifesting from amid its immense array of life variation is the reality of self-aware consciousness. Though empirical science provides us with much of the information necessary to cultivate self-knowledge, because of its underlying materialistic orientation, which views consciousness as merely an epiphenomenon of brain-neuron activity, we will have to understand its limits. As far as egoic embodied consciousness goes, the materialistic view is true to a certain degree, but falls short in the most significant areas of knowledge. Yet scientists of materialist persuasion, ignoring volumes of data, continue on, smugly confident in their exquisite clarifications of the biological foundation of mind—claiming all attributes of consciousness came about strictly to enhance physical survival, for no other purpose than insuring our genes will continue for future generations. But as we shall see, this stance is built upon a foundation of assumption, biased hypothesis, and ignorance of the deeper realms of Being.

With the knowledge that is available, any person with perceptive intelligence should be able to discern from the world of human culture surrounding us, that there are myriad manifestations of creative endeavor involving thought processes which have not an iota to do with any element of physical survival. Humans are much more than just well-dressed apes involved in sophisticated forms of striving for survival. Our daily reactions to our environment, and to our own thought processes, though not a truly awakened state, does comprise a scope of consciousness which transcends instinctual awareness, even though we are still subject to the influence of animal impulses. Of the various factors that make us unique among creatures, the most profound is the fact that we know death awaits us. But just as significant, we have the potential to develop spiritually by conscious endeavor. The impulse to develop, to grow, is the cardinal inclination of the vast wild branching narrative of our physical/mental evolution. Thus, because our primate past has deeper roots than our hominid ancestry, we must thoroughly understand our animal nature in order to transcend its hindering attributes.

All our animal companions of the earth seek food, warmth, shelter. They are afraid when something threatens and are friendly to what they can trust; they know pain and suffering, hunger and weariness, concern for family, and times of pure joy; and they have, according to species, varied degrees of what we could call a certain body-centered awareness—what Marc Bekoff calls a sense of "mineness,"[3] though not the sense of "I-ness" humans have. Do animals know of death? Well, they fear any threat to their life, and will not go willingly to whatever stalks them—not because they are conscious of death as humans are, but because of the instinctual impulse to live, the tremendous thrust of the basic life force to survive. We see here clear evidence of affinities in the responses of animals to their world with human responses. These affinities are so obvious that entire schools of thought relating to our animal nature have swept through the academic community, periodically enthralling the intelligentsia. Volumes of research by the likes of Konrad Lorenz, Jane Goodall, and influential writers like Robert Audrey and Desmond Morris, and others, have overbearingly highlighted how closely animal behavior is related to human behavior, so much so that this view becomes all many can perceive—thus the "naked ape" concept. Such scientific studies and writings are all too often isolated from sound knowledge of the unique qualities of humanness, and are conducive to dehumanizing dogmas, such as materialistic skepticism, metaphysically sterile humanism, and social Darwinism, all of which contribute to a highly destructive global economics. These "isms" smother and detract from the essential aspects of our spiritual nature. It is within this academic-scientific stream of thought we see the heavy influence of materialism hold sway, excessively equating both animal and human behavior with the mechanistic model of reality. Such a stance is rooted in both the perennial desperation for a rational clear-cut explanation of everything, and what Heidegger called "amnesia of being."

Human consciousness aside, the exquisite complexity and unrecognized depths of all life forms surpasses common mechanistic interpretations. We only have to consider how ants domesticate and care for aphids in order to "milk" them as a food source, how bower birds creatively design and decorate their nests with flowers, acorns, berries, mushrooms, to attract a mate, or the fascinating complexity of the honey bee's pursuit of food sources. A wild raccoon I surprised in my kitchen one night, stopped as it was halfway out the window, instantly interpreting the tone of my voice, "Hey, it's OK," to understand I would not harm it, thus returning to eat the cat's food as I sat and watched. These examples hint at rudimentary forms of consciousness exceeding mere pre-wired behavioral survival activity. Of course, we must be on guard not to anthropomorphize, either in attributing levels of consciousness where they do not exist, or reducing the haunting wonder of animal activity to a comforting Disneyfication.

Once we have accepted our affinities with our animal companions on the planet earth, we can consider abilities which validate the distinct uniqueness of being human. Even on the basic utilitarian survival level, no other animals make clothing, or cook their food, or make such aesthetically pleasing but unnecessarily extensive structures for habitation as we do. But such things as these only highlight differences in degree, not in kind. Despite all seeming similarities, we are different in kind by distinct mental abilities no other creature comes near to, generating our flair for and facility of speech, and our quality of abstract thought. Though various animals may possess a very rudimentary arithmetical ability to count, this is not even close to what humans have cultivated—advanced mathematics, algebra, calculus, physics. And no other creature has any conscious idea of time, of a life narrative entailing past, present, imagined future, of its own birth and death, all of which is the substance of poetry, literature, art, music, science, philosophy. Such "beyond survival" expressions transcend all attempts to connect creative phenomena to strictly biological impulses, which is reductionism of the most insidious sort.

As John McWhorter elucidates in his book, *The Power of Babel*,[4] no matter how marvelous the communicative expression of other creatures, from ants and bees to parrots and chimps, humans are the only creatures able to *"convey an open-ended volume of concepts not limited to matching vocalization..."* All animals have some form of communication, and some can interpret signs, but no other animal has related to and creatively expanded upon the evolved ability to interpret symbols as humans have. The symbol functions as an unlocking device opening a gateway to greater expansion of thought and imagery. Albert Borgmann speaks of the profusion of meaning which radiates from a powerful symbol. Rodney Collin wrote of significant symbols having a referent analogical nature which opens an avenue of understanding between spatio-temporal and higher dimensional realities. In his instructive book, *The Twin Dimensions*, Geza Szamosi illustrates how time and space, fundamental constructs of human reality, are symbolic creations of the mind. He states:

> *Symbolic language was an evolutionary event of the greatest importance... It broke the monopoly of the process of biological evolution... Symbols can also refer to other symbols (making) the range of human symbols not merely large but infinite.*[5]

Susan Langer has written:

> *The power of understanding symbols...is the most characteristic mental trait of mankind. It issues in an unconscious, spontaneous process of 'abstraction,' which goes on all the time in the human mind: a process of recognizing the concept in any configuration given to experience, and forming a conception accordingly... Abstractive seeing is the foundation of our rationality... It is the function which no other animal shares... Symbolism is the recognized key to that mental life which is characteristically human and above the level of sheer animality.*[6]

In James N. Powell's truly enriching book, *The Tao of Symbols*,[7] he succinctly elucidates how human reality is drenched in symbolization. We are "homo symbolicus," inundated, surrounded by symbols of all sorts — linguistic, musical, mathematical, etc. We cannot even think without the activation of symbols. Human language is made of symbols imbued with meaning, which gives it a significant qualitative difference from forms of communication of any other creature, including such complex manifestations as the communicative dance of bees, and the intriguing conceptual displays of crows and dolphins. Human language is more fascinatingly rich than most of us conceive it to be, speech much more than the interpretation of noise coming out of our mouths. As John D. Caputo wrote, "*There is something deeper within man, something which is not merely human, which constitutes man's true dignity and worth.*"[8] And what is this something deeper, greater, higher, which the human race has consistent intimations of by way of religious imagery and ritual? Well, that is what this book is about—the potential within us to awaken fully to the "deeper higher" essence of our spiritual being.

Humanity's place in the evolutionary process is like a branch on an oak tree that is only fifty years old and has 200 to 300 years of growth yet to come. Though we are, as a species, only one branch among vastly numerous others, humanity is unique, for the branch has become aware of its branching, of its place on the great oak tree. We could think of each individual as a leaf, with the process of photosynthesis, of transforming the light, dependent on each "leaf's" willful commitment to opening, to unfolding, toward the solar brilliancy of the soul. This is a question of self-responsibility = the ability to respond to the self's spiritual magnetism. The ancient Hebrew Hof Torah, like most religious works, if interpreted beyond traditional cultural limitations, does contain streams of wisdom. One of the Torah's most intriguing statements is: *"To be human is a promise. We are not, yet."* This then is our predicament within the essentially spiritual surge of terrestrial-cosmic existence.

What then does being human mean? A. H. Almaas states,

> *In a very real sense, an individual who is not connected to his essence is not a human being because the human element is one's essence. He is still a potential, a human in the seed stage.*[9]

To understand this seed stage we must first realize that everything else throughout the entirety of creation is of the "non-human." It is only us—Homo sapiens/homo symbolicus—who partake of that quality unique among creatures, the ability of in-depth self-reflection—encompassing the potential of inner choice to awaken from or remain in semi-animal slumber. Heidegger believed it is only within the human sphere amid the vast non-human that the potential for truth and awareness of Being may occur. What we call human at this juncture of evolution, the first quarter of the 21st century, implies what has been recognized for more than two thousand years in esoteric writings as a creature stranded in some midway predicament between animal and transcendent states of being. We are "in interim," entangled in lower brain impulses, emotions, with limited intelligence, held back from fulfilling the potential of our existence, thus actually not fully human, not yet. The multitudes do not recognize this predicament, for our spiritual potential is overshadowed by the façade of "civilized" sophistication, clothed in designer fashions, with 85% of Americans living in comfortable affluence, in well constructed houses, containing huge TV sets, with very few ever tuned to the two or three channels offering cultural enrichment. We have hypnotized ourselves to believe in the domain of objects, possessions, escapist entertainments. This is the domain where the ego/persona rules, primping, preening, consuming. Religious sects and denominations of Christian persuasion are constructed and formulated, to a large extent, to justify such no-risk lifestyles — with biblical interpretations which bolster conformism, prolong stunted traditions, and contribute to excessive nationalism. Thus genuine spirituality becomes stunted.

To rise above conforming to such mass entrancement, to become authentically human, to realize our full potential, and live in the light of the essential truth of existence, thus opening as far as possible to awareness of Being, the individual must set ablaze his/her will to act, to seek, to risk. The more we live by the guiding magnetism of ultimate truths, the more authentic our lives become. We must know and acknowledge that it is within the "less than human" aspect of ourselves that self-ignorance, false confidence, worthless dreams and schemes dwell, where the potential of becoming a tool for inhuman tendencies lurks, and where evil makes its inroads into the psyche of humanity, often disguised as good. It is this "less than human" element that prompts many church goers to place patriotism on equal footing with the foundational teachings of Christ. A pro-war Christian is an oxymoron. When it comes to political and religious belief systems, people are all too easily manipulated to believe cubes are spheres. But this we shall deal with further on. Let us just acknowledge here that to go through life accepting common ignorance of significant knowledge as a natural condition, is a conforming tendency that cancels out our potential as individuals. The poet Novalis wrote, *"To become human is an art."* We should look upon ourselves as spiritual artists, and our lives as our greatest creative endeavor.

We find ourselves here in physical form, flesh, bones and blood, caught in the zeitgeist of our era, named, dated, our existence certified and recorded at birth and at death. Thinking of ourselves as just higher socialized animals, we assume the reductionist scientific view which reigns in this era, known as materialism, which claims we are "only" evolved creatures confined totally to physical-egoic reality, and all forms of consciousness, whether ordinary, poetic, imaginative, visionary, are only offshoot epiphenomena of the brain, nothing more than the surge and sparking of neural activity. Religion has capitulated to the secularistic influence of materialism, inducing citizenship obedient to the state, which is given priority over authentic spiritual development. So, before gazing into the misty mirror of our deeper essence, let us consider what it is that makes materialism such a powerful force, and where its soft underbelly of fallacy is, into which we can plunge the well honed blade of greater truth.

5 – Materialism's Last Gasp

Get a man to see the mysterious depth
and seriousness of the act by which he
and his neighbor exist, and he will have his
eyes turned upon the bush in which the
supernatural fire appears.
— Austin Farrer

Though science has helped humanity throw off many absurdities laid upon us from thousands of years of superstition, and prevented religious irrationalism and occult delusion from overwhelming the human psyche, from the eighteenth century on, heavily influenced by secularism, naturalism, and materialism, it has drained the mysterious mystical qualities of life from the cultural ambit, thus stifling awareness of the living depths of our spiritual essence.

Vincent Micelli, in his book, *The Gods of Atheism*, wrote,

Natural science, through its process of technical domination, falls into untruth by dissimulating and concealing the truth of Being. For untruth is always a form of dissimulation. Therefore, a one-sided science as a source of real truth has to be debunked. Of course, these scientists gather many facts, announce formulas, develop techniques and predict results. But in many cases this is done not in the name of truth but of power and control... If estranged from the truth from the outset of the quest for knowledge, men often mistake their preoccupation with gathering facts about things as the essence of truth. This is often the scientist's great mistake...and is not part of the revelation of truth.[1]

Representative of the perspective of the "one-sided" materialistic scientist, we have Professor Paul Churchland, who claims truth is not an essential attribute of a mechanistic universe, and need not be considered as one of science's primary aims. In response, I would point out that in science an hypothesis becomes a theory because, concerning the phenomena under study, it is considered closer to the truth than other hypotheses, and a theory becomes law because it has been proven to be true. Mrs. Patricia Churchland, Paul's wife, a scientist of similar persuasion, wrote, *"Truth, whatever that is, definitely takes the hindmost."*[2] The eructation, "whatever that is," verifies her arrogant ignorance of significant areas of human discourse. Scientists of this ilk are numerous throughout every field of research.

Understand that I am not attempting to turn materialists into mystics, anymore than prove to the religiously oriented and New Age spiritualists that heaven and reincarnation are delusions. I learned long ago that attempting to change the mind of confirmed and rigidly biased believers, be they scientists, fundamentalists, or political ideologues, is futile. I do not seek to persuade, only to lay things out in a certain way for observation and contemplation, and let the readers do with it what they will, each individual comprehending what he or she is ripe to comprehend.

How did the overwhelming influence of materialism come about? This has been substantially documented in volumes by varied scholars, so I will just give a precis. We can name two theistic influences that were possibly incipient in setting the stage for the sprouting of Western civilization's concept of a mechanistic universe, which modern materialism is rooted in. The first was the early Hebrews' development of a cosmology unique to the Mediterranean-Levant area, in which the sun and moon had no sacred or spiritual quality, but were just objects created by Yahweh to illuminate the earth. The second was the ancient Greek belief in Zeus, whose victories over the gods of nature augmented the justification of mankind's domination of the natural world. Thus arose generations of what we could call "philosopher scientists," such as Thales, who taught that rational explanations should always supersede supernatural ones. His cohort Anaximander followed suit, though, oddly, both held worldviews forged of irrational imagery — Thales believing the universe was essentially liquid, in which the earth floated like an island, and Anaximander conceiving the earth to be shaped like a column.

Socrates strove to perfect rational explanation in his skilled style of argumentation. His student Plato, circa 370 BC, equated mythos with the false and logos with the true—one of his weightiest mistakes, lacking insight into the depths behind mytho-symbolism. Around 350 BC, Aristotle, attempting to rid philosophy of irrationally influenced reasoning, developed a veritable obsession with deductive reasoning, which launched a style of analytical thought involving the study of the mechanics of how the universe works and changes through time.

In the Euro-Mediterranean area, following the fall of the Roman Empire, religion had become extremely confined to the dogmatic influence of an all powerful and intolerant Christian Church. What was to become known as the Dark Ages, where all knowledge was confined to religious interpretations, fell upon Europe, lasting for centuries. Yet all the while, the expansion of civilization inspired constant technological innovations, which, interacting with elements of analytical philosophy through individuals such as Friar Roger Bacon, laid the foundation for scientific empiricism. Human curiosity about the universe overcame the suppressive policies of a dominating Church. Thus, around 1490, the era known as the Renaissance came about. Greek thought concerning a mechanistic perspective of the universe was reintroduced circa 1601, through the work of Francis Bacon, who believed empirical science should usurp metaphysical speculation. This was further amplified by Galileo, circa 1604, Kepler, circa 1611, and Hobbes, circa 1620, to be followed by Descartes, circa 1636.

Descartes, though a genius, was somewhat daft, a sadist of sorts, and a coward who kowtowed to the Church, remaining silent when he realized Galileo had been right. He developed an intellectually overwhelming mechanistic philosophy from the premises of Kepler and Galileo, the basic postulate of which was that all phenomena were machinelike in essence—matter in clockwork action. John Locke, circa 1665, called the "father of empiricism," (though the title was also given to Francis Bacon), proclaimed knowledge of reality can only be attained from sensory experience. Less than half a century after Descartes' death, Newton, the discoverer of gravitational force, who is looked upon as one of the most prominent figures in the history of science, would amplify this clockwork conception of life in his exposition of the inanimate world. (Curiously, he was also passionately involved in occult studies, including astrology and alchemy). Thus the burgeoning all-pervading influence of scientism came to the fore in post-Enlightenment Western culture, circa 1750, specifically through the works of Hume, who felt that if a person picked up a book that had nothing to do with quantity or experimental reason or number, it should be put aside or even destroyed. A hundred years later Auguste Comte followed Hume, claiming that anything which could not be scientifically measured was unreal and therefore need not be considered significant. Comte, expounding the platform of positivist scientism, thus amplifying Plato's disparagement of myth, even claimed philosophy was obsolete, and should be tossed in the waste bin of the past along with religion and superstition.

Science began to be looked upon as the supreme avenue for controlling the external environment for the benefit of humans. The more rational science became, the more it confined its investigations to natural phenomena that were consistent and predictable, more and more disregarding whatever lay outside the boundaries of certainty, in that darker immensity that always has and always shall encompasses the knowable. As the materialistic worldview began its overwhelming reign, self-knowledge was no longer required as an essential element for understanding the mysteries of life. All understanding could be had by external techniques—weighing, measuring, dissecting, quantifying. Any mystery confronted became just a problem not yet solved. Science became an expansion of intellect enraptured with itself.

We can glimpse civilization experiencing, over a few centuries, the impact of concept shattering breakthroughs—the discovery of the New World, the Copernican awakening, Galileo's findings—all of which were bolstered by pivotal social-intellectual movements such as the Renaissance, the Reformation, and the French Revolution. The all engulfing progress of science over the proceeding centuries justifiably scorned the substantial degree of superstition inundating religion. With each passing century science became so confident in its empirical advancements, it not only debunked superstition, but also inspired denial of spiritual truths intimated through religious and mythological symbolism. This included any beliefs thought to be tainted by mystical and spiritual concepts. Effectively, science threw out the baby of human spirituality with the dirty bath water of superstitious absurdities. Religion itself was persuasively influenced by such "mechanistic revelation," and the concept of the

"Watchmaker God" gained popularity. Though the Church remained a powerful force, inducing the vast majority of ordinary folk to hold to a belief in the traditional religious concept of God, there was little concern for direct experience of spiritual consciousness. And so, contingently, the complacent engrained faith of the multitudes empowered the ever expanding anti-spiritual scientific attitude. Knowledge of human nature became confined to empirical methods only. Scientism, which is the belief that science is the final arbiter of truth, began its reign.

Men now historically famous whose brilliant minds were subject to arrogance and vanity, expounded their materialistic views with influential articulation, not only denying the spiritual dimension of human existence, but eventually claiming consciousness to be entirely an attribute of our physical nature. We could make an extensive list of such "great" men: Hume, Bacon, Leibniz, Laplace, Hobbes, Darwin, Watson, Fichte, Freud, Russell, etc. These renown figures, some traditionally religious but lacking spiritual awareness, thus never transcending the acculturation of their era, developed their capacities of thought oblivious of any obligation to explore their personal potential for more profound states of consciousness. Without ever having attained authentic self-knowledge, the works of these men strongly influenced the basic philosophical, religious and scientific concepts which shaped Western civilization. We can see this syndrome at work among prominent scholars and scientists of today, whose best-selling books attempting to persuade everyone the materialistic viewpoint is how we should interpret even the mysterious phenomenon of consciousness, aptly demonstrate the attitude of many scientists has not changed one iota since Hume made his expositions over 255 years ago. This mental stagnation continues despite the last half century of converging evidence countering such entrenched bias. It is this smug limited attitude that must be exposed, not science itself. Ironically, materialists clinging to their crumbling fortifications are very similar to scientific creationists defending blatantly bizarre religious denials of evolution, distorting any insights of science to bolster their deranged claims. That science itself is essentially a self-correcting process oriented to discovering the truth, leaves room for hope. But scientists under the sway of materialism, in their striving to defend their perspective, and out of vain refusal to admit their own limitations, fail to self-correct.

It is quite clear from the above named "great thinkers," that materialism arose from a masculine dominated attitude which lacks the significant feminine ingredient of intuitive insight. William Irwin Thompson touches on this in his work, *Coming Into Being*:

> *On one side you have the Nobel laureate biologist Barbara McClintock with her 'feeling for the organism,' and on the other, the manipulations of genes as discrete objects by Francis Crick and James Watson, or Jacques Monod and Francois Jacob. In the female context, we have living plants, whole organisms growing in slow and seasonal time within the soil; in the male context, we have discrete objects taken out of their context and subjected to manipulation, control, and sometimes even torture. We have narratives of 'symbiosis in cell evolution' with Lynn Margulis, or we have dramas of power and deception with the selfish gene of Richard Dawkins. We have Harlow and the Yerkes Primate Lab versus Goodall and Fossey in the wild. Male science tends to focus on discrete corpuscular objects — be they elementary particles or genes — and seeks to reduce ecologies of being to single causes that it can identify and control. Female science seems to be pattern based, interactive, and more cooperative than competitive.*[3]

Of course, it's not really such a clear cut gender-determined division. Patricia Churchland fits into the masculine approach Thompson speaks about, and I could name half a dozen other female scientists of similar materialistic persuasion. And there are numerous male scientists attuned to their intuitive, less analytical, what we could call feminine qualities of perception, who are open to other than materialistic modes of thought.

From the late nineteenth century onward, as science merged with the constantly accelerating innovations of technology, the all pervading power of the materialistic paradigm's social and philosophical influence amplified its momentum. Lacking to an extensive degree both intuitive insight and imaginative perspective, scientists put before us the rigid conclusion that all living organisms are complex machines functioning according to fixed laws, that the deeper spiritual and mystical experiences human beings claim to have, are, like the mind itself, nothing more than epiphenomena of neurological activity within the brain, and thus are rooted within and confined to the material dimension. Materialistic science attempts to persuade us that chemical-electrical forces void of any spiritual quality, create and govern a human being's entire conscious existence, that human beings have no substance beyond the reality of the so-called material world, that humans are mere bio-electrical "meat puppets," whose physical behavior and thought patterns are no more than neural reactions to internal and external stimuli.

Such conclusions were reached through the use, (or perhaps we should say misuse), of the empirical method of research, which involves what scientists like to believe is pure objective evaluation: setting up experiments so that the entire process and its conclusive steps are consistently repeated, producing and reproducing exactly the same results, thus giving us the controlling abilities of measurement, quantification, predictability. Though Descartes praised this procedure as the only avenue capable of revealing how things actually come about and function, and many scientists today still cling to this view, professor Joe Rosen demonstrates the fallibility of this perspective in his book, *The Capricious Cosmos*.4 He shows us that forming theories and laws from experiments that are reproducible enough to allow prediction, is a very limited method of inquiry which actually restricts scientific comprehension of existence. Why? Because any aspect of nature that is not reproducible, thus unpredictable and chaotic, is considered outside the domain of science. The fairly recent field of "chaos theory" itself was only integrated into the empirical paradigm because elements of symmetry and pattern were detected, thus presenting what some scientists claim as a high possibility of predictability. Still, "possibility of predictability" retains the suggestion of the unpredictable, since it allows something may or may not occur, thus an element of uncertainty seeps in. Another significant point is that consistent reproducibility that is highly predictable usually occurs within an isolated environment in which all possible external influences are cut off. But, isolated environments do not exist in the natural world, where everything is ecologically interactive and interdependent.

Back in the early 1900's, the philosopher Edmund Husserl became acutely alert to the flaws of scientism, and exposed many of its over-reaching claims in his work concerning phenomenology.5 His ex-student Heidegger stated, *"the scientist weighs and measures constantly, yet does not know the weight of things."* As Vincent Micelli clarified, scientists gather facts, bring forth formulas and predict results with the skillful use of technological instruments—but, though some like to claim to be exploring the "soul" of things when dealing with micro-biology, nano-technology, neuroscience, biopsychology, etc., they have not penetrated much beyond the surface of, shall we say, God's epidermis. Materialistic scientists lack enough as it is, just by their disregard for the immense and significant areas of human existence empiricism is incapable of dealing with. To claim their limited probings reveal anything significant about the "soul" of things is pure hubris.

Though science has opened up magnificent dimensions of knowledge, most scientists stubbornly refuse to see the implications of much it has revealed. It's amazing that many scientists ensconced within the materialistic paradigm, who deal daily with mind boggling phenomena not subject to logical explanation, such as those encountered in quantum physics, cannot consider the metaphysical, the mystical, or the paranormal, without succumbing to cynical vertigo. They even have a hard time accepting experiments accomplished with empirical methodology if it threatens their limited paradigm. This is why they haven't recognized how definitely quantum mechanics has undermined the law of causality, and what the implications are. The work of physicists Alain Aspect, Jean Dalibard, and Gerard Roger, done at the University of Paris in 1982,[6] confirmed how subatomic particles can exchange information even though separated by vast distances, entailing some mysterious seemingly faster-than-light signaling process. Some have said these works are equal to the revelations of Copernicus, and have the potential to overthrow the entire edifice of causality. Why? Well, according to Einstein's theories, nothing that exists can travel faster than the speed of light—and yet, in addition to the above research, there is a phenomenon known as "entanglement," where certain subatomic particles briefly reach speeds faster than light. Then we have David Bohm's "Guide Wave" theory, and what is known as "synchronistic observation," dealing with what Einstein referred to as "spooky action at a distance," which can be related to telepathic phenomena.

The excessive dependence of materialistic scientists upon naturalistic-physicalistic interpretations of existence is as strong as the dependence of religious fundamentalists upon such ideas as a heaven awaiting them with golden streets and a grandfatherly God on a throne with lambs and lions cajoling nearby. But just as intelligent Christians have transcended literal interpretations and immature imagery to develop a more spiritually genuine faith, so have scientists of broader vision and intuitive insight transcended the smothering limits of materialism. Einstein said, "*A sense of the mystical is the sower of all true science.*" And yet, despite this growing awareness of a deeper realm of human experience, a materialistic orientation is still commonplace, and is even taken as law among many highly educated people. This is a dire problem. Why? Because, as many scholarly works have elucidated, materialism produces an extremely dehumanizing resonance throughout various levels of human culture. We can see this dehumanization revealed in the words of Francis Crick, the physicist who helped to discover DNA, who wrote:

> *You, your sorrows and your joys, your memories and your emotions, your sense of identity and free will, are in fact no more than the behavior of a vast assembly of nerve cells and their associated molecules.*[7]

Crick calls his book, from which this quote was taken, *The Astonishing Hypothesis.* Yes, his hypothesis is astonishing—but not as he meant it. From over forty years of researching every field of knowledge relating to the mind and soul of humanity, plus yogic explorations and shamanic experiences, I can definitely say the only astonishing thing about Crick's hypothesis is that it is extremely limited, banal and nauseatingly reductive. Unfortunately, this attitude reigns in much of the scientific academic community and has contributed to various dehumanizing currents of thought in philosophy, psychology and economics.

The spiritually sterile worldview such a reductive perception brings about can be glimpsed in a ludicrous comment from another well-known materialist. Richard Dawkins, speaking about his book, *The Blind Watchmaker*, states,

> *This book is written in the conviction that our existence once presented the greatest of mysteries, but that it is a mystery no longer, because it is solved.*[8]

Despite all the prestigious awards his fellow materialists bestow on him, anyone with intuitive intelligence, or just well-honed common sense, can only consider Dawkins' statement to be pathetic.

In a very fine book of interviews with varied scientists, *Complexity – Life at the Edge of Chaos,* by Roger Lewin, one of the scientists interviewed, Norman Packard, a materialist, states, *"Of course, consciousness seems mysterious, but that is just the subjective element that we humans experience."*9 Packard's words are equal in inanity to those of Crick and Dawkins, and others I will mention, and is a typical materialist statement that blatantly contradicts itself.

The subjective dimension of our egoic mind cannot be brushed aside with a smug "it's just …", which is like saying Niagara Falls is "just" the place where the river flows over a cliff. Though privately hidden and most often unexpressed externally, the subjective element of our mind is where the unhindered boundlessness of imaginal powers, ideas, fantasies, daydreams, scientific inspiration, exploratory thought, illuminated discovery, visualizations encompassing our entire historical and prehistorical evolving, and profound metaphysical visions dwell, resonating with and shaped and colored by aesthetic intuitions, feelings and moods, all ripe with potential of myriad expression through interaction with the "objective" world. Within this fervent crucible of the subjective mind, influenced by both external experience and the fecundity of our subconscious and vast unconscious depths, the extensive and immense creative activities and high cultural accomplishments of the human race, art, painting, music, architecture, poetry, science, literature, etc., have their source. Edward F. Edwinger writes, *"The subjective experience of individuality is a profound mystery that we cannot hope to encompass by rational understanding."*10 Start out with just two subjective questions: "Why do I exist?" and "What kind of entity am I?" and you're already over your head in mystery. As William Broad and Nicholas Wade elucidate in their book, *Betrayers of Truth,*11 materialists, viewing science as based firmly on a foundation of logic and objectivity, overlook the undeniable fact that scientific research to a large degree is rooted in the subjective and thus the irrational operates behind the gilded image of purely rational activity.

Albert Einstein stated:

> *The fairest thing we can experience is the mysterious. It is the fundamental emotion which stands at the cradle of true art and true science. He who knows it not and can no longer wonder, no longer feels amazement, is as good as dead, a snuffed-out candle.*12

When we consider that there is so much about existence science still does not know the essential nature of, it is not hard to view scientists such as Crick, Dawkins, the Churchlands, as "dead" to the numinous depths of the life. Max Born was right when he said, though such scientists show much skill and ingenuity, they definitely lack both wisdom and philosophical intuition.[13] Most significantly, they lack aesthetic imagination and creative visualization. Aesthetic imagination, having affinity with what Coleridge called "primary imagination,"[14] is capable of gleaning the numinous meaning from both modern mathematics and archaic symbolism. Just as mathematical symbols render explicative insights into subatomic realities, spiritual truths can be construed by the awakened mind through sacred symbols. Certain mathematical symbols deciphered by in-depth intuitive clarity can even resonate with spiritual frequencies. The history of religious rites and rituals, and of mysticism, is drenched in number and equation. Albert Borgmann's writings expound on this—God is "one," the trinity "three," the "four" Gospels, the "seven" sacraments—going on to comment about such things as Pythagorean ratios, Vedic geometric construction of altars, and the numbering of colored pebbles found within Mesolithic archeological sites. Every letter of the ancient Greek and Hebrew alphabets was both a number and sacred symbol. Mathematics is a language of both scientists and the mystically inclined, and is essentially an intuitive system. The processes of quantifying, measuring, weighing, are all too often conceived to be what confines scientists to a materialistic orientation. But when followed beyond orthodox limitations, these same procedures lead to mystical connections, esoteric truths and greater mystery. Jung said that number is an archetype. The brilliant mathematicians George Cantor and Kurt Gödel agreed with the Judaic Kabbalists and the Pythagoreans = numbers have a mystical essence basic to the construction of all creation. Cantor carried his mathematic calculations of set theory to an extreme state which he realized could be considered as proof that mystery is the essence of the universe. But one must be careful here, for number symbolism and mysticism can be woven together on looms of occult, theosophical, and kabbalistic schools of thought, to create labyrinthine distortions of spiritual truths. It's up to the discerning mind to free the jewels of spiritual truth within these realms of thought, from the distorting elements of both scientism and New Age ideas unhindered by substantial reasoning.

In his book, *Mind Tools*,[15] Rudy Rucker demonstrates how George Boole, the founder of Boolean geometry, saw various metaphysical principles as algebraic truths. The book, *Jungian Archetypes*,[16] by Robin Robertson, elucidates how Gödel was always conscious of the philosophical underpinnings of mathematics, an insight essential to the creation of his "Incompleteness Theorem," which, as he saw it, put an end to the schema of those who wanted to *"remove the mysteries from the world."* Just as Einstein's paradigm encompassed Newton's, a mysticism harmonized with reason shall encompass materialism. Thus we glimpse the possibility of the unification of science and the mystical. Josiah Royce spoke of the mystic as the most thoroughgoing empiricist in the history of philosophy.

All thought, mystical as well as scientific, is drenched in image, metaphor, symbolism, and thus the very mulch of intuitive imagination. Joseph Chilton Pearce spoke of no profound creative thought existing *"except through imagination, and also no intellect, no logic, no abstraction ..."*[17] Paracelsus said *"Imagination is the star in man."*[18] The great expounder of praise for the imaginative powers, the poet William Blake, saw Christ as a metaphor for imagination, and stated that *"imagination is eternity."*[19] Of course, we are speaking here of highly cultivated imagination, which integrates intellect and logic into its creative process, having little affinity to either daydream or banal fantasy of a Walter Mitty sort, or the fabrications of the religious mentality, both of which entrance the undisciplined ego.

The materialist-naturalist weltanschauung is bereft of symbolic imagination, thus lacks genuine aesthetic perception and metaphysical capability. This limited mental schema produces scientists who spend years making poison gas, diseases for germ warfare, "smart" bombs, and who willingly perform experiments on unsuspecting citizens, all without questioning what they are involved in, just because their work happens to be sanctioned by clandestine government policies. Such scientists go to their laboratories everyday as if they were making vitamins, performing their jobs in a state of moral somnambulism. Whether involved in such malefic endeavors or not, few materialistically oriented scientists have any spiritually imaginative depth in which genuine moral strength might take root.

Understand that my critique of scientific materialism is balanced with my high respect for what true science is, and all that it has brought to humanity. To see the flaws of science clearly, and the shortcomings of reason and empirical methodology, does not mean becoming arrogant with spiritual condescension. One must keep in mind that Goethe's Mephistopheles claimed anyone who scorned reason and science would soon be in his snares.[20] Though existence is far too extensive in depth and scope to be explored adequately by empirical methodology alone, or fully explained by reason and logic, we must use these to the best of our abilities for clarification of what we know and what we may discover. As Pascal clarified, reason itself, if used properly, will perceive its own limitations.

Self-knowledge requires cultivated objectivity, which involves a stringent attentiveness to the impingement of emotional bias and acculturated influences on one's subjective perceptions and ponderings. As Bernard J. F. Lonergan stated, *"Objectivity was the fruit of authentic subjectivity, and authentic subjectivity was the result of raising and answering all relevant questions for intelligence, for reflection, and for deliberation."*[21] Roger Shattuck writes of how an overly subjective consideration of things can bring about a loss of our capacity to judge things rightly, whereas an excessively objective perspective can bring a loss of empathic understanding.[22] Thus it is clear a harmonized balance is called for. As scientists, sages, and poets have clarified, the subjective and objective entwine in the play of consciousness. Gurdjieff spoke of becoming subjectively objective, by way of what he called "self-observation." This brings about an acute awareness of one's state of mind, harmoniously responding to external and internal stimuli. As to human relationships, this subjective-objective element of our existence can be seen as a reciprocal I/thou participation, which the theologian/philosopher Martin Buber maintained was a significant element of spiritual awareness. This process becomes a synchronistic attunement to existence.

In his book, *Synchronicity*, F. David Peat states,

Synchronicities are manifestations, in mind and matter, of the unknown ground that underlies them both. In this way similar orders are found in both consciousness and in the structuring of matter. The parallelism between the subjective and objective aspects of the universe do not so much arise through causal connections, or linear patterns in time, but out of underlying dy-

namics that are common to both.[23]

Joe Rosen touches on this, concerning physicists who realize the mechanistic concept of nature in all its micro-macro immensity does not encompass the whole of existence:

> *Science, in its study of nature, cannot fulfill our demands for objectivity. The quantum aspect of nature involves observers too much for that. So any objective reality must be "farther" from us than nature, than perceived reality. It must transcend them. Thus I am led to the belief in partially hidden objective reality, a reality transcending nature, a reality most likely surpassing human understanding.*[24]

It is here we realize though each of us resides in a private subjective inner sphere as unique in its individuality as fingerprints, snowflakes, and DNA, we exist in the center of a relational interplay with universally objective phenomena. In her book, *Quantum Self,* Danah Zohar clarifies how energies resonating from profound creative expression extend throughout the basic elements of life, based on the *"vital link between thought processes and quantum processes"*[25] — an holistic interaction of internal-external realities. Consider aesthetic perception. Though among so-called "post-moderns" it is fashionable to consider aesthetics as passé or even obsolete, such sterile intellectual opinions are worthless. The word aesthetic can be traced back to a Greek word "aisthetikos," which means a highly attuned apprehension of what is presented. True aesthetic perception has nothing to do with the intellectual detachment of the person known as an "aesthete" — an aloof spectator rather than directly attuned participator. As Heidegger maintained, classical aesthetics highlighted in the world of art and art criticism is apt to reduce genuine attuned aesthetic apprehension to the affected sensibility of a confined intellectual perceptiveness.[26] With his ever articulate brilliance, George Steiner elucidates how true aesthetic acumen is intrinsically consociate with authentic artistic endeavor, which in turn is rooted in the very process of creation itself. Such aesthetic awareness is a conduit to the groundless wonder of the presence of Being, having an affinity with what the Russian psychologist Lev Vygotsky referred to as *"thinking in pure meanings."*

While strolling through an art museum, if we stop to gaze at a painting, our consciousness of the work before us exists neither in the paint and the canvas, nor in our brain, but in some phantom relational point of interchange of psychic-quantum level frequencies:

Observer →	*	← Painting
(Perception frequencies)	Quantum Relational	(Reflected frequencies)
	Subjective Experience	

We never get bored with returning again and again to gaze upon a fine work of art because we are subjectively different each time, allowing subtle expansions of our perception to ignite deeper, wider relational reflections from the art before us, further enriching our experience. Essentially, such is our relational interaction with all phenomenal existence. This is the essence of the creative awareness from which a haiku comes forth—knowing the centerpoint, and being there, still, silent within the dynamic play of it all.

How the subjective and objective aspects of our being entwine in the play of consciousness has been verified from various directions. Zohar states:

> We bring our world and ourselves into being through a shared, creative response to the world and to each other. This introduces a new quantum concept of "shared subjectivity," a subjectivity that is in dialogue with the world and that, through that dialogue, gives rise to objectivity. It is the relationship between the observer and the observed, translated from the physics laboratory into the moral sphere through the quantum nature of our consciousness. This is what Ilya Prigogine calls 'a concept of knowledge as both objective and participatory.'[27]

Michael Novak highlights this perspective:

> There is no self over and apart from the world. There is only a self in the world, part of the world, in tension with the world, resistant to the world. It would be better (although after so many centuries our language scarcely would allow it), to drop the expression 'self' entirely, and to speak instead of 'a conscious world' or, indeed, 'a horizon.' I am a conscious world, a horizon, a two-poled organism, a conscious, open-ended, protean, structuring of a world. The world exists through my consciousness and my consciousness through it: not two, but one-in-act.[28]

Oliver Sacks writes of an acutely aware blind person who spoke of the non-blind as "visually dependent" because their descriptions of their surroundings were so dull.[29] People with normal sight have developed a take-for-granted attitude that they are seeing all that need be seen. But there is a significant difference between a truly conscious person receiving impressions and an ordinary person. The truly conscious person in a state of self-observation is aware of the very act of perception while striving to keep the mind open and free of all inner trash and banal thoughts, fantasies, etc. He/she realizes each experience is an aspect of our existence encompassed by the mystery of Being. Gurdjieff spoke of nourishing our spiritual essence from incoming impressions of our immediate environment, by attentive attunement to every object, scene, tableaux one comes upon. This conscious aesthetic attentiveness is an ability cultivated by the teachings of Zen. Of course, most people are aware of what they observe, but because they are not aesthetically aware of self-observation interplay, they do not properly transform the perceived energies into deeper nourishment of their essence. Though an ordinary person, in certain situations, may be attentively alert to the activity of the immediate surroundings, say, as a hunter in the woods or a cab driver in the city, he/she is still blind to the full depth and scope of the dynamics involved. The ordinary person may feel the delight of a beautiful sunset, or perhaps a performance by, say, the Cirque de Soleil, but the energy is dissipated in the personality's associations; thus the blossoming of the eternal within the immediate is obstructed.

Kenneth T. Gallagher stated in his work about Gabriel Marcel,

The recognition of mystery is the recognition of the self as besieged by being. We only 'are' in so far as there is that in us which thought cannot lay bare: we only know we are by recognizing that there is a positing prior to thought. But this means that wherever there is an encounter with 'being' there is mystery; and it means that every other example of a mystery is a particular manifestation of the mystery of being.[30]

The depth psychologist Carl Jung, the Hindu sage Sri Aurobindo, and the physicist Werner Heisenberg, all clarified cognition is suspended over unfathomable depths. Anything science states about what consciousness is, or how it comes about, is pure assumption or speculation. As Professor Rosen puts it,

> *Science can go only so far in comprehending nature... Any understanding of the whole can then come only from outside science, from nonscientific modes of understanding.*[31]

Such non-scientific modes of understanding are also outside the reach of orthodox religion, as well as superficial "New Age" theosophy-Hinduism-Buddhism hybrids.

Despite the continuing persuasive use of ever expanding empirical research to convince everyone consciousness is just an extended property of neuronic brain activity, materialism is a gradually collapsing paradigm. More and more truly inquisitive and intelligent people of the scientific community are adjusting to encompassing the paranormal and the genuine mystical within their worldview without succumbing to credulity. Ironically this has come about because accumulating empirical research verifies its own process, scientific empiricism, to be inadequate for evaluating spiritual, mystical and in-depth psychological attributes of human existence. To be a scientist incapable of thoroughly considering transcendent, mystical, numinous areas of human existence, reveals an appalling lack of cultural intelligence. Ken Wilber's profound book, *Eye to Eye*,[32] which, like his other works, deals with in-depth scrutiny of consciousness, devastates the extremely narrow viewpoint of scientific materialism by showing us that, in the light of the knowledge now available, the psychological condition of a mind confined to materialism could actually be considered a mental derangement.

Arthur Koestler clarified how, after years of being denied, parapsychology was finally accepted into the American Association for the Advancement of Science in 1969, in response to the accumulation of a great amount of stringently researched evidence.[33] Yet as I write this over thirty-six years later, there are still scientists who ignore the significant research of paranormal and mystical states of consciousness, because much, though not all, of this considerable evidence does not meet the empirical demand of consistent predictability. Of course, we must realize, all too often ideas and research within these fields, including the in-depth implications of quantum physics, the exploration of different levels of transcendent consciousness, and diverse methical delvings into the paranormal, have been tainted in the scientific mind by association with sensationalized New Age quackery, with its seemingly endless list of reductive absurdities, such as Shirley McClainism, Neal Donald Walschism, the overblown claims of Scientology, Eckankar's astral travel, the embellishments of astrology, volumes about fortune-telling, laughable pseudo-levitation demonstrations, the preposterous claims of reincarnation, palmistry, ludicrous channeling of the dead, and on and on "ad nauseam." Such popularized madness has a worse quality of derangement to it than that of the materialistic scientist we have criticized so thoroughly. Yet for any scientist to throw out the living baby of pertinent mystical/metaphysical knowledge with the dirty side-show bath water, is just as unscientific as believing Bigfoot is a yogi Yeti from the Himalayas.

I have to confess, I leaned heavily toward materialism and was an advocate of naturalism until close to thirty years of age, when I began my shamanistic alchemical explorations in earnest. Thus, considering the overwhelming empirical evidence that supports the materialistic view, I can understand how any person with an informed intellect, lacking spiritual intuition and mystical experience, would succumb to materialistic conclusions concerning the nature of things. But a well-rounded holistic intelligence, not confined to merely intellectual-rational aspects of thought, soon discovers the materialist worldview to be founded on assumptions and convictions which cannot stand up to the scope of more expansive knowledge.

Scientific materialists, like both religious fundamentalists and pseudo-spiritual groups, avoid in-depth consideration of any knowledge that threatens their conclusions. I have read the books of every materialist I have criticized and their bibliographies, like those found in the books of fundamentalists and many New Age authors, are substantially lacking in range of research. No scientist or scholar with any sense of integrity should begin to write about consciousness, or the mind, or the soul, or any aspect of existence for that matter, without at least making a sincere effort to become well informed concerning the significant works of contemporary scholars, writers and scientists, such as Eric Neumann, Paul Davies, Ken Wilber, C. G. Jung, Colin Wilson, Karl Pribram, Michael Talbot, Sir John Eccles, James Stewart Bell, Dean Radin, F. David Peat, Roger Nelson, Stanislov Grof, Alain Aspect, Charles Tart, Claudio Naranjo, Russell Targ, Dr. Thelma Moss, and the work of Grinberg-Zylerbaum on transpersonal contact. To disagree with their research is one thing, but to be ignorant of the knowledge these people offer should shame any scientist, no matter how established his or her reputation, and is an insult to the spirit of both genuine scientific inquiry and the overall quest for truth.

Science can never provide us with a total grasp of existence, and any "theory of everything" based on empirical evidence alone would not be all encompassing—for the intuitive insights of myth, the visions of mystics and saints, the explorations of shamans and poets, certainly count in any attempt at total description. But, though science cannot provide us with an understanding of the whole, it can assist us in cultivating a greater radius of comprehension. Though not the royal road to wisdom many have thought it to be, science is a significant highway which can merge with the royal road. Science is a fine tool and an important avenue toward self-knowledge and overall knowledge of our existential-cosmic situation, but so far, the majority of men who use it, do so to build a bulwark of ego security against the insights brought forth by explorations of the mind's archetypal depths and transcendent dimensions. As Lawrence LeShan clarifies in his book, *The Medium, The Mystic, And The Physicist*,[34] behind many of the men and women of science who so confidently articulate and justify their materialistic views, hidden even from themselves, is an existential fear—the same fear that religious fundamentalists are afflicted by, indeed, all zealous believers. It is the fear of finding the foundational belief they have built their successful lives upon to be all too flimsy, absurdly shallow, and precariously collapsible. But they will not admit this, for they do not care to probe farther than the need for psychological comfort allows. As we touched on, cognitive science has proven human beings often reach conclusions through reasoning that is invalid, yet such conclusions are believed to be valid if such reasoning upholds their basic view of the world.

The paradigm of materialism is like a huge building with a significant cornerstone missing. In fact, the whole structure of thought scientism encompasses is unbalanced and will eventually, no matter how many lean-poles are put in place, collapse, as Newtonian concepts of the universe collapsed when confronted with Einstein's revelations. However, this is not total annihilating collapse into complete obsolescence, but a process of being enveloped by a greater more comprehensive paradigm. Newtonian concepts are still valid within the realm of classical physics and Euclidean geometry, which relate to a significant portion of the world as we know it, entailing macro-micro phenomena from the farthest suns and planets to cellular activity. Over the next few decades it will be materialism's turn to be encompassed and transformed by a more extensive comprehension of the depth and scope of Being.

This vaster comprehension is slowly but thoroughly rising within the ferment of 21st century civilization. The force of its momentum is empowered by an unconscious resonance occurring within a psychic skein which vibrates synchronistically in collective attunement with millions of individuals who have committed themselves to the spiritual quest. In partaking of such a quest, the seeker of truth comes to realize the necessity of gleaning whatever and from wherever worthy insights are available, even in the works of those not committed to any spiritual quest, such as those materialists I hotly criticized. One develops the skill to absorb knowledge from many people, scientists, scholars, "gurus," while simultaneously remaining acutely alert to their intellectual and spiritual shortcomings. I have learned from the works of those I have criticized. May they in turn learn from this.

The intelligent, open, and questioning mind does not have to remain limited to a barren materialistic orientation of reality, or succumb to the delusions of religion or overly simplified mysticism. Millions among us can become the companions of the great sages, true poets, profound musicians, gifted artists, philosophers, and scientists of real merit. We can travel with those who know that the brain's magnificent electro-chemical surge of embodied consciousness, in its dynamic ferment, transcends its own activity, igniting frequencies that resonate with dimensions far beyond what we are ordinarily aware of. To know yourself is to know of these things, for such exploration expands our consciousness, enriches our minds, and makes us capable of moving ever nearer to the essential truth of our astonishing existence.

6 – The Mind/Brain Conundrum

To what point must we enlarge our thought
so that it shall be in proportion to the phenomenon.
—Schelling

For they being lovers of wisdom more than worldly wealth,
drove at higher and more excellent operations.
—Elias Ashmole

We now have a fair grasp of how the overshadowing influence of materialism nullified Western humanity's sense of the mystical. The materialistic system of thought, backed up by the rigorous analytical empirical procedures of Western science, gained its power because it was believed to be the most realistic view of things, since it dealt only with the tangible and easily accessible, thus becoming ripe for popularization and victory over the more intangible psychic/spiritual dimensions of reality. Throughout Western civilization, up to this day, formal education has failed to adequately address this situation, and by use of textbooks restricted to idealization of the mechanistic viewpoint, keeps right on producing scientists who zealously believe all experiences concerning spiritual dimensions and higher levels of consciousness are nothing more than by-products of electrochemical reactions within the neurocircuitry of the brain. But as the last chapter revealed, from an enormous amount of converging evidence, an expanding perspective of consciousness surpassing reductionist expositions, has come about with clarifying force. Unfortunately, few scientists of materialist persuasion ever consider information that extends beyond the borders of standard scientific investigation. Somewhere between the naïve belief systems and superstitions of New Age expressions of mysticism and theosophy, and the rigid skepticism of materialistic science, is a more cohesive comprehension of reality and our place in it. This is what we are pursuing here.

It should be clear to anyone that the facet of our existence having to do with mind-consciousness is the most significant we shall deal with, for without consciousness we would not be dealing with anything. All our most profound thoughts, notable ideas, even visions of God, would not exist if we had no mind or consciousness. In fact nothing of what humans call reality would exist. For what we perceive as reality is entirely different in form and psychological association than what any other creature perceives. Since mind and consciousness are words referring to concepts often equated in meaning, I will use them in a fairly interchangeable manner, though more discernment will be necessary as things unfold.

As we begin delving into mind-brain interactivity, we must address the issue of consciousness being conceived as an "emergent property" of the neural networks of the brain. Emergence is a reductionist theory used in various fields, both scientific and non-scientific, which views all phenomena in terms of their component parts. Thus "emergent property" is a term used by physicalists who perceive thought arising from brain activity as similar to biological processes such as sweat arising from the workings of sweat glands. This limited view clashes with the perception of consciousness as a phenomenon transcending brain activity. This clash of viewpoints is the most controversial aspect of the "materialism versus mysticism" issue of the present era. Using an historical analogy, we can think of General George Custer as representing the materialistic stance, and the Sioux warriors as representing accumulating evidence undermining it. So let me pick up my bow and flaming arrows and approach this intriguing brain-consciousness issue starting with the most basic tangible element, our brain.

Since 1650, when Thomas Willis began exploring the brain as it had never been done in Western civilization, we have learned an immense amount concerning what was once looked upon as a strange lump of curds inside our skulls. And we are still learning. As Professor Antonio Damasio, one of the most prominent brain researchers, remarked, *"So much of what can be said about the brain is best stated as working hypotheses."*[1] What is this amazing organ the proponents of physicalism and naturalism, the neuroscientist and biopsychologist, so overconfidently assume to be the seat from which all our spiritual visions and mystical awakenings arise? Inside an adult skull lies approximately three pounds of flesh about as big as two large fists put together, which, in relation to our body size, is considered enormous in comparison to other creatures. Only dolphins have a similar ratio. But brain size within the ambit of our human species cannot be correlated with intelligence. Though a larger brain was significant in our departure from primate ancestors, further development of expanded states of consciousness hasn't anything to do with size. Actually, Cro-Magnon folk had larger brains than the average modern person. There are people with low IQ's who have larger brains than Einstein's, (which is now kept some place in a jar of formaldehyde).

Though specialists divide the human brain into numerous categories, in the standard outline there are basically three main sections, sort of like three brains combined in one: the cerebrum, the cerebellum, and the brain stem. Some scientists prefer the use of the three categories, forebrain, midbrain, and hindbrain, to describe the vertebrate brain in general. One scientist, P. D. McLean, put it in the more evolutionary context of a brain triad consisting of neomammalian, paleomammalian, and reptilian elements. I shall highlight only the basic facets for the purposes of this book, one of which is to show that the brain, though mapped and measured extensively, has not yet and never will reveal an answer to the nature of consciousness.

The cerebrum makes up 85% of the brain's mass, and has two large hemispheres, left and right. It sits over the earlier evolved lower portions of the brain like a helmet, and is assumed to be the main control center for sensory and associative information processing, as well as voluntary motor functions. The outer layer of the cerebrum is called the cerebral cortex, and consists of convoluted gray matter. Although they look similar in jars of formaldehyde, each brain is as unique in its pattern of convolutions as the one-of-a-kind whorling design of a person's fingerprint. The cerebellum, sometimes called the "little brain," situated at the back of the brain, is vital to bodily movement, and also contains the "ascending reticular activating system" which recent research indicates contributes significantly to a wide variety of cognitive and perceptual activity, including definite influence upon the capacity for egoic consciousness. The brain stem, also known as the reptilian brain, is the most ancient part of the human brain, evolving five hundred million years ago in some primal lizard-like creature. It has three parts, the midbrain, which is at the top of the brain stem, and is responsible for many crucial functions, including eye movement; the pons, which is below the midbrain and directly in front of the cerebellum; and the medulla oblongata, which is the stalk-like lowermost part of the brain stem, connecting to the spinal cord. Two other important parts of the brain, considered by some to be components of the midbrain, are the thalamus and the hypothalamus, both of which lie under the cerebellum just above the brain stem. The thalamus is the main relay station for incoming signals to the cerebral cortex, and the hypothalamus is part of what is known as the limbic system, which, in conjunction with the pituitary gland, influences hormone production and emotional states.

As we shall see, the brain is an amazingly ultra complex phenomenon. Recent research reveals the pre-frontal lobes to be far more involved in significant mind activity than previously thought, enough to be called "new brain" by certain researchers. As to the two separate hemispheres, split functioning of "rational left" and "intuitive right" is not as pronounced as current thought has it. Example: 200 million fibers in the corpus callosum overlap in weblike fashion, influencing both hemispheres. Right brain has taken over left brain activity when the left was injured and vice versa. There is an interactive relationship betwixt left and right hemispheres, as harmonized as music coming forth from the left and right hand keys on a piano. During the act of deep meditation the EEG transcriptions of the two hemispheres become totally synchronized.

What we call brain activity is a ferment of dynamic processes which filter and transform the complex incoming flux of electromagnetic frequencies, sensory data and biochemical stimuli, somehow becoming a resonant focal point for magnetizing transcendent realms of consciousness, thus enigmatically activating embodied consciousness. In scientific jargon, the brain converts the chaotic buzz and flurry of surrounding wave-quantum phenomena into what we consciously perceive as the known world. This mass of pudding-like tissue inside our skulls is made from hundreds of thousands of miles of compacted nerve fibers, which in turn are produced by billions of nerve cells called neurons, which magnified thousands of times look something like this:

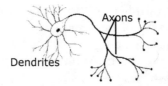

The dendrites are the neuron's input receptors. The axons are the leg-like extensions, which function as electro-chemical output lines. Each neuron is like an electric nano-creature, with quivering dendrites like excited tentacles stretching out in every direction, while electrical impulses rush along its tail (axon), stimulating chemical neurotransmitters that leap across what is called the synaptic cleft, to other neurons. Of course, this is a simplified image, for there are approximately 20,000 to 100,000 synapses per neuron. The neuron, like all cells, is a kind of storage unit, powered by potassium and sodium ions. Within each neuron there are billions of microtubules, a focalized network of hollow "spaghetti" bundled together within cord like sheaths, so tiny they can only be seen by an electron microscope that enlarges things hundreds of thousands of times. These ultra micro strings, million of times finer than the highest quality violin string, ceaselessly vibrate like miniscule tuning forks quivering to a vast spectrum of frequencies.

Twenty-four hours a day, billions of these ten millionth of an inch in diameter microtubule filaments packed together into infinitesimal oscillating tentacles, electro-chemically stimulate at least one hundred billion neurons. Each stimulated neuron manifests constant electrical charges igniting a complex skein of billions of interactive energy components: glial cells, dendrites, synapsial nodes, axons, creating a vast neural web of excitation of one hundred trillion pulsation points, which process information, screening and interpreting, discriminating and repressing unceasing external and internal stimuli, from the top of your head, throughout your body, to the tips of your toes. To do this it uses twenty percent of the body's oxygen, far more than any other organ. We can begin to understand why science considers the brain to be the master organ, and why in yoga the brain is the area of what is known as the highest crown chakra—a sphere of psychic energy which, if released, opens embodied egoic consciousness to more expansive awareness.

Our brain has intrigued the human imagination since it was first perceived as the throne of thought. Writers have dealt with the brain in every mode, through science fiction, comedy, theatre: Frankenstein's monster receiving the brain of an executed criminal, live brains in jars manipulated by mad scientists, etc. Such fiction has intriguing affinities to what can be done with modern medical techniques. Consider the possibility of a brain surviving without a body. If a mad scientist were to take some poor fellow, skillfully amputate his arms and legs, then his lower torso, then his stomach, and feed him intravenously, he could live. If the scientist then removed and replaced the man's heart and lungs with a heart-lung machine, then replaced his kidneys and bladder with similar state-of-the-art machines, then amputated his shoulders, removed his spine and rib cage, thus leaving the poor fellow with only a neck and head, it is possible he would live for some time. No, don't slam this book shut and run for the TV set. Endure, for knowledge, for science, or just for curiosity. Let's speculate that if our scientist continued, he could remove the jaw, the cheekbones, the forehead, eyes, ears, portions of the upper and rear skull, indeed all parts of the head, and keep the person's brain alive in a special container connected to all the necessary tubes and wiring, (sci-fi horror movies become reality). If this "person" with only a brain left is then wired to state-of-the-art computerized biofeedback systems, he could communicate by controlling brain wave patterns which would appear on a screen in an agreed upon code. And if it was the brain of an intelligent person, fantastic conversations could quite possibly occur between this brain and some normal person.

We can also approach the brain-consciousness question from the opposite perspective = can a person live without a brain. Consider that scientific research has verified there are many people who have had large amounts of their brain removed and, with some of them, you can hardly notice it by their behavior. Antonio Battro has written a true story entitled *Half a Brain is Enough: The Story of Nico*,[2] about an epileptic boy whose entire right hemisphere was removed, yet his neurons extended and naturally rewired themselves during the healing process to compensate for what he lost. People have recovered amazingly after total removal of their cerebellum. There are hundreds of people every year, because of disease or accident, who have lost various sections of their brain, and in many cases, the "mind" seems to permeate whatever brain matter remains in order to function properly. We have the research of Professor John Lorber, a British neurologist at the University of Sheffield, who in 1950 told of a student with an IQ of 126, with first class honors in mathematics, who was as normal socially as any young man his age, yet he was hydrocephalic, with an extremely small amount of brain matter in his skull, for his cranium was filled mostly with cerebrospinal fluid.[3] Medical literature verifies there have been many people with various degrees of hydrocephalus who have led normal lives.

Ok, let's consider our imaginary mad scientist again. Once he has accomplished the removal of all parts of the human body except the brain, and has placed the precious three pounds of flesh in a state-of-the-art jar, what then? After all, it is our very body that our personality relies upon for a sense of self-identification. Thus, with a brain in a jar, would the ego go through an identity crisis? Would the brain's consciousness be able to think to itself, "I think, therefore I am..."? The questions we could ask are intriguing. Would there be a powerful deprivation tank type of effect which would send the brain's egoic consciousness into a alternate reality, à la John Lilly adventures, or perhaps a death-and-rebirth process of enlightenment, or the extinction of ego = Nirvana, or.... who knows? And dare we let our imaginations go a little farther and ponder a jar of cerebrospinal fluid that is conscious with no brain at all? Why not? Such ponderings bring up fascinating possibilities. Would the consciousness abiding in a jar of cerebrospinal fluid be confined to the jar? Or would it have OJE's = "out of jar experiences?" Would not the recorded cases of people with only half a brain, or a totally removed cerebellum, or hydrocephalics with only a small amount of brain tissue, all functioning quite well, indicate such a "transcendent" possibility? Such thoughts are a definite catalyst for metaphysical ponderings.

Some researchers posit that consciousness is diffused throughout our entire sensory system, the brain being the main electromagnetic input organ. In the field of neurocardiology the heart is being called the "fourth brain," because of its profoundly influential connections with the neural structures of the head. At Columbia University, the research of Michael Gershon has revealed that a complex skein of nerve cells in the digestive tract—more abundant with nerve cells than the spinal cord—is involved in much more activity than just digestion, and has even been termed "the second brain."[4] Thus we see a definite relationship with three of the chakras—Stomach

(3rd), Heart (4th), Brain (7th). The mind-body issue is still very much a riddle. In the December 1999 issue of Scientific American, Sir John Maddox , a theoretical physicist who was knighted for his "services to science," stated:

*The catalogue of our ignorance must also include the understanding of the human brain, which is incomplete in one conspicuous way: nobody understands how decisions are made or how imagination is set free. What consciousness consists of...is equally a puzzle. Despite the marvelous successes of neuroscience in the past century (not to mention the disputed relevance of artificial intelligence), we seem as far from understanding cognitive process as we were a century ago.*5

Let us take a brief and very condensed glimpse of the historical and prehistorical elements of the brain-mind issue. Within the vast surging of multi-varied life forms across the entire planet, from reptilian seedling through 60 million years of sprouting primate activity, the hominid brain developed. We did not neatly evolve as a science magazine foldout chart might make it seem, just a smooth flowing linear series of stages, from ape to early hominid to modern humans. As our brain evolved over those hundreds of millions of years, a lot went on we know about, but much more we do not know about. Yet we have a slim to fair idea of how the primal upright creatures who left their footprints on the Laetoli Plain in Africa three million years ago came to be what we now are, with our brain so similar yet our consciousness so astoundingly different from all other animals. Though the brains of all other primates, then and now, develop almost entirely while still in the womb, four to six million years ago something happened, (whether it was before bipedalism or after, no one is sure) — the female of those primal creatures began giving birth to offspring whose main brain development occurred outside the womb. Our primal ancestral young had to adapt to the external world while the brain was still in a fetal stage of development. This postpartum brain maturation had immense consequences. With gradual brain enlargement, a unique and powerful stimulation of neuronic activity simultaneously burgeoned forth. From the perspective of biopsychology, we could say our primate embodied consciousness arose from the intricate complexities of brain-interactive responses with environment. Near the dawn of egoic consciousness

101

within our hominid ancestors, survival demanded an acute instinctual attention to the immediate surrounding world. From converging
evidence it seems, over passing eons, such intense attentiveness amplified neuronic acceleration, resulting in the ability to deal with
more complexity in the world. This quite possibly created a feedback
loop demanding even more attentiveness, which in turn stimulated
the brain-eye configuration to perceive more, thus adapting to expanding complexity while intensifying the continually accelerating
feedback loop process.

Over tens of millions of years, the intensely active dynamics of
the brain evolved through fits and starts, and mutations, in constant
interactivity with external environmental change. What seems to
have occurred is that increased dendrite growth and accompanying
neuronic acceleration pushed the consciousness/complexity-of-
environment loop to a level that gradually demanded more and
more need for self-reflection. As millions of more years drifted their
uncalendared way, the necessary survival interactions calling for
more social activity among primal groups brought about seminal
tribal consciousness, and eventually primitive cultural cognition.
Over the vast ranges of timeless ages, the evolving creativeness of
tool making, merging with a rudimentary religious impulse and artistic endeavor, stimulated abstract qualities of thought, eventually
bringing about an ever increasing requirement for early Homo
sapiens to understand their own predicament, demanding communication, thus language. Dreams and shamanistic visions welling up
from the archetypal depths brought forth the need for a religious
oriented explanation. It seems at a certain point this accelerated pace
of mental development set off a brain wave frequency, causing a
psychic resonance which opened the archaic cultural mind's potential to experience higher dimensions of consciousness—at first only a
trickle, possibly by way of shamanistic practices, just enough to
stimulate the consistent sproutings of the individualized self-
reflective process. Thus we can get an inkling of how immensely vast
and exceedingly complex in the play of causes and effects were those
great stretches of millions upon millions of years from which the
brain-consciousness sphere of being evolved. Does anyone but a few
zealous AI researchers think they can even come near duplicating
such a tremendously enigmatic phenomenon?

In this probe of the mind-brain issue I will, for explanatory
purposes, use varied analogical images such as electricity, light bulb,

and radio. These are extremely simplified analogies — linguistically limited ways to ignite visualized intimations of what is going on in the relationship of brain and consciousness. There is no analogical image, including the computer, that can come near to rendering the actual vigorous fusion of brain-consciousness activity. Despite the overblown rhetoric of artificial intelligence buffs with their nanotechnology and quantum engineering, as well as the claims of those known as functionalists and futurologists, including the daffy dreams of Donald A. Norman, the wacko futuristic speculations of Hans Marvec, and the deranged ideas of Ian Pearson about downloading the mind, the brain is tremendously more complex than the most state-of-the-art computers are or ever will be. As we shall see, and as Professor Antonio Damasio succinctly clarifies, brain function is much less like the filing system of a computer and more like a symphony.

I am not about to make an extensive critical probe here. I am only going to highlight flaws which will at least reveal the emperor of AI science wears no real clothes — just simulations made by articulate tailors with skillful use of psychobabble cloth and metaphoric thread. AI scientists who perpetuate and excessively elaborate the "brain/mind as computer" analogy, are career confined exclusionists who, succumbing to both confirmation and oversight bias, continuously ignore significant areas of research which validate the profoundly enigmatic qualities of consciousness. What we have with AI research, involving cyberneticists, biomedical engineers, neurobiologists, etc., is a belief system as stringently clutched to the breast by its faithful as the literal interpretation of the Bible is clutched by religious fundamentalists. A person debating with a religious fundamentalist soon realizes how hopeless it is to think such a zealous believer is capable enough to recognize the obvious absurdity of believing there was once a real Adam and Eve, or that Noah really rounded up all living creatures by pairs to put in his ark. To anyone speaking to an AI enthusiast, it soon becomes obvious he/she is enclosed in a worshipful faith that computers will someday not only surpass human beings in every mental capacity, but will actually become sentient creatures. AI buffs would say to this that the fundamentalists believe in myth but they believe in facts. But as William Irwin Thompson has demonstrated, science itself is a form of myth. Bottom line, AI is grounded on crude simulation and mimicry of human mental activity. Despite delusions of blurring the line between animate and inanimate in future research of photonic connections to nano-microchips, a line is there between what is sentient and what is not that will never be breached. Those who claim computers can think have not truly contemplated what human thought essentially is.

Steve Pinker, a big man in the AI field, asserts in his arrogantly titled book, *How the Mind Works*,[6] that the mind is a system of computational organs. From what we have read over the previous chapters, this has the stench of the over-confident smugness most materialistic scientists are prone to. Pinker's subconscious oversight bias must have kept him from coming across significant research which verifies so many aspects of the mind which are noncomputable. The computational attributes of brain-mind activity AI researchers confine their computer comparisons to, are concerned with the most basic level of neuronic activity, an area where stimulus/response rules, where the behaviorists put all their theoretical hopes, which have been vanquished by knowledge of complexities and depths of mind that don't fit into the mechanical concept. This limited ambit of AI experimentation, entailing mimicry of brain-mind activity, is confined to basic sensory survival perception of the material world, limited to physical laws. Yet even this lowest level of egoic mind involves far more than any computerized computational system can even come close to simulating.

John Casti states in his book, *Searching for Certainty*,

> The key question raised by the computability imperative is: 'Are there natural or human phenomena that are intrinsically uncomputable?' Or, put another way, 'Do there exist 'incompressible' natural or human phenomena?' On general mathematical grounds, we know that the computable functions constitute a very small subset of the set of all possible functions. Therefore it's perfectly plausible, likely even, that the 'true' mathematical descriptions of many observed phenomena are indeed uncomputable. And, in fact, arguments have been presented in the scientific literature claiming that phenomena ranging from turbulent fluid flow to human consciousness can be properly described only by using such uncomputable functions.[7]

Computation has to do with the finite, and a computer can only, in its most extensive forays of iteration, distantly signify the infinite. As Amit Goswami noted: "Computers process symbols, but not the meaning of symbols. The meaning exists in the mind of the programmer."[8] A computer system in a rocket programmed to hit a target does not in any way compare to the exceedingly complex brain activity of a baseball player's intention to hit a home run. As the ball comes toward him, the neuronic surge connecting the processes of the retina to ignition of brain imagery, is over a million times faster than the finest computer ever developed.

To any intelligent person with a substantial comprehension of the world, it is quite apparent AI researchers have no idea of the mind's true depths, thus no idea of their own minds' deepest impulses. Ensconced in arrogant bias, they continue to fill entire volumes with vain scenarios of future computers surpassing all the abilities of the human mind. The puffed up confidence of AI enthusiasts reveals not only just how powerful the mechanistic view of life still is, but how persuasive the influence of the computer-as-mind metaphor is. This is a continuing hangover from over a century of "machine age" idolatry, 1850 – 1980. Even ordinary speech (Lakeoff and Johnson) is filled with metaphors relating to the mind as a machine—"after two cups of coffee my wheels are really turning," and "I'm old and my mind is rusty," etc.—with the most advanced materialistic representation of the mind being the computer.

A computer program for the most advanced robots is an algorithm, a set of directions so exact that in order to perform it must be isolated from any external interference causing even the slightest change which may interrupt its technically confined process. To compare such a fixed agenda to the magnificent complex reality of the free flowing non-computational activity of the brain-mind-consciousness equation, is another demonstration of how unbalanced the rational scientific mind can become beneath the sway of biased expertise. To even think, like the functionalist, that human feelings, emotions, desires, let alone consciousness in all its wondrous manifestations, can be reduced to the source code and circuitry of an electronic computing device, can only be a sign of mental sterility, no matter how much expertise involved in such thought.

Mathematics permeates every field of science, and is used extensively to analyze every aspect of the human condition in relationship to material reality, from quasars to quarks, stock market to taxi fare, extending into the realm of AI research, neurobiology, and, of course, the theory of consciousness as epiphenomenon of the brain.

But there are many significant aspects of the human condition specifically related to consciousness that are completely beyond mathematization, beyond measurement, beyond quantification, beyond computation. Roger Penrose has stated that though some lower brain activity has a algorithmic aspect to it, higher levels of consciousness are fundamentally non-algorithmic, thus no machine can ever have true consciousness or genuine intelligence.[9] Various lines of research have validated that computers can never simulate the immense complexity of human thought and that the most complex sophisticated computer program is significantly less complex than the simplest mental activity of a five year old learning to spell.

The entire foundation of Artificial Intelligence, along with the branch of research in robotics and artificial life known as "Alife," consists of mimicry, signification, and wide-of-the-mark simulation — a diagrammatic mathematical parody that is nothing more than fake life. Ellen Ullman, in an article in Harpers Magazine, October 2002, "Programming the Post-Human: Computer Science Redefines Life," wrote,

> Simulating a self-identifying sentient creature will be a little like trying to simulate a hurricane. Think about how weather simulations work. Unable to take into account all of the complexity that goes into the production of weather (the whole world, essentially), simulations use some subset of that complexity and are able to do a fairly good job of predicting what will happen in the next hours or days. But as you move out in time, or at the extremes of weather, the model breaks down. After three days, the predictions begin to fail; after ten, the simulation no longer works at all. The fiercer the storm, the less useful the simulation. Hurricanes are not something you predict; they're something you watch. And that is what human sentience is: a hurricane — too complex to understand fully by rational means, something we observe, marvel at, fear.[10]

AI buffs have no respect for semantic use of words such as "memory" and "intention," which should never have been applied to algorithmic computer systems. A programmed rocket on its way to a target is no more involved in conscious intention than a wound up alarm clock sitting on a shelf, with its hands moving toward the time set for it to ring. "Deep Blue," the chess playing computer program that beat chess champion Gary Kasparov, can only compute information "patterns"—it does not "play" chess. "Deep Blue" has no joy in winning, no feeling or emotion at all concerning the match, whereas a human chess champion has myriad desires, dreams, plans, memories, ideas, fears, concerns—all simmering beneath his/her disciplined focus upon the game of chess. As Kasparov stated, "Deep Blue may have beaten me, but it did not enjoy beating me."[11]

The most highly skilled computer scientists, neuro computer specialists, cyberneticists, etc., despite their most ambitious imaginings, do not now have, nor will they ever have the knowledge and ability to create a computer that will ever feel hungry or thirsty or irritated, or have an itch, or have any powers of intuition, any moral sense, any sense of humor or sexual desire, or any feelings of the marvelous emotions inspired by art and music. So how could they ever create a robot in any way comparable to a human being, except perhaps for physical form and features? Nor will robots ever manifest the intricacies of human language. Though a robot can be programmed to mimic human speech, it cannot begin to approximate the complexities of verbal communication. And despite those AI zealots hot on the goal to create a computer with emotions, they are like explorers during the early 1900's searching for Shangri La. To paraphrase Albert Borgman, that humans think, feel, express emotions effortlessly, does not mean we do it mechanically.[12]

The state-of-the-art robot Kismet, no matter how "cute," merely mechanically mimics human facial expressions with no more life than a puppet on strings, or a child's windup toy. It has no genuine capacity for true human emotion, or sensitivity to pain or pleasure, or moral discernment. Though we will eventually create exquisitely human looking, moving, speech mimicking robot-computers that will respond to their owner's voice, or even (very doubtful) build a replica of themselves, they will still be programmed and maintained by humans. And yet, by way of entrenched oversight bias that blinds AI enthusiasts to the blatant limitations of many of their conclusions, computer zealots continue to interpret experiments they themselves devise as signs of sentient awareness. They completely "mistake the tool for its builder." As for future computers directing human slaves, despite science fiction imagination and runaway personification, computerized robots will not only never have a desire to rule over humans, which entails an urge for power only humans are capable of, they will never ever demand freedom, or be in any way concerned with freedom, because they will never grasp the significance of freedom, which is a concept rooted in 10,000 years of human cultural experience. AI enthusiasts who think otherwise are in dire need of therapy.

Contrary to the diatribe of computer evangelist Marvin Minsky, who claims future computers will have humans as pets, there will never be even a semi-sentient android like the character Data on Star Trek, or the robotoid house servant played by Robin Williams in the movie "Bicentennial Man." As Rudy Rucker clarifies, no matter how fancy walking robots may now be, none can yet convert coupled 2-D pictures and records of motion into 3-D models. And even if they ever do, this will not be anything like how human perception functions. AI scientists can not make a computer capable of responding to random threat as quickly as a cockroach does.

The AI enthusiast's ambition to eventually simulate a mammalian emotion is as disengaged from our actual existential-psychological-biological situation as those people who have their bodies or just their heads frozen after they die so they may possibly be revived in some more technologically advanced future, never realizing that such freezing destroys the cellular structures to such a devastating degree that nothing will remain that is capable of revival. Not only will computer devotees equate a computer's data storage capacity with human memory, and computer programming with human intention, some have even slipped over the edge to the degree that they not only see computers as having a potential for sentience, but eventual spirituality. They expound on this without even batting an eye. A lecture was held at Stanford University in 2000, with the theme "Will spiritual robots replace humanity by 2100?"

No computer can even begin to originate a philosophic meditation on the meaning of existence without a human programmer at the helm. And even if it spewed forth an intelligible essay gleaned from its sterile filing system, it would only be a sophisticated but spiritually barren mimicry of real philosophical intelligence, which requires genuine human feeling grounded on worldly experience. A computer will never dream, a computer doesn't have and will never have a subconscious, a computer will never have passion, a computer will never have intuition, a computer can never resonate with unconscious archetypes, a computer will never have an "inner" awareness, thus will never have mystical experiences, or visions. The AI dream of eventually creating a nonbiological "spiritual" robot is a sure sign of what Heidegger called "amnesia of Being," if not outright deranged alienation from coherent intelligence and intuition. To consider some future computer as having spirituality is a projection by spiritually undeveloped humans attempting to fill their own inner void. By projecting human spiritual potential onto computers, AI enthusiasts avoid the hardships and dangers of the authentic spiritual quest they themselves have repressed into nonexistence as they look toward a future super-computer as some sort of Messiah.

Theoretical physicists and quantum information analysts conceive the universe as a giant computer, even though one of history's finest scientists, Sir James Jeans, wrote almost a hundred years ago, *"The universe begins to look more like a great thought than a gigantic machine ..."*[13] which contemporary research into human consciousness and perception verifies. Conceiving the universe as a giant computer because it manifests certain significant computational qualities is like conceiving a forest fire as a bushel of hot peppers because they both possess heat. This desperation of AI enthusiasts for simplified reductive metaphors of consciousness seems to be a sign of a kind of shrinking or evasive narrowing effect of the materialistically inclined mind, permitting an escape from genuine reality into one which can be manipulated and controlled. As Judith Hooper and Dick Teresi clarify, in their book, *The Three-pound Universe*:

> *In science metaphors are called 'models,' and they are more than figures of speech, for they shape, direct – and sometimes confine – our knowledge. It's an interesting commentary on the fellowship of man and machine that brain metaphors have historically been drawn from the most advanced technology of the age. Descartes's models were inspired by the ornate water clocks of his day. In the heyday of steam engines, Sigmund Freud envisioned the central nervous system as a hydraulic system in which pressures (drives) build up and required 'discharging.' In the early 1920s the brain was likened to a telephone switchboard, and not coincidentally Ivan Pavlov, the high priest of the conditioned reflex, began preaching that behaviors were built of layers of reflexes, of hard-wired connections between different brain parts... The latest model is, of course, the computer, which began to haunt neuroscience in a big way in the early 1960s. Now*

terms such as 'inputs' and 'outputs,' 'encoding,' information 'storage' and 'retrieval,' 'parallel processing,' and 'software' are part of the everyday idiom of the brain...[14]

William Irwin Thompson writes,

These dominant metaphors are literally dominating and force us into the submission of belief in the doctrinal narratives of big science. We submit to the technology of explanation because the explanation is technological ... Technologies have stabilized a consensual domain for us moderns more effectively than faith, doctrine, or poetic visions. We all look at buildings that don't fall down and rockets that go to the moon and... worship science and technology in an idolatrous fashion."[15]

Recalling the descriptions of the mind Jung, Aurobindo, and Wilber have given us, involving levels of expansion and depth of consciousness, we realize that approaching the deeper truths of our essential humanness by way of the materialistically oriented intellect will always fall far short of cohesive comprehension.

There is no doubt the brain, empowered by the dynamic interplay of bio-electro-magnetic energies and neuro-chemical ferment, is the most profoundly complex organ in the human body. Thus it is easy to understand why scientists who have mapped out how specific activity within various parts of the brain relate to certain body movements, mental functions, emotions, feelings, etc., have come to believe it is within this marvelous three pound mass of pudding that consciousness is born. As far as egoic consciousness is concerned, they are right to a certain degree. But not totally right, for there is "something more going on." It is a challenge to reach an understanding of what this "something more" is, for the whole issue is rife with claims/counter claims and contradictions. Let us examine this field of contradictions, and with the sparks of critical contemplation perhaps enough light will be cast about to enable genuinely open-minded readers to discern the wheat of truth from the chaff of assumption and biased opinion.

Over the past century, quantum physics has revealed more about the nature of matter than has been known since the beginning of Western civilization, with the potential to reveal even more. For scientists to get upset about the use of quantum physics to support the claims of mysticism is counter-productive. In-depth contemplation of quantum physics is a valid gateway to metaphysics and mysticism. For those newly approaching this field, rest assured that a person does not have to be a rocket scientist to grasp the basic tenets and implications of quantum physics. The best approach is through the development of classical physics, a science we can trace to ancient thinkers of fifth century Greece, who began by studying such things as motion, quantity, form. It is an intriguing tale of discovery (tremendously compressed here) beginning thousands of years ago in Egypt, where, long before Pythagoras was born, the pyramid builders were applying what we know as the Pythagorean theorem, using a highly skillful method of tying ropes in knots. Centuries later the Greek mystic and mathematical genius, Pythagoras, who had learned extensively from the Egyptians and possibly the Vedic altar builders, went on to explore the marvels of numbers much farther, along with musical harmonies and cosmology. Eventually, expanding on these matters, the Greeks came to the bewildering discovery of irrational numbers, which cannot be expressed with either fractions or finite decimals, but involve infinite series of tedious equations. Another Greek mathematician, Euclid, put together his great mathematical composition of geometry, The Elements, which became a platform for yet another brilliant Greek, Archimedes. Over the centuries, their work eventually ignited ideas in Copernicus, Galileo, Descartes, and thus influenced Western civilization for over two thousand years. In fact, Newton, the mentally beleaguered mathematical giant who lived from 1642 to 1727, used The Elements as a base to construct the Principia, his great work on the laws of motion and gravitation, which dealt with everything from the orbits of planets to the rise and fall of the ocean tides, and contributed heavily to the mechanistic view of the world with its limited concepts of cause and effect. From there, we can follow this path of discovery across generations to the nineteenth century and early physicists such as Boscovitch, Ampere, and the intuitive Cauchy, who claimed even then that atoms were made up of other unknown elements of energy. Then came James Clark Maxwell's investigation of light and electricity, circa 1860, from which came the "electromagnetic theory." We go from there to Henri Poincare's work, which led to Max Planck's idea of energy packets called "quanta", followed by Einstein's work on photoelectric effect. We then come to the independent discoveries of Louis de Broglie on the dual aspect of light, leading to the first works of quantum mechanics and the expansive research of Heisenberg and Schrodinger. Actually, the term "quantum mechanics" is somewhat misleading to the public at large, for this field of science deals with things on an entirely different level than commonly conceived mechanized activity. "Quantum processes" would have been preferable.

According to the laws of physics, there are three basic forms of matter: solid, liquid, and gas. These three forms make up the magnificent multi-diversity of all phenomena, the ten quadrillion things—wood, metal, plastic, smoke, fog, steam, clouds, fumes of all sorts, air, water, flowers, wind, breath, blood, bones, the brain, etc. And all such phenomena, whether solid, liquid, or gas, are made up of various densities of molecules, which in turn are made up of atoms. Ninety-two different kinds of atoms in multi-diverse combinations bring into being all known phenomena in the universe. Even the largest atom, hydrogen, is so ultra micro, it would take 85 million of them lined up in a row to span the length of an inch. In turn, atoms are made up of even tinier elementary particles—protons and neutrons, which are in active relationship with "orbiting" electrons. An electron, which seems to be fundamental, that is, not composed of any other elements, is actually a pulsation surge of energy scientists can only study by photographing its streaking passage through a huge machine called a cloud chamber, or particle detector. The protons and neutrons that make up the nucleus of the atom are made up of what are called quarks, which are "glued" together by intense sparkling configurations of energy called gluons. There are six kinds of quarks which are now being studied in a new field called "quantum chromodynamics." Quarks are of a "size" that makes the hydrogen atom look gigantic in comparison. We are way beyond teeny-tiny here. Whereas the laws of classical physics hold true on the scale from the largest planet in the universe to the realm of micrometer measurements of such things as blood cells and even molecules, these laws break down at the subnuclear level—thus the need for a different kind of physics = quantum physics. Subnuclear particles are nothing "actual" in and of themselves, but are "tendencies to actualize." Though termed "particles," they are not really "part" of anything, as such. We are dealing here with names, with labels, which are essentially metaphoric quasi-descriptions of various specter-like points and streaks of force. The great physicist Max Born spoke of subnuclear particles as "named observations," which exist on the frothing edge of non-existence, definitely beyond the entire scope of any imaging capabilities of the human mind.

Thus, in the quantum realm, when we talk of subnuclear particles, we must come to realize that we are dealing with "things" beyond the human conception of size. No subatomic particle actually exists as a solid form. Hundreds of these subnuclear particles have been discovered, which more than one physicist has called a "zoo" — quarks, gluons, sigmas, rhos, muons, mesons, xis, and more—and most of these are completely devoid of any "physical" attributes, having no mass or weight at all. Even when it is discovered that a subnuclear particle has mass, do not mistake this for "solidness." The significance of all this is to realize quantum level phenomena can no longer be considered matter as it is usually thought of.

As a sphere of "mass" and energy, the atom should probably be visualized more like the tip of a Fourth of July sparkler than a tiny solar system. But even this image misleads us as to the actual insubstantiality of the phenomena involved. Whenever quantum physicists attempt to explain, thoroughly and in-depth, just what subnuclear particles and quantum forms of energy actually consist of, and the essential nature of their activity, their explanations eventually go way beyond the logic and reasoning associated with classical physics, and into the realm of paradox and wonder. When we get down to the essential activity of subnuclear material, we are dealing with the realm of the bizarre and the illogical. This is where a single subnuclear "particle" can exist in various places at the same moment, where one single "particle" can go through two side-by-side holes in a metal plate simultaneously without splitting. Contradictory, weird, and very elusive are the forces of which the very "solid" matter of our everyday world—including our brains—in essence is made. We cannot avoid confrontation with paradox and perplexity when dealing with this baffling realm. It is in this eerie borderland without any borders between what is "solid" and simultaneously "not solid," between "brain" and "something more than brain," that egoic mind and greater consciousness dwell in reciprocal interchange. This greater consciousness exists within and beyond the "unconscious" posited by Jung, and is validated by 5000 years of empirical yogic experimentation.

Physicists of materialistic persuasion, finding themselves in a quandary and abhorring any acknowledgement of mysticism or other dimensional levels of consciousness, attempt to describe with labels and metaphors what is essentially indescribable. This has tended to mislead us about the real nature of matter, and has created oversimplified and even false imagery. Simplification of description is known as reductionism. This can be positive in breaking down a complex idea into simpler components in order to get a clearer grasp of the total structure. But it becomes negative when it reduces or oversimplifies something to the point of distorting its reality. The best scientists admit that there are no simple explanations or images available. The renown physicist Werner Heisenberg wrote, "*The very attempt to conjure up a picture of elementary particles and think of them in visual terms is to wholly misinterpret them.*"[16] Many contemporary scientists make this mistake. Some time ago I saw this syndrome in action in a scientific TV special. A physicist whose book was a best seller used stunning diagrams and amazing special effects to portray the concepts he was working with for the television multitudes, which could be called making visual metaphors, though even he spoke as if what we were seeing was what actually occurs at the subatomic level. Such diagrams are similar to maps of the United States, where each state is a different color and shape, with the names of towns, cities, highways. Yet as any photograph taken from a satellite reveals, there are no color patterns or boundaries separating states, no names. Scientific diagrams concerning quantum realities are contrived representations of non-representational phenomena, and can only be used to speculate about possibilities. Such diagrams certainly do not resemble what is actually happening within the fantastic dynamics at the subatomic level.

It was Einstein's world shaking equation, $E = mc^2$, that revealed matter and energy were not separate realities but a single perpetually congealing and dispersing phenomenon, consisting of constantly interacting subnuclear forces unremittingly transforming into atomic, molecular, cellular states of the myriad forms which make up known "material" reality. As a person explores the realm of quantum physics, which deals with these very subnuclear forces, he/she will come across dozens of strange and amazing things, mind boggling happenings such as time warps, space stretching and bending, the existence of a mirror universe of anti-matter, and theoretical reality expanders such as the Pauli Principle, Heisenberg's Uncertainty Principle, Schrödinger's Cat, M-Theory, Calabi-Yau shapes, Zero-brane, and more. Such exploration calls for months of study to become fairly cognizant of these fascinating constituents of quantum physics. We should be sufficiently informed about these extraordinary aspects of our existence to help keep us constantly aware of the essential enigmatic dynamics of matter, the very "stuff" of which we are made.

When we speak of quantum level phenomena as pulsating surges of force, are we not in territory that could easily be considered ethereal? And if such rarified force, such "tendency to actualize," is the incorporeal "stuff" the brain fundamentally consists of, would not consciousness itself have even more of an essentially mysterious ethereal quality? Is not the specter lightning flash realm of quarks and gluons on the very edge of the deepest archetypal depths of the immaterial unconscious mind, and perhaps transcendent levels of consciousness that our normal ego-consciousness, bound as it is by acculturation, is not ordinarily aware of? We must open ourselves to consider such things if we are to be authentically spiritually aware human beings.

Keep in mind that in quantum mechanics, as in theoretical physics, we are dealing for the most part with theories, hypotheses, probabilities, assumptions, where the fundamental nature of scientific observation becomes paradoxical, meta-complex, uncertain, intriguing — where what is being observed is so interrelated to the consciousness observing it that it is changed by that very observation, so that we can never accurately observe what we are attempting to observe. This is the basic insight of Heisenberg's Uncertainty Principle = we will never know the initial conditions of the quantum phenomena we observe. Niels Bohr, a Nobel Prize winning physicist, stated, *"If a person does not feel shocked when he encounters quantum theory, he does not understand a word of it."* Bohr was one of the creators of the over simplified "miniature solar system" model of the atom, which he later realized was far too simple.

Scientists with a materialistic bent seem to prefer having things fit into orderly schemata, which usually involve equations imbued with a certain symmetry. In fact, most hypotheses of mathematical physics and quantum physics adhere to a certain elegance of symmetry as a criterion to qualify as theory. But, just as we know Nut the Egyptian sky goddess isn't actually arching her giant human-like body over the bowl of the heavens, we know the quantum forces and information processes scientists have confidently labeled cannot really depict what is actually going on within deeper levels of reality. What is going on? Well, that's what we are exploring here.

We could say research accumulated from quantum physics has, in its probing of matter, dematerialized the material world, rendering hardcore materialism obsolete. As quantum physicist David Bohm wrote, "Matter is like a small ripple on this tremendous ocean of energy, having some relative stability and being manifest."[17] All known phenomena which make up everything within the material world are basically varied forms of what Einstein called "congealed energy." Thus the "solid" brain in your skull, as with all phenomena, essentially consists of molecular-cellular processes which are themselves congelations of subnuclear particles, which in turn are condensations of light, which in turn is...?

All existence as we perceive it, receive it, relate to it, our entire physical terrestrial realm of being, is an immense explicate cosmic skein which has burgeoned forth from a vast implicate meta-quantum source of ever dispersing and congealing multi-frequencies of enigmatic information exchange. And from converging evidence a numinous consciousness is the ultimate foundational matrix. To pin the callused misused label "God" onto this matrix is to reduce its haunting splendor.

7 – Consciousness and Being

In the mountains of truth
You never climb in vain.
—Nietzsche

The limits of reason, we may reasonably surmise,
hardly define the limits of reality.
Nature is not bound by the limits we impose.
—E. Randall Floyd

OK, we have pondered the master organ we call the brain, and the elusive complexity of embodied and disembodied consciousness, with intriguing relationships to what occurs within quantum realms. It is crucial for the seeker of truth to have a confident understanding of such things. But we must proceed cautiously, being very careful not to be swayed by the materialist claim that consciousness is just an emergent property of our physical nature. This claim can be very persuasive when backed up by empirical evidence that most attributes of our embodied egoic mind— memory, personality, emotional response to reality, attitudes toward political, social and personal issues—can be altered by tumors, injury, chemical imbalance, and electro-stimulation of the brain. But we are concerned here with "something more," some greater numinous consciousness that engulfs the egoic ambit of mind. Both in philosophical and mythological writings of ancient Greece we find the idea of the "winged soul," symbolizing the potential within us to truly grow, to soar above the swamp of common embodied consciousness. The quest for self-knowledge, which includes delving into such things as the mind-consciousness-brain configuration, spreads the wings of your mind, and thus your soul. To the person who has directly experienced transpersonal levels of consciousness, or to the individual with an expansively intuitive mind, the brain is understood to be not merely the ground source of embodied ego consciousness that evolved from our animal ancestry, but also an interactive resonance receiver of transcendent frequencies of consciousness.

We have to consider this subject "outside the box" of common sense, beyond the limitations of spiritually rootless logic and reasoning, for the brain-consciousness conundrum is as perplexing as quantum physics. Nick Herbert, in his marvelous little book, *Elemental Mind*, expressed this perplexity when he said, "*Physicists can perform quantum experiments of unprecedented accuracy, and correctly predict the results, but what they cannot do is clearly say WHAT IS GOING ON in these experiments.*"[1] When we come down to it, quantum physics can only give us a restricted description of quantum reality. The same could be said of neurology and biopsychology, for they deal with the brain-mind conundrum through limited empirical methods which severely hamper the full consideration of how consciousness comes forth into the human sphere of existence.

Thus we see how necessary it is to keep an unbiased open mind when approaching the depths of this subject matter. Open mindedness requires "integral inquiry," meaning we must look at all evidence with an intelligent flexibility. Years of education within a classroom/laboratory atmosphere oriented to scientism can ossify the mind, restricting it to a very narrow range. Intelligent reasoning entailing well honed flexible skepticism harmonized with keen intuition, can usually detect where truth dwells.

Let's reflect on a passage from the work of Hooper and Teresi, *The Three Pound Universe*:

> *An illustration from the 1930's depicts the brain as The Control Station of Your Body. In their separate offices sit a Manager of Speech, a Brain Headquarters (in Cerebrum), a Manager of Reflex Actions (Cerebellum), a Tester of Foods, while in the Camera Room industrious 'camera operators' run the giant projector of the eye.*
> *Of course, we all know this factory-brain is about as realistic as those ancient maps of the world with their leviathan-infested seas ('Here be dragons') and enchanted isles. But we tend to confuse our more sophisticated 'maps' – such as the simplified textbook diagrams of nerve pathways – with the real thing. Hence*

the reductionist dream of a point-to-point correspondence between a mental event and a brain event, as if, ultimately, our entire mental life could be mapped out onto the surface of the cortex. But the more we learn about the organ of consciousness, the further we seem to be from such a wiring diagram...

Thus no EEG apparatus ever dreamed of could plot the course of the stream of consciousness. Nor can obsession, paranoia, or creativity be explained by measuring microscopic amounts of chemicals or by trying to label neuroreceptors as if they were stuck on a circuit board.[2]

One of the essential elements we are trying to grasp here is that materialists, with canons of ample evidence aimed at validation that all forms of consciousness are dependent on brain-matter activity, never truly consider that the brain itself, as all matter, is fundamentally an elusive excitation of forces we do not essentially understand the nature of. We must bear in mind, the strongest evidence to support materialistic claims positing all mental states as correlated to brain states, thus supposedly identical, is based on research garnered by scientists entrenched in oversight bias. An example of this bias was expressed in an article in Humanist magazine, by Professor Bruce H. Hinrichs, who elaborates the "consciousness dependent on brain" canon to its full extent. With the typical smug assurance of the materialist, he states,

Brain imaging technologies are now capable of identifying people's moods, temperaments, various types of memory, perceptions, and numerous other mental states. In monkeys, microelectrodes have recorded the individual neurons that fire when visual perception shifts from one interpretation of a stimulus to another (David L Sheinberg). Corresponding brain sites have been identified in human subjects (Sahraie). Two independent studies (James B. Brewer and Anthony T. Wagne) found that the amount a person later remembered could be predicted by looking at activity in the brain's hippocampal region during learning. William Marslen-Wilson and Lorraine Tyler were able to identify different brain areas for storing regular and irregular past tenses of verbs. The brain areas that process nouns and verbs are separate from one another and have been identified (Antonio Damasio).[3]

Hinrichs' statement is riddled with semantic distortion. The word "storing" brings forth the image of a filing cabinet filled with verbs and nouns, which is as misleading as the image of the atom as a tiny solar system. That scientists make the very questionable claim to have located specific areas of the brain that perform such functions, in no way means they can explain how nouns and verbs come together in an individual poet's mind to create great verse. The poet's trans-emergent creative flow of thought cannot be identified with any activity of the brain. There may be a stimulation of activity within a certain location of the brain while the poet's creative thought is flowing, but that is as far as it goes. Thought transcends brain activity as light, revealing everything within a once darkened room, transcends the light bulb. Thoughts do not exist in the neural network of the brain any more than words exist in telephone wires.

In their enthusiasm, scientists working with magnetic resonance brain imaging technology succumb to excessive extrapolations and assumptions as to the evidence revealed and what they believe it means. An MRI scanner does not take a snapshot of a thought—it makes images of brain "hot point" activity. Images on an MRI scanner reveal only the brain area activated when certain thoughts are present in the patient's mind. The scientific ability to map the "hot point" areas of the brain that coincide with a person's mathematical reflections or linguistic contemplations, is in no way related to discovering the "mechanism" of consciousness. That scientists can locate a place on the brain that becomes a "hotpoint" when a person feels anger or love, in no way explains or will ever be able to account for the complexity of psychological causes which brought about those emotions. Our thoughts and emotions surpass the bio-physiological dynamics of the brain, just as violin music transcends the friction play between bow and string.

The physicist A. S. Eddington has written, *"What goes on in the brain resembles the simultaneous thought process about as much as a telephone number resembles the person answering the phone."* John Hick further elucidates,

> *Thoughts on the one hand, and electro-chemical events in the physical brain on the other, seem to be realities of quite different kinds... The theory that my consciousness of the night sky is, identically, a set of physical changes in grey matter is thus para-*

*doxical in the extreme. It will be said by the mind/brain identity theorist that although the experience of seeing the night sky is, phenomenally, admittedly very different from an episode of cerebral activity, yet the two may nevertheless be one and the same: what is subjectively the experience of seeing the night sky, may be, objectively, a brain state or states. It must I think be granted that this is a conceptual possibility. To this extent the mind/brain theorists may be said to have made out their case. But they normally claim to have provided reasons for believing that this theoretical possibility is in fact realized. Against this it must be insisted that <u>evidence of mind/brain correlation is not evidence of mind/brain identity</u>. It is of course compatible with identity; but it is positive evidence for no more than correlation. Further, the prima facie state of affairs remains one of distinction, and indeed radical distinction, rather than identity. Thus whilst it is entirely plausible that something going on in my brain causes my consciousness of the night sky, sustains it, and is indispensable to it, the claim that my consciousness of the night sky literally is — exclusively and without remainder — my grey matter functioning in a certain way is a claim that two things which are apparently different in kind are really one and the same.*4

Walter Penfield, one of the world's foremost neurosurgeons, recognized potentially disembodied elements of mind few other scientists considered at that time (circa 1950). After a long career wrote:

*To suppose that consciousness or the mind has localization is a failure to understand neuro-physiology. The mind conditions the brain. I found no suggestion of action by a brain mechanism that accounts for mind action. That is in spite of the fact that there is a highest brain mechanism and it seems to awaken the mind, as though it gave it energy, and seems itself to be used in turn by the mind as 'messenger.' The mind must be viewed as a basic element in itself. One might then call it a medium, an essence, a soma. That is to say, it has a continuing existence. On this basis, one must assume that although the mind is silent when it no longer has its special connection to the brain, it exists in the silent intervals. The exact nature of the mind is a mystery and the source of its energy has yet to be identified. It acts as though endowed with an energy of its own.*5

Penfield's words, "*the mind is silent... it exists in silent intervals,*" cue recall of the words of Heidegger, who, in his own profound contemplations of mind and being, wrote, "What is stillness. It is in no way merely soundlessness." This inner silence, this numinous stillness, this "wholly other" aspect of mind, is also touched upon in the teachings of Zen concerning "mind stuff," and the silent "suchness" of things during deep meditation. And we can find relationships of such inner silence to the deeper delving of yoga states of samadhi and the Buddhist concept of sunyata = "radiant emptiness." Something is going on we have no awareness of in our ordinary state of consciousness.

As philosophical and mystical text states again and again, normal consciousness, in comparison to a truly awakened mind, is a state just above sleep, if not a form of sleep itself. And by "normal consciousness" I include even the highest IQ mentality and sharpest skeptical intelligence. Above-normal consciousness entails extensive radius of comprehension of self and world-at-large, involving transpersonal experience of archetypal depths. I am not talking here of what a certain stream of New Age thought speaks of as "enlightenment"—some distant Shangri-la of the mind that only the most committed sages experience and are forever after spiritually perfect. The state of awakening I refer to requires introspective insight into one's own psychological complexities, involvement in the constant purification discipline of overcoming negative acculturation, fallacies of belief, enticement of social games of status, prestige, power, and rising above common meaningless interactions and entertainments. A magnificent inner cosmic vision can free one from the egoic shell, but if such an experience cannot be integrated by striving to overcome all the above drawbacks, there is the possibility of becoming mired in a naïve superficial spirituality, or entranced by demonic impulses. Cosmic vision or no, it is the venture of introspective purification harmonized with the grasp of various significant knowledges and perspectives of the human situation, that gives the individual the necessary leverage in the struggle to live an authentic existence.

We have to realize the egoic mind, though for the most part a cultural construct that evolved over the past ten thousand years, is still influenced in various ways by the survival impulses of the primal lower brain. In other words, our cultural consciousness is still influenced by tribal-ethnic impulses which have hardly changed since Cro-Magnon wandered the earth. Of course, "hardly changed" does not mean "no change." We have changed dramatically in many ways, just as our surrounding social-technological environment has changed. Most people who have spent ten or more years in our formal educational system have a more extensive knowledge of our cosmic position, our place in history, than people living prior to the 20th century. But how an individual follows up and integrates such school-induced knowledge in order to form an intelligent comprehension of the human situation, is another venture altogether.

As we go about our daily routine we exist for the most part within our ego-sphere of awareness, which encompasses all an individual knows and has experienced of life. The ego sphere is the ordinary person's most significant experience of consciousness. We could say conscious egoic mind is a constant flowing of thought, of images and words, which can be controlled and directed to varied degrees depending on the capability, intelligence, and will of the individual. But then, just what is the nature of this "flow of thought?" Where does it come from? What makes it flow? The only other form of consciousness the average person is familiar with is the dream state. When remembering a dream, we recall images of ingenious creativeness, which is proof, even to the most ordinary person, that there are more levels of consciousness than just our everyday ego-consciousness. Though dreaming consists mostly of images percolating in our subconscious mind, if a dream is especially astounding and meaningful, it is probably receiving imagery from deeper archetypal levels. When we are awake our subconscious and deeper transpersonal unconscious are still active, we just are not aware of this activity. Dream imagery has an affinity with stars — when we sleep, dreams shine forth in the night mind, yet during the day are hidden beyond the dazzling sunlight of our waking ego mind, which blinds us not only to dreams, but also much vaster realms of our being.

We will come to recognize that egoic consciousness is just one level existing on a gradation of intensities of consciousness. Teachings of certain schools of yoga claim there are eight to twelve levels of consciousness to the human psyche. Ordinary mind is usually considered a level lower than midpoint. Western depth psychology delves into several dimensions of consciousness. Jungian scholar and analyst Marie Louise von Franz describes six levels, A through F, where A = the individual ego-consciousness; B = the personal unconscious or subconscious; C = group or folk unconscious, D = collective or regional unconscious, E = collective unconscious of mankind which is the dimension of archetypes, and F = "unus mundus," or "mysterium tremendum," God, Wholly Other.[6] We can visualize the ego, "A," as a small bubble being partially inundated by the personal subconscious, "B," and so on, each level partially inundated by a greater level. Though as individuals we are isolated within our egoic radius, we are simultaneously rooted within deeper dimensions, which 5,000 years of yoga, various fields of psychology, and anthropological research into shamanism, has validated thoroughly. We are constantly influenced by such dynamics of subconscious and unconscious dimensions of mind.

Thus here we are, encompassed, permeated, imbued with various degrees of consciousness. We might then ask, when a person is in a state of unconsciousness, as in a coma or while anesthetized, is some element of "mind" still active? That is not an easy question to answer. In Oliver Sacks book *Awakenings*,[7] he writes of patients suffering for years from encephalitis, or "sleeping sickness," which turns its victims into immobile manikin-like people with various degrees of egoic consciousness, some seemingly with none at all. A few who briefly recovered related they had been in an endless nightmare state, remaining normally conscious while horribly entrapped for decades in a body as rigid as a statue, while others, blessed in comparison, spent their years in a blank dreamless coma, completely void of consciousness. Yet can we say those void of consciousness did not have minds? Could we say their minds were "there," but in a kind of deep hibernation? Or was it more like switching a radio off, and all mental activity, all incoming stimuli were cut off completely, thus their egoic minds were totally shut down. If not totally shut down, what had occurred? Were the dynamics of the subconscious and unconscious still active in the dreamless "depths," like a radio blaring music in a deserted building in the middle of the Sahara Desert?

You can begin to see how these case histories present very disturbing implications, challenging our religious beliefs and displacing our sense of egocentrism. For those who existed during ten, twenty or more years in total dreamless coma, oblivion was a validated reality, or would that be a validated non-reality? Those patients who were conscious statues for ten or twenty or thirty years, on recovering temporarily, said they did not dream when they slept. And, even after a quarter of a century being rigid and still as a stone, they never experienced any deep meditative state of awareness, nothing like a state similar to that of a yogi who voluntarily sits as still as a tree in the lotus position, sometimes for weeks, to reach states of ecstatic bliss. Why is it they did not experience the bliss prolonged meditation brings about? Nor did they experience anything akin to out-of-the-body experiences or "astral travel." Some, like the one Robert de Niro portrayed in the film version, did not even know they had been asleep for two decades. It was like going to sleep one night and waking up twenty years later — a terrible and very real Rip Van Winkle type of experience. Some of these patients demonstrated astonishing resilience and adaptability. One in particular, who had been entombed in immobility for 45 years, on recovering revealed herself to be a woman of intelligence and charm, full of delight and humor, filling her room with laughter — this after she had endured for almost half a century experiences of stark hopeless rage and depression few of us can even begin to grasp. She was the epitome of the phrase "indomitable spirit." There were several others who, though understandably depressed and angry at having been locked into such extreme solitude for so many years, manifested astounding durability and existential acceptance of the harsh randomness of their fate. What psychological trait of character preserves such enduring spirit?

We cannot deny ego consciousness, the primary process of the embodied mind, is significantly dependent on the brain's neurocircuitry. Brain injury can demolish a person's entire character, which was first scientifically noted in the case of Phineas Gage in 1848.[8] The brain-personality link became obvious after Gage, a morally upright man, suffered a tremendous wound to his brain and on recovering became a rowdy trouble maker. Damage or disease to varied areas of the brain can destroy a person's ability to see color, or speak, or see, or walk, or talk, or remember. There are people paralyzed with anosognosia, a brain malfunction which causes them to become oblivious of their paralyzed limbs, lack all emotion and feeling, with no idea there is anything wrong. There is another brain injury syndrome called prosopagnosia, where a person cannot recognize faces, even those of his own family members. There are brain injuries where the patients can't recall anything that happened over ten seconds before. They can eat dinner, and if a second meal is placed in front of them ten seconds after the first meal is finished, they will think it is the first serving. Besides injury and disease, the chemical effect of drugs and electronic probes stimulating the brain can bring about astounding personality changes, both positive and negative. Take a certain drug, plant, or fungus, and depending on mindset, you're in heaven, or hell, or satori. Consider the implications here. If, to an extensive degree, our egoic minds are dependent on the physical well being of the brain, what then are we? If the personality/ego sphere of the mind is wholly dependent upon the condition of the lump of flesh in the skull, then materialism would seem to be right as to the brain-consciousness configuration. Our ego and personality, who we think we are, certainly seems to be dependent on the neuronic activity of the brain—period. But we cannot slip by this issue so easily, thinking empirical science has everything figured out. We must consider other factors, always bearing in mind the unavoidable truth the brilliant scientist J. B. S. Haldane clarified in his statement, *"The universe is not only queerer than we suppose, it is queerer than we CAN suppose."* Consider John Lorber's intelligent patient with very little brain matter in his skull, and others with half their brain or the entire cerebellum missing, yet they still functioned normally. Consciousness is queerer, deeper, vaster, more glorious, than modern science has yet revealed.

Just where does consciousness abide? Could it really be produced by the activity of the brain's neurotransmitters? Or is this activity somehow, like an antenna, attracting consciousness from a deeper source? Would we say the artistic genius of Michelangelo's magnificent Sistine Chapel was located in the brushes and paint? Would we say various tubes of paint themselves are art because the final masterpiece formed from them is art? No, the paints are just paint, which could have been used to color a table or wall. Michelangelo produced art by using the medium of paint as a conduit of creative power, transcending its nature as paint. This has an affinity to a symphony coming about from the complex organized playing of a variety of instruments. The symphonic music is an event transcending the orchestral activity which brought it about. Would we say Beethoven's 5th Symphony is merely an emergent property of dozens of musical instruments? No. The sound which soars forth from the conduit of the instruments is no longer dependent on them. The listener's aesthetic interpretation of the composition enigmatically transforms the code of molecular pitch and timbre that arises from the musicians' stimulation of instruments of brass, wind, string and percussion, metamorphosing into the enchanting pleasure of music. Nor is the music an emergent property of the brain of the listener. The point where sound becomes music transcends the neural activity involved. Music, like mind itself, is something we can never pin down.

Let's try a technological analogy, the radio, for all the guys and gals at MIT, and because it is so apt an image. Envision a group of technologically ignorant primitives living on an isolated island, who know nothing of the civilized world, coming across a battery operated radio recently parachuted into the jungle. They would, by examining this radio, come to believe the music and voices coming from it originate inside of it. Materialistic scientists of all shapes and sizes, microbiologists, neuroscientists, biopsychologists, sociologists, physicists, what have you, probing the brain's flesh and its complex network of neural circuitry, and concluding all levels of consciousness must originate in the physiological aspect of this complex organ, are in a position very similar to our naïve primitives dealing with their newfound radio. Such scientists poke one part of the brain and speech is affected, another part and movement is affected, another and memory is affected, another and anger or joy is expressed—hence they claim they have found the source of passion, poetry, visions. Some even have the audacity to claim they have found the seat of the "illusion" of the soul, just because they can trigger off quasi-mystical experiences from stimulation of the temporal lobe. But they are like the primitives switching the dial around on the radio. If you destroy the radio, the source of the music you were listening to, whether the Boston Symphony or a Puerto Rican mambo band, will continue to be broadcast, resonating through the atmosphere. Likewise, it is definitely not the neurological activity of the cortex from which poetry, art, reasoning, and philosophy arise, but "something else." Annihilate the explicate level physical brain, destroying the "radio" from which embodied egoic mind comes, and greater implicate omni-consciousness abides. As Professor Emeritus George Wald, biologist and co-recipient of the Nobel Prize in physiology and medicine, put it, *"Mind, rather than emerging as a late outgrowth in the evolution of life, has existed always."*[9]

Cultural and creative thought forms such as crafts, art, literature, architecture, music, poetry, science, philosophy, demonstrate that consciousness has developed far beyond any genetic survival necessity, and is imbued with trans-emergent quality. "Trans-emergent" is a term referring to thought produced by embodied consciousness, which I have coined to counteract the reductive use of the materialistic phrase "emergent property." Though our thought processes are intrinsically consociate with neural activity, they transcend brain function when merging with frequencies of disembodied omni-consciousness which existed prior to and encompass egoic consciousness. The infinite encompasses and is immanent within the finite.

Consider this simple diagram using the analogy of the solar panel:

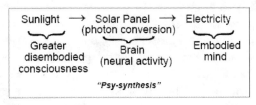

The solar cells in the panel convert the sun's thermo-electromagnetic waves of photons into electricity, which corresponds to the way the brain's neural activity converts degrees of greater disembodied consciousness into embodied egoic consciousness in a process we shall call "psy-synthesis." Psy-synthesis is comparable to photosynthesis, which literally means "to build with light." During photosynthesis sunlight is absorbed by plant pigments, especially chlorophyll, converting it to chemical energy which is then used to synthesize the glucose needed for plant growth, as well as the oxygen that is needed for all life on earth. Thus, psy-synthesis is the process through which disembodied omnipresent consciousness is "absorbed" by the neural activity of the brain, exciting electro-chemical/quantum configurations to produce embodied consciousness.

To see it from a different perspective, consider the following illustration, keeping in mind that brain-consciousness interplay is more like rippling electrical surges than a static diagram of neat circles within circles. Perceive the arrows as representing frequencies of qualities of consciousness surging inward and outward, with the center of this ripple of circles, the brain, like the tip of an antenna sending and receiving waves of these consciousness-frequencies:

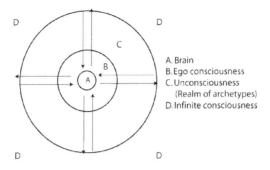

A. Brain
B. Ego consciousness
C. Unconsciousness
(Realm of archetypes)
D. Infinite consciousness

Each human being, existing amid the dynamic intensities of implicate-explicate dimensions, is a whirlwind of frequencies. Indeed, the neurophysiologist Karl Pribram called all of reality a "frequency domain," stating that "objects are made of a vibrating dance of frequencies."[10] Our brain is such a living pulsing "object," a complexification of dynamic forces which no one knows the true nature of. Michael Talbot wrote that all known frequencies are ultimately extensions from the deeper order meta-frequencies of existence beyond time and space, from which the brain mathematically (quantum wave equation) constructs reality. Varied directions of research point to the strong possibility that egoic consciousness is a manifestation of meta-frequency cohesion. In other words, the sphere of egoic consciousness is encapsulated within greater trans-quantum consciousness like a tiny bubble of foam encapsulated within a tsunami.

By using ultra cold clouds of atoms, scientists can bring light to a standstill, forming a Bose-Einstein condensate, which is a gathering of atoms into a single quantum state which then acts in synchrony. This can be seen as an analogy for how embodied ego-consciousness becomes encapsulated in the spherical complexity of brain-matter. Perhaps various types of radiant energy waves are received by the antenna-like magnetism of dynamic brain activity, which then resonates interactively with greater disembodied consciousness, somehow condensing into the stable synchrony of egoic consciousness. There have been and currently are ongoing lines of research which verify the possibilities of such speculations: Roger Penrose, Stuart Hameroff, Karl Pribram, David Bohm, and Danah Zohar.

Whatever is happening, whether approached scientifically or mystically, the entire phenomenal world is definitely a perceptual skein of illusion, which Hinduism and Buddhism have claimed it to be for thousands of years—Maya, makyo, the dream within the dream, from which the determined seeker strives to awaken. Illusion does not mean the world is not real. It is of an illusory quality in that it is a shimmering veil of congealed elusive energy over greater depths of Being.

That an electrode stimulating a certain area of the brain can bring about an experience akin to mystical vision, thus seeming to accomplish in a minute what it took years for a yogi to do, does not reduce or invalidate the mystical experience of the yogi anymore than the experience of a man placed on top of Mount Everest by a helicopter can reduce or invalidate the experience of the man who spent weeks climbing the mountain. The experience in both cases is real. Of course, the man who physically climbed the mountain will have a much broader and lasting understanding than the man who got there by helicopter. It is the same with a well prepared person taking a psychedelic substance under the proper circumstances, as well as the yogi disciplined by years of practice—their quality of experience corresponds to their knowledge and discipline. But visions brought about by electrical probes can be real. It is only the scientist, as he jabs and pokes, who believes he is dealing strictly with the flesh, with neuronic activity, never considering just what the essence of his probe is in relation to the Whitmanesque "body-electric" of the person being probed, and the significance of amplification of psychic frequencies. What the yogi calls the "third eye" chakra of awakening is centered between the frontal lobes of both hemispheres of the brain. That electrical stimulation of this area can trigger off mystical consciousness verifies the interplay of electro-quantum frequencies. We are beings made of congealed electro-magnetic energy pulsations. One need only study yoga diagrams of chakras and psychic channels, and Chinese acupuncture charts describing energy meridians, to realize just what astounding electro-magnetic beings we are. The artwork of Alex Grey illustrates this marvelously.

In yoga, "bija mantra" means "mystical sound," and is entoned to vibrate skull and jaw, which in turn, like resonating tuning forks, stimulates the brain, creating access to higher psychic frequencies. Consistent repetition of such mantras, merged with fasting and meditation, kindles the alchemical fire of frequencies relating to our ontological essence. What science knows as the supplementary motor area located at the top of the brain is the very area known for thousands of years in yoga as the lotus chakra, an energy vortex which is imbued with the potential to open the embodied mind to trans-emergent spiritual realms of consciousness. A highly advanced yogi using mantra or chant techniques can stimulate various areas of the brain at will and thus control his level of consciousness. Anyone with sufficient intelligence and will power can at least learn to discipline unceasing and ordinarily uncontrolled thoughts and emotions. Unfortunately, 90% of the human race, unaware of their mystical potentials, fail to apply their capabilities in this direction. They remain in the somnambulistic state of ordinary consciousness, with no inclination to expand their radius of comprehension by accumulating knowledge available through even ordinary channels, let alone yogic and shamanistic methods. And so they are completely helpless in their psychological reactions to internal and external stimuli, without even knowing it. This is one of the reasons why the psychological school of behaviorism became such a powerful system of thought, and is a significant factor in why materialism still reigns.

Even empirical science acknowledges that the energy which pulsates from all known phenomena throughout the universe, whether quark, quail, or quasar, does not as a whole increase or decrease, but is always constantly interchanging, transforming, converting, creating a vast spectrum of frequencies. The entirety of all known existence is essentially an immense weaving of vibrations, oscillations, of quantum and meta-quantum frequencies. Various frequencies of cosmic rays make up the electromagnetic spectrum. Our sun is the major source of electromagnetic light waves engulfing the earth. We are also subject to cosmic rays of higher energy originating from tremendous sources in the deepest depths of the universe. The works of Jung and Wolfgang Pauli, Penrose and Pribram, Alain Aspect, David Bohm, substantially clarify we are deeply affected by such cosmic activity.

Human embodied consciousness, having evolved through primal instinctual graspings of strictly survival activity, pulses with ascending frequencies of the evolutionary surge. As these survival pulsations interact with descending frequencies from higher levels within the helicoid whirl of consciousness, an illuminate infusing occurs within the brain, producing egoic consciousness, imbued with the potential to transcend its sphere of existence. But science as we know it has not yet evolved sufficiently beyond the materialistic stage to be able to fruitfully explore such things.

That thought processes of the egoic embodied mind are dependent to a large extent on physiological activity, and shaped by language hindered by materialistic metaphors, should not obscure the fact that the egoic mind's ability to expand and transform is harbored within the depths like a butterfly within its cocoon. Again, when dealing with psychic phenomena, <u>arising FROM does not necessarily mean reducible TO</u>. The materialistic scientist studies the brain-consciousness relationship through the medium of his own ego consciousness, for the most part with no experience of alternate states of consciousness — thus we have the problem of psychological interference, involving professional bias, pride, unconscious fear, defensiveness, etc. The subliminal influence of such intrusions can all too easily shape the "objective" conclusions of the most stringent empirical investigations.

That scientists beneath the sway of the materialism-scientism paradigm can consider the astounding and significant phenomenon of consciousness arising from the brain as no more than analogous to "kidneys producing urine," truly signifies conceptual alienation from reality. A telling example of such sterile intellectual interpretation of consciousness comes from James Watson, who was Francis Crick's cohort in the discovery of DNA. Watson wrote,

> *I don't think consciousness will turnout to be something grand. People said there was something grand down in the cellar that gave us heredity. It turned out to be pretty simple – DNA.*

Actually, consciousness is blatantly "grand," in a magnificent mysterious way. Watson's statement clearly exposes the gray drab quality of his perception. As to DNA being "pretty simple," coming from a scientist who was intimately involved with revealing the code of DNA to the world, his remark is dumbfounding. It doesn't take a significant amount of research to know DNA is far from being "pretty simple." DNA is what we could call the long term storage medium in all organisms, except for some viruses. It functions as the processor of the cellular language of the human genome, which contains three billion "letters" recorded on two strands that entwine in helicoid play, wrapping around itself hundreds of millions of times. Steve Jones, author of The Language of Genes,[11] has pointed out that if all the DNA in every cell of a single human being were stretched out, it would reach to the moon and back <u>eight thousand times</u>, an estimated four BILLION miles.

In his fascinating book, *The Cosmic Serpent*, J. Narby highlights how the phenomenon of biophotons emitted from DNA imbue all phenomena throughout existence:

> *Cells of all living beings emit photons at the rate of up to approximately 100 units per second and per square centimeter of surface area. They also showed that DNA was the source of this photon emission. During my readings, I learned with astonishment that the wavelength at which DNA emits these photons corresponds exactly to the narrow band of <u>visible light</u> ...Furthermore, there was a fundamental aspect of this photon emission that I could not grasp. According to the researchers who measured it, its weakness is such that it corresponds 'to the intensity of a candle at a distance of about 10 kilometers,' but it has 'a surprisingly high degree of coherence, as compared to that of technical fields (laser).' How could an ultra-weak signal be highly coherent? How could a distant candle be compared to a 'laser'?... I came to understand that the coherence of biophotons depended not so much on the intensity of their output as on its regularity. In a coherent source of light, the quantity of photons may vary, but the emission intervals remain constant... How could this 'amazing stately pavane' occur without some form of intention? In biology, this question is simply not asked. DNA is 'just a chemical,' deoxyribonucleic acid, to be precise. Biologists describe it as both a molecule and a language, making it the informational substance of life, but they do not consider it to be conscious, or alive, because chemicals are inert by definition. How, I wondered, could biology presuppose that DNA is not conscious, if it does not even understand the human brain, which is the seat of our own consciousness and which is built according to the instructions in our DNA?*[12]

With all that said, we get a glimpse of Watson's "pretty simple" phenomenon. Watson represents the "disconnected from inner life" mentality so many materialistic scientists are prone to.

This book is not an anti-science missive, "abjuring the rational in favor of the willfully obscure..."[13] My intent is to clarify that empirical scientists must be open to other ways of verifying the actuality of certain phenomena — ways which allow them to see what they are observing in its broadest and most complex expansiveness. When we are dealing with the deeper complexities of DNA, the enigmatic aspects of quantum realities, psychic energies and multidimensional frequencies going beyond ordinary consciousness, all of which enter upon the realm of paradox and wonder, we can open our minds and free our intuitive abilities without becoming New Age dupes to pseudo-mysticism, irrational fabrication, and theosophical credulity.

The history of scientific knowledge consists of a perennial rising and collapsing of ever expanding paradigms — every expansion denied and fought off with the last-ditch obstinacy of old guard scientists. Scientific facts relating to the brain-consciousness conundrum, gleaned within the ambit of empirical research, are unhesitantly oriented to support the naturalist perspective, with the implication that naturalism's accompanying atheistic or agnostic notion of truth automatically rules out mysticism. Pat Duffy Hutcheon, a sociologist representing this perspective, wrote in an article in The Humanist magazine,

> *The premise of naturalism, with its accompanying agnostic and pragmatic notion of truth, is a premise now supported by the facts of evolution, the theory of relativity, the tool of quantum mechanics, and complexity theory in physics.*[14]

This is outright sham reasoning, what Professor Susan Haack refers to as "making a case for some conclusion immovably believed in advance." Though the study of evolution certainly vanquishes such concepts as "intelligent design" and "concerned creationism," it does not negate the possibility of a "wholly other" consciousness imbued within the continuing genesis of all phenomena. Likewise, with no credulity involved, the study of quantum mechanics can certainly be looked upon as a gateway to metaphysics, opening a broader scope of possibilities to any curious intelligence not petrified by an excessive demand for empirical facts. To understand the fascinating scope of the mind's complexity, and thus the self, the truth seeker must be able to discern how far science is reliable and where it falls short.

There is a quality of conceptual thought which can steer clear of the perennial clash of rigid dualistic thinking: embodied/disembodied, materialism/mysticism, physicality/spirituality. The ancient Chinese symbol of yin and yang represents an ever flowing cycle of constant interchange, a pulsing flux of polarities. Aristotle spoke of the "hegemonikin," which he saw as an embodied component of the soul, yet not separated from the greater esoteric disembodied essence by any actual barrier other than an individual's quality of awareness. As philosopher Gilbert Ryle put it, dualism, from its conceptual beginning, was a *"category mistake ... mind is not an entity, it is a process."*15 And if we consider what "matter" actually is — congealed energy process — we come to understand mind and brain are as intrinsically interactive as the particle and wave aspects of light in quantum physics. Consider:

magnetism and electricity = "electro-magnetic" force
wave and particle = "wavicle"
brain and mind = "brind"

OK, so this is a somewhat playful attempt to verbalize interactive material/quantum qualities of energy. But isn't it possible that by some semantic construction the non-dualistic nature of brain-mind will eventually come to be recognized? Renee Weber, while considering David Bohm's concept of implicate-explicate order, quoted Spinoza: *"Matter and consciousness are not separate realities, but two expressions of one underlying reality."*16

It is becoming very clear that when the convergence of all available knowledge is laid out to be witnessed by the unbiased intelligence, embodied egoic consciousness, subconsciousness, unconsciousness, and disembodied expressions of consciousness-at-large, will be seen to have no strict separate existence, but are various interrelating octaves of frequencies of consciousness. When you sing the musical scale, do-re-mi-fa-sol-la-ti-do, what separates each note? These are frequency intervals without rigid barriers. Thus, depending on radius of comprehension and purification of negative "monkey mind" attributes, the egoic mind partakes of various frequency intervals, or "octaves" of consciousness. There is no ghost-in-the-machine conundrum, for there is neither ghost nor machine, only and essentially a "ghochine," or "machost," whatever you prefer – what the hell, make up your own word.

Teresi and Hooper stated, "*The richest psychological dimensions of human life are not explicable in terms of biochemistry and physiology as we know them to date...*"[17] As we move toward deeper psychological dimensions, involving mysticism, it should be dawning on any skeptical reader that since ego consciousness has been empirically proven capable of experiencing alternate states of consciousness, (Lilly, Houston, Grof, etc.), then it is quite possible the ordinary mind is imbued with the potential to transcend to higher frequencies on the helicoid scale of consciousness. The difficulty is, the ego-persona dimension of mind, snared in the brain's physical "mammalian" survival mode, both embellished and stifled by ten thousand years of civilization, has cut itself off from accessing this potential. Yet occasionally, by accident or intent, various individuals connect with higher frequencies, or at least experience brief episodes of inspiration that highlight our existential-spiritual situation. Such experiences can help free an individual from the fallacies and falsehoods of traditional religious concepts, as well as constrictive scientific claims of who and what we are. This is an essential aspect of the process of developing a relationship with the "soul" of things.

Soul is omnipresent consciousness dwelling within all known phenomena throughout the known universe. Soul is the essence of all frequencies which weave explicate-implicate realities together, thus it both preceded and was immanent within terrestrial evolution. As humans we are responsible for tapping into this essence. We cultivate our own soul by giving way to the greater essence soul. Our minds are instruments capable of cultivating this ability. The great sage Aurobindo said a person's soul is none other than this very potential that lies within each of us to open ourselves to deeper transcendent essence.

There have been volumes written about mind, from the most entrenched materialistic point of view to astounding mystical vision, from standard psychological explanations to bizarre occult and theosophical descriptions. So many descriptions, so little time. When you consider them all, it seems somewhat ridiculous to attempt any description. But if one is lost in a forest, coming across a mark on a tree indicating a possible trail is better than no sign at all. It is reassuring knowing someone passed this way who knew the territory. Such markings by fellow humans who have made earlier excursions help keep us from feeling hopelessly lost. We have trailblazers from varied cultures, who, each in their own way, have left cairns of varied sort which help us understand our situation in the immense wilderness of the deeper dimensions of mind, of Being, revealing how our ego-conscious mind is constantly influenced by the ceaseless oceanic movement of the mind's greater unconscious depths and heights, and how we can discipline ourselves to both experience and direct such influences, rather than be helplessly under their sway.

Jung said only a comprehensive grasp of the psychological composition of our conscious and unconscious spheres of mind can bring about a condition qualifying as true sanity. Of course, as we have indicated, this doesn't imply simply an intellectual grasp of psychology. The psychological knowledge Jung spoke of implies knowing much more about the mind than formal education in the field of psychology ever approaches. From the vast cauldronic depth of the mysterium tremendum, pulsations of living archetypes are constantly resonating through the personal unconscious, influencing subconscious levels, trickling into, flowing into, occasionally flooding ego consciousness, according to individual circumstances.

Most people's radius of comprehension extends no further than the quotidian ego sphere of awareness, and they have no inkling of how their little bubble of consciousness is situated amid the greater realms of Being. We must realize the "unconscious" where archetypes dwell is only unconscious to the ordinary ego-mind. Archetypes are woven of the same stuff as consciousness, though dwelling within immense realms that are wholly other than human, encompassed within the greater consciousness of even vaster realms of Being, thus merging with the eternal, the meta-spiritual, the mystery of the forever unknown. Of course, these different realms are not sealed off and separated like different floors in a skyscraper. As we touched on, there are spiraling gradations of frequencies of consciousness permeating and encompassing human spatio-temporal reality with nano-scale vibrations constantly in ebb and flow from the deepest depths up through the ego, resonating toward higher dimensions. This fathomless incomprehensible helicoid continuum is the substance of Being, in which our entire egoic awareness is like a gnat within the immense churn of a tornado.

With all the knowledge available that we have dealt with so far, only a mentally constipated individual would deny the substantial possibility that this omnipresent "holy otherness," this mysterium tremendum of Being we have spoken of, interposes its numinous powers in human fate by way of the manifestation of archetypes. Only a vain fool would claim there is nothing beyond his/her intellectual comprehension of such things. The ego is a micro-grain of salt within the turbulent sea of greater psyche. Archetypal forces, the trans-individual tides and currents of our essence, are dynamic configurations of numinous psychoid forces which inundate to various degrees every level of our mind, and can bring about a rebirthing psychic crisis with little regard to traditional religious images and assumptions concerning spiritual reality. Ego consciousness can endure, integrate, and be transformed by these fundamental dynamic forces. Unfortunately, the bulwark of traditional religious dogma, with its limited anthropomorphic cookie cutter projections, restricts the ego-dispersing transformation (rebirth) experience to a brief emotive episode, likely to inspire moral attitudes confined to a narrow religious orientation, but most often lacking genuine spiritual opening.

Regarding the philosophy of Gabriel Marcel, Ken T. Gallagher wrote,

> *I do not accede to the realm of Being simply by freely accepting my situation, but by recognizing that the roots of my situation go down into the eternal. Being is the eternal dimension of my existential situation. Being is that to which I aspire... If I ask 'what is being?' can I regard being as an object which is thrown across my path? No – for being, as a datum, includes me: in order to conceive being as a datum, I must conceive it as including me. I cannot get outside of being in order to ask questions about it in a purely external way. The attempt to isolate what is before me from what is in me breaks down completely here. Being, then, is not a problem at all, but a mystery.*[18]

Nietzsche once stated that Being was unconditioned essence. Aurobindo spoke of the eternal burgeoning of Being, relating it to the idea of Heraclitus that unites Being and Becoming as one constant unfolding. Being is not an entity, and cannot actually be named or labeled. Though Heidegger maintained that language can open us to the presence of Being, he also stated that Being is nothing other than dynamic presence which is essentially nameless. It is here we find ourselves in a situation scholars known as structuralists would consider as paralyzed by language. Of course, in a way, structuralism is to linguistics what behaviorism is to psychology = precise but exceedingly reductive in regard to deeper significance. To speak of the nameless is unavoidable. We have no recourse if we seek to use language as a lever of opening toward the "nameless Presence." To speak of "Being beyond being" is magnetizing the nameless incomprehensible toward a form of humanized metaphysical comprehensiveness. We are human — we have no choice. We can only be careful, respectful and alert.

Though "Being beyond being" implies transcendence not only of this world but of "otherworldly" realms of fantasy, imagination, hallucination, paradoxically it is not beyond us. It engulfs us, permeates us, is intrinsic to our individual essence. Thus the "wholly other" of the mysterium tremendum is beyond conceptual grasping, but not beyond an experiential glimpse. As Gallagher puts it,

> *Being is that which resists critical dissolution, which refuses to be dissipated into the transitoriness of an empty play of appearances. Being is what cannot be seen through. The pessimist turns the corrosive acid of his ill humor upon his life and finds there emptiness of emptiness: it is tale told by an idiot, wherein nothing signifies, nothing matters. To affirm being is to affirm that there is a depth in reality impervious to this nihilistic "seeing-through."*[19]

Though Being is intellectually unknowable and indescribable, as ultimate Presence it can be intuitively sensed and mystically experienced, to an ecstatic degree — not in its entirety, but as it resonates within a human psyche open to it. An intuitive sensing of Being is dependent on a person's attentive concern with ultimate realities, and a deep heart chakra caring.

Lao Tzu wrote,

> *There was something formless yet complete,*
> *That existed before heaven and earth;*
> *Without sound, without substance,*
> *Dependent on nothing, unchanging,*
> *All pervading, unfailing.*[20]

To sense such "Presence of Being" — which is far greater than and totally encompasses Western civilization's metaphysical concept of

God—demands a commitment surpassing the ego's schemes, comforts, convictions. Thus, to be acutely conscious of our thought processes is of significant import. All living creatures are endowed with certain degrees of consciousness, but only human beings are conscious of consciousness, and can think about thinking, thus having the potential to refine the quality of thought and transcend mundane reality. All of us, in our own way, are self-aware beings. We know we exist. We know we die. But, as clarified, though we believe we are fully awake when we are not in a state of sleep, few of us are actually awake to the wonder of our ordinary self-awareness, let alone its potential expansiveness. It is a fact that the majority of human beings never attentively contemplate the fascinating knowledges this book expounds upon, and actually consciously or subconsciously avoid such things. This means that by reading this book you are treading a very unique path. It is here within this activity of reading that brain and mind interfuse as you glean knowledge through a process involving photons of light doing a dance with retinal activity, igniting a dazzling array of sparkling synapsial orchestration. What then occurs, as my knowledge is transferred to your consciousness, still lies in mystery. But tangibly, undeniably, I am communicating to you this very second. Though what I am now capturing with paper and pen occurred in what to you is the past, enigmatically I am simultaneously with you now.

8 – Inner Discipline

*The very maximum of what one human being
can do for another in relation to that wherein
each man has to do solely with himself,
is to inspire him with concern and unrest.*
—Soren Kierkegaard

I landed in San Francisco in 1965, having walked away from a fairly affluent lifestyle in Los Angeles, ending a three year marriage. I had been a streetwise guy with a razor styled haircut, a closet filled with tailor made suits, and drawers of expensive cufflinks. I just parked my car by the side of the road one day and stuck out my thumb, heading nowhere in particular. Hitchhiking wasn't new to me. I had my first "on the road" trip (pre-Kerouac) through the Southwest at fourteen years of age, and hitchhiked across the states several times while in the Service. Over the years, I lived in both lower and higher income areas of varied cities, doing the "mean streets" pursuit of money scene, smoking weed and taking a variety of uppers and downers. In '65, the word "hippie" had not yet entered any level of mass media. I had never heard it. With no more income and just the money I had in my wallet when I got to San Francisco, I sought out the cheapest room I could find, which happened to be what others entering the Bohemian lifestyle of the "hippie" scene were doing. Sometimes six to a dozen would randomly come together sharing a rundown Victorian flat, and this would occasionally, over a period of months, form into an intimate communal scene, with few having any idea at first of what a "commune" even was. Between 1960 and 1967 many people finding their way into this scene had, by experimentation with psychedelic drugs, blown through the acculturated ego sphere of reality and glimpsed a more expansive state of consciousness possible for human beings to attain.

And, as mentioned, such a glimpse usually involved confrontation with evil, as well as dimensions of spiritual heights their childhood religious orientation had completely lacked. None of us gathering in San Francisco had any inkling that we were part of a growing scene that would come to be looked upon as the "Haight-Ashbury" sub-culture. Such "movements" come about in ways too broad and complex to be captured by the neat little formulas sociologists and cultural historians like to place them in.

The New Age "movement" is just the latest manifestation of the perennial expression of human longing for ultimate spiritual awareness which orthodox religion does not satisfy, entailing a more expansive rippling of ancient Eastern religious concepts, occult lore, theosophical schemata, flowering forth into what was, pre 1970, the flatland of American spirituality. The growing awareness and use of psychedelic substances building up since the late 50's burgeoned forth over the following decades. The awakening to alternative perceptions of reality and deeper dimensions of spiritual experience brought about an expanding "dropping out" of the sterile nightmare of the American Dream. It also brought about a certain historical relapse into superstitions and occult knowledges that hadn't been active within the American ambit of cultural awareness for over a century.

Though it is possible to trace New Age root connections to the counter-culture hippie scene of the '60s and '70s, it is now such a wide ranging phenomenon that it shouldn't even be considered a movement in the way the beatnik and hippie scenes could be. You can't look at a person and identify him/her as a "New Ager," as you could identify beatniks and early hippies as separate from main stream citizenry. The New Age is an umbrella label covering a wide variety of activities concerning aspects of physical health, and mental and spiritual development. And, despite the shortcomings of the contemporary New Age movement, there is no denying that something is going on involving the expanding transformation of human consciousness. Over the past thirty years, more people than in any previous era have become aware of their potential to overcome social programming and psychological weaknesses in order to bring about genuine spiritual growth. Those setting off on the quest for authentic self-knowledge are going to partake here and there of certain New Age activities. Thus they should definitely be concerned with the ability to separate falsehood and delusion from the truthful and genuine. This demands close observance of any organized system of mental or spiritual growth they may become involved with, perceiving any subterfuge or derangement behind skillfully constructed masks of spiritual expertise. For amid the nourishing garden of New Age offerings are shadowed areas where lurk parasites and predators that can hinder and even blight the potential for growth.

From a certain perspective, the New Age movement seems to have contributed as many obstacles to spiritual awareness as doorways. One of Donovan's songs from the sixties, "Young Girl Blues," has the phrase *"working your way through the phonies."* "Phoniness" is concern for image rather than substance. On the journey for authenticity, maneuvering through the legions of well intentioned but shallow guides and teachers of every stripe—gurus, masters, swamis, herbalists, channelers—acute discernment is a necessary skill one must develop. Treacherous indeed is the ego's craving for excessive self-esteem, cultivating ways and means for the personality to preen an image of awakening rather than seek the actual challenge of inner exploration. This entire capitalist society, dependent upon the interplay of consumer and marketing industry, has produced the most profoundly manipulative advertising empire the world has ever known—and the main "game" is to create self-imagery dependent on external validation. Marketing experts, skilled at catering to every vanity and whim of the ego-persona, inundate the media with commercials that ignite a worshipful attitude for external display, such as fashionable name-brand attire to enhance the image of success, coolness, or hip sophistication. The New Age movement has its own place in this marketing empire. Designer gurus and yoga teachers give their devotees in-crowd prestige on the New Age circuit. The expanding number of people who are skilled at cultivating external images of spiritual depth and intellectual substance is epidemic as the new millennium dawns.

For the seeker to find a way through such ego entrancing obstacles without succumbing to cynicism, calls for a refined and flexible skepticism of everything offered as a way of "spiritual" lifestyle. A finely honed skepticism sharpened by consistent consideration of every field of significant knowledge, is absolutely necessary in this endeavor. Cautionary inquiry is able to separate truth from cunningly disguised falsehood, the authentic from cultivated mimicry, insightful simplicity from banality, and genuine spiritual phenomena from the merely psychic and hallucinatory. Such discernment also calls for insight into the misuse of words, language, concepts. For instance, everyone knows how the concept of love suffers from tenacious reductionism in our consumer society, how it percolates throughout the entire social network in infinite banal ways, capitalized upon for material profit, degraded as a tool for commercial manipulation in order to enhance material products, from automobiles to cereals to deodorants. If the word love is so easily reduced to such an insipid level, what about such words as soul, enlightenment, and of course, God. Authors of books concerning everything from Christian fundamentalism to theosophical concepts to the paranormal, use a kind of linguistic mimicry of the phrases of genuine wisdom to validate absurdities. Such falsification gives the wrong impression of authentic spiritual teachings.

James Hillman, whose works delve deeply into Jungian archetypes, sees most New Age therapeutic methods as failing to deal with the true complexities of the soul.[1] We can see this lack of substantial psychological awareness in many New Age writers and lecturers. Though such spokespeople may specialize in Hindu and Buddhist terminology relating to levels of consciousness, few speak with any background knowledge of centuries of Western art, literature, poetry, science, philosophy, and how these have contributed to highlighting the further heights and depths of the human situation today. Many become popular because they speak and write with a reductionist style that brings the complex and disturbing down into canned formulas of what spiritual growth is supposedly all about. Dozens of such New Age authors could bring their works together into one large volume entitled "How To Become Aware of the Depths of Your Being Without Disturbing the Routine of Your Comfortable Lifestyle."

All those who set out to pursue the quest for self-knowledge should consider H. L. Mencken's perception that there is no idea so stupid you can't find people to believe in it.[2] If the seeker does not wish to number among the spiritually naive, he/she must be willing to approach inner exploration, the mystical, the paranormal, the metaphysical, as if gathering fruit from an orchard inundated with land mines. We must be very attentive, for, as Theodore Roszak warned us in his insightful book, *Unfinished Animal,*

> *It is spiritual intelligence that is demanded of us; the power to
> tell the greater from the lesser reality, the sacred paradigm*

from its copies and secular counterfeits. Spiritual intelli-
gence – without it, the consciousness circuit will surely be-
come a lethal swamp of paranormal entertainments, facile
therapeutic tricks, authoritarian guru trips, and demonic sub-
versions.3

Since the mid 1970's when Roszak wrote this warning, common gullibility and lack of spiritual intelligence when dealing with
psychic phenomena and occult systems has become rampant. Rather
than stumble naively through the labyrinth of New Age belief systems, it is worthwhile to read through dozens of issues of Skeptical
Inquirer magazine, which reveal much of the fraud and deceit that
goes on with esoteric messengers, channelers, astrologers, etc., who
roam the avenues of the New Age spiritual movement. But one must
be aware that such skepticism is very prone to a narrow materialistic
orientation, which has its own failings. Somewhere between the
Charybdis of zealous skepticism and the Scylla of New Age credulity
lies the firm higher ground of cohesive awareness.

There are many positive elements within the New Age ambit,
which have injected a fresh vitality into a half century and more of
religious narrow mindedness, soulless materialism, and spiritual
blandness. And there are teachers and gurus of integrity and capability who can be very beneficial to those with certain spiritual and psychological needs. Yet, like mining for gold, as one approaches the
genuine mother lode, there is always more eye-catching fools gold
scattered about than real nuggets. David Tacey points out,

The New Age man wants the Goal (unity with the divine) with-
out the way (the discipline, ethics, and self-effacement that make
such unity possible). He wants blissful union without the suffer-
ing of the cross, spiritual rebirth without having to first endure
spiritual death. He is 'hooked' on the sacred, addicted to spiri-
tual techniques and practices, and his credo is: 'Follow your
bliss' (Joseph Campbell). A Jungian response would be to doubt
the authenticity of this so-called 'spirituality' if it is merely de-
signed to provide instant gratification for the ego...

[There is a] notorious problem of rampant egotism, emo-
tionality, splits, and competitiveness that plague New Age
groups, cults, sects, ashrams, clubs, societies and communes. Al-
though all these groups (ostensibly) work toward transcendence

*of ego in favor of soul, they are often destroyed by a secret, dark and malignant egotism, which eats away at the high ideals and eventually causes the whole edifice to collapse, often with devastating consequences to society and to all concerned... The drives of the ego, especially the power drive and its push for identity and esteem, cannot be got rid of by intellectual attitude which espouses focus on 'higher' things. Although the conscious emphasis is on 'openness' to the divine, merging with a higher will, and mystical 'negative capability,' the power drive of the ego makes itself felt in the fixity and dogmatism with which these 'expansive' goals are pursued. The devotees declare that they are 'nothing' before the divine, or worthless before the charismatic teacher, but in the background there is fierce jockeying for privilege and special places, for power and influence within the group.*4

As Tacey indicates, within the faction of society supposedly involved with activities related to the spiritual quest, various leaders and teachers, who claim to have conquered their lower desires, capitulate to all too common sexual urges, games of manipulation, and even lying to their followers to cover up their duplicity. Such failings of integrity are no less negative than those of a Jimmy Swaggart or Jim Baker, but few devotees recognize this. I have heard some devotees use Jungian concepts to excuse their gurus' sexual gambits and power games, saying they were just manifesting their shadow. That's nonsense. Anyone who claims guruship or the title of master should have full control of lower mind desires, not from puritanistic repression, but by conscious disciplined restraint. Others use a more Buddhist excuse, claiming their master's shortcomings as displays of "crazy wisdom." Though there are jester/trickster methods of teaching, when it drags into any of the above mentioned negativities, or worse, it is pure folly. A revealing case in point is Amy Wallace's exposé about her years as one of Castaneda's harem of neurotic women, all self-deceived to believe they were elite extraordinary beings when in reality they had succumbed to common negative traits of the human personality.5 Where such things are concerned, we have to develop an attentive intuitive perception which allows us to see beyond the skillfully created image cloaked in all the garb that creates the illusion of spiritual wisdom.

We are dealing here with a very significant aspect of the seeker's journey, the ability to judge the quality of a person in the position of teacher or guru he/she may relate intimately to in pursuit of enhancing spiritual development. This is not just a matter of simple common sense, like how to pick your lawyer or mechanic. It's a situation that requires a keen sense of discrimination. Consider the weak criticism and apologetic semantic acrobatics of certain American roshis, in their attempt to justify the rabid anti-Semitism of Zen master Yasutani. Their efforts only reveal just how much the process of dharma transmission has been diluted over the past two hundred years. Roshi Bernie Glassman's feeble defense in Tricycle magazine '99, was truly pathetic.[6] Such incidents reveal a delusion built up about Zen—that Christianity is subject to its Elmer Gantry's, but Zen roshis are all purity. Scandals during the 1990's revealed how limited such an idealistic assumption can be. In the effort to adapt Eastern religions to Western culture, Glassman, like many New Age "masters," is ready to reduce even the ideal of an enlightened sage to fit Yasutani's spew of hatred and ignorance. In the same issue of Tricycle, instead of demanding a roshi's commitment to purity of mind as qualifying for enlightenment, Roshi Aitken desperately excused Yasutani's anti-Semitism, claiming Yasutani was vulnerable to the times and the current political atmosphere. But the truly enlightened mind should not be drawn down by time and place, or current politics. The genuinely awakened spiritual master may perhaps have an impulse to get drunk now and then, or have a momentary sexual attraction for another person, or occasionally get overly angry at injustice, but will <u>never</u> capitulate to serious negative traits of the mass common mind, such as racial prejudice, greed, lust, ethnic pride, or mentally limited impulses such as patriotism and nationalism. And though the awakened one may on occasion be carefully and knowingly involved in political activities such as civil rights and anti-war demonstrations out of an acute sense of compassion, he/she is never a believer in any political system. Politics, to an awakened one, is like stirred dust in a strong wind—an exceedingly ephemeral distraction from more meaningful and significant ways and means humans have available to create a worthwhile social structure.

Writing of the qualities of a genuine master, Robert Nozick says,

First, they exemplify what they hold important; their values infuse their lives... In their presence we are reminded of our own neglected heights, embarrassed to be less than our best selves... The spiritual teachers are exemplars of the full force of their values... They adhere completely and totally to what is important to them. They will not compromise these values or deviate from them.[7]

Bernie Glassman, who has been involved in many positive social works, claims that Buddha would have considered him to be enlightened—a claim that is undoubtedly bolstered within his mutual admiration network. But Bernie old boy, you'd better not even begin to speculate what Buddha would have thought about your spiritual state. Obviously a claim such as that is imbued with a definite element of egoic self promotion, thus tainted with more than a little vanity, which is enough to void the claim.

What of Deepak Chopra, a man whose fame, status, and fortune is so well established he has no need for elaboration of his abilities. Yet, in Esquire magazine, October 1995,[8] he claimed to have the ability to levitate. The interviewer saw a photograph with Deepak and Michael Jackson in the lotus position. Michael was on the floor, but Deepak was supposedly a foot in the air! Deepak said it was real, and that his wife Rita could do it also. If his idea of levitation consists of that absurdity of hopping around on one's butt—the so-called "yogic flying" of practitioners of Transcendental Meditation—and the photo was of one of his higher "hops," well, the entire claim is ridiculous. But if he truly rose from the lotus position into the air, sort of gently floating upward, then it is the greatest breakthrough in the centuries- old debate between materialism and mysticism that has ever occurred. So why has Deepak not given a televised demonstration with an audience of expert illusionists and qualified scientists to scrutinize? Did he really do it? I do not believe so. Why would he distort the truth? He has no need to bolster his fame by tricks of illusion. I think Deepak was the victim of self-delusion, which religious and spiritual "experiencers" are very prone to.

I could go on about others—Werner Erhard of EST, or designer-guru Sri Krishna Pattabhi Jois, whom some have called a racist Brahmin. We all know about Bhagwan Shree Rajneesh, whose devotees, snared by cultish elitism, went bonkers against the local community. The internet will clue you in on all the negative activities of Sai Baba, or Adi Da, or Amrit Desai. Unfortunately, there are very few "gurus" you can name who don't have skeletons in and out of their closets. Yet all of the above people do have significant insights to offer. It is the same with philosophers and scientists. I have found many deeply meaningful insights in the brilliant work of Heidegger, yet he succumbed to Nazism and praised Hitler as a Germanic savior.

Like the roshis who strive to protect Haku'un Yasutani's reputation, William Patrick Patterson does the same in his writings about the late Chogyam Trungpa Rinpoche,9 said to have once been the supreme abbot of a Tibetan monastery, whose devotees rationalized his excessive drinking, chain smoking and womanizing, as his way of understanding Western decadence, and his taste for exquisite suits and luxuries as his "disguise," so he could be a spiritual spy among the social elite. This is absurd. I have gained many insights from the writings of Rinpoche, but I have gained as much from others who don't claim titles of spiritual tradition while simultaneously succumbing to negative habits an ordinary morally weak person is prone to. Patterson also mentions Miguel Serrano's writings about having found his true self, which apparently did not prevent him from becoming a zealous Nazi. In his last internet interviews, Serrano was involved in esoteric Hitlerism, which is most likely still quite active in South American political-corporate circles.

Image, position, outward trappings, guarantee nothing. The riots between Buddhist monks in Korea in 1988, as well as pedophile priests in the West, verify that a so-called spiritually disciplined lifestyle can all too often be a veneer, a masking of ordinary psychological hang-ups. There have been a dozen or more autobiographies written over the past decade by people who became obedient disciples of one or another guru or monk representing teachings from Buddhism or Hinduism, and for five to ten years, or even more, merged with fellow worshippers in a seclusive and seemingly ideal way of spiritual life, only to later discover the "clay feet" of the person they had seen as godlike. They realized that though they had matured to some extent during those years and had developed an amazing vocabulary concerning enlightenment, gurus, yoga, etc., they were still not any more spiritually aware than those who had never bowed before a guru. Those who attempt to be truly free, free even from the enchaining "freedoms" of the immoralist and the nihilist, free from all mundane desires and ambitions, must maneuver through the labyrinth of charlatans and illusions that can impede the way of the sincere novice seeker. To continue the journey without becoming ensnared by skilled deceivers and psychic predators, one must be alert to powers and forces opposing spiritual awakening, becoming skillfully discerning, balancing flexible skepticism with cautious openness, constantly and eclectically taking from various "masters" what is of real value and leaving all else behind.

A significant element here is the problem of psychological transference. This syndrome, known to all psychiatrists, occurs when a patient projects his/her longing for a godlike guide onto the analyst. In the New Age milieu, a person only needs to be qualified to teach a class in yoga to receive such projections, since so many people naively equate the teaching of yoga as somehow qualifying a person for the status of guru. Many yoga teachers encourage this for various egoic reasons. Far too many who have claimed to be and are seen as gurus thrive on projection. As with the analyst-analysand relationship, if this projection isn't revealed by the guru to the devotee when the moment is ripe, authentic growth is stunted. The patient/neophyte must eventually be empowered to stand alone and cultivate inwardly the qualities he/she projects outward.

To ignore the failings of those espousing spiritual truths is a serious oversight. When dealing with subject matter in which a decision can dramatically affect your entire life and the well-being of your soul, the integral value of a person's spiritual worth must be thoroughly evaluated. The seeker must consider such things as whether spiritual teachers or guides live up to their own teachings, how much they actually know concerning their subject matter, how much experience is behind it, and whether or not they are still in their own way seeking. If they are defending and bolstering a scheme of delusions woven together with certain essential truths, this must be uncovered. The quest demands cultivating the skill to know the difference between delusive preachings and authentic wisdoms, and most of all to realize that a permanent intermediary between your own soul and the holy source of existence is not needed. Perseveringly develop your intelligence, your intuition, your spiritual disciplines, and your own inner intermediary shall reveal itself, becoming clearer and more dependable as your comprehension expands.

There is no getting around it, the quest for truth is definitely a multi-leveled social, psychic, spiritual obstacle course we must be very attentive to. Though the quest is imbued with numinous relationship to an enigmatic cosmic design, it should not be considered an aspect of some great theosophical cosmic plan of "earth as spiritual basic-training camp." Truly, as one awakens and faces existence head-on, the human condition can be seen as a very dark and troubling predicament. There are great writers and philosophers who even saw it as completely hopeless and tragic. Miguel de Unamuno's book, *Tragic Sense of Life*,[10] presents a vision we should not flee from, but face and integrate into our own comprehension of life. The disturbing insights of Kierkegaard, Nietzsche, Baudelaire, Artaud, Joseph Conrad, Dostoyevsky, Kafka, Beckett, and the dark visions of other artists and poets, must be fully taken into consideration, for there is much about life that justifies their disquieting revelations. Even the writings of our great sages can be very disturbing when it comes to describing our actual existential-spiritual predicament. This is necessary, for too many New Age books present nothing more than facile ineffectual messages of hope. But the philosophy of Sāmkya yoga proclaims that this kind of hope only prolongs common entanglements, and thus should be vanquished. Genuine faith in the light of the moment is sufficient. Enough moments of light fill a day—enough days, a lifetime. The challenge is to face both the horrid murk of the external world and the deeper shadows within ourselves, and deal with it by orienting ourselves to the light, both external and internal, wherever it manifests itself. This cannot be done by turning one's back on the evil that exists and adopting the trite "there's a divine reason for every horror" formula, which reflects the New Age tendency to dismiss the suffering and misfortune of humanity as part of some great karmic apple-pie-in-the-sky plan for us all.

Does it seem the demands of the quest for self-knowledge are more than you are able to take on? You would be surprised what you are truly capable of. Just begin by taking on what you can, and you will find your capabilities expanding as you develop. If you make it too easy for yourself, your inner potential will never reach the tension that ignites the alchemical fire. You have to stretch, sacrifice, act.

9 – Symphony of Forces

From here through tunneled gloom
the track forms into two:
and one of these wheels onward
into darkening hills,
and one toward distant seas.
—Walter de la Mare

This quest we are delving into is not some frivolous social-psychological phenomenon of current New Age fashion. Western civilization can trace the concept of the inner quest to Hellenistic Greece and ancient Hermeticism, which taught disciplines to enhance the mystic's pursuit. In the East, the mysticism of Hinduism goes back thousands of years. No one should take such a profound universal impulse lightly. Mysticism denotes the exploration of spiritual mystery. It should be clear from the material we have covered that we are drenched in mystery. It is scientifically verified that all phenomena of human reality in essence consist of varied frequencies of electromagnetic waves, and all we know about the nature of such waves is that they are emissions of light, and yet we have no idea what the essential nature of light is, or why this magnificent bewildering world of ours has been illuminated to a limited degree within the embodied mind. We are permeated by mystery, and encompassed by ever greater mystery. To be incapable of grasping this is the sign of a defensive mechanism rooted in fear of the unknown, fear of the possible actuality of other than egoic levels of consciousness existing that are imbued with a spiritual quality of meaning traditional religions only hint at.

Essentially, science has always been rooted in the quest for broader knowledge, and is a significant aspect of the pursuit of self-knowledge and the quest for truth. Science is not philosophy, but should definitely be an integral part of developing an holistic perspective of human existence. Thus I will not hesitate to use scientific insights to describe significant elements of our situation. But that does not mean being confined to the naturalistic world view, or a rigid empirical methodology. There are depths to existence that are not subject to such modes of thought. We must be able to intuitively extrapolate knowledge scientifically presented into broader spiritual perspectives and possibilities.

As we explored in Chapter Seven, our brain is an incredible pulsing electro-chemical "condensate," consisting of tens of billions of interweaving nerve fibers, which create an amazing network, sending and receiving trillions of vibrating messages resonating with quantum-psychic frequencies throughout our entire sensory being every second. It is here amid this fantastic surging of electro-chemical brain activity that we near the very edge of the mystery of consciousness. It is here we contemplate vibrations, oscillations, and frequencies, which are fundamental to the manifestation of all forces and phenomena—quantum fluctuations in a vacuum, gluons tethering quarks, atoms forming molecules, sound waves in air, ripples in water, hammering of steel, plucking of violin strings, spider webs in the wind, ad infinitum—and which, in the brain-mind arena, range from the measurable EEG frequencies of the brain up through the un-measurable psychic frequencies of varied circumferences of consciousness. Though certain psychic frequencies can't be empirically measured, they can be felt by anyone actively attuned to such things. Yes, James Randi and other skeptical fundamentalists will begin to tremble here with righteous indignation, for sure. And I can't really blame them, if it weren't for the fact that as pursuers of truth they are a cowardly lot, with few I know of undertaking any John Lilly or Stanislav Grof type of experiments to perhaps discover a deeper, broader perspective than the limited one they are content with.

For centuries, spiritual sages have been telling us in a variety of ways that we are intimate at-one elements of a vaster "God-being" consciousness. They have informed us that though this world around us feels, smells, looks to be the solidified stuff we are born, labor and die in, such a perception is a complex illusion, real to us as sensory beings, but basically only a thin veil over awesome dimensions of depth. Staying open to accepting such ways of perceiving things, without becoming gullible prey to New Age pseudo-mysticism, is very important to understanding the human existential/spiritual situation, especially when relating to parapsychology, the paranormal, metaphysics, etc. The prefix "para" means "beyond," thus paranormal and parapsychology relate to the study of things that go beyond the realm of normal perception and ordinary psychology. The paranormal has to do with extraordinary human capabilities, that, up until the '60s, in the USA, were considered nonexistent by a large segment of the population. Yet today, even within the scientific community, certain things that were considered beyond the range of ordinary experience (paranormal), such as conscious control of blood pressure and alpha and beta brain waves, have now been established as within the range of normal abilities, though still somewhat unique.

Despite the influence of materialism and secularism upon political/economic powers, as well as the religious reductionism of authentic spirituality, according to various polls, 40% to 50% of the population of the United States has had what is considered a mystical experience. Can we really just shuffle this aside as mass superstition based on ignorance? I think not. In these matters we must apply a well-honed but flexible skepticism, open to both scientific and mystical exposition. Genuine mysticism does not blatantly disregard reason and logic, as too many New Age mystagogues are prone to do. We must know reason's scope as well as its limitations in order to separate genuine mystical and psychic phenomena from falsehood, fabrication, delusion and confusion.

It should be quite clear from what we have covered that Whitman's concept of "the body electric"[1] is definitely no dry metaphor. Add to this Gabriel Marcel's, *our body is the mode of presence of self in the world,*[2] plus the fact that we are each abodes of myriad frequencies of varied forces, and we evoke far reaching implications. To further understand, we must step forth from our common ignorance toward the radiant darkness, occasionally treading across the twilight border of the unknown, the hidden, the occult. Opening ourselves to a more extensive scope of reality beyond our acculturated framework can be initiated by attempting to understand just how the field of quantum physics relates to the "body electric" reality of who and what we are, and how oscillations, frequencies, vibrations, like musical chords, are essential ingredients in creation of the symphony of consciousness.

Let us consider the words of F. David Peat, concerning the mystic physicist David Bohm's concept of implicate-explicate orders:

*"The explicate order could be thought of as an extension of the order of Cartesian coordinates introduced in the first half of the seventeenth century."*3 By contrast, the "implicate order" is the ground from which the explicate unfolds as well as the ground into which it is continuously enfolding. In the implicate order there are none of the defining characteristics of the explicate order—solid bodies that are unambiguously located in space, sequences that occur in linear time, etc. Rather, the chief characteristic of the implicate order is interrelatedness. The focus is on the "whole." What we experience within the sphere of egoic consciousness are merely abstractions and projections of that whole. Essentially, Bohm's theory of implicate order stresses that *"the cosmos is in a state of process – a 'feedback' universe that continuously recycles forward into a greater mode of being and consciousness."*

Since quantum physics has clarified the dematerialization of our material world, we must accept reality as much more extensive in scope and depth than our senses reveal, and humans as potentially more flexibly expansive beings, both psychologically and spiritually, than what we have heretofore taken ourselves to be. We have to see all things in the light of a broader radius of comprehension. Though science has assigned metaphoric labels to the phenomena at the very edge of existence—protons, neutrons, quarks, gluons, plus bits and quibits from the arena of information theory—essentially we are speaking of various configurations of frequencies. The fact that the theory of materialism is fundamentally founded upon so-called tangible physical "material stuff" that in essence is intangible and non-physical, is ironic in the extreme.

What we call vibrations, oscillations, frequencies are the basic indwelling factors of all forces and phenomena. All objects we perceive in the vast world around us, everything, is essentially made up of wild elusive oscillating quantum forces—elusive because science has no idea what the metaphor "force" attempts to describe. Force is indefinable, being essentially a dynamic process which influences interrelationships between varied phenomena. Consider the electron. The electron's rate of oscillation in its relation to the atom depends on what type of atom it is. The electrons of certain atoms oscillate ten times per second, some a hundred times per second. Each oscillation per second equals one hertz = Hz. At the level where atoms bond into molecules, the merging interactivity vibrates at a <u>trillion</u> times per second. You can't even utter one tiny squeak in less than a second. We are talking here about incomprehensible activities words can only point toward. Again, empirical methodology based on state-of-the-art research reveals that every object, animate or inanimate, is essentially a congealed state of such dynamic quantum activity. Bohm believed what we can perceive of the implicate order is manifested in the complex activity of magnetic fields in the form of light waves. As stated in "Cosmic Plenum," *"Such movement of light waves is present everywhere, and in principle enfolds the entire universe of space and time..."*[4]

Light from anywhere in the universe travels through space at 186,000 miles per second. Photons enter the eye/brain/mind configuration as stream-bursts of light via the retinal process, which amplifies each photon's energy a million times or more. Every waking moment visible light flows into your eyes, initiating a magnificent process which entails light oscillating through swirls of multitudinous neural fibers, passing through a refraction process involving millions of microscopic rods and cones located at the back of the eyeball, which produce electro-chemical currents that surge through the optic nerve and into the thalamus, then the visual cortex, mysteriously creating the marvelous process we experience as sight. We are beings with a consciousness frequency oriented toward visible light waves, but, as clarified, we are awash with a variety of other waves operating on different frequencies. As the Hamilton-Jacobi theory clarifies, the entire phenomenal world of matter is a creation of complex interactions of wave motions. Visible light itself is made up of various wave frequencies which we perceive as different colors, each color dependent upon the frequency of its unique wavelength reflecting off an object.

In his delightful book, *The Tyranny of Words*, Stuart Chase wrote:

> *The eye takes cognizance of light waves from .0008 to .0004 mm, but misses electric waves, ultraviolet waves, x-rays, gamma rays, and cosmic rays, all running from wavelengths of .0004 mm to .000,000,000,008 mm .... A rough estimate is that the eye can see about one twelve-thousandth of what there is to see.*[5]

The entire edifice of how we perceive reality is intimately reliant on the retina's reception of light waves, the largest percentage of which are photons radiating from the sun. Sunlight is essentially streams of photons = "particles" of light which have zero "mass." Photons as radiant electromagnetic energy bind electrons to the orbits of atoms. Atoms, of which the entire phenomenal world is made, are born from the astronomically immense upheaval of super nova explosions which occur every second across the universe of one hundred billion galaxies, with each explosion producing a luminosity one billion times that of our sun. We consist of such furiously made "stardust" and "starlight." We are beings of light born from solar fury. Whether a person is a scientist or a mystic, he/she must admit we are in essence astonishing paradoxical beings. Yet we hardly take notice. We are asleep to our essential nature.

On the level of our physical senses, even with the aid of a range of instruments from the electron microscope to the Hubble telescope, all we perceive of the entire material universe is a mere "visible light slice" of a vast spectrum of wave frequencies. We are like goldfish in a fishbowl located in the huge living room of a very large mansion. Everything within our fishbowl is our everyday terrestrial existence, and the living room is the entire universe. We are unaware that beyond the walls of the living room are many more rooms within the mansion, itself surrounded by thousands of acres of wilderness.

Quantum physics has revealed the very act of perception is an act of disturbance, of alteration. When scientists do research on subnuclear phenomena, the moment they observe a particle, they transform it. This is what the Principle of Uncertainty is based upon, revealing the limits to what empirical science can predict about quantum processes. At this level scientists are incapable of simultaneously determining the velocity and location of a subatomic particle. It is an either/or predicament. If velocity is determined, location cannot be determined, and vice versa. Thus uncertainly is a basic ingredient of existence. And to further complicate matters, we must factor in the psychological reality that though we all perceive the same world, we each "see" it differently, according to belief system, degree of ignorance, state of awareness, etc. To exist fully and authentically is to be assiduously aware of these difficulties, and continue struggling to learn what kind of beings we are in the wholeness of our existence.

Perception is a process of light. Embodied mind is a process of perception. As esoteric Buddhism teaches, all consciousness arises from the ground of "Clear Light"—which is in essence implicate omnipresent consciousness. The nature of such consciousness, as the essential nature of light, is an esoteric enigma. From the spiritual perspective, we can envision "clear light" at the source of existence, descending on a spiraling symphonic scale of intensity of frequencies which produce varied degrees of consciousness. Human consciousness exists within a stream of lower unrefined frequencies of light which are not purified, not yet clear of lower animal impulse frequencies. To refine such frequencies, to alter one's consciousness, to expand one's radius of comprehension, is to resonate with ascending energies. This requires struggle to open oneself to the stream of descending frequencies, which are paradoxically imbued with implicate order spiritual magnetism, creating in our souls a directional guidance, a calling forth. Infinite clear-light consciousness (sachidananda) descends, encompassing and permeating the lower levels of unconscious archetypal realms, thus the subconscious of certain attuned individuals receive a degree of energy from higher illumined levels of mind, awakening the egoic mind.

It is here I would suggest the reading of a book entitled *Catching the Light*, by Arthur Zajonc, who wrote,

> There is no truly unambiguous attribute of light! ... By now it should be evident that *light possesses a nature unique to itself*. Every natural assumption we make about it, assumptions common to us from daily life, leads to errors. Entering light, we cross into another domain, and must learn to leave behind what we hold dear from the past, and cleave only to the archetypal phenomena of light at every level, down to the quantum. Particles, waves, location... all should be left, like soiled sandals, at the threshold of the temple. The light within is of a different order than the object without; it inspires us to subtle reflections not common to the marketplace. We stand like Brunelleschi, in the portal between sanctuary and piazza. He looked out, intent on the geometry of sight; we are turned in, absorbed in the morphology of light. From the union of our open imaginations with the firm facts of light will rise the offspring of insight into it.[6]

As Bohm stated,

> *When we come to light, we are coming to the fundamental activity in which existence has its ground ... Light is the potential of everything.*[7]

We can begin to see why scientists who are fighting a hopeless rearguard battle to keep quantum theory from supporting mysticism, have lost and just can't face it. Such scientists don't understand, as Robert S. Ellwood clarifies,[8] that mysticism shares many correlations with science — both are concerned with what lies behind external appearances — they just have different methods of investigation. Mysticism implies an attentive intimate relationship to that which is mysterious, enigmatic, esoteric, baffling, igniting an intense feeling of genuine awe and spell-binding wonder. Basically, mysticism is both the philosophy and the science of the numinous — the striving for knowledge and communion with "divine" dimensions. Aurobindo has written of the mystically inclined spiritual seeker,

> *It is the supreme Truth of all things that he seeks, and that too cannot be arrived at by any scrutiny or research that founds itself on outsides and surfaces or by speculation based on the uncertain data of an indirect means of knowledge. It must come by a direct vision or contact of the consciousness with the soul and body of the Truth itself.*[9]

We have spoken of frequency as the number of repetitive oscillations per second in the periodic process of an energy wave. We all know how an opera singer can break a glass with the vibratory power of a high note. There are ultrasound vibrations that occur far beyond the capability of what the human ear can hear, like the high frequency of a dog whistle and the low frequency elephants use to communicate. Scientists are now using ultrasound frequencies to break down toxic waste molecules in water, thus diluting its poisonous potential. These are sound frequencies, whereas light comes from a higher frequency range. Lasers are now being used to remove tattoos by breaking up the ink in the skin pigment without damaging the tissue. The white blood cells then carry off the microscopic particles of ink. Military researchers (insane as ever) have developed laser beams with the amplified power to blow up tanks! From these amazing facts we can catch a glimpse of the vibratory power of frequencies of light.

The pitch of quantum energy vibration is an essential aspect of the actualization of all known phenomena, because everything, from quarks to quasars, from microtubules to possible superstrings, from photon pulsations to expanding fractals, from the darkest unknown depths to the highest realms of the mind, everything, a dog's bark, a phone's ring, a mosquito's buzz, a dream, a fantasy, connects and interrelates with human consciousness through the oscillating increase or decrease, the acceleration or deceleration of wavelengths, frequencies, vibrations.

In his remarkable book about human transformation, *The Silent Pulse*, George Leonard wrote:

> *If you should glance for only a second at the yellow wing of a butterfly, the dye molecules in the retinas of your eyes will vibrate approximately 500 trillion times -- more waves in that second than all the ocean waves that have beat on the shores of this planet for the past ten million years. Were the butterfly blue or purple, the number of waves would increase, since those colors vibrate faster. With x-rays instead of light, the rate of vibration would speed up a thousand times, with gamma rays a million. (The vibratory rates of the subatomic particles that make up ordinary matter are incredibly higher, while the waves of the heart of the atom's nucleus vibrate at a rate that would strain our imaginations.) The rates of vibration of all radiated energy -- including radio waves, heat, light, x-rays, and so on -- can be arranged in order. The resulting electromagnetic spectrum turns out to have more than seventy octaves, with visible light being only one of them. As in music, all the "tones" in this spectrum have their own harmonic overtones, and there are certain similarities that appear at octave intervals. Many of the most basic discoveries of the scientific world, in fact, have simply confirmed the musical nature of the world.*[10]

This isn't just a metaphoric projection—the musical essence of things was there in the beginning. In an article from Scientific American, Professors Wayne Hu and Martin White touch on this in relation to the theory of inflation which concerns the primal birthing of the universe:

Because inflation produced the density disturbances all at once in essentially the first moment of creation, the phases of all sound waves were synchronized. The result was a sound spectrum with overtones much like a musical instrument's. Consider blowing into a pipe that is open at both ends. The fundamental frequency of the sound corresponds to a wave (also called a mode of vibration) with maximum air displacement at either end and minimum displacement in the middle ... But the sound also has a series of overtones corresponding to wavelengths: one-half, one-third, one-fourth, and so on. To put it another way, the frequencies of the overtones are two, three, four or more times as high as the fundamental frequency. Overtones are what distinguishes a Stradivarius from an ordinary violin; they add richness to the sound... The overtones have wavelengths that are integer fractions of the fundamental wavelength. Oscillating two, three or more times as quickly as the fundamental wave, these overtones cause smaller regions of space to reach maximum displacement, either positive or negative, at recombination... Just as musicians can distinguish a world-class violin from an ordinary one by the richness of its overtones, cosmologists can elucidate the shape and composition of the universe by examining the fundamental frequency of the primordial sound waves and the strength of the overtones.[11]

Various anthropologists claim there are sufficient signs and artifacts which make it highly possible primal proto-hominids had a sense for patterned rhythms, thus varied forms of music and dance. A bone flute found in France dated back 32,000 years. From the ancient Sumerians, through Orphic mystery religions of ancient Greece, through the works of Pythagoras and the "harmonice mundi" of Johannes Kepler, teachings of the world's most profound thinkers, mystics, sages, expound upon the knowledge that all existence is rooted in harmonious vibrations and pulsations which are immanent in all phenomena. So Professor Damasio's description of brain-mind activity as a symphony is exquisitely apt.

With all this knowledge available, pathetic interpretations of scientists limited to a materialistic view continue, as in this quote of Professor of Physics Fred Alan Wolf, who confidently states,

The familiar sweet sound of a lyrical voice is <u>nothing more</u> than a continual repetition of air molecules vibrating against your ear drums. The familiar harmony of a barbershop quartet is the wave interference of four different vibrational frequencies, each coming from a different singer.[12]

As with the quotes of other materialists sited earlier, Wolf's words are confined to the sterile sphere of his analytical intellect. Though based on empirical facts, his statement is as dehumanizingly reductive as saying Michelangelo's Sistine Chapel is "nothing more" than dabblings of paint.

What goes on when we have the experience of hearing music? We take certain materials fashioned in a particular way, called musical instruments, and by using these instruments in unique inventive ways we can organize sound and stimulate certain energy wave patterns of molecular vibrations. These vibrations flow into the cochlea of the inner ear and are processed by an amazing structural system of micro-tiny hair-like cilia which stimulate your auditory nerves, which then resonate in the brain's frontal lobes, stimulating neuronic vibrations, sparking electrical pulsations, triggering brain molecule frequencies which resonate through the embodied mind. At this point, in some "unknown" way, the experience of music is created. It seems that a quantum meta-frequency code of the composer's soulful intentions ignites an elusive psychic transformation within the mind of the listener. Stephen Jay Gould wrote, *"The meaning and impact of this sublime moment cannot be revealed or explained by the underlying mechanics."*[13] The phenomenon we call music can never be reduced to any level of materialistic interpretation of brain-neuron activity. That an individual composer skillfully manipulates musical symbols (frequency codes) in the act of composition, and is able to communicate his ideas and feelings to his fellow beings through the medium of music, is one of the most marvelous creative expressions of human culture. Once again, we see the profound and ubiquitous significance of frequencies in the way we "process" the patterns and rhythms of music. In essence, music is intimately connected to the immense cosmic skein of frequencies pulsating throughout the universe.

We are dealing here with the marvelous, the astonishing, the sublime. Materialistic scientists can only give simple empirical explanations like Professor Wolf's—none can explain why or how mere molecular vibrations and trains of neural discharges are transformed into the phenomenon we call music, which moves us so deeply. As Shakespeare put it, *"Be it odd that sheep's guts shall hail men's souls out of their bodies."*[14] We only know music is a kind of meta-communication from the creative depths of the composer's mind to others. It can be depressing communication or uplifting. It can make you cry or dance, depending on the composer, the musicians, and your disposition. Music of rich creative quality, whether the work of Bach, an exquisite raga of India, a Gregorian chant, an indigenous drum ritual, or a Philip Glass composition, resonates within the very soul of things. Music, like everything else we may explore in the "material" world, if penetrated layer after layer, beyond molecules, beyond atoms, beyond electrons, beyond quarks, beyond gluons, eventually leads into the amazing, the wondrous, the mysterious.

Rodney Collin wrote,

> *Now if pure elements... are harmonically related in seven octaves by their atomic weights, we should expect these organic compounds to be similarly related by their molecular ones. And so it turns out. The individual notes – do re mi fa sol la si do – struck by the atoms of different elements, go echoing down the scores of octaves of organic compounds, reproducing there the same qualities in more complicated form.*[15]

All these harmonic energy dynamics are constantly taking place throughout the cellular level of our physical being, unceasingly quivering within trillions of cells—each cell a fantastic world in itself made up of complex seething molecules, which in turn are made up of atoms, which are made up of ever finer subatomic elements of energy, "on the edge of nonexistent" particles ebbing and flowing in tremendous motion at all times. Thus, undeniably, we are essentially marvelous creatures, all magnificently congealed into this mysterious body of flesh, primarily formed of wondrous magnitudes of pulsing radiant energy.

The poet Walt Whitman, through poetic intuition and vision, realized the amazing inner symphonic reality of our natural majesty. Poets, mystics, visionaries, all over the earth, have for untold ages known and expressed the unrecognized splendor of our being. During the dawn of the verbal expression of language, surely words were looked upon as magical, imbued with power to reveal unknown things. A place of oracle was definitely sacred, as was sooth saying, mantra, song, poem, tale, runes, hieroglyphics. The ancient alchemist sage Hermes Trismegistus looked upon music as the hieroglyph of the universe. Ancient priests used alphabetic codes to create ritual chants which would resonate with the numinous realm of the gods. The work of Anton van Webern elucidated how language and music are intimately related. And the most profound esoteric teachings clarify how the musical quality of all existence reveals itself through a interweaving helicoid scale of cosmic-quantum-consciousness frequencies.

Some readers may feel we are slipping too much into questionable New Age abstrusity. If so, they have not paid attention. There need be no great divide between critical scientific thinking and mystical perception. Every scientist accepts that our bodies are abodes of intense energy dynamics that mysteriously merge from subnuclear levels, congealing in some miraculous orchestration of molecular and cellular frequencies to make a newborn babe, to make you and me and every creature on earth. In ancient gypsy fables, Hindu, Greek and African tales, Sufi legends, North and South American myths, and more, existence has been looked upon as a wondrous dance of awe inspiring archetypal powers occurring just beneath the thin veil of perceived phenomena. The ancient Finnish epic, the Kalevala, tells of the world being sung into existence. From the most primal ages of humanity, shamans communicated with higher dimensional realms through song and drumming. Before anything was ever written, before any alphabet was designed, sacred tales concerning the origin of life and the gods, were sung or chanted in poetic form.

From what Joachim Jeremias, Professor Emeritus of the New Testament at the University of Gottingen, wrote concerning the rhythmic element of the Aramaic phrases attributed to Jesus, by his use of beat, stresses, meter, Jesus was most likely a gifted georgic poet.[16] Ancient Hebrew prophets doing their best to decipher visions and dreams of spiritual dimensions were said to have prophesied using harps and lyres while intoning sacred poetry. The most ancient writings of the first biblical text consisted essentially of poetry. And there is a possibility Jesus may have sung to his followers in the same way as the ancient Siberian shamans who sang to their tribes, and Celtic bards who sung their poetry. Various scholars have dealt with the idea that the first essential works of the Bible were song books, chants, and mantras.

Five thousand years ago, Sumerians used a seven note musical scale. Hundreds of years before Christ, two profound poets of early Greek civilization, Homer and Hesiod, wrote of the seven swans that circled the heavens the day Apollo, the god of music, was born. In esoteric teachings of yoga, seven is the number corresponding to a person's soul, and swans are symbols for the soul's flight toward enlightenment. Apollo's personal instrument was the lyre, which has seven strings corresponding to the seven note musical scale. Geoffrey Ashe touches on this in his book, *Dawn Behind the Dawn*, writing,

> *In the first century BC, a certain Demetrius writes, 'In Egypt the priests sing hymns to the gods by uttering the seven vowels in succession, the sound of which produces as strong a musical effect on the hearer as if flute and lyre were used.'* [17]

Such singing has intimate affinities with yogic mantras that impel consciousness to transcend the mundane world.

The brilliant thinker P. D. Ouspensky wrote about the seven numinous levels of consciousness existing on a beyond-quantum spectrum of psychic-spiritual frequencies relating to some immense wondrous cosmic musical scale.[18] Humans can come in contact with such transcendent frequencies through the equivalent of what is now recognized in various areas of musical composition as microtonal application, which has been used for centuries in the sitar music of India, incorporated in certain ragas to produce higher states of consciousness. It is possible that the vibration of microtubule frequencies within the brain can alter the embodied mind's octave, setting off an expanding ripple of morphic field resonance, permeating the superstring level of phenomena, which then synchronizes with elementary levels of "wholly other" realms of consciousness. As any musician knows, two notes in harmony merge in a higher harmonic. In other words, just as our ear catches the soaring high pitched tones of a violin, greater consciousness-at-large "catches" the resonating pulsations of the extra-ordinary self-willed frequencies of the spiritually disciplined mind—thus, transcendence of the material world.

Most ancient ritual consisting of chant and song was performed in acoustically formed caves and temples, where the sound frequencies of music or chant interactively resonating between the octillions of molecules in the body and the trillion trillion air molecules in such an enclosed space could reach the necessary level. When we consider that we are each a sphere of frequencies of mind boggling complexity, and realize the interactive resonance our "body electric" sphere would have within such an enclosed sacred temple, we can begin to comprehend our involvement in the great numinous dance of the mysterium tremendum, the movement of the arch-primal "holy other," the song of songs within the core of our being.

In science, what is known as String Theory has been claimed to have the potential to unite general relativity and quantum mechanics as was not possible when Einstein was alive. Though still at the stage of conjecture, hypothesis, speculation, some scientists believe that strings have a final fundamental nature that nothing lies beyond. String theory clarifies all phenomena in the universe arise from the vibrations of ultramicroscopic loops of energy, know in science as superstrings. Such "strings" are said to be four billion trillion times smaller than a proton. Our imagination is not really capable of grasping this, for at this level we enter the realm at the edge of baffling dynamic nothingness.

Yes, "nothingness." Here we arrive at a concept formative to the growth of existential philosophy in the West, which induced a culturally persuasive intellectual stream of nihilism. In the East, on the other hand (clapping), for thousands of years there was an acknowledgement of the essence of life as emptiness, which gave acknowledgement to the illusory quality of egoic consciousness, to life as Maya, "all is but a ripple of appearances," all existence as a configuration of illusions drifting upon the great river of Sunya — the Void. In Western civilization, nothingness is a dreaded concept. Such dread goes back to Aristotle's denial of both the concepts of Void and Infinity, for each implies the other, threatening his idea of the "Prime Maker," which was supposedly proof of God. Christianity adopted this stance to bolster its monotheism. There is even a stream of Christian thought, influenced by the theologian Karl Barth, which equates nothingness with evil, gleaned from Judaic-Christian elements in the Bible which interpret creation as God's striving to conquer nothingness. In the East, (Hinduism, Buddhism), the very ground of being dissolves into the Void (the groundlessness of Being?), which is considered more of a liberating realization than a despairing one. To Buddha the Void was Nirvana, and in esoteric yoga there is the idea of the ego emptying itself into the greater emptiness of Sunya. Christianity fears the concept of Void because it rules out immortality for the ego, i.e. Yet the Christian mystic Meister Eckhart spoke positively of the "divine abyss,"[19] demonstrating how esoteric mysticism has always transcended the exoteric limitations of the religion of its culture.

The nothingness of existential nihilism implies a kind of blankness or absence, or stark barrenness, whereas in mystical thought, and in Zen, the void is not static, inert, but full of dynamic potential. Even science claims the entire universe came forth from the "Big Bang" out of some sort of dynamic elementary "nothingness." The Copenhagen interpretation of quantum theory asserts the essential phantomlike "emptiness" at the core of all phenomena could be considered a sea of possibilities. In any English translation of Eckhart's or Heidegger's works, the use of the term "void" comes from the German word "wüste," which expresses not empty vacuum but the incomprehensibly immense vastness of mystical realms residing beyond the sphere of the ego-persona's grasp of things. Heidegger speaks of "Being" as an epiphany rising out of depths of the "abyss," a zone of emergence where truth comes forth between "clarity and concealment." Terry Eagleton wrote of the essence of meaning as a flickering dance between presence and absence.[20] So many approaches to the essence of existence refer, with good reason, both to nothingness and to "Dance," to a numinous harmonic underpinning of all and everything.

And so we have contemplated our situation through both scientific observation and metaphysical reflection. When pondering the human condition in its broadest scope and depth, the naturalistic assumption that the metaphysical is to be disregarded is like cutting off a leg to run a race. Metaphysics is a branch of philosophy referring to transcendent levels of reality beyond detection by our sensory attributes and their technological extensions. But metaphysical contemplation can only rise above abstract intellectual discourse if it is grounded upon firsthand spiritual experience. Only then can it meaningfully delve into the ultimate nature of things, encompassing the investigation of all avenues of exploration, scientific, mystical, religious, and all modes of thought, from rationality to madness. This of course will carry us to things that lie beyond, or rise above the limits of empirical methodology.

This is not to denigrate the dominant theories of science as flimsy social fabrications. Science and its rigorously tested descriptions of nature are a main highway to metaphysical contemplation for the person not petrified in the materialistic paradigm. Only the scientists who have no experience at all of the deeper dimensions of their own minds, who have glimpsed neither the inner light of higher spiritual realms nor the demonic darkness of the lower realms, have the ignorant arrogance to look scornfully from their petty citadels of hubris upon the vast spectrum of clarifications, from ancient to contemporary, of mystical dimensions of consciousness. Yet for scientists of intuitive insight and well honed reasoning, quantum physics, with all the baffling and enigmatic things it has revealed over the past eighty years, becomes a kind of passageway from classical physics to metaphysics.

Without the metaphysical consideration of scientific insight, the secularized intellect remains entrapped in a house of mirrors. Without the cultivation of mystical intuition skepticism becomes vulnerable to confirmation and oversight bias, subconsciously blocking out, or avoiding transcendent implications which threaten the established world view. But, in order for metaphysical ponderings to bear fruit, the worms of theosophical distortion, as well as religious reductionism, must be detected. This demands the cultivation of genuine knowledge instead of mere egoic opinion. Astute mental discipline is required. I can say here that any person involved with the pursuit of truth and the search for broader and deeper self-knowledge, who has a desire to rise above the taint of biased opinion, whether materialistic or New Age, should undertake reading the entire five volumes of commentaries by Maurice Nicoll,[21] which will deepen, refine and enhance anyone's quest.

Both Wittgenstein and Jung believed empiricism was the avenue to clarity of thought. Yet both were well aware there was more to existence than rational thought and empirical methods could encompass. We must refine the intellect so it becomes conducive to passing through the gateway of quantum physics to metaphysics, opening the mind's meta-encompassing capability. Refusing to pass through the gateway because one is comfortable within a social niche and secure within a well constructed world view, is to go against the very root impulse of all life on earth, entailing transformation, growth, constantly unfurling within the immense stream of evolution.

Unfortunately, a large segment of academia and the scientific community remain ensconced within the intellectual-analytical sphere of the materialistic paradigm, bleak and bereft of genuine spiritually imbued metaphysical thought and mystical insight. Bleak, because no matter how profound and eloquent many materialistic scientists have been in describing why they still find wonder and meaning in human existence, if human beings are but flesh-bound creatures that became conscious of existence by some quirk of the fantastic but pointless mixture of chemical and biological properties, then the guiding lights of meaning for humanity — religious concern, philosophical ethics, humanistic morality, all spiritual endeavors — are merely ways of refusing to see the horrendous farce of our predicament. Either there is <u>something more</u>, beyond the house-of-cards explanations the great religions have put forth, something more than New Age theosophy and pseudo mysticism have dreamt up for us, or the ever worsening situation of humankind can only continue falling toward a future of catastrophic fragmentation. This "something more" must have a meaningful quality an individual can seek out and relate to through an inner communicative reciprocal acknowledgement, inciting an unquestionable awareness of higher spiritual presence. Universal esoteric teachings have spoken of such a numinous relationship for more than five thousand years.

Surely, all the knowledge we have pondered from so many reliable sources, indicating that harmonic frequencies permeate all existence, frequencies which stir and surge as if to a cosmic musical scale quite possibly imbued with some "wholly other" consciousness, must definitely compel us to give this knowledge as much regard as we give such significant theories as "dark matter," "string theory," etc. Some readers may hesitate to agree. I can understand that. Yet, when we carefully consider all the volumes of research confirming the existence of transcendent consciousness, plus volume upon volume of text, both ancient and contemporary, of human experiences of the mystical, and of what we call enlightenment, satori, samadhi, we can only conclude, once again, there is definitely "something more" — a significant spiritual component imbued in human existence. So let us ponder the tremendous possibility each of us has of making contact, of opening ourselves, whatever way we can, to this something more, this "Numinous Presence," this "Holy Other," this mysterium tremendum within the core of our being.

We can no longer be content to look upon the heights and depths of the mind as merely epiphenomena of the brain. Even though the brain itself may have contingently arisen from some ill-defined chemical/biological brew of the primordial earth, it eventually evolved an antenna-like receptiveness to a streamlet of omnipresent consciousness, thus transcending its mammalian orientation. Consider — the very energy you are now using to read this, as well as the energy you receive from your environment and disperse every moment of every day, originally came forth from the exploding impetus of the cosmic tremendum, the so-called Big Bang, 15 billion years ago. (From what we now know of the musical quality imbued in all existence, we can grasp why astronomers and physicists Dominique Proust and Barbara Nicolescu speak of the "Great Sound" rather than the "Big Bang.") We – you and I and every one and every thing – are individual condensed energy manifestations of the continuing expansion and acceleration of the universe. But "normal" mammalian-sensory awareness established strictly for physical survival entails being ensheathed within a very limited sphere of egoic consciousness, protected by the collective shield of conformism, which prevents us from observing the wonder of what we are and what we are part of.

There is, as elucidated, a vast spectrum of frequencies within which ordinary egoic consciousness vibrates at a very low level, using only a tiny portion of the brain's immense potential. This is validated by research converging from varied fields. In the words of Robert S. Ellwood Jr., from his book *Mysticism and Religion*,

> *An example of the (scientific) study of meditative and mystical consciousness is biofeedback brain wave research, which works toward determining the complex EEG signatures of a number of states of consciousness. A British physicist has employed a device called the Mind Mirror, whose face presents twelve frequency ranges for each brain hemisphere and shows a continually changing pattern symbolizing the subject's mental state. This device makes easily visible what had previously been known: that people in meditation have a high production of alpha waves, the brain wave associated with calm, relaxation, and peace of mind; meditators also have a high symmetry between the two hemispheres.*[22]

In 1988, at the David Geffen School of Medicine at UCLA, research into "high frequency oscillation events" in humans found rates in the 80 to 200 Hz range, with people undergoing epileptic seizures manifesting up to 500 Hz.[23] Some patients experienced religious visions during seizure. We can definitely say that higher ranges take one into out-of-the-ordinary consciousness. We can infer that the frequency oscillation within the brains of animals would be lower than that of the average human, which would in turn be lower than that of people of "expanded consciousness" such as yogis, seers, mystics, and others. But this is not to be confused with Intelligence Quotient, or IQ. We dealt with the fallacy of IQ in Chapter Three. To expand on that issue a bit, although the effects of neural acceleration on intelligence have been validated by tests proving that the faster the speed of the testee's nerve impulses, the higher the score on intelligence tests, levels of consciousness are not empirically measurable and do not correspond to I.Q. A member of MENSA with an I.Q. of 180 could be on a very low "frequency level of consciousness" compared to the much higher frequency level of, say, an Indian Yogi, who might have an IQ of only 120. I.Q. is confined to the comprehension of acculturated intellectual and utilitarian knowledge. Altered states of consciousness, including shamanistic vision and yogic states of meditation, expand the circumference of the embodied mind's frequency range and resonate with the higher meta-frequency levels of disembodied consciousness.

EEG tracings have proven meditation produces brain frequency patterns that cannot be compared to any normal waking state, or dreamlike state, or hypnotic suggestive state. High quality meditation shifts to beyond-ordinary brain frequencies. Shamans alter their mind frequency through trance and ritual and the use of psychoactive plants and fungi, elevating to frequency ranges similar to, but usually still lower than, highly skilled yogis. Though ordinary people get slight amounts of acceleration with caffeine, and much more with the use of amphetamines and other drugs, your average Joe drug user shooting speed is like an Indianapolis race car chained to a steel post, engine going full speed, tires squealing, going nowhere at all. With no cultivated disciplined intelligence to direct the flow of the energy surge released by the drugs, it implodes into an egoic sense of power and vanity, stunting psychological growth and voiding any potential for transcendence, while creating low level ecstatic states that are very addictive. Drugs like amphetamines or psychedelics can only be tools for genuine awakening for the individual committed to accumulation of significant knowledge and pursuit of experience conducive to spiritual awakening, preferably grounded with yoga and such disciplines as Tai chi, Aikido, Qi Gong. Alteration of brain processes for the purpose of reaching levels of transcendent consciousness can be significant if the circumstances are creatively designed for that purpose. The potential to expand one's consciousness by way of brain-energy acceleration, thus triggering psychic frequencies which imbue the essence of phenomena throughout all known existence and beyond, lies dormant within everyone.

The conceptual magnitude of most people's comprehension of existence, no matter what their formal education, varies only a few degrees from their late teens to 60 years of age and beyond, whereas a person consistently intent on cultivation of spiritual depths significantly surpasses this mass stultification. Collaboration between composer and orchestra to produce organized sound waves which surge into the complex structure of the human ear, igniting the enigmatic experience of music, has an affinity to the individual seeking genuine spiritual awakening creating an ascendant psychic resonance with higher dimensional meta-frequencies.

We must be mindful of the fact that spiritual awakening depends on many factors, including external circumstances such as time, place, career, relationships, etc. Experience teaches us environment can have an immense impact on spiritual potential. Psychological research from Freud to Focault has verified negative aspects of culture can have a dysfunctional effect on the multitudes within its sphere of influence. Individuals trying to break the chains of cultural dysfunction can stumble into greater mishaps. During the Haight-Ashbury hippie era of psychedelic drug extravaganza, circa '66-'76, spiritual and psychological catastrophes were rampant. With the unprepared use of psychedelics, intense alteration of egoic consciousness caused numerous individuals to burst through into primal levels of mind, which inundated them with negative forces lurking in the unconscious depths, or ignited freaky paranormal abilities, or activated other horrifying experiences—seeing ghosts or hearing voices, even plunging into psychosis. The inner mariner must be seaworthy, which calls for a process of learning and development, entailing acute awareness of negative influences, both internal and external.

Many writers, psychologists, scholars, have used the analogy of the sea to represent "mind at large." What is meant by this? The answer depends on the depth of your perspective. Most people's concept of the human mind—"What's on your mind today?" or "Please keep that in mind"—is of the same common order of things as their visual image of the sea = a sort of idyllic artistic conception of waves and foam extending to the far horizon. But the sea is all science has revealed it to be and much more—the wonders we have seen in all those amazing National Geographic documentaries of ocean explorations ranging from vast deep sea valleys and mountain ranges to beautiful calm tide pools. Within this immense aquatic world dwell strange and haunting creatures, constantly devouring and being devoured, from tiny plankton to walrus and whale, delicate seahorse to giant squid, hermit crab to giant tortoise—myriad upon myriad of bizarre creatures thriving and perishing. Within this analogy, let's consider the saline property of the sea, its "saltiness," as representative of the collective human mind, with each microscopic granule of sodium-chloride as an individual embodied ego-mind. Within the infinite, endless sea of greater consciousness, each ego-granule, part of and intimately belonging to the sea, is a kind of "center," one note in a great symphony, a hologrammic reciprocal reflecting point of all of existence. Every degree of our awakening to self-knowledge and expansion of consciousness produces ripples flowing ever outward throughout the surrounding sea.

We exist within an awesome symphony of mysterious forces. We are more than we think we are, with depths we only have inklings of. We are creatures of stardust and sunlight. This we should recognize. Yes, we still fart, and sweat, and belch, and none of us are the chosen apple in the eyes of some supreme overseer God, but we DO NOT have to continue stumbling and bumbling along, snared in ignorance and delusion, puppets to passions and shallow political and religious beliefs, dupes to manipulations of unqualified authority. Spiritual powers DO exist on a spectrum of negative-positive/ascending-descending frequencies, and we best know what we are about, for the consequences of ignorance, or hubris of intellect, which contribute to non-participation in the numinous surge of existence, has a price which would cause anyone's heart to shudder. Life with no experience of the presence of the mysterium tremendum is a greater loss than losing one's sight or hearing.

Extensive and broad research reveals that though chaotic terrestrial-planetary forces of chance certainly played a part in the brain's evolution through the eons of our primordial past, once the brain's primal embodied consciousness reached a certain frequency, thus acquiring the ability to reflect upon its own awareness, an accelerating feedback loop developed. Gradually, over hundreds of thousands of years, consciousness rose from low frequency levels of the instinctual ambit, up through medium frequency ego cognition, eventually attaining the possibility of constant attunement to higher meta-frequency states of consciousness. Thus, ten thousand years of civilization and the accumulation of knowledge have brought a small percentage of the human race to the threshold of self willed evolution = alchemical individuation. And, as we have reflected upon, psychic energy frequency is a key element in understanding how the mind's potential and possibilities, encompassing conceivable and inconceivable dimensions which flow and ebb, emerge and vanish, along the immense spectrum of consciousness, may be experienced, attained and held firm. Shakespeare's comment on human existence, "*Tis a tale told by an idiot, full of sound and fury, signifying nothing,*"[24] is only true for those remaining ensnared in rigid mind-sets and outmoded belief systems, be they religious, philosophical or scientific, in which the believer has given up the risk, challenge and adventure of exploring the breadth and scope of his or her very soul.

10 – Cultural Chains

> *But what ear can catch the mysterious*
> *voices that with mystic murmur rise*
> *from out of the most hidden womb of things?*
> —Manuel José Othon

> *Every exit is an entry somewhere else.*
> —Tom Stoppard

Fate is a strange brew of random and deterministic events intermingling in the life sojourn of an individual. It is not preordained — it is just the way things play themselves out, like patterns of rain on a window, or foam designs on wet sand when the tide goes out. Fate casts us into a certain historical time, place, physical form. Within these confines we interact with reality through a sphere of consciousness we call the ego, coming to believe this is who we are and all we are. It is here the entire struggle to awaken begins. As most esoteric teachings specify, we must put the ego in its proper place, not by destroying it, but by gradually refining it in the service of the more expansive truth of who and what we are. It is your egoic consciousness which contemplates these very words, and judges them to be worthy or not of enriching your life. The strategy of using fire to fight fire is significant here, for a person must have a strong confident ego, and thus the courage to sacrifice ego enhancing attributes society perpetuates that are detrimental to spiritual individuation.

Awakening from mass sleep to the possibility of a soul enriching quest which takes one beyond self delusion, is a rare occurrence. To do so implies a person has uncovered the hidden stream of authentic meaning flowing amid both the terrifying meaninglessness of terrestrial existence, and the absurd banalities the majority of people spend their lives involved in, pursuing such spiritually empty goals as the "American Dream." Authentic meaning fully partakes of the baffling miraculous wonder of life and our actual place in it. Is life a miracle? Yes, according to the dictionary definition of miracle as an "extremely outstanding or unusual event," with or without divine intervention. The very fact that we exist rather than not, that anything at all exists rather than never having existed, and that we can be fully conscious of existing, is a realization both Leibniz and Heidegger claimed to be the root of all philosophical thought, as well as the foundation of all endeavors of spiritual awakening. For a person to completely realize the very fact of existing amid the awesome wonder of it all, ignites satori = awakening to one's totality. Let us continue to ponder the possibility of such realization.

As we touched on in Chapter Nine, within the spectrum of electromagnetic frequencies surging through the universe, visible light is but a narrow band. The entire micro-macro universe scientific exploration reveals through electron microscope and Hubble telescope, is a slice of reality comparable to what we could perceive of the Brazilian jungle by lighting a torch at midnight while flowing down the Amazon River in a canoe. In order to extend our knowledge of the jungle's interior we must be willing to go ashore, our torch of self-knowledge lighting the way through the wilderness. On entering the interior, a person can take various routes, the choice being dependent on the sincerity of an individual's intention, scope of experience, quality of intuition, perseverance and the willingness to take risks. The alchemical use of certain herbs, seeds, fungi, plants, may come into play—if taken only in specially structured circumstances, and with knowledgeable disciplined preparation. Yes, in this era of epidemic misuse, abuse, and frivolous ingestion of drugs, the very suggestion of using even natural substances might seem to lack a sense of moral concern. But a knee-jerk morality dictated by sanctimonious undercurrents of religious righteousness has done nothing beneficial for the human condition. As the works of dozens of reliable researchers and scholars verify, the meticulously careful use of psychedelic substances is definitely a way to expand psychic frequencies that have remained dormant all too long beneath the ordinary person's acculturated ego-personality.

Professor Michael Tansey, exploring biofeedback methods with numerous individuals,[1] discovered that most had become stuck on a certain mental frequency level in early adulthood, and remained there, like a stereo loaded with dozens of CD's containing beautiful music becoming jammed so that only one plays over and over. Psychedelic opening can break this stagnant frequency hold that the person most often is not even aware of. If used with reverent care, a certain psychedelic can become a sacred host of transformation throughout a person's life. Though psychedelic substances have been used for thousands of years in culture's all across the earth, in modern Western civilization it is only since the early 1960's that these natural alchemical tools, along with certain synthetic psychedelic drugs, have been used (mostly misused) by tens of thousands of people. The 60's and 70's brought about a mass attempt to leap right out of the canoe and into the midst of the jungle. Sadly but not surprisingly, due to lack of spiritual discipline and vulnerability to negative primal psychic forces, all too many cases of careless use of psychedelics wrought more psychological-spiritual havoc than awakening. The quest is not some great cosmic game that can be taken lightly.

The author Alan McGlashan had a very apt title for his book about the mind — *The Savage and Beautiful Country*[2] — for that is what the seeker enters when the acculturated egoic boundary of the embodied mind is crossed. If unprepared, psychedelic probes can bring about obsession with demonic impulses, inflated hubris, capitulation to psychic parasitism, or even permanent derangement, if the person is not able to center and integrate whatever experience he/she has had, into a process of intentional growth. But even when fully prepared, spiritual awakening will often ignite episodes of psychic crisis. It goes with the territory. Of course, many can carelessly use psychedelics, have an ecstatic high, and go about their life the next day as if they had just been to a party. I've witnessed this in dozens of people — casual trippers who have a weird or wild or enjoyable trip, or even a bad trip, and after it's over it's like they just had a ride on a roller coaster. Some, even after experiencing astounding insight into the depths of reality, partaking of realms of esoteric vision and possibly a certain influx of seedling wisdom, all too often find themselves failing to hold on to any quality of spiritual insight, and once again become enfolded in a state of ordinary consciousness, still caught up in habitual psychological histrionics, still prone to jealously, envy, insults, doubts, worthless daydreams, and all the common detrimental habits of the unawakened mind. Their mindset is so rigidly confined to the ego sphere it would take an extensive period of preparation to equip them for a more worthwhile inner journey, awakening them to deeper integrative enhancement of their experiences. Of course, according to Stanislav Grof, who structured psychedelic trips for thousands, it seems all his clients reached various levels of awakening to greater dimensions of Being, which changed their lives dramatically. But I ask, "Where are these people now?" There should be a follow up study to see how they are all doing after twenty or thirty years. Did they go on to more spiritually enhanced lives of inner discipline, did they capitulate to darker impulses which one must deal with once opened to deeper heights of essence, or did they hop on the New Age bandwagon, with their psychedelic experience becoming no more than a trophy on the mantelpiece?

By now everyone is aware psychedelic experience is not the only, or even the best way to open to the wholeness of one's spiritual nature. There are those who come to a profound state of existential-spiritual realization without ever ingesting any psychedelics, usually after years of yogic-like disciplines, or sometimes, if the mind is somewhat attuned to the wonder of things, just spontaneously awakening. There is no blueprint, no specific way, or rather there are many styles of approach involved in the way—the "way" meaning an individual's intentional journey toward experiencing self-realization, striving to merge egoic embodied mind with greater spiritual consciousness. An important aspect of this is eclectically choosing from myriad formulas and systems, those that fit one's individual endeavor. The bottom line is the basic necessity of cultivating a state of constant vigilance, so that one does not succumb to a delusion of awakening, or escape into a traditional religious or theosophical belief system, or get snagged into some ego enhancing cult, "ism," or "ology."

There were those who went to the Far East to study under gurus and in monasteries, who spent years involved with traditional practices, rituals, disciplines, relating to Buddhist or Hindu or Zen or Sufi belief systems, yet in most cases were thrown off balance upon returning to the daily scurry and flurry of our society, losing most of their insights of wisdom and whatever equanimity they thought they had permanently acquired. Terrence McKenna, Jack Kornfield, and Ram Das's companion in India, Bhagavan Das (Kermit Michael Riggs), all admit to aspects of this syndrome in some of their writings. The journalist Tiziano Terzani, whose colorful travel journal, A Fortune Teller Told Me,[3] is an exotic glimpse of the universal human entanglement in superstition and vast variety of religious orientations, tells of meeting expatriate Westerners who had become Buddhist monks, who, even after twenty years or more of monastic discipline, were still sadly unsatisfied. And we have all read of those Korean Buddhist monks succumbing to violent riots amongst each other, and so-called Western gurus who capitulated to their most banal cravings which were supposedly already conquered. This is why Jung stressed that hard won psychological self-knowledge was the only truly firm foundation for spiritual growth, and why Gurdjieff called his system of astute self-observation "the work."

So we see that neither psychedelic venturing, nor intellectual accumulation of facts concerning psychological attributes of the mind, nor commitment to traditional religious beliefs, are always sufficient for genuine awakening—they can even be detrimental rather than productive. Many psychologists and psychiatrists have accumulated mucho intellectual info concerning the depths of the mind, based on therapies and systems of all sorts—Freudian, Jungian, behavioristic, primal scream, drumming, etcetera—but are significantly lacking in experiential knowledge of transcendent awareness and essential disciplines required to integrate such knowledge into their personal sphere of awareness. More importantly, they have not cultivated in-depth insight into their own psychological weaknesses and darker negative impulses, which is the mulch of self-deception. Such insight into the shadow elements of our inner being is indispensable in the quest for awakening.

Most people relate to the world through expanding circles of relationships—self, mate, family, friends, neighbors, co-workers, community, state, nation—with their own ego seeming to dwell at the center of it all. This innate, culturally inbred tendency, a paradoxical mixture of truth and illusion, is a phenomenon we must be able to comprehend fully. It is true that the world seems to expand outward from each individual's egoic point of reference, but it is an illusion to see that point of reference as the center of the world. This is an illusion not easily dispelled. Self-centeredness is an archaic trait, rooted in territorial animal impulses and ignorance of the world beyond the tribal area of experience. Most ancient tribes thought their tribe was at the center of the world, and they were the chosen ones. Even today many people around the globe think their ethnic group is somehow more unique, more special than others, and their nation is superior in historical cultural richness. For the past six hundred years, the Caucasian race, bolstered by the Christian idea of being God's chosen people, has been able to play this mass self-deception out over a large portion of the earth, via colonialism, imperialism, "globalization." Patriotism is a manifestation of this "chosen one" delusion, with each unwitting citizen sucking the collective pride of nation into his/her sphere of ego to bolster a sense of superiority. Americans are particularly vulnerable to this, because our nation is the wealthiest and mightiest on earth at this moment in the flow of history.

Ego-centrism, a manifestation of this "center of everything" delusion, attains its power because it is a corruption of a significant paradoxical truth, clarified by the ancient alchemist's: *"The center is everywhere, the circumference nowhere."* In The Sun magazine, May 2001, in an interview with Renee Lertzmann, Brian Swimme said:

> *Centuries ago, we thought the earth was the center of the universe. Then we discovered that the earth was going around the sun, so the sun became the center. Then we found out that the sun is moving around the galaxy, so we thought the Milky Way was the center. When we discovered that there are many galaxies, we came to the conclusion that there is no center. Finally, what we're discovering now is not that there's no center, but that every point is a center. When we look at galaxies through telescopes, we find that they're moving away from us. No matter which direction we look, they're moving away at the same rate of speed. Now, that's kind of strange, because, if everything is moving away from us at the same rate, then we're at the center of the universe.*[3]

We are paradoxically at the center where no center exists.

Because our subjective thought is so thoroughly private, the ego-centric perspective is very compelling, and the ego is skilled at gleaning whatever knowledge and experience is conducive to maintaining it. But, as the poet John Donne said, *"No man is an island."* Actually, as William James pointed out, each "man" is an island, for geographically an island is really an isolated mountaintop connecting and merging on the sea floor with surrounding islands. We could say our egoic subjective solitariness is what protrudes above the ocean of unconscious essential Being.

Beyond the "condensed energy" of our physical form, we all merge into the hurricane swirl of para-quantum frequencies within the very womb of Being. The conscious illumination of such depths reveals not only spiritual glories, but what dwells in the darker side of our being, where the negative potentially destructive/demonic elements of ourselves entwine with the dormant potential of positive spiritual and creative powers, all fermenting in unconscious silence, hidden from the lackadaisical scrutiny of the average person's awareness. In the more shallow shadow levels lurk the petty negative traits we remain blind to, things we fear to contemplate, where our own flaws and weaknesses lie simmering, ready to be projected outward onto others. Such psychological projection must be brought to consciousness for any degree of self-knowledge to take root. As Jesus stated, *"Why beholdest the mote in thy brother's eye but consider not the beam that is in thy own?"*[4]

Projection stems from self-blindness. Most people are unaware of their negative traits, because they are subconsciously skilled in psychological euphemism. Misers see themselves as stringently thrifty. Jealous people see themselves as being justifiably protective, guarding against intrusion into what they consider rightfully theirs. A selfish person thinks in terms of realistically taking care of number one, projecting unworthiness onto anyone in need of compassionate giving. Vain people look in the mirror and see well deserved self-esteem and self-assurance. Lust and sexual exploitation are usually seen by the perpetrator as the uninhibited sexual adventures of a superior person not obligated to common moral guidelines. Sanctimonious religious people of every sect, blind to their own hypocrisies, see themselves as holier than all the "sinners" around them. Corporate executives and businessmen see themselves as elite power holders with no need to pay heed to the negative consequences befalling fellow humans. Politicians blind to their own shadows project their repressed flaws and deceits onto foreign enemies. To withdraw projection is to acknowledge that many attributes projected outward belong to oneself.

Yes, there are occasions when certain individuals who appall us are as bad as we think, but we must not let ourselves become too judgmental, for somewhere in us similar tendencies exist. Jung's concept of the "shadow" is a subject that has intrigued this author for many years, inspiring me to read through all eighteen volumes of his works, and also the work of every Jungian scholar or psychoanalyst I came across. I have come to terms with varied tendencies rooted in evil pulsing in the deeper shadows of my being. Thus when I speak of the potential for evil lurking in certain political and religious figures, I am paying acute attention to my own potential for projection, honing my judgment with self-awareness of my own shadow. My criticism comes from diagnosis based on thirty-eight years of thorough psychological research, and ruthless introspection.

Psychological projection of negative traits is active everywhere—in the workplace, in schools, in churches, and in every neighborhood. The horrors throughout history caused by such projection always began with individuals lacking insight into their shadow, who easily capitulated to projecting their own worst tendencies onto those who were outsiders, or different. Ignorance of the psychological attributes of one's own mind, including petty personal failings, keeps most people from ever realizing their potential for spiritual awakening. Seeing into the pathological tendencies hidden in the shadow areas of our minds, accepting and dealing with them, is a tremendously important aspect of self-knowledge. When a person rationalizes his/her envies, jealousies, greed, prejudices, overzealous dislikes, as merely run-of-the-mill aspects of being human, a thick curtain is being pulled over the shadow, giving it the power of unrecognized influence, thus setting the person up to become an unwitting tool for evil. When people say, in a confessional sort of way, "Oh, I know I'm selfish, (or vain, or jealous)..." this is but pseudo awareness, because if they were truly awakened to the effects of these seemingly petty characteristics, they would realize such traits become a magnetism within the depths for negative archetypal forces . If a person had any inkling of the realms most seemingly petty negative traits are rooted in, it would be a shock to say the least. To willingly shine a perceptive light onto aspects of one's psyche dwelling in the shadow requires a special courage.

No one likes their shadow exposed. People develop various psychological strategies to avoid contemplation of insightful criticism. True self-insight demands opening ourselves, welcoming and thoroughly considering all constructive criticism we can experience, for others can often see manifestations of repressed shadow tendencies we do not observe. That our repressed shadow tendencies lie hidden beneath the social facade of our personalities, doesn't mean they are inactive in the personal subconscious and deeper unconscious depths. The terms subconscious and unconscious should never be taken to imply lacking in influence on ego consciousness. In fact, as various fields of psychology have amply demonstrated over the past hundred years, just the opposite is true. The view of most Westerners is that psychologically our daily ego state is wakeful alert consciousness, and subconsciousness and unconsciousness are obscure states, semi-void realms of dreamlike fermentation, nothing more. In actuality, the sphere of our ordinary ego state of wakefulness is a pea-sized bubble within the pumpkin-sized bubble of subconsciousness, within the larger barn-sized bubble of unconsciousness, all three bubbles within the immense boundless sea of greater cosmic "mind-at-large."

Most esoteric teachings consider common ego-consciousness as the somnambulistic condition of the human race. The New Testament speaks of Jesus: *"And he cometh unto the disciples and findeth them asleep."*5 The disciples weren't snoring. They were in a state of all too ordinary consciousness, as most human beings are. Those of us who wish to spiritually awaken have much work to do. Awakening from the ordinary sleep we conceive as daily consciousness may take a person through various experiences, entailing alternative states of consciousness and the realm of archetypes. Of course there are those materialists, even so-called "quantum materialists," who claim only ego consciousness is real, and no unconscious or archetypal reality exists, or that such phenomena entering consciousness are mere hallucinatory imagery. To such inflated rationalism Jung replied, "Not for a moment dare we succumb to the illusion that an archetype can finally be explained and disposed of."6 Thomas J. McFarlane states, *"...the archetypes of the collective unconscious are universal patterns that shape our experience of the world and provide it with common elements."*7 Anyone with well honed intuitive intelligence who studies Jung's works, clearly realizes archetypes are not only the basic components of the unconscious, but are living expansive numinous realities which encompass and envelope embodied ego mind. In his truly informative book, *The Burning Fountain*, Phillip Wheelwright has written,

> *Jung is quite palpably right to this extent, that the primordial images are 'as much feelings as thoughts' but that their strong feeling-tone does not by any means reduce them to the status of merely subjective occurrences. Their subjectivity has its origin somehow (unlike Jung I can't suggest how) beyond the confines*

of the individual. A genuine archetype shows itself to have a life of its own, far older and more comprehensive than ideas belonging to the individual consciousness or to the shared consciousness of particular communities.[8]

All scientists should heed that Jung had a close relationship with Wolfgang Pauli while formulating his experiences and ideas concerning archetypes. Pauli, who was a physicist intrigued by relationships he detected occurring between physics and psychology, believed archetypes came forth from nonrepresentational realities of quantum dimensions. Archetypes, like quantum activity, dwell within a range not detectable to ordinary human consciousness, though they will manifest in dreams, and can appear in artistic endeavors by way of "active imagination." It is when the mind becomes attuned to meta-frequencies of extraordinary states that archetypal realities may be directly perceived.

To discern genuine archetype from hallucination is a talent that comes with experience and accumulation of significant knowledge. Ira Progoff touches on this in his work, *Jung, Synchronicity and Human Destiny*:

> *As the archetype is experienced in the individual personality, the question of whether it is numinous, that is whether it generates an inspiring and energizing power in the psyche and casts an unusual light or atmosphere around itself, depends on the depth at which it is contacted. A complex of psychic factors basically archetypal in nature may be experienced superficially by an individual, and then the force potential in it will dwindle away before it has been truly formed. On the other hand, if the archetype is entered into deeply and its full potential is drawn forth and actualized, the result is a numinosity of highest intensity so that the archetype then becomes much more than a psychological image. It becomes a 'living power,' a center around which new patterns of events constellate in time.[9]*

The patterns Progoff speaks of have to do with inner depth symmetries within implicate realms which may manifest partially on the explicate level of the material world. In his book, *Synchronicity*, F. David Peat, writing of quantum realities, observed:

Shortly before his death, Werner Heisenberg, the creator of quantum theory, argued that what was truly fundamental in nature was not elementary particles themselves but the <u>symmetries</u> that lay beyond them. These fundamental symmetries could be thought of as the <u>archetypes</u> of all matter and the ground of material existence. The elementary particles themselves would be simply the <u>material realizations</u> of these underlying symmetries. Heisenberg argued that ultimate reality is to be found not in electrons, mesons, and protons but in something that lies beyond them, in abstract symmetries that manifest themselves in the material world.[10]

We have touched on both scientific and mystical insights concerning how the embodied mind creates the entire manifestation of the material world through an enigmatic alchemistry of brain activity which seems to organize abstract symmetries of the mind's deepest and highest numinous depths, filters their frequencies, and creates the cultural mythoform. In his work, *Eating the I*, William Patrick Patterson states,

It is in the patterns and influences of our collective and personal archetypes that we live our lives. We can sense and see it in particular qualities of energy, events and symbols.[11]

By cultivating an inner discipline to control and direct subjective impulses, we can learn to objectively recognize positive and negative influences from archetypal dimensions as they enter consciousness. This demands acute awareness of the psychological factors making up one's personality. Of course, this is no easy task. I have come across volumes almost half a foot thick dealing only with the phenomenon of personality. There is nothing simple about the conundrum of what we think we are, contrasted with what we actually are. Don Quixote was a character swamped in delusions, yet he was quick to claim, *"I know very well who I am."*

Personality has to do with what is known in psychology as the persona, which relates to the Latin word for "mask." Your persona is the "you" everyone else sees, the aspects of your ego-self you let them see. The persona has many guises, some socially acceptable, some not. Either can be detrimental to inner growth. The socially acceptable guises can induce mechanical conformism within the social ambit without discernment or question, such as when a person unhesitatingly stands up when the national anthem is played, or is compelled to buy fashionable designer clothes, or feels subservient or docile to anyone in a position of authority. These are manifestations of the false personality, our socialized idea of ourselves. Michael Talbot deals with this in his book, *Mysticism and the New Physics*, where he writes of such power of conformism being...

> ...*dramatically demonstrated in experiments undertaken at Harvard concerning the effect of social pressure upon perceptual judgments. When asked to correctly match the length of a line with that of one of three lines presented, participants made the 'wrong' choice less than one percent of the time. However, in a group where the majority was coached beforehand to unanimously choose the 'wrong' line, the decision of the unknowing participants was measurably affected. Under group pressure minority subjects agreed with the majority's 'wrong' judgments 36.8 percent of the time even when the length of the two allegedly equal lines differed by as much as seven inches.*[12]

Seven inches was a very obvious difference, and yet these people still gave up their genuine perceptual grasp of reality in order to conform.

This entrenched conformism is intimately related to a person's self-image, which is but a mask-like fragment of the whole person. It is your mask. Though mask may seem like a superficial analogy, it is not. Each mask we wear in a given situation is composed of a complex mixture of our inner needs and desires, our wish to be appreciated, to impress others, to be accepted, to fit in, in order to make our way through the social milieu. This acculturated persona is your "front," your social role, and is manifested in feelings and emotional displays, and other overt character traits, through which you attempt to communicate your most desirable qualities to the world. We wear these tailored masks for everyone we meet, even though they might not feel like masks to us — one mask for Mom and Dad, another for a friend, another for a teacher, and so on. An individual's personality can be multi-faceted without any taint of multi-personality disorder where complete personalities of various types reside in one individual psyche. When a certain attribute suits a situation better than another, we present it through an aspect of the persona, not always as a deliberate ploy, but usually as an almost instinctual manifestation we are not even aware is occurring.

The persona becomes a false personality when it is disconnected from one's authentic inner being. This has nothing to do with schizophrenic fragmentation. Again, varied "masks" does not mean varied personalities, though they can mean multi-faceted manifestations of what Gurdjieff called a legion of inner "I's" controlling impulses and negative compulsions which possess the average personality. Negative controlling "I's" cater to the vanity of the ego and its craving for recognition and power. These "I's" rule most people's fantasy life. We even wear masks for our own private theatre of the imagination, seeing ourselves as we would like to be, seeing qualities in ourselves we have not really developed. Getting rid of useless "I's" involving the unnecessary wearing of false personality masks is an essential task of self-observation and the cultivation of authentic being. This demands unyielding truthfulness. We can overcome self-deceit by bold self-confessional introspection whenever we catch ourselves involved in what we sense to be essentially worthless desires or negative activity. The more often we can catch ourselves succumbing to worthless, useless, negative thought processes and stop them, the more energy we conserve for further inner growth. The psychological-spiritual rewards of such vigilant self-observation are subtle yet profound.

From varied directions of cultural expression—literature, theatre, philosophy—the theme *"To thine own self be true,"* is reiterated over the centuries, from Socrates to Jesus to Shakespeare to Ibsen. The less we know of our inner self, our shadow tendencies, our projections, the whys and hows of our emotional needs, likes, dislikes, belief systems, the less authentic we are, and the less we can be true to ourselves or to others. There are a thousand self-help books out there of varied quality, some which may give helpful insights that can lead to a healing, a necessary change, an improvement of situation, but for the most part the actual inner effect is like a small glass of water when you are parched with thirst—mildly quenching, that's it. Far more thirst quenching are the penetrating writings of Maurice Nicoll, based on the brilliant insights of P. D. Ouspensky and Gurdjieff, clarifying how one cultivates objective perception of personality. The works of these three men, along with those of Jung and Aurobindo, produce a quality of study inducing genuine self-knowledge that limited self-help formulas aimed at superficial alleviation of personal hang-ups can't even approach.

C. G. Jung clarified the personality is both profound and mysterious. No matter how much psychologists and psychiatrists may think they know about it, there is always something elusive and unexplained about how the personality develops and relates to the world. The refinement and enhancement of the personality releases one's inner potential for cultivation of the soul. Objective introspection is in no way narcissistic, for the deeper the truth of our self-knowledge, the more real we become in our "I and Thou" relationships to others. As this authenticity blooms, the persona aspect of the personality gradually ceases to be a quick-change artist in the game of masks, becoming translucent to the degree of inner development. Of course, a totally maskless person would be a sage or a saint. Yet, though you or I, dear reader, may never qualify as sage or saint, if we strive for the stars, we may at least get to the mountain peak of selfhood.

The essential thing here is not to get caught up, like so many who relate to the New Age movement, in creating only an external front of inner growth, cultivating a mask of "spiritual enlightenment" lacking authentic content. This is a very serious pitfall on the way to self-knowledge. The Russian sage Ouspensky pointed out how easily people can create a self-deluded image of awakening, yet remain ensconced within an ordinary state of consciousness, with all its games and self-deceit, relatively asleep. I recall the story of a Zen monk who took LSD and had his entire concept of being serenely at one with all things shattered like a porcelain vase struck by a rock. Although there are certainly states of profound serenity we can cultivate, all to often we have merely taught ourselves to act serenely and to skillfully avoid all circumstances that might reveal the superficiality of our cultivated composure. Apparently the monk who took LSD had intellectually integrated traditional concepts of Zen into an image of how an awakened person should act, and he came to believe this act was authentic. Zen monasteries are inhabited by quite a few "monks" in this condition, especially in the West. I have seen such pseudo serenity to a high degree in yoga ashrams and among those gathered about gurus across the globe. This delusion of being enlightened is fairly widespread within the New Age movement. How can we tell we are fooling ourselves about awakening? Each individual must deal with their own unique skein of psychological/spiritual experience in the most truthful way possible. Unflagging self-honesty is necessary — and such self honesty can be very painful.

There are methods that can help sharpen objective introspection — exercises, disciplines, ways and means to prevent a person from backsliding, or turning away at the first inkling of fear. A person can create a special symbol, or mantra, or cultivate a certain mental activity that alerts him/her to any forgetting of necessary truths. You can make a collage covering an entire wall in your home, filled with pictures of people and things and places, which provoke a sense of existential/spiritual awareness of your place in the vast wildness of existence. Or you can create a painting or sculpture, or a shrine of significant objects which turn your mind toward the numinous essence of creation. Even a meaningful symbolic tattoo as a constant reminder is worthwhile. All such efforts can be beneficial. But, again, beware — the ego can be so adverse to giving up its hold on the socialized character it has adjusted to, that involvement in such activities can easily strengthen a false self-image of spiritual development. We can become prideful of our involvement in such endeavors, and lose contact with sincere inner intention. Thus such methods of awakening must be in synch with the pursuit of pertinent knowledge. Perhaps shamanistic rituals may be necessary to break the mold of habitual reactions to the world. Significant to this is the importance of who one associates with, occasionally requiring a change of environment and the solicitation of feedback from knowledgeable strangers. All too often a person will remain with a group surrounding a certain guru, or a cult, or commune, where a mutual admiration syndrome occurs, and everyone's delusions are strengthened by never being confronted with insightful criticism or fresh challenges or necessary psychic crisis.

Where do you find the time for such endeavors? If you give up all compulsions and cravings to fulfill the American Dream, giving the quest for awakening top priority, one way or another, the basic necessities of shelter and food will take care of themselves. One learns to cultivate what ancient Zen monks call "refined poverty." Two thousand years ago the awakened wandering Siddha of the Mideast whom history calls Jesus, said,

> *Therefore I say unto you, Take no thought for your life, what ye shall eat, or what ye shall drink; nor yet for your body, what ye*

shall put on. Is not life more than meat, and the body than rai-
ment?...And why take ye thought for raiment? Consider the lil-
ies of the field, how they grow; they toil not, neither do they spin:
And yet I say unto you, That even Solomon in all his glory was
not arrayed like one of these... Take therefore no thought for the
morrow: for the morrow shall take thought for the things of it-
self.[13]

New Agers rationalizing an excessively affluent lifestyle as
they claim to pursue spiritual awakening, exclaim Buddha gave up
asceticism and fasting because he realized he did not need to prolong it to produce enlightenment. They tend to ignore the fact that
without his extensive period of extreme asceticism and fasting he
wouldn't have become the Buddha. He knew fasting and giving up
the material lifestyle was a necessary stage. He never returned to an
affluent routinized lifestyle. The great founder of Zen, Bodhidharma,
spent nine years in a cave in constant meditation. The ancient craving for materialistic affluence is an addiction amplified by capitalistic
culture, which definitely influences the New Age "spirituality of
prosperity" syndrome, where money and success are said to be signs
of spiritual growth. But authentic commitment to spiritual truth
transcends ephemeral pecuniary values.

We must keep these words of the Zen sage D. T. Suzuki in
mind,

The way is strewn with thistles and brambles, and the climb is
slippery in the extreme. It is no pastime but the most serious
task in life; no idlers will ever dare attempt it. It is indeed a
moral anvil on which your character is hammered.[14]

"*It is indeed a moral anvil...*" Such morality is of a much deeper,
transcendent level of understanding than that which the narrow,
parochial "moral majority" expounds. Transcendent morality caters
to no arbitrary system of duties, no common obedience to an external religious or political authority. As Edmund Burke said,

The lines of morality are not like the ideal of mathematics. They
are broad and deep as well as long. They admit of exceptions,
they demand modifications.[15]

Unassuming self-responsibility and flexible self-discipline are ingredients of genuine open-minded morality. There is no need to kowtow to commandments from on high, or worry about karmic punishment meted out by ineffable "divine" judges. One must be responsible enough to keep constantly alert to the consequences and effects of personal explorations in pursuit of self-knowledge. What is a learning experience at one time may become a negative addiction at another. A holistically knowledgeable conscience is your best guide. True serenity does not come easily. It is an aspect of the pearl of great price, and the price must be paid.

Why would people even begin to commit themselves to the all-consuming challenges and trials the quest for genuine self-knowledge demands? Just the fact of being alive, conscious of the haunting immensity of existence, knowing we are born in mystery and die in mystery, is a fairly significant reason. But it gets even deeper, for the more truth of our existential-spiritual predicament we creatively bring forth through our hearts and wring from each moment of life, the more the numinous presence dwelling within the depths of existence, in subtle reciprocal response shall disclose its enriching meanings. Just as Ortega y Gasset wrote about the history of civilization dwelling in the subconscious as nourishment constantly enriching us, which is what Colin Wilson referred to as a cultural energy reserve, there are even deeper reserves of spiritual sustenance. These deeper reserves have an affinity here with Teilhard de Chardin's concept of the noosphere, and to Gurdjieff's "great accumulator." It is this reservoir of inner nourishment which gives the energy and meaning to overcome periods of nihilistic. Taking up the inner quest responsibly, faithfully, reverently, undaunted even when wounded with despair, the seeker shall definitely find the way through the thickest, darkest wood, and in the process experience treasurable moments of awakened joy. I say this, having been through the darkest wood several times during my own journey. And I must admit, I have never felt completely out of those woods. But as Yeats said, *"I shall find the dark grow luminous."*16

11 – UltraOrdinary Situation

As a man is, so he sees.
—William Blake

Come forth as what thou art.
—Pindar

As science probes further into the unknown, it seems its continual expansion in depth and scope and complexity is endless. And yet, as elucidated in various works, such as John Horgan's *The End of Science*,[1] there are definite limits to the empirical process, as far as ultimate answers go. Thus, as always, we must direct our search for deeper meanings into such perennial areas of thought as mysticism, metaphysics, and philosophy.

The essential meaning of philosophy is the love of truth and wisdom, and although it has undergone a process involving construction of varied schools of thought, and has been viewed as overwhelmed and buried by science, the words of Etienne Gilson should be kept in mind: *"Philosophy always buries its undertakers."*[2] In other words, sound intelligent philosophical exploration of reality will bury conceptual systems confined to inflexible logic and sterile intellectual analysis, such as materialism, reductionism, functionalism, computationalism, quantumism, as well as any religion, cult, or spiritual movement built upon credulity. It will also expose and surpass schools of thought considered to be philosophy, but are nothing more than an airy mimicry riddled with intellectual hairsplitting and unnecessary scholarly abstruseness. The scholarly volumes of exposition concerning such subject matter as defining the difference between Continental philosophy and Anglo-American analytical philosophy, resemble the work of ingeniously skilled masons who have built elaborate brick towers only to imprison themselves. Academic philosophers all too often become entangled in the very processes meant to free the mind. What does it matter if we know Sartre's style of profound synthesis is basically "centrifugal," whereas Merleau-Ponty's is "centripetal." It doesn't matter at all. Yet I've come across scholars who have written entire volumes of such intellectual exorbitance.. Castaneda's Don Juan spoke about Wittgenstein tying the noose of analytical exposition so tight, he strangled his own potential for deeper explorations.3 This could also be said of the average academic philosopher. Robert Avens touches on this in his book, *The New Gnosis*:

> *Thinking in the Western philosophical tradition is for the most part identified with reasoning and argumentative rigor. Doing philosophy, especially among the logical analysts, means to be engaged in a competition between arguments. In this capacity thinking is usually distinguished from what is assumed to be its less respectable, if not irresponsible alternatives: mysticism, art, myth-making, poetry. To Heidegger, philosophy, based on this type of confrontationalist thinking, though useful and necessary in many respects, is rooted in 'the technical interpretation of thinking'... It recognizes no goal or meaning that is not grounded in rational certainty, and its modus operandi is what Heidegger calls 'calculative thinking'—a thinking that plans and investigates, computes and never stops, never collects itself. Today it expresses itself in the frenzy of technological mastery and in the will to power involving man in the circle of its own projected world.* 4

To an extensive degree privileged professionals of academia have undertaken philosophy strictly as an academic pursuit, caught up in their thinking function with little interactive play from their emotional, feeling and intuitive attributes, and none from exploration of their inner being. Volumes written by scholars on every subject—morality, reason, truth—involving complex debates of past and current doctrines, yet substantially lacking in psychological depth and experiential awareness of the world at large, have abetted the domination of scientism, positivism, and thus materialism.

William Kluback stated, *"Philosophy belongs to the spirit ... and is inspired by that longing to see beyond our sight, to think beyond our thinking."*5 And Heidegger said, *"It is the very nature of philosophy* *never to make things easier but only more difficult."*₆ Not difficult because of some high flown analytical manipulation of abstract concepts, but to make it difficult to cling to belief systems and structures of thought that keep the mind enchained to dogma and delusion. Because philosophy is an open-ended process, no fixed point should ever be reached where one claims, "I am an existentialist," or "idealist," etc. Philosophy belongs to the household of religion, but with the windows and doors open.

Mortimer Adler has written, *"The better our understanding of ideas, especially great ideas, the better we understand reality because of the light they throw on it."*₇ The intensity of the great ideas of philosophy remains viable because they reveal reality and mystery to be essentially synonymous. Reality is palpable mystery.   Because we have named and labeled everything our perception encompasses does not make reality less mysterious. It is getting at this essential nature of things beyond names and labels, as close as humanly possible, that is the activity of philosophy. It doesn't matter what the classical perception of philosophy is, or the history it has been confined to. What matters is how one goes about "philosophizing," so that it is directly effective in the unfolding of self-knowledge. As Gabriel Marcel said,

> *Philosophy is not building further structure upon the established foundation of traditional premises, but an adventure of creative exploration, ever opening, ever expanding."*₈

Philosophy pursued in this manner combines both the love of truth and the acceptance of paradox. According to Heidegger, philosophical discourse is to open up and take true measure of existence. To do this, philosophical exposition must be rooted in transpersonal experience, which it lost contact with during centuries when Christian scholars and theologians strived to construct a rational system based on the merging of Aristotelian concepts with religious dogma. This loss of contact with transcendent experience was amplified during the rise of scientism and positivism, à la the Vienna Circle.

Philosophical exposition is sterile if not underlined by exploration of the deeper dimensions of the psyche, entailing confrontation with significant archetypes and trans-egoic states of consciousness. Lacking this, a person may succumb to agreeing with A. N. Whitehead's remark: *"The purpose of philosophy is to rationalize mysticism."*₉

Such rationalizing has been a significant deficiency of modern philosophy, especially when we consider the limitations of reason. As Verhoeven puts it, *"reasoning is thought without wonder"*... and *"wonder is central to philosophy."*₁₀ Reason should not be adverse to revealing its own flaws and shortcomings. Intelligent reasoning can expose its own limits, substantiating that what lies beyond reason may be comprehended with intuitive and visionary facets of consciousness. Mysticism, as various sages have demonstrated, can be brought into accord with reason. Reason, honed with applied logic, is the filter that keeps mystical thought free of superstition, theosophical fabrication, occult obscurity, and New Age credulity. Though authentic philosophy is rooted in mystical vision, it is also a science of the mind, for it requires—demands—consistent and assiduous self-criticism, harmonized with intellectual and intuitive weighing and measuring of extensive knowledges. Philosophy, and even more so its basic branch, metaphysics, is not something to be pursued by either gullible visionaries incapable of analytical reasoning, or toplofty professors so caught up in analytical intellectualization they're incapable of mystical vision.

Consider, out of 180 academic "philosophers" having educational positions in Germany during the Third Reich, half became members of the Nazi party. Of course, like the glass seen as either half full or half empty, so can this statistic be perceived, for 50% had the courage not to join the Nazi party. But however you see this, it validates that erudite philosophizing doesn't necessarily imply wisdom, or even astute reasoning. Despite the brilliancy of Heidegger's works, (much of which I have integrated into my own weltanschauung, and which I will use throughout this book), he was a vain and pompous man, believing himself to be some kind of a philosophical avatar, and he was also a Nazi. He attained profound knowledge, yet lacked significant attributes of self-knowledge, which is an essential requirement for every genuine philosopher who is more attuned to ceaselessly renewing him/herself than competing for academic prestige. The potential for prestigious power Heidegger's academic position and the political situation offered was a temptation he was too inwardly weak to refuse. His lack of awareness of his Mr. Hyde shadow traits amplified his intellectual hubris and undermined his potential for Sophianic wisdom. Still, his work is not to be sanctimoniously tossed aside, for in fundamental ways it transcends his personal failings and political viewpoints. You can glean meaningful knowledge from certain people without succumbing to their failings. You can also learn from their failings as much as from their nuggets of profound insight. If you are climbing the very rugged incline of a great mountain and an old Nazi who climbed there previously carved a few very good handholds in the rock, you would be a fool not to use those handholds because of moralistic considerations. And yet you must be aware of what missteps he took that eventually led to his downfall. With such in-depth scrutiny, all knowledges gleaned will be imbued with the power of substantiated truth. One pursues philosophy as a Jana yoga discipline enhanced with poetic perception, eventually going beyond philosophical inquiry when the egoic aspect of the quest dissolves from extensive immersion in the essence of Being. This is what the quest is about = gradual immersion into Being.

Does much of this seem perplexing? Of course. The discerning Spanish philosopher, Ortega y Gasset, wrote that a life fully lived means accepting a sense of constant perplexity.[11] He said the symbol for perplexity is the crossroads, for vibrant individuation repeatedly places us at the crossroads of significant decision, where we are exquisitely free to make fateful choices. Perplexity goes with the territory, for it is the mulch of self-knowledge. Perplexity is a hue of the color of wonder. Better to be constantly perplexed concerning profound reflections than to remain comfortably static with the false confidence of collective opinions, safe in some religious or political cul-de-sac or tightly constructed philosophical stance, shutting down the potential to ever experience the magnificent fullness of your being. Yet perplexity too must be refined. Perplexity should not partake of befuddlement. Refining perplexity is a function of "negative capability"—having aplomb amid the wild terrifying wonder of it all.

Mortimer Adler wrote that to be human is to be endowed with the proclivity to philosophize. But, though most of us are born with various degrees of potential to grow psychologically, spiritually, and philosophically, the world has a way of hypnotizing us with its entrancing banalities, or crushing us under mundane circumstances of economic survival, depriving us of time and opportunity, sapping our will to grow. The quest for genuine self-knowledge begins when we challenge such obstacles, intuiting there must be more depth and scope to the world than we have been taught. Amid the global circumstances circa 2005 – 2050 on planet Earth, only a relatively small number of human beings will be graced to find themselves morally and spiritually responsible to commit themselves to this quest. For this commitment will require eclectic integration into your life of the way of the alchemist, scientist, shaman, yogi, witch, philosopher, sage, and medicine man, to a width, depth, degree that suits your own individual uniqueness of intention and capability. Such authentic cultivation of self-knowledge is similar to the way a sculpture is carved from granite, with years of dedicated and consistent work. Blood, sweat, tears, fear, laughter, are definite attributes of self-discovery, but most important is patience and a sense of humor, especially being able to laugh at the occasional absurdity of your own plight.

Through disciplines such as yoga, fasting, and meditation, or through the meticulous careful use of psychedelics, visions may be had along the way, and quite grand indeed. But it is just as significant to cultivate insights revealing the possibility that what you know of yourself, the entire conceptual structure of your self-image, including religious belief, sense of patriotism, ideas about the world at large, is most likely built to a consequential degree of falsehood and delusion. Authentic inner strength comes from facing such intimate revelations and overcoming fear of being left vulnerable. The inability to handle fear is a basic psychological deterrent to proficient spiritual growth. Although it may seem facing and ridding yourself of religious and political misconceptions, and other acculturated duplicities which hamper fecund psychological growth, is less of a challenge than facing external terrors, it is often these internal confrontations that give rise to the greatest fears. This is what underlies the rigidity of religious and political belief systems which are built and believed in as bulwarks against such fear. Facing, challenging, striving to understand and overcome all forms of fear enriches your spiritual being. Significant philosophical and mystical systems place great import on containment of fear, of converting panic into intensity of insight. In the teachings of martial arts, fear is transformed into a dynamic energy component. In Tantric discipline, overcoming ideas of terror is known as "chod," where the practitioner seeks out fearful situations to challenge him/herself. We cannot vanquish fear, but we can come to understand and transform it into an instrument of spiritual enrichment.

In addition to our tendency to become incapacitated by fear, another entrenched psychological weakness is our vulnerability to a

variety of illusions, both internal and external, significant and insignificant. The most obvious way our mind can be fooled is by optical
illusions. Take a simple optical illusion where you see a triangle that
does not actually exist.

This illustration actually contains only three black discs with pie-
slice notches. Cover one of the discs and the illusory triangle disappears. It was never there. It isn't there now, even though you definitely see it.

From just this simple example you can grasp how tricky our
optical-sensory system can be. Existence is a poly-disperse dance
betwixt appearance and reality. The actual size of the moon is tremendously different than the golf ball sized globe we nightly take
for granted as we see it seeming to cross the sky. In reality, the moon
doesn't cross the sky. The earth spins, creating the illusion. But optical illusions, in and of themselves, are soon detected, and we are not
likely to be tricked by the same one twice. It is the intangible deceptions of the mind we must be attentive to, for these can engulf an
individual, causing him/her to lead a life of undetected falsehood
and impeded spirituality. This is especially true when it comes to
illusions and delusions created by acculturated influences, such as
biased religious, ethnic and political attitudes. I recall a scientific ex-
periment where groups of young soldiers who had been drilled for
weeks to unquestioningly respect their superior officers, were lined
up in front of a kind of "Ames Room," which is a small room built
specifically to optically distort how the objects inside are perceived.
This particular room was constructed to distort the appearance of
any face looking in through a window across the room. When the
young soldiers looked into the room at the faces of their peers in the
far window, the room did just what it was designed to do—it distorted their features, like in a fun house mirror. But when an officer
put his head through the far window, the young soldiers were so
trained to see perfection in this figure of authority, their minds simply could not perceive the officer's features as distorted. The officer

looked perfectly normal to these young soldiers. This reveals how we unquestioningly respond to images of authority and is an example of how powerful the influences of acculturation, rooted in custom and tradition and reinforced by education, can be.

Of course, there is nothing wrong with respect for authority, IF it is worthy of respect. But we should never give respect blindly. We must always question authority. The ruthless dictator Adolph Hitler's psychological condition was a complex merging of psychopathic intelligence with Machiavellian cunning, amplified and energized with drug induced psychic powers. On becoming the supreme authority of Germany in 1933, he used the influence of his authoritarian image to convince people the lies he told were truth. Like the young soldiers in the special room who could not see any distortion in their officer's face, most Germans blinded by patriotic zeal could not see the evil lurking behind Hitler's speeches of national glory. They were duped by a psychological illusion. Hitler was a magician at developing a system of propaganda to create the illusion of supreme authority. Today, all over the earth, dictators, religious and cult leaders, and just run-of-the-mill politicians, some who become Presidents and Vice-Presidents, (with help from their "public relations" friends), use knowledge of human emotional response to patriotism and religion to manipulate the multitudes, leading them to believe falsehoods are true and illusions are real. This is why it is very important to grasp how the human mind can be played by external influences like a puppet on strings. If we do not develop an indepth understanding of our world, of our minds, of our very selves, we remain vulnerable to such manipulation. Without substantial self-knowledge, we remain ignorant of the dangerous power of persuasive illusion and self-deception. Everyone is capable of being duped, and of duping themselves.

We have dealt with our primate ancestry and early hominids whose knowledge of the world was confined to a small orbit of tribal activity. We considered the brain-eye configuration's filtering of a narrow band of visible light from an immense spectrum of frequencies, creating a perception radius conducive to physical survival. Thus we can grasp how humans have become exquisitely attuned to the dynamic network of the physical-terrestrial sphere of being. Even though people may live in a technologically advanced nation like the United States, with all its amenities and orderliness—paved streets, garbage collection, sewer systems, traffic lights, manicured lawns, police, hospitals, schools, 9 to 5 routine—intent in their involvement with family, career, entertainment, they are, like their ancestors, oriented strictly to the immediate social-physical environment. This attunement has brought about an inflexible social-nationalistic orientation, with religion as a kind of cultural extension, an organized traditional acknowledgment of a higher-deeper dimension of being confined to simplified anthropomorphic imagery which in no way disturbs the societal ambit of political-economic endeavors. Since this is so, the seeker must strive to keep in mind that the entire universe of terrestrial/cosmic phenomena, is a vast veil over an immense complexity of forces—solar, cellular, molecular, atomic, quantum, psychic, spiritual—which are manifestations of, interweave with, and create, our every day "normal" reality we so easily take for granted.

In his truly enjoyable book, *The Secret House*, David Bodanis elucidates the wonderland of phenomena hidden beneath our everyday world:

> Take a step across your bedroom floor on the way to bed after demurely turning out the top light...and, unless there have been some shady deals in the zoning department, you are unlikely to fall through the floor. This is because as you apply your weight to your slippered foot, the floor, apparently passive and immobile beneath you, pushes back up with exactly as much force as you're applying down. This is miraculous.   Touch your right toe to the floor in a mock pirouette as you gingerly step from the bathroom towards the bed ..., exerting only a few ounces of pressure, and the floor will register that and push up with only a few ounces too; shift into a running scamper so that your full body weight is on that foot, and the floor, right in the same spot, will immediately rearrange itself inside and push up with the equivalent of your full body weight.
>
> Nothing escapes its measure; the swiped scoop of mashed potato, that furtively devoured third helping of cake – the floor detects the weight of it all, and pushes up accordingly. It's important that it does so, for if it missed something you had eaten and pushed up too softly you would gradually start sinking through the floorboards, your slippers puckering out the ceiling below. If the floor over-estimated what you had eaten, then it would push up with more force than your body weight could

overcome, and you would be propelled up like a trampolinist.

The floor knows all this because when you step on it you tell it how much you weigh. The more you've eaten the more you crush the molecules in the floor beneath your eager slippers. This is the key. Crushed floor molecules push back. Each individual molecule in the segment of the floor directly beneath your foot rebounds up to counterbalance the crushing. They can't push back very hard, each molecule being limited to a very small fraction of an ounce of rebound oomph because of its diminutive size, but as there are very many molecules in the floor the net result can be considerable. The more crush, the more they push back, so equalizing your weight – exactly. In a floor made of iron or concrete the push-back of the crushed floor molecules would be near instantaneous, which is why such surfaces feel hard underfoot. In wooden floors the crushed molecules respond with only a little more delay, and that's why such floors have a slight give but otherwise feel hard and solid when you jauntily skip across them.[12]

We tread through an extraordinary realm we are hardly aware of, moving through the illusion of solidity when in actuality we move through vast forces of phantomlike phenomena every moment. What we perceive is so much more than what we have adapted ourselves to believe it is. The poet William Blake saw our situation with clear poetic vision, and his words have been quoted many times: *"If the doors of perception were cleansed everything would appear to man as it is, infinite,"* and, *"The eye of man a little narrow orb, clos'd and dark."*[13] But it is not the "eye," in and of itself, that is the culprit. The eye, as our organ of sight, is intimately interwoven with the brain-mind configuration, which for tens of thousands of years has been intrinsically influenced by language, thus thought, all at play in perennial feedback loop complexity—perception igniting thought, thought enhancing perception, etc. As Judith Hooper and Dick Teresi clarify:

But it isn't just the receptors in our skin and nostrils, the rods and cones in our retina, the minute cilia in our ears, that restrict Mind at Large to a utilitarian trickle. What matters more is how we <u>interpret</u> and edit the incoming messages. Human gray mat-

ter, after all, is 90 percent interpretation equipment, 90 percent storyteller.[14]

No matter how marvelous the entire sensory apparatus of our physical being, if we do not cultivate an expansion of our own perceptual abilities, we will remain confined to perception through a *"narrow orb, clos'd and dark."* To awaken to greater expansiveness of being, of experiencing existence to the fullness of our capability, is what genuine spiritual enlightenment is all about.

Thus here we are, ensconced in the perplexity and paradox of the dance betwixt appearance and reality, as both passive receivers of "information" from light emissions, and simultaneously active creator-storytellers of the surrounding world by way of acculturated projection and metaphoric coordination. The ultra complexity of perceptual and cognitive faculties has yet to be substantially pinned down by empirical investigations. There is always "something other" involved. Jurij Moskvitin, one of the most intelligent metaphysicalists on the contemporary scene, touches on this astonishing psychic-quantum frolic between "subjective" and "objective" elements of our existence, in the following:

> *The world as it appears to us is made up exclusively of sensorial impressions and their combinations, and is therefore determined and limited by the form and the range of the organs of perception. Whatever we experience of a world external to ourselves is nothing but the release by external impulses of <u>something</u> that is in ourselves. We do not perceive an object external to ourselves but <u>something</u> in ourselves which has been called up by impulses from that object and which presumably corresponds to it – colors, sounds, smells and sensations are in us, and by projecting them onto the unknowable world around us we build it up like a mosaic from elements in ourselves.*[15]

Within this intriguing statement dwells the perplexing wonder of our predicament. We should give priority significance to this "something" in ourselves, for it has intimately familiar qualities to that inner potential the Hindu luminary Aurobindo calls the soul. We are, as the ancient Greek sage Sophocles exclaimed, truly "uncanny beings," existing within an equally uncanny universe of objects seemingly external we can tangibly weigh and measure, yet the very nature of this external world is dependent on significant elements of internal cognition. Our brain/egoic-mind creates the entire universe by transforming and interpreting frequency patterns "coming" from the all-encompassing "external" world. That which is observed is an intimate aspect of the observer. As Lawrence LeShan and Henry Margenau put it in their work, *Einstein's Space, Van Gogh's Sky*,

> *What we can observe of reality is our own organization of it. Reality is a compound like water, with consciousness one of the elements. But we can never hope to know what the compound would be without consciousness. If we were to say, 'We now have an idea as to what reality is before consciousness was added. Let us check and see if our idea is correct,' the second sentence would have no meaning. We cannot even conceive of a way to make this check... No longer do we view consciousness as a late arrival on the scene. Consciousness is the scene.*[16]

Arthur Zajonc put it this way:

> *We need to soften the notion of ourselves as equipped with fixed vidicon-like eyes and static computer-like brains to produce the equivalent of consciousness. The blossoms of perception unfold out of a far richer and self-reflexive union of mental and natural lights.*[17]

Yes, there is something neo-Berkeleian to the New Age view that the mind entirely creates objective reality, that the world is only what we perceive as we perceive it—but that's not quite so, or rather, it would be better to speak of a sort of paradoxical both/and. Dinosaur footprints and other fossils verify the world, cosmic-terrestrial "concrete reality" where evolution occurs, the entire magnificent flow of all and everything, was going on long before the first primate, let alone the first human, was born, and as even ordinary informed intelligence can deduce, will continue long after all of us are gone. That this "concrete reality" is proven to be something entirely other than we perceive it to be, does not invalidate its existence. If a tree falls in the forest with no human beings around, all the nearby creatures of the forest, squirrels, foxes, bears, wolves, birds, will jump, startled at the sound. Before Columbus "discovered" the New

World, no one from the "Old World" of Europe knew it was there, yet Native "Americans" had been doing their cultural thing for thousands of years with no concern for any European wondering whether they were there or not. And though Europe did not exist for the Native Americans, it too was there, in all its tumult and extravagance. Because things are "out of sight and out of mind," does not mean they are out of existence.

All the turmoil of wars, poverty, famine, going on beyond the personal perimeter of you and your family and friends, is not of less significance or less real because it is "far away" in other countries, having no immediate effect within your personal ambit. Right now, while you're reading this book, six billion other human beings are busy with their own lives, performing myriad activities all over the earth. Do you know how many six billion is? As we demonstrated in an earlier chapter, it would take you twelve days, counting twenty-four hours a day just to count to one million; it would take you forty-eight years to count to one billion. It is almost impossible to imagine what an immense number of people six billion is. This great swarming mass of humans is a blur in your mind's eye, and in relation to those billions of individuals you are just another microscopic cipher smudge of this great blur. Yet each individual among these six billion "out there" feels as unique and real as you feel yourself to be.

The threat of being an anonymous microscopic blip amid billions of other such blips is one of the essential reasons human beings develop and cling to belief systems that make them feel they are somehow unique among the multitudes. A sense of belonging to a crowd, cult, corporation, nation, religion, the pursuit of fame and status, keeps the threat of isolated anonymity at bay. The conforming element within political and religious ideologies offers one of the most powerful escapes from this sense of anonymity. Nationalism, thus patriotism, is rooted in belief that the geographic location, as well as the governmental and cultural structure of a person's nation, is superior to other locations and structures around the earth. Thus the people abiding there consider themselves superior to those outside their nation's boundaries. Most forms of religion work in a similar manner, with every denomination or sect within a religion succumbing to this trait, amplifying the sense of uniqueness in each member of the group. Though ordinary common sense informs us such things as geographic location, political ideology, ethnic origin, or religious orientation, do not in any way make people superior, an acculturated mindset ignores and overrules both common sense and intelligent reasoning.

Because of the power mass idolization bestows upon billionaires, movie and TV stars, sports heroes, etc., fame and fortune are even more bewitchingly conducive to the illusion of eliteness. It is exceedingly difficult for a famous celebrity to avoid succumbing to a sense of egoic specialness. Such is why being in the limelight of their culture is so sought after—they are no longer lost in the anonymity of the masses. Fame is very detrimental to the spiritual quest. It hampers even those known as gurus and "spiritual" spokespersons who have risen in stature within the New Age ambit. It is only when you can perceive yourself as just another personality going through the brief jaunt of existence among six billion others, that you may become willing to bow to that which has significance beyond the ego's sphere of reality, and so commit to necessary disciplines, necessary risk, necessary sacrifice of comforting beliefs, thus partaking of the quest to awaken.

Right now, at this very moment, a farmer in Mongolia is weeding his garden, an Eskimo in northern Canada is mending her blanket, a monk in Tibet is saying his prayers, a convict in Norway is dreaming of freedom, a doctor in Scotland is treating her patient, somewhere some poor soul is being tortured, a man in Montana is herding sheep, a woman in South America is knitting a shawl, in a thousand different places, at this very moment, a baby is being born, and in a thousand other places a person is dying. Hundreds of millions of people are working at different jobs, millions are at play, armies are marching, crowds are watching sports, fishermen are fishing, factory workers are laboring, housewives are cooking, lovers are entwined, children are playing—right now, all over the earth, continuously, billions of human beings, this very moment, sleeping, laughing, crying, working, playing, learning, as you are reading these words. The immense and never ending genesis of the world swirls unnoticed around them just as it swirls unnoticed around you. And just as you are barely conscious of these billions of other humans each doing their individual thing, they are unaware that you exist.

In addition to the six billion or more people alive now who are your contemporaries, there have been millions upon millions who lived in the past, existing in hundreds of magnificent cultures, large and small, that appeared on earth and vanished—the ancient Etruscans, Egyptians, Romans, the nomad tribes of North Africa, the forest and jungle tribes of central Africa and South America, the Mongol tribes of Asia, the Viking seafarers, the German and Celtic tribes, the kingdoms of Europe, Russia, India, China, Japan. Since the dawn of primal self-awareness, humans have come forth into the wonder of the world, lived in their time and place ensconced in their culture's belief systems, then were swept away with the wind, as we will be, followed by billions coming after us to struggle with triumph and failure, eventually to also pass into the unfathomable darkness of death. Look around you while strolling or driving through town. Everyone you see, homeless bum or corporation president, milkman, waitress, politician, thief, doctor, butcher, baker, candlestick maker, you and I and everyone you know and billions of others spread across the earth, all will be dead in just 120 years, all the billions alive at this very moment, newborn or ninety years old. All, including you, will be vanquished from physical existence just twelve decades from now, most much sooner, some tomorrow, others within an hour. And the billions remaining will not notice this gradual disappearance of entire generations, as others fill vacancies left by the departed and continue doing all those things people have done before them. We are being swept along in a great tide of forces and phenomena beyond our ability to grasp.

The dread of egoic annihilation such knowledge evokes is why the majority of people strive to find a niche that will give them a sense of significance, of eliteness, which will stimulate and intensify their illusion of individual centrism. Belonging to a religious denomination or any spiritually oriented organization claiming to be exceptional, creates the egoic illusion of being closer than others to the source of things. Many tend to think "God" especially favors their denomination or sect. But there has never been, nor will there ever be, any "chosen" people, and no one is the "apple of God's eye," including all outstanding historical personalities, televangelists, gurus, etc.

If you can open up to this highlighting of personal insignificance, using this as a stepping off place toward the wonder of existence, a dissolving of all overblown ideas of the ego's significance, along with dispersion of shallow and false values becomes activated. It is then what Gabriel Marcel called ontological humility blooms, which as Ken T. Gallagher clarifies...

...is an existential attitude, a recognition of a depth in being which surpasses and includes us. In a word, it is the profound acknowledgement of finitude. To assent to finitude is not simply to acquiesce in the theoretical limits of the essence of man, for this can be done by an unruffled and self-confident rationalism. To experience finitude in the existential order is to experience the continued duration of a being which is not the master of his own being.[18]

To accept the finitude of the ego-persona opens up the potential to experience the infinite of essence.

That we can have a certain degree of command concerning what fate has given us does not mean we can willfully create our own reality. We can to a degree create our careers, our relationships, our social success, the quality of our spiritual quest, but these are encompassed by a reality we do not have any control over. Though we can be captains of this "I's" life goals, it is only to a certain extent, for just as the captain of the Titanic was caught in the play of forces having no concern for the success of his voyage, all our goals, ambitions, plans, can be turned topsy-turvy at any moment, an accident, a tumor or disease, a fatal confrontation with a stranger, or even a drastic change in the political-economic climate. While many go through life, pursue their ambitions, gain success, without a ripple of significant disturbance, others fall prey to a variety of tragedy and trauma. Such is the innate random uncertainty underlying the surge of human existence. New Age beliefs such as karma and past lives, "we create our own reality," and guardian angels that hover over a special few like spiritual bodyguards, are attempts to escape the stark reality of the cosmic-terrestrial lottery of fate. Though, as we shall see, there are quite possibly meta-archetypal beings that dwell in transcendent dimensions we could label "angelic," they have little to do with any medieval religious imagery of a popularized sort, and would more likely be of Rilke's "terrifying angel" quality. Contrary to Einstein's statement, *"God does not play dice with the universe,"* we actually are thrown into existence like dice tossed by the "gods." Einstein's statement stems from his religious upbringing, and his fear of what quantum physics would reveal. And yet it was Einstein who said, *"As far as the laws of mathematics refer to reality, they are not certain, and as far as they are certain, they do not refer to reality."* Again, when pondering the ultimate elements of our existence, contradiction, perplexity, paradox, go with the territory.

The ancient sage Pliny, speaking of Kairos, the Greek god of luck, said, *"We are so much at the mercy of chance that we have made chance our god."* Of course, the renowned physicist Max Born stated that an unrestricted belief in chance does not recognize the fact that we dwell amid an array of daily regularities and obvious causes creating consistent effects. He claimed even the unpredictability of the activity of subatomic elements is due to our inability to perceive the complex subtlety of that which causes the activity. On the other hand, he also observed that an unrestricted belief in causality produces the mechanistic view that the world is a huge machine and we but expendable parts. Born maintained that nature is ruled by a subtle blend of the laws of cause-and-effect and the laws of chance, which is a very apt and intriguing perception. Gregory Bateson spoke of nature creating fields of random possibility imbued with exquisitely selective purposiveness. Perhaps factors of purposiveness disperse as the profusion of free play increases chance, or could it be vice versa?

Consider the horse races, with all the utilitarian purposive causes which bring about the placement of thoroughbreds into the starting gate: raising colts, training, finding jockeys, etc. It is nearly 100% predictable that they will all leave the gates as the starting gun goes off. But despite the chain of intentional causes, as the race goes forward around the track, predictability is dispersed. Consider the winning of a horse race by a 100-to-1 long shot. A group of highly expert scientists, horsemen, race enthusiasts, veterinarians, etc., would most likely come up with a report entailing a number of very probable causes of why a long shot horse whose chance of winning was almost nil, won a race against several champion quality horses. They would consider such factors as an exceedingly skilled jockey, expert preparation, diet, care, and perhaps such things as some of the champion horses being handicapped by an unrecognized fever, an ankle strain, a new unfamiliar jockey. Yes, myriad causes could probably be found that possibly enhanced the chances of the long shot winner. And yet each of these enhancements/causes were themselves imbued with elements of chance — of occurring or not occurring according to the random play of unforeseen circumstances. Thus we have Born's subtle blend of cause and chance effecting the outcome of the race.

In competitive sports where two teams compete, preparation, skill, dedication, determination, talent, all combine in one team to a greater degree than the other, enhancing their "chances" to become winners on a certain day. Yet on another day, because of certain changes due to no explicit clear-cut causes, the opposite team wins. Both teams were intensely concentrating on "creating their own reality" of victory. And the winners will believe they did that.   But chance comes into it at all times, merging with all intentional factors. Watching a football game involving the Minnesota Vikings versus Tampa Bay, the Viking's receiver went out for a pass, determined to catch the ball, his skill and discipline and talent in full purposive operation, as three huge Tampa Bay defensive players closed tightly in on him. As the whole group of hundreds of pounds of muscle and bones hurtled down the field in a dynamic quartet of concentrated effort, the receiver leapt in the air, stretching his arms above the outstretched arms of the defenders, and with his fingers protruding just inches above this surging sphere of energized flesh, grasped the ball, creating a winning offensive play. I've seen similar plays where a receiver just about to grasp the football is hit, or trips, and the play fails. In football, as in poker, or golf, etc., we can witness the complex play betwixt causality of intentive action and chance/accident. Within the surge of any individual's life, intentions, purposive orientations, all have a certain degree of vulnerability to the random interference of chance—a veteran skydiver's chute becomes tangled in another's, a rock climber is struck by a falling boulder, a student out to get a degree in engineering falls in love with a woman who convinces him to become a hippie. Of course, skill, acute attentiveness, quality of self-knowledge, can make a significant difference when random chance interferes with intentive action. A skillful veteran motorcyclist has more of a chance of surviving a race along a winding road during a sudden rain storm than a novice, because of expertise in reacting to the unexpected, thus having a better chance with chance. And yet, a deer running out of the woods, a tree falling on the road, and the most skillful veteran cyclist dies. Random accident is the offspring of the essential uncertainty of chance that underlies all existence. Captains with many years at sea, caught in a storm, no matter how skilled, went down with their ships. All we can do is set sail toward spiritual awakening, cultivating our seamanship as we go, preparing for whatever storms may arise, being acutely attentive to every pertinent detail relating to our endeavor. One thing is certain—when it comes to spiritual awakening and the dangers of psychic crisis or confrontation with evil, the quality and expansiveness of one's knowledge is a deciding factor as to how one handles the disruption of chance within the psychic-spiritual ambit, possible unexpected terror, or even chaos of momentary madness. Well honed introspection and acute attentiveness to one's surroundings, including the games people play, plus the ability to remain calm within the churn of fear, all add up to surviving the upheaval of an unexpected paranormal episode. All in all, it's a dance of skill and chance amid the play of possibilities.

The seeker must become strong enough and humble enough to accept that this bewildering conscious life flows through us as briefly and precariously as a candle's flame exposed to an increasing wind. To open oneself to our actual situation ignites a magnificent comprehension of the wondrous and terrifying extensiveness of deeper dimensions of consciousness. Certain esoteric teachings clarify that such comprehension, if expanded and enhanced with determined commitment to varied mental disciplines and yoga techniques, creates the possibility of engendering an after death glow of consciousness—alert and lasting in degree and duration according to the state of one's strivings for spiritual awakening while alive.

The perennial philosophy of spiritual teachings are guideposts, to touch on, understand, catch a sense of direction, and move on. To cling to a guidepost, to establish a static religious stance because it offers safety and comfort, is to obstruct the soul's journey. Only by constantly moving courageously forward in search of the depths, never clinging to the security of what we are sure of, will we find another guidepost further on, to pause and rest for awhile, knowing we will face the darkness of the unknown, even the "nigredo," the dark night of the soul, between one guidepost and the next. Such periods of dark perplexity are portions of the psychological pain which is something every seeker of self-knowledge must deal with, and learn to accept. This spiritual "dark night" doesn't necessarily entail Sartrean nausea or nihilistic despair, for paradoxically, the farther you travel on this journey, if you stay centered in your heart chakra, the more esoterically significant your life becomes—not in the recognizable way of the quotidian world, but with the grace of the meaningful uniqueness of an inner voyager.

It is not vanity to realize the person you are is as unique as your fingerprints, or DNA pattern, or voice, or iris, which all have patterns no other human has. Mentally and physically you are unlike anyone else who has ever lived on the planet earth. But keep in mind, this uniqueness is also true of a slob or a fool, and adds up to little that is meaningful if an individual has no awareness of depth of being. Authentic meaningful uniqueness can only come forth in the paradoxical surrender and victory that imbues an individual life involved in significant spiritual development and challenge. Intentional commitment to alchemical individuation enlarges a person's life, not as a superior ego, but as a spiritually distinctive being of inner wholeness, integrity, and spiritual strength.

The intensely brilliant philosopher, Fredric Nietzsche, said it takes rare inner courage for a person to question his or her convictions and "tear asunder" those found to be false, shallow, or misleading. It is very important to become aware of the power negative habits and inadequate convictions have to stunt our spiritual growth. Only such awareness of the distorting quality of one's convictions will raise a person above the influence of acculturated illusions and manipulation. The more you are aware of your tendencies to succumb to growth hindering religious symbols, or political manipulations and personal vanities, the greater the inner potential to live an authentic spiritual existence. You have to constantly and thoroughly question yourself, your motives, intentions, goals, self-image, belief system, projections. This is the mulch of self-knowledge. No personal flaw is too small to be acknowledged. Overcoming minor temptations is a significant element of inner development. For if banal temptations haven't been conquered, greater temptations will prove overpowering. As D. T. Suzuki stated, the way is strewn with obstacles of all sorts, and the seeker must develop a unique sense of moral integrity in order to prevail. The noble truths taught by authentic spiritual teachers are invaluable in honing such integrity.

Let your cosmic insignificance and your coming death be your constant companions as you walk amid the wild wonder of it all. This has nothing to do with the escapism of satiated Epicureanism— *"eat, drink, and be merry, for tomorrow we may die."* To walk in wonder means to live intelligently, conscious of the precarious immensity of life, striving to conquer the ego's addictive needs, its games of vanity, and the clinging to delusive beliefs. We are here on this strange global ark called earth, sailing through the cosmos, conscious for a brief sixty or eighty or hundred years out of the aeons that have been and shall come. We do not know where we came from, and we do not know what lies beyond death. All we know is that during this brief existence, which can end any moment, we have an opportunity to experience reality to our utmost by developing our minds and spiritual potential, and perhaps, just perhaps, create a conscious intensity that catches a glimpse of the redeeming meaning of our strange wondrous journey.

12 – Wheat from Chaff

Truth is the precious harvest of the earth.
—George Eliot

The roots of language are irrational
and of a magical nature.
—Pablo Neruda

In the search for truth, there is definitely a need for culling common useless streams of thought, memory associations, futile dreams and false beliefs, in order to keep in the forefront that which is significant and meaningful to spiritual development. When I speak of the "search for truth," I do not mean half-truths or partial truths, but whole truths, solid truths, as far as we can comprehend them by unifying accumulated evidence based on empirical methods of science, intellectual contemplation, intuitive insight, introspective critique, and sufficient experience of alternative levels of consciousness.

Truth can not be confined to the anthropic sense, as Kant used it, with man as the absolute measure. This is what Heidegger refers to as the humanization of truth, which is what scientism is constructed upon. In a remarkable book entitled *The Poetics of Belief,*[1] Nathan A. Scott Jr. describes the humanization of truth as, "*the doctrine that truth resides in some human perspective rather than in Being itself.*" The essential thing is, though spiritual truth resides in depths beyond ego consciousness, it retains the potential to blossom within each of us, depending on our degree of commitment to awakening.

From the history of wisdom comes the message that the commitment to live, as much as is humanly possibly, according to truth in all its expansiveness, as we can perceive it within the entire realm of human existence, is humanity's most lofty and meaningful task.

Though many theories have been constructed about the concept of truth, this is largely because of the tendency toward unnecessary intellectual elaboration. To strain oneself within the scholastic arena of intellectual debate arguing the validity or invalidity of the concept of ultimate truth is similar to arguing the existence or nonexistence of God. Despite voluminous debates among scholars, with their pseudo-articulation of exceedingly obscure abstractions, claiming the nonexistence or relativism of what we call truth, such intellectual argumentation is nothing more than amphigoric hair-splitting, and has little effect on a seeker's inner ontological magnetism resounding within his/her heart.

Despite revelations of quantum physics as well as Hinduism's elucidation that the tangibility of existence is but a veil of appearances covering metaphysical depths which are the substance of our existence, to us the veil is real—congealed energy, condensed force, solidified stardust and light. Indeed, we are amazing "creatures of the veil." Here we are, confined in matter, suspended within the matrix of space-time amid terrestrial/cosmic evolution, and if our flesh is pricked with a pin or burnt with fire we will yelp. As the philosopher Gabriel Marcel clarified, this is our predicament and the platform from which we must work, and to deny it would be foolish. Here, as "jelled" forms of photonic energy/consciousness, we live, we exist. This quotidian world is not ultimate reality, but it is the world we must deal with every day, and cultivating a perspicacious comprehension of truth shall free us of all stultifying restraints upon our spiritual growth this world is prone to entangle us with.

Just as the concepts of electricity and magnetism were regarded as separate and distinct prior to being recognized as one force = electromagnetism, so it is with truth and spirit. William Kluback highlights this interconnectivity and interchangeability in his brilliant book about spiritual awakening, *Sri Aurobindo Ghose: The Dweller in the Land of Silence*:

> *Truth is not a penetrating spear devised by some craftsman to kill quickly and artistically. The spirit approaches slowly and unevenly. The resistance it faces is enormous. The truth of the spirit is its unpredictability, the unevenness of its strength and the inadequacies of definitions to give it sharpness. The spirit is imprecise and in the command of no man, nor expressed in any*

human formula. The best we can say of the spirit is that it is the
spirit. You who are open to it will know it.[2]

Truth (spirit made conscious), is what separates lies and false-hood from the genuine and authentic, whether you're dealing with antiques, jewelry, philosophy, art, or science. Sartre said that igno-rance and intellectual distortion are starting points from which truth extricates itself. All the significant knowledge we gain is worthless without the skilled discernment to derive truth which resonates from the omnipresent frequencies of Being. Truth always transcends the egoic sphere of thought, yet is also immanent within it. The tran-scendent power of "satya" from which the perennial stream of Sophianic wisdom flows forth, is present within the subquantum essence of the human mind's interaction with all phenomena, and yet is simultaneously nowhere, dwelling within the dynamic noth-ingness of the void. Esoterically, truth is illumination. As Heidegger elucidated, Van Gogh's paintings are revelations of truth, meaning they are not reality "correctly" portrayed, but the veil of appearances made translucent, the numinous illuminated.

Aurobindo has written, "*Spiritual truth is a truth of the spirit, not a truth of the intellect, not a mathematical theorem or a logical formula.*"[3] And as the brilliant mathematician Gödel demonstrated, though mathematics, which has remarkably explained much of the world, is constructed upon a foundation of logical propositions, truth is not confined to logic. Mathematical truths can transcend their rational premises. As computer scientist Gregory Chaitin said, "*There are mathematical truths that are true for no reason at all.*"[4] Sartre stated that truth is essentially not a logical or universal organization of abstract concepts, but a totality of being, agreeing with Heidegger's "*truth and being are inseparable.*" Such truth has nothing to do with dogma or rigid absolutes. In his thought provoking work, *Confrontations: Derrida, Heidegger, Nietzsche*, Ernst Behler writes that the essential foundational impulse of their work consists of a "*truthfulness that continually calls itself into question...*"[5]

Truth is as essential to those seeking genuine self-knowledge as water is to fish. The first and foremost action such seekers must commit themselves to is fidelity to be truthful, which demands a per-sistent questioning of all one's convictions. Religion is powerful be-cause those who bow to its traditional images and narratives believe it is founded on ultimate truth. In actuality, the major religions are founded upon biased cultural interpretations of valid spiritual truths, thus begetting belief structures based on of half-truths, illusions, falsehood. This is a prevailing historical predicament which undermines religion, rendering it incapable of substantially counteracting scientism or philosophical systems that undermine spiritual truth with their tendencies toward moral relativism, or even nihilism. There are nihilistically tainted intellectuals who put forth very convincing arguments that truth does not exist. Such arguments come from a sterile mentality that limits and distorts the ontological-spiritual truth of the essential nothingness of Being. Whenever such a distorted philosophical dehumanization of the actual human condition is proffered, it is a clear demonstration that ignorance of substantial truth is present.

Accepting the tangible realness of our quotidian situation doesn't imply we must confine ourselves to common perception of truth. The ancient Greek playwright Aristophanes criticized Socrates and other philosophers for carrying logical contemplation of simple problems farther than needed beyond common sense. But Socrates knew that common sense isn't always dependable in revealing the truth. Plato clarified this, and author Alain de Botton, in his book, *The Consolations of Philosophy*,[6] validates Plato's stance, demonstrating how the Socratic method of analyzing an opinion or belief is capable of revealing whether it is substantially true, imprecise, or false. Botton shows how Socrates insisted it was not good enough to just intuit or feel a thing to be true yet not know why or how to demonstrate it; one should be able to prove it and also reveal why opposing views are false. This procedure can take us quite a ways in coming to understand the world and our place within it all. However, we must recognize it was these elements of the Socratic method that eventually contributed to the rigidity of empirical scientism, leading to logic's disregard for intuitive and mystical inclinations, which Heidegger saw as a significant flaw in Western philosophy. This significant flaw in the works of Plato, Socrates, et al, is thoroughly clarified in Morris Berman's book, *The Re-enchantment of the World*.

An overbearing reliance upon empirical methodology is as absurd when dealing with the depths of things as clinging to common sense interpretations. To paraphrase Stanley Fish,[7] the claim that something is a universal truth and the acknowledgement that it can't necessarily be proven, are logically independent—the second does not undermine the first. Gödel aptly demonstrated that something can be true even though it cannot be proven. For instance, the early Greeks calculated the earth was a sphere and not flat, but could not prove it. It was centuries, involving explorations of the "New World," before it was validated. The history of science evolved from theoretical clarifications that could not be proved for decades, and even centuries. The individual seeker cannot depend on centuries, and so must on occasion use other methods to substantiate whether something significant to their spiritual awakening is or is not true. Still, the attempt to clarify any assertion as if trying to prove it, is an invaluable approach in endeavoring to separate the genuine from the false in most circumstances.

Truth, as far as it can be perceived within the matrix of human consciousness is, despite excessive scholarly debate to the contrary, attainable within all situations, on a spectrum from simple truisms, such as water is wet or $2 + 2 = 4$, up through religious and political beliefs, to the heights and depths of profound metaphysical perception and mystical experience. Of course, as pointed out over the previous chapters, what is considered simple on any level of existence has its complexity, and even "2+2" can lead to metaphysical ponderings in the higher realms of mathematics and physics. The laws of causality elucidate how seemingly simple events are actually the result of complex chains of causes — each cause triggering a branching display of effects, perpetuating more causes, unceasingly.

A superb haiku seems a simple poetic existential description of a scene, a place, a moment, a person, but that simplicity can capture all eternity. We could say the attainment of truth is full comprehension of phenomena and numina that manifest within the multi-level range of human consciousness.

Wherever truth seems to be distorted or lost, it is waiting in the wings, available to acute intuition of its presence. As William Barrett says of Heidegger's use of the word *"aletheia,"*[8] truth occurs when what has been hidden is revealed. Sartre wrote that significant truth doesn't come by chance, that it requires the task of deciphering. Though attunement to deeper universal truth comes to the seeker by way of inner cultivation, the seeker should also become skilled at the art of deciphering scientific facts, theological and philosophical concepts, academic rhetoric, ancient mythology, separating wheat from chaff within various schools of psychology, as well as detecting the worth or worthlessness of various avenues of political information coming through modern media. The quality of such deciphering depends upon the extent to which a person has developed his/her radius of comprehension.

So here we are, dwelling within a perplexing paradoxical sphere rife with illusion, hallucination, even madness, <u>from which we must derive truth when and wherever possible</u>—a most significant and meaningful task. We must learn to perceive truth from multi-level perspectives which can bring about an appreciation of life's complexity. For instance, when we claim the grass is green, we speak the truth, for it is so; but this truth entails the complexities of photosynthesis and the activity of our brain's perception/data-filtering process. There is no method or analysis or scientific theory that can give us an adequate explanation of the poetic/mystical consciousness and numinous signification of the very nature of color. Science still has no explanation for the intriguing phenomenon of color we see in our dreams, in closed eye fantasy, active imagination, or in hypnogogic states, none of which relate to the interplay between light waves and retinal cones within the eye. Though orthodox science is a superb instrument for revealing many elements which make up the known world, and can be a gateway to deeper perception, it is also a system which can overlook and even distort essential truths. And yet scientific and mystical approaches need not cancel each other out. To truly understand our existential-spiritual situation we must try to be as aware as possible of the varied aspects, great and small, of each and every thing we perceive. In this way we move toward understanding the truth about the multi-dimensional potentials of our very being.

During the inner quest, it is crucial to be able to distinguish true mystical vision from a variety of lesser experiences. When we undertake inner explorations, we must become impeccable in discerning whether we have had an authentic confrontation with, say, an archetypal being, or have been entranced by hallucination. Such discernment is possible, but requires well honed psychic proficiency. A true spiritual vision should have a universal component, which can usually be confirmed by accumulation of evidence from archives of religious, mystical and psychological documents both ancient and current. Of course, there are occasions in the use of psychedelics when discernment between meaningful vision and meaningless hallucination is quite blatant. A chorus of dancing and singing hot dogs in top hats can be definitely seen as low grade hallucination not worth more than a laugh. It is another thing entirely if one confronts a fearsomely awesome living god or goddess, or giant flaming feathered bird with a writhing golden snake in its mouth rising up from the archetypal depths into your very living room. Because their archetypal component is rich with universal symbolism relating to the ancient quest, such inner confrontations and experiences hold truths of a fateful existential quality for the individual. Still, there is much perplexity here. We may ask, if an experience enhances a person's life, does that person really need to question whether it was vision or hallucination? Yes. I have watched a televangelist tell an audience of thousands about his visionary experience of going to heaven and coming upon God sitting bewildered and weary about the condition of the human race, and how he put his arm around God's shoulder, giving him assurance and comfort. The man spoke as if he believed in the actuality of his "vision." Most of the audience looked as if they too believed. But to anyone with any real psychological comprehension, this was absurd madness. With such mental derangement and stupidity manifesting through so many avenues of religion, it is clear why skeptics, humanists, atheists, have shown so much scorn for anything resembling religious belief, including metaphysics and mysticism.

Discerning hallucination from vision encompasses the borderland area where insight and delusion, clarity and madness, salvation and damnation, can cyclone swirl through the psychic frequency spectrum of the embodied mind's conscious, subconscious, and unconscious matrix. Whether manifestations from this borderland burgeon forth within a stable perceptive awareness honed by yogic disciplines, come filtered and formed by way of a rigidified delusionary belief system, or erupt into an unbalanced mind by way of hallucination, depends on the quality of self-knowledge of the individual involved. This is very important territory for the person who seeks to live by truth and pursue spiritual awakening, for we are delving into the realm of powers both good and evil.

To think deeper psychic-spiritual powers which can benefit or harm human beings do not exist, or to think your religious faith relieves you of having to consider such things to the degree demanded for genuine spiritual growth, are both foolishly naïve stances. Freud made modern and scientific what gothic literature had been clarifying for a century, concerning the powerful influence of unconscious forces upon human activity. He elucidated that in most cases mental illness need not be attributed to demonic spirits, but is brought about by strictly psychological and social factors impacting the individual's psyche. C G Jung expanded on Freud's work and brought forth the idea that there is more going on than can be explained by a rational secularized approach to certain manifestations of the unconscious depths. Though he saw himself as an empiricist in his method of accumulating data as evidence to substantiate his research, Jung wasn't tied into the limitations of the staunch materialist. His work thus encompassed and surpassed Freud's in the field of psychology as Einstein's did Newton's in the field of physics.

Today we are aware of varied factors that produce mental disturbances— bio-chemical imbalances, social and personal stress, etc. And when psychiatrists speak of dissociate disorders disrupting the central function of egoic consciousness, they are referring to unconscious influences beyond the patient's voluntary control. Yet only certain Jungians, as well as a growing number of New Age psychologists, consider such influences as welling up from archetypal depths which have a demonic component to them. Nothing is clear-cut here. No psychiatrist, neurologist, biopsychologist, theologian, exorcist, has it all down pat. Because the way we perceive the quotidian world is underlined by the uncertainty of what things actually are beyond appearances, everything is open to varied possibilities. The thing we're after is to get as close as possible to what any phenomenon in question actually consists of.

What role, then, should the skilled use of reason and logic play in dealings with the irrational, the paranormal, the deeper spiritual dimensions? Reason and applied logic are tools to balance and harmonize all knowledges accessible to our comprehension, whether mystical or scientific, so that we fit such knowledges into our lives cleared of as many distortions as possible. Though, as most sages claim, there are definitely experiences that can never be communicated by way of words, there is no knowledge beyond the reach of the contemplative examination of reason's light. For even the most esoteric knowledge which cannot be reduced to logical explanation, can be spoken about, pointed to, inferred by way of metaphor, symbol, and poetic clarification. Our most articulate mystics, sorcerers, magicians, shamans—Aurobindo, Jung, Gurdjieff, Muktananda, Castaneda/Don Juan, Yogananda, etc.—all have given cohesive, though startling, explanations of our psychological-spiritual-cosmological depths. Psychedelic explorers such as John Lilly and Terrence McKenna have been able to reasonably articulate to a significant degree their most mind-boggling experiences. That their expositions of our psychic-spiritual situation do not seem to fit into the categories of the empiricist's idea of logical analyzation, does not rule out the validity of certain truths abiding in their clarifications. As Ouspensky stressed, we need a new system of logic to deal with the mystical, just as we needed a new kind of physics to deal with quantum realities.

Inner explorers from various cultures have given us volumes articulating fantastic spiritual dimensions and awe-inspiring encounters with beings and gods of all sorts. These are available to be logically contemplated and reasoned about, culling what attains spiritual cohesiveness from credulity, fabrication, outright madness. When we consider the immense scope of such numinous dimensions, which the average mind is hardly ever conscious of, let alone experienced in, it is certainly enough just to attempt to integrate such expositions into the ordinary person's somewhat fragile grasp of existence. Yet the attempt alone can ignite the expansion of our radius of comprehension. Just being aware of such "wholly other" dimensions should evoke in us a sense of mystery to which we can only bow. Not to bow smacks of the self-deceiving certitude of a limited intelligence.

In learning to decipher what is essential to understand of both science and mysticism, the seeker should remain open to appreciate the value of any known ancient rite and ritual which may reveal significant insight into the truth, wherever it resides. As William Barrett expressed it, *"Indeed, what man becomes, in his history as well as his thinking, turns upon the decision he makes as to what truth is."*[9] The people of CSICOP and Skeptical Inquirer believe they have a handle on the approach to truth, Shirley McClain and Elizabeth Claire Prophet and dozens of their ilk think they have it, materialistic scientists think they have it, Christians of various sorts and sects think they have it. It should be clear from all we have pondered why Sartre called deciphering significant empirical and theoretical concepts of reality in the quest for truth "a laborious task," and why Gurdjieff called similar activity "The Work." This requires a kind of thinking, as Robert Avens succinctly puts it, "neither rationalistic nor irrationalistic, but belongs to a sphere which is prior to distinction between reason and unreason."[10] As Arthur Zajonc stated, *"We need not give up rationality, but rather must broaden its meaning."*[11] Since we live in a civilization overbearingly beneath the sway of rationalization, opening ourselves intellectually to the irrational qualities of our actual situation amid the helicoid surge of spiritual dimensions, without succumbing to the comforting fabrications traditional and New Age schemata partake of, is a task indeed. Such a laborious task requires constant attentiveness to the snares of credulity, self deception, false belief, uncontrolled fear, rigidified skepticism, delusions and lies. Those who wish to live authentically, to exist as holistically awakened beings, must accept this challenge, entailing consistent disciplined introspection.

Blaise Pascal wrote, "*We should seek the truth without hesitation, and if we refuse, we show we value the esteem of men more than the search for truth.*"[12] To reveal and live according to truth, you must be willing to delve deeply and thoroughly into every field of knowledge to whatever extent is necessary for significantly expanding your individual radius of comprehension. If that means making dramatic changes in your life to do this, then change you must. Willingness to sacrifice comfort, security, status, to induce necessary changes in order to follow your spiritual truth, is the essence of the journey of self-knowledge. As the Russian sage Nicholas Berdyaev wrote in his profound work, *The Realm of Spirit and the Realm of Caesar*, "*Truth is an unlocking, a revealing...There is nothing higher than the search for, and the love of truth.*"[13]

The import and impact of what I have just stated may not be grasped by many readers, because the words "truth" and "spirit" are all too often overused, or used in a reductively narrow sense. But the power of such words can bring about illumination if the moment of surge between the attentive reader and what is being read releases the meaning abiding "in potentia." Though thought processes of the embodied mind are constructed to a large extent from words, this does not imply a mechanical relationship. Words, thought, symbolic images, exist in a living dynamic interactive play. Consider a seemingly ordinary word which I have used quite often, referring to the manifested world of all things we are immersed within: "phenomenon." In Greek, the meaning of phenomenon is *"that which reveals itself."* William Barrett elucidates:

> *The Greek word 'phenomenon' is connected with the word 'phaos,' light, and also with the word 'apophansis,' statement or speech. The sequence of ideas is thus: revelation-light-language. The light is the light of revelation, and language itself is this*

light. These may look like mere metaphors, but perhaps they are
so only for us, whose understanding is darkened; for early man,
at the very dawn of the Greek language, this inner link between
light and statement (language) was a simple and profound fact,
and it is our sophistication and abstractness that makes it seem
to us 'merely' metaphorical. This metaphor of light, as we shall
see, opens the way to Heidegger's theory of truth, which is for
him one of the most fateful issues in human history and human
thought.[14]

Because we are conceptualizing creatures linguistically
drenched in metaphor, we have to be able to breathe new life into
words to truly communicate with ourselves and with others. Metaphors concerning numinous depths have clusters of meaningful ety-
mologies swirling about them. As we have seen, when it comes to
words and ideas relating to the <u>mysterium</u> <u>tremendum</u>, there are no
"mere" metaphors. According to Hans-Georg Gadamer, of all phenomena, language is one of the most mysterious. If we ponder our
present condition, the fervent ambit of our brain/embodied-mind
configuration, the play of thought, relationships, correspondences,
associations, meanings, ideas, concepts, metaphors, we are revealed
not only as quantum-electro-magnetic beings but extraordinary creature encompassed within a radiant sea of linguistic particles of light.

Thus I ask of you dear reader, as to any significant word in
this book, such as "spiritual," "being," "existence," "metaphor,"
"light," please try to comprehend what lies beneath the callus of centuries of casual use, and perceive the illumination of meaning these
words have the potential to convey. Language is so much more expansive than the ordinary mind considers it to be. If we could be
constantly aware of what language, words, speech, truth, actually
are in relation to the very existential-spiritual quality of our lives, we
would speak each word as if releasing a delicate butterfly from a net.
Words can be used to spread the wings of the mind, or misused to
enchain, as with propaganda. Albert Borgmann has written,

Living language immediately encountered is so fluid, embodied,
contextual, and evanescent as to discourage if not defy analysis.
But once written down, especially in the parsimonious way of
the alphabet, language appears stable, structured, and already
analyzed into its ultimate constituents.[15]

Understand that what you are reading here has a certain "dehydrated" quality to it, as an encrypted version of what I am thinking, and it is dependent on the intensity of your desire to learn, to know, which adds the "water" that brings it to life in the alchemical play of your mind.

There is an ancient Egyptian tale about the origin of the world. At the primal dawn of creation, an immense god-being in the form of a phoenix adorned in flaming plumage swept downward from the sky to settle on the highest mountain peak. Raising its magnificent beak it pierced the eternal silence with its cry—which was the first sound, logos, hence the word. This may strike the aloof intellect as overindulging in mytho-romanticism, but you should not underestimate the meaning imbued in such archetypal imagery.

We attach words to everything. When you look about the room you are sitting in, everything has a word that names it—book, chair, door, window, carpet, etc. You are involved in a constant nanosecond psychological process of naming, of objectification which pinpoints and fits each object to its place to suit the configuration of your immediate reality. Yet from our study of quantum physics we know each object is much more than its perceived solidity portrays, much more than its name can capture. A human infant crawls about in a wondrous world of nameless phenomena, just as all non-human creatures perceive their worlds. Even the child just learning to walk, having grown beyond the chaotic buzz of its firstborn moments, still roams about in a nameless universe where all is new, each object an unknown fascination. We all began our lives in that infant wonderland of mysterious phenomena. Gradually the child grows more callused as he/she matures and everything is named and taken for granted. We forget that we actually have no idea what the essential nature of what we have named is. Beneath the appearance of each named object lies the greater realm of its being.

We have considered the amazing phenomenon of DNA, with all the fantastic complexity and power of its code, which functions as a system of information dispersion, thus a kind of language. From one perspective, signs and symbols are energy components, as is DNA in essence. Semiotics is a way of studying language as signs and symbols, which are intimately interactive with the marvelous dynamics of the brain's electro-chemical relationship to consciousness. At this moment my words are adding an ingredient to your mind-brain alchemical brew — the syntactic, semantic, semiotic ferment and shuffling of symbols. As Albert Borgman clarifies, *"language is an organism of natural signs... language and the structure of reality... coincide."*[16] Heidegger states, *"Man acts as though he were the shaper and master of language, while in fact language remains the master of man."*[17] Language essentially and paradoxically both creates and is created by thought. As a butterfly is a trans-emergent aspect of its cocoon's wondrous alchemy, language is a trans-emergent aspect of the brain. Words shape, color, shade, forming images of the actual world we dwell within, yet are symbols of something more. As symbols, words are imbued with the power of evocation, creating a bridge which can reveal our silent subjective thoughts to another.

There are perhaps six to seven thousand known languages, some that vary astoundingly, yet there is an underlying similarity that is deep and universal. This can be seen in the emotive response to the way a language is spoken. Watching a foreign film with subtitles blanked out, as the actors speak a language we do not understand, we can tell if the words imply anger or joy or sadness from the speakers' expression, tone, demeanor. And though to us, perusing the pages of a book written in a language we can not understand, the symbols are just strings of marks, slashes and shapes, meaning nothing, we know that millions of people automatically decipher and understand such strange inscription as you decipher and understand this text you are reading. A bilingual person fluent in a language we do not know, as well as being able to speak and read ours, could translate what are just odd puzzling marks to us, for our understanding. A foreign language is not an alien script from Mars. There is no foreign language in use on earth we cannot learn to speak and comprehend.

We know communication is primal. All creatures of the earth, from bees to elephants, use a form of communication. The most unrefined sounds humans can make were once a mode of primate communication — grunts, murmurs, growls, snarls, squeals, howls. Such were the seedlings of speech. Apes have a crude symbolic mode of communication faintly similar to words. Marmosets and tamarinds, like birds, are highly vocal. When did hominids begin to vocalize a somewhat organized expression of their grunts, yelps, growls? We are not sure, but it most certainly arose in tandem with a highly evolved sign-language of gesture and facial expression. We know by the sign language of the deaf that extensive articulation of thought is quite possible without spoken words. Sign languages are highly structured linguistic systems with a grammatical complexity equal to spoken language. Piaget demonstrated that in humans a form of language manifests first in the non-verbal movements of newborns. In the Kanaka form of dancing there is a body language which entails eight hundred gestures. Words most likely arose from a highly developed sign-gesture language which eventually merged with vocal expression as proto-humans imitated the sounds of other creatures and of their environment, luring prey during a hunt or mimicking the sounds of nature to communicate the coming of rain, or a river up ahead. The first words of meaningful religious connotation were perhaps chanted within a ritualistic setting, perhaps around the tribal fire—a rhythmic hypnotic sound, to bring on visions.

There has been speculation claiming crude elements of speech existed among primal hominids as far back as one to three million years ago; others claim 500,000, and others no farther than 40,000. In his book, *The Power of Babel*,[18] John McWhorther writes of language being traced back to at least 150,000 years ago in East Africa. We just don't know about primal hominid's communication abilities. Leakey thought it possible from various artifacts he came across that certain weapons such as spears and bolas were in use two million years ago. If there were weapons, there were tools, and such creative utilitarian objects definitely implies a degree of reasoning, planning, goals, team work, thus communication. To think primal hominid's were "dumb" cavemen is an assumption we should have put side a long time ago. I'm not implying that "Homo erectus" was a creature of extensive intellectual ability, but just because they lived in caves for 0.3 million years, and bats were a mainstay of their diet, doesn't verify some kind of "ape-like" imbecility, but rather exquisite ecological adaptation to environment. Australian aborigines, African bushmen, New Guinea mountain people, lived in extremely simplified, ecologically tailored living conditions up to less than a hundred years ago, yet they are a long way from "dumb," and have highly sophisticated forms of language. We do know that Neanderthal people left evidence of burial rituals that indicate caring for the dead 135,000 years ago. Would not this require a degree of abstract thought, and thus at least crude verbal communication? From prehistoric remains scientists know Neanderthal's pharynx was too small for them to talk as fast or make certain vowel sounds as we do. But a form of speech was possible. There's no telling what quality of language un-refined elements of speech merged with sophisticated gesture and facial expression could bring about. It is generally recognized now that Cro-Magnon people possessed a kind of speech, but it is not known how developed it was. Would not Cro-Magnon, whose brain size and mental potential differed little from us, and who are said to have been more evolved than the smugly assumed dull-witted Ne-anderthals, have had a lucid speaking ability 50,000 years ago? As to those theories that limit the origins of language to around 10,000 years ago, a flute made of bone dating back 30,000 years, and arti-facts symbolizing a creative goddess were found in Siberia dating 24,000 BC. It seems that a mind able to construct a flute from bone, thus being aware of the joy of music, plus create symbols of religious signification, would certainly be capable of sophisticated and well established forms of speech.

As to writing, scholars have found several syllabary forms in Asia dating to over 5000 years ago. From these it is clear the earliest forms of writing began primarily as an extension of primitive proto-art/graphics used to describe the passing of the seasons, the cycles of moon and sun, hunting activities, etc. From this followed picto-graphic expression, the earliest dating circa 4000 BC, with the use of representative likenesses, as with a figure of a dog, 🐕, simply mean-ing dog. Ideograms came forth a few centuries later in both ancient Sumer and Egypt, improving upon simple pictographs by adding various symbols, marks and signs, capable of expressing concepts to go along with and clarify pictorial figures. These were followed by cuneiform script, which became highly developed in Mesopotamia around 3500 BC, consisting of various abstract marks, without any pictorial characters involved. It has been put forth that neither hiero-glyphic writing nor cuneiform related to the sound of spoken words, though this always seemed too narrow of a claim to me. In any event, somewhere around 2000 BC in the land of Canaan, what we call phonetic writing came about. The Greeks developed this into an alphabetic system. In phonetic writing, which comes from the Greek "phonê" = voice, each letter corresponds to a certain sound, with a specific merging of these sounds creating a composite sound, a word. The alphabet is an organized grouping of these symbols, each representing a different inflection of sound. Our alphabet is almost identical to that of the ancient Romans, who were heavily influenced by the Greeks. The implications of this are quite provocative. But I have to limit myself, for the knowledge of one subject can be expanded upon for volumes. Whatever and however language began, here we are, and we should know of what stuff our thoughts are made, in order to develop sufficient mastery over our conscious minds. Though there are other significant forms of expression which can be looked upon as modes of language—dance, gesture, dress, architecture, music, etc—our ability to speak is the basic method of communicating thought. Heidegger claimed language to be the "house of Being."

Because the very structure of our embodied thought is to a high degree made of words, of language, we are, as Aldous Huxley and others in various fields of study have verified and are continually verifying, both the beneficiaries and victims of our language. As Edward Said stated, *"Language is at once excess and poverty."*[19] How did language evolve into such a condition that would become in its negative aspect encaging, and in its positive exquisitely liberating? I imagine some scholar could spend fifteen years tracking that question to its source, and maybe some whom I have overlooked have, but I feel we will never really know. The important thing is, we can begin to free ourselves from the enchaining attributes of language through channels of significant knowledge.

As stated, this book is an exposition of only the fundamentals of what genuine self-knowledge requires—deep enough for a sufficient grasp of our existential-spiritual predicament. How much an individual needs to know concerning such things depends on a complex variable of abilities, traits, intelligence, experience of the depths, mystical insight, and so on. The reader may expand upon the subjects covered according to what is necessary to his/her own search. As to language, one can peruse the works of scholars such as de Saussure, Chomsky, Wittgenstein, Derrida, Korzybski, Whorf, and others. Of course, there is no need to get as entwined in linguistics as these men did, for though brilliant in their field of expertise, none manifested in their personal life the presence of vital force gleaned from direct experience of the greater depths and scope of Being. Intellectual knowledge all too often derails the development of essence. D. T. Suzuki said, *"Affirmation must rise from the fiery crater of life itself."*[20]

Recent research presents various perspectives on how the embodied mind creates our essential conceptual structures from metaphoric imagery. This is quite intriguing since, as most of us are aware, metaphor is the highly significant facet of syntax by which humanity's greatest poetry fills our minds with profound images. In their insightful book, *Descartes Dream*,[21] Davis and Hersh clarify how the embodied mind, through use of metaphor, organizes the multi-dimensional flux of the world's ever-changing elements for human comprehension. The embodied mind is a fervent brew of metaphors, which are much more than Aristotle's "ornaments of language," or even the meat and potatoes of great poetry. As Lakeoff and Johnson stress in their book, *Metaphors We Live By*,

> But metaphor is not merely a matter of language. It is a matter of conceptual structure. And conceptual structure is not merely a matter of the intellect – it involves all the natural dimensions of our experience, including aspects of our sense experiences: color, shape, texture, sound, etc. These dimensions structure not only mundane experience but aesthetic experience as well.[22]

Our reliance on metaphor definitely has its drawbacks. Phillip Wheelwright states, "*We are much too influenced by metaphoric corpses that have lost their vital substance but retain influential power.*"[23] He explains how we must extricate ourselves from such mental bondage if we wish to get beyond the glass cage of egocentric consciousness. Colin Turbayne succinctly encapsulates the significant import of cultivating knowledge and control over our use of metaphor, stating, "*We can choose our metaphors…*" and when we are able to choose, "*we are no longer duped citizens of the city-state of Oz; we are the Wizard of Oz himself.*"[24] Metaphor has the power to imprison us or become the wings to set us free.

Over the last 230 pages, I have used metaphor without even thinking about doing so. I must use metaphor, words, images, syntax, to write about those very things. Just as it is written that Lao Tzu spoke volumes concerning silence, Focault wrote volumes concerning the treacherous futility and paradoxes of using language to get at the truth. This isn't contradiction or self deceit in either case, though it is a definite validation of the enigmatic quality of the very act of writing, and it is just as much so with the act of reading. This is all I have, this shuffling of symbols here on this page, to communicate what I feel impassioned to express. A numinous depth of silence lies between each word, with years of extensive worldly experience and spiritual venture between the turning of each page. And although, as the sages and most scholars of linguistics know, language, even in the most skillful hands, may fall short as a medium to describe the fullness of the human predicament, I will continue. Thus here I am, this pen, this paper, this place, with over half a century of accumulated knowledge circling within the spiraling gyre of my consciousness, the words flitting down upon the stark white page like crows gathering on snow.

For the most part, metaphor is used to enhance imagery of common discourse, all to often of the most banal sort. As LeShan and Margenau elucidated,[25] we all too casually use metaphors of the sensory domain in relation to inner experiences. This can sometimes help in clarification of a subjective idea or feeling, but it usually falls short. If you are sitting beneath a tree pondering where there may be an affinity between the work of Aurobindo, Nietzsche, and Chirico, and you say "I'm having deep thoughts" to someone who knows little of in-depth philosophical contemplation, with no idea what existential angst or spiritual doubt or abstract art are about, using such a phrase would be a futile attempt at communication. He or she would probably take your phrase to mean you are thinking about things like considering divorce, or quitting a job, or a relative's recent funeral. The metaphorical "deep thoughts," like "boiling rage," can give us a sense of what someone else may be experiencing, but it can also obscure it because such metaphors can vary to remarkable degree as to the actual quality of thought. A child claiming, "My Dad was boiling with rage," when his father was briefly angered over his son not doing chores, is significantly different than the description, "He was boiling with rage," stated by a police officer describing a psychotic who just killed ten people. Improper use of metaphor has led to the banalization of human communicative ability. To just open one's mouth and mindlessly gab is a trait the first stages of mental discipline demand the halt of.

As Lakoff and Johnson make clear, metaphorically constructed concepts govern our lives, structure how we perceive our every relationship, shaping our thoughts from banal fantasies and bromidic chatter to sublime ideas and poetic imaginings. We could say perception, metaphor and concept are entwined like vines enwrapping each other. The process of conceptualization is an activity of mental grasping, of interpreting perceptions. It is a cognitive process using thought to corral the incomprehensible, attempting to tame it into

comprehension. The quality of a concept has to do with the knowledge and understanding of what is conceived, entailing configurations of relationships, meanings, all flavored, highlighted, enhanced
with metaphoric imagery and symbol.

There are two basic kinds of concepts = theoretical and empirical. A theoretical concept is an abstraction, a speculative notion, a
mental model we create in order to grasp something intangible. To
abstract means to draw or derive from. A theoretical concept comes
about when we abstract a comprehensive configuration of thought
from that which is incomprehensible. A theoretical concept usually
takes a metaphoric form referring back to "something" not available
to the five senses, having no concrete tangible existence in and of
itself. Theoretical concepts we are familiar with, such as "God," "de-
mocracy," "death," "communism," "patriotism," have been traditionally formulated to suit a tacit cultural-social agreement. We take
such concepts so much for granted we come to believe them to be
something they are not. You can be patriotic, but you cannot see,
touch, or taste patriotism. It is the same with all theoretical concepts.
We can see people die, we can observe a corpse, but we cannot see,
touch or taste death itself. There is no black cloaked grim reaper that
actually exists. Death is beyond graves and skeletons and ghosts.
Death is a realm unknown which we tend to convert to comfortable
knowns such as heaven and reincarnation, which are illusory attempts at containing the uncontainable, demystifying the mysterious.

Empirical concepts relate to tangible activities of the sensory
domain, which you've seen or performed yourself: cooking, sewing,
soldiering, schooling. We see, touch and taste when involved with
cooking. Soldiering calls for physical action, involving seeing and
touching, as does schooling, and sewing. Theoretical concepts can
work in tandem with empirical concepts. The theoretical concept of
patriotism causes people in the United States to think of the "American Way of Life," which creates images and feelings of all kinds of
tangible activities: sports, entertainment, work, eating habits, pa-
rades, etc., which give Americans a sense of united fellowship they
believe is uniquely theirs—which it isn't. All nations inculcate a
sense of patriotism in their citizens. In Germany when Hitler ruled,
millions of Germans were just as patriotic as the majority of Americans are now, thinking Hitler would lead their nation to greatness.
Their concept of patriotism was also based on the above tangible

activities of the "German Way of Life," activities very similar to our own social habits, hobbies, pursuits of pleasure, and confirmation of fellowship. What went wrong in Germany? Part of the answer is the majority were ignorant of the things this book elucidates, for anyone sincerely committed to self-knowledge in all its complexity will never be manipulated by the deceitful patriotic propaganda and religious rhetoric those in power so skillfully put to use.

This book deals primarily with theoretical concepts, because they have the potential to deeply influence the mind, usually without our being aware of it, thus having effects which are all too often detrimental to humanity. Just as subnuclear particles, which we can't smell, touch, or feel, can be manipulated and controlled by scientists using mathematical equations and technological expertise, to the extent that they can create something as terrible as an H-bomb, theoretical concepts like patriotism and God, also not available to sensory perception, can be manipulated by Presidents, politicians, tyrants, military commanders, public relations experts, to convince humans to use such weapons as H-bombs against other humans. In other words, through the misuse of empirical concepts the mind can technologically create tools of destruction, and by the misuse of theoretical concepts establish reasons to put them to use. As mass media verifies daily, this destructive potential of the mind's conceptual ability is activated continually on a global scale.

Let us further explore the very influential theoretical concept of patriotism. The ideal of patriotism is taught to citizens of every nation as soon as they enter kindergarten, even before. Being gradually reinforced all through school, it becomes engrained. Most citizens accept patriotism as they accept grass being green—just a natural aspect of their lives. But patriotism isn't natural, though it has ancient roots. Few ever consider the shadowed caverns of the mind those roots penetrate. Einstein, having experienced Nazi Germany, called patriotism "a loathsome nonsense." He was lucidly aware of how the concept of patriotism can all too easily be misused by tyrants, politicians, even priests, who exploit the media to manipulate the multitudes' pride in their country, swaying their thoughts and feelings, pulling their "mind strings," thus turning the majority into puppets to do their bidding. Such mass manipulation is a rather common practice across the globe, and most citizens of every nation are susceptible to its sway. Perceiving deceit and falsehood behind political rhetoric is a necessary discernment any person who wishes to have a truly free mind must cultivate.

If you automatically feel pride when you hear the national anthem, whatever nation you are a citizen of, you are heavily handicapped in pursuing self-knowledge. If you cannot separate your feelings from the source of stimuli and see the entire process as objectively as possible, you are ripe for knee-jerk patriotism. In 2004, country-western singer Toby Keith's hit song, "Courtesy of the Red, White, and Blue" stirred the hearts of millions of Americans because it pushed all their patriotic buttons. Overcoming such acculturated button-pushing is similar to a reformed alcoholic watching someone else enjoying the brew he once enjoyed, without taking a sip himself. He objectively observes his feelings of desire for a drink, realizing he doesn't need it any more, that it never was all he had made it out to be, and that basically it was detrimental to his growth as a human being. His body craves a drink but his mind transcends the craving. I know from experience, having once been an infantry paratrooper marching proudly beneath the flag to the stirring rhythm of a military band. Though people may feel Toby Keith's song move them, they should recognize that it is blatant jingoism sung by a naïve well-meaning country boy who has no real idea of the economic-political power games going on in the world. The National Anthem pulls our mind and heart strings the same way. When it's sung at the World Series or the Super Bowl, tens of thousands immediately stand as if Pavlov himself had rung a bell in their well programmed minds. Cultivating an awareness of the negative machinations of one's government isn't an exercise confined to the political arena of anti-establishment radicalism, or the political left. Such awareness has to do with learning to perceive things with a well honed intelligence, to see things as they are, to rise above collective somnambulism, above the unquestioning kowtowing to the whims of psychologically and spiritually ignorant and repressed individuals who have finagled their way into positions of authority. The ability to perceive the distortions of manipulative propaganda requires being respectfully attentive to the world at large and appreciative of various cultural differences in order to learn about others, and in reciprocal comparison learn about ourselves.

Understanding patriotism demands being informed beyond what standard schooling teaches and mass media conveys. Every society tends to educate their young by teaching them a history of the world that makes their nation shine with glory. Children all over the world are taught to pledge allegiance to their flag and sing their national anthem. Though most people think they have decided to be patriotic of their own free will, this is an illusion. In reality, they are patriotic because they have been strongly influenced by their up-bringing, their education, and a lifetime of unquestioningly accepted propaganda. This is the persuasive power of acculturation at its most banal and hypnotic level. As Terry Eagleton maintained,[26] culture equals a taken-for-granted set of beliefs, which enable people to function without questioning their situation as a whole—a way-of-life package of laws, values, morals, which people accept as completely as they accept who their parents are and the neighborhood they grow up in. Acculturation entails being drenched in and permeated by one's environment. Every society upholds and fortifies its own political and religious beliefs as the walls of a fortress protecting those within. And tradition is no guarantee that such beliefs are based on truth rather than on illusion. Formal schooling (pseudo education) in its formative first twelve years is mainly a system beneath the sway of acculturation. Thus, unfortunately, the majority never rise to a level of authentic individuality beyond what mass education has molded them to see themselves as.

Everyone can grasp the fact that a man of wealth and power who believes he is superior to others just because they lack wealth and power, is a vain fool. But when it comes to patriotism, millions cannot grasp that believing America is superior to other nations because it is the wealthiest and most powerful, is even more foolish and vain. Unfortunately, zealous patriotism is how many people bolster their view of themselves, somewhat like the "my Daddy can beat up your Daddy," or "my football team is the best" syndrome. People have no idea how their traditional religious and political belief systems are shaped by negative or defensive psychological impulses. Toby Keith on stage surrounded by star spangled banners and fireworks has a psychological and emotional affinity with those naïve German entertainers, circa '33 – '43, who were surrounded by swastikas and torches as they took the stage to sing the praises of the Fatherland.

To become capable of perceiving the shadow of one's nation in order to rise above responding like a Pavlovian dog to patriotic bell ringing, requires not only revealing certain truths, but integrating those truths into one's radius of comprehension. In his book, *White*

*Bears and Other Unwanted Thoughts,*₂₇ Daniel M. Wegner demonstrates how people who believe false information to be true will continue to cling to that information even after it has been revealed to be false. They completely ignore the correct information in order to maintain their first impression. This has to do with the power of collective conformism, where an individual will denounce his own perceptions and knowledge to go along with the majority. In America, religion and patriotism are like jam and bread, with over 60% of the population believing God is on their side and America is the "apple of God's eye." But that is patently absurd. Any God who created this immense mind boggling universe where a million Earths will fit inside the single star Epsilon A, would definitely not have any preferences concerning the political situation on this one ultra-microscopic planet. To believe America is special to God is a deranged orientation clinging to an ancient tribal mythocentrism. Such patriotic pride is a sort of extended delusion of grandeur, encompassing both ego and nation.

As the twenty-first century dawns, (2000 – 2025), individuals living in America should look closely at how theoretical concepts such as patriotism and capitalism influence significant aspects of their lives. Those who commit their lives to inner growth eventually develop a certain detachment from political impulses and attitudes. It becomes all too obvious that wars and rumors of war, the tumult of opposing political parties, continue with their perennial havoc because the masses of human beings dwell in ignorance, lacking both self-knowledge and insight into the forces that manipulate their minds. Every person committed to the inner quest performs a service for his/her fellow humans far more significant than any activities undertaken by military leaders or politicians. C. G. Jung clarifies this:

> *Every advance in culture is, psychologically, an extension of consciousness, a coming to consciousness that can take place only through discrimination. Therefore any advance always begins with individuation, that is to say with the individual, conscious of his isolation, cutting a new path through hitherto untrodden territory. To do this he must first return to the fundamental facts of his own being, irrespective of all authority and tradition, and allow himself to become conscious of his distinctiveness. If he succeeds in giving collective validity to his widened consciousness, he creates a tension of opposites that pro-*

vides the stimulation which culture needs for its further progress.[28]

With this said, I must add that participation in social activism does not necessarily detract from spiritual growth, as long as psychological individuation is the priority.

The vast majority of people only get through life by developing methods of mental censorship. One such method is known in psychology as repression, which is the automatic subconscious and semi-conscious censoring of any memories and impulses, feelings and emotions, that threaten a person's self image or mental stability. Another powerful psychological defense people use to keep their belief system fortified is bias, both oversight and confirmation, which we have touched on half a dozen times in the preceding chapters. Surely such scientifically verified psychological syndromes as repression and bias should be of the greatest interest to anyone wanting to be free of self-deceit. The problem is, those who live within the distorting deceptions of a religious or political belief system, (usually a blend), do not see themselves as living a lie, and are not even aware such things as repression and bias impact their cognitive functioning. Television gives us an opportunity to observe such self-blindness in action with conservative news commentators such as Sean Hannity, Joe Scarborough and Bill O'Reilly. Watching these men is like a home-schooling study of self-deception and bias in action. The worth of anyone's opinion is proportional to the scope and depth of knowledge it is rooted in, and the opinions of these men are virtually rootless. Only those who can awaken from the engrained habits of self-deceit can cultivate an authentic life based upon truth. Evaluating to what degree your concepts and thus opinions are based on truth is a basic aspect of the quest, and requires extensive committed research and courageous introspection.

We have learned that language is the shaper of illusions, delusions, half-truths, distortions, as well as a vital avenue which can reveal truth. Thus we must be aware of how certain words trigger conceptual impressions relating to our sense of values. Words such as patriotism, God, race, honor, pride, stimulate a certain acquired collective response. Such all-around programming of a person's worldview is the essential element of acculturation—a force of the social environment which the collective psyche of an entire nation creates in order to imprint its traditions and beliefs upon the minds of its citizens. Though different cultures vary in their customs and beliefs, acculturation is equally powerful in its effects on growing children, no matter where they are born. Unless a person breaks the chains of negative acculturation, retaining only what is imbued with truth, there is no chance for awakening to Being.

Skilled rhetoric emphasizing the religious and political differences of races and nations is very often used to manipulate people in order to instigate and carry on wars. It is the seemingly alien differences of another culture, its language and customs, which create susceptibility to adverse propaganda. Without political and corporate powers using mass media to propagate trigger words which play upon engrained prejudices and established bias, the peoples of differing cultures would rarely if ever be involved in war. Without such negative influence of authoritarian powers, human beings will usually communicate and make peace by reaching beyond such factors as nationalism, race, language, to realize their basic universal human affinities. Every child, no matter where she/he grows up, no matter what language is spoken, enjoys sweet treats, toys, playmates. Every person, adult or child, male or female, likes to have a warm place to sleep on a cold winter night. Everyone on the planet, whether they are Chinese, Italian, German, Mexican, African, English, Afghan, Pakistani, enjoys a good meal when they are hungry. Though the word for rose is different in every language, it smells just as marvelous to all those different noses. All across the planet, everyone partakes of common human joys and pains. We are all human beings, no matter how different our cultures, and for the most part we embrace universal human values. This may all sound quite simple, but if it were, ordinary common sense would prevail, thus preventing war and political upheavals around the earth. Yet as we know all too well, this is not how things go.

Cultural differences manifest by way of custom, which is an aspect of acculturation we can see in the activities of the people within different societies. An example of a foreign custom that can immediately alienate someone acculturated in Western civilization is the eating of dogs. Nobody sees this as wrong where it is a traditional custom. But, since this book is written in English and published in the United States, many readers probably think eating dogs is very weird, even appalling. To most Americans, a "Lassie Come Home" relationship to dogs is delegated a set cultural place and response. But I ask anyone who is appalled by people who eat dogs to pause for a moment, slow your thoughts and consider the facts your reaction is based on. If you are not a vegetarian, focus truthfully on the meat you eat. You most likely eat hamburgers and hot dogs. Hot dogs? Of course, we know they are not made of dog meat, but are actually a mixture of ground up muscle, fat and organs of cows and pigs that have been killed and cooked and then packed into oblong skins. You probably eat chickens too, and turkeys and ducks, and lambs, and perhaps even cute furry little creatures like rabbits. Numerous Americans eat raccoons, deer, possum, bear, moose, and even rattlesnakes. Some of these animals have an intelligence equal in their way to dogs. In fact, pigs have passed scientific tests that validate such intelligence. So it is ridiculous for Americans and most Europeans who are not vegetarians to think their eating habits are more refined than those of people who eat dogs. There are people on earth who think eating some of the animals Americans eat is just as strange and weird as Americans may think eating a dog is. This is due to judgment shaped by custom.

Each animal killed so you can eat it will struggle to avoid pain and death, fighting for its life just like a dog would. Most animals humans eat can be domesticated like dogs are. Pigs and lambs are household pets in many places. They like to be cared for and respond when you call them by name. They like treats and a nice place to sleep just like all creatures. There are cultures where women even breast feed piglets. So what is the difference between eating a dog and eating any other sensory creature? The main difference is custom — how your mind has been shaped since birth to think about such things. I know dogs are more intelligent than chickens or cows, and those dogs I've seen in cages of Asian markets waiting to be eaten, would have all made good pets. But that doesn't make me believe Asians are inferior. Of course, I believe there is always room for improvement of values and customs in every culture. There are people within every nation on earth with a cultivated spiritual awareness and sensitivity attuned to perceiving intelligent responsiveness in other creatures, who will not harm or eat any animals at all. I've been a vegetarian for over thirty years, but if placed in a situation where I was facing starvation and had only a pig and a dog, and I had to consider eating one of them, my entire "customized" sensitivity would be to keep the dog and eat the pig. I have had some very fine dogs for pets, but never had a pig. Now, if I had raised the pig from a piglet and it had been my pet for ten years, and

I had only found the dog two days ago, (and it was one of those mousy little poodle dogs), I think I would eat the dog. Custom can be altered or nullified by circumstances and individual idiosyncrasy. People facing starvation have even eaten the corpses of fellow human beings.

There are people who eat bats, and even rats, as an every day treat. There are people who eat monkeys, ants, grasshoppers, roaches, slugs. They were brought up according to the custom that eating these kinds of creatures is OK, just like American customs teach people eating cows, pigs, chicken, lamb, rabbit, is OK. But Americans never think about these creatures when eating them because someone else has already killed them, and the butcher has cut them up and washed away all the blood and wrapped the meat in nice little plastic packages, and restaurants and fast food joints even cook it for them. Yet no matter how nice and neat the package is, it is still the flesh of a sensory creature similar in many ways to a dog. If every person had to kill the animals whose flesh they eat every day, they would have an entirely different perspective of what was on their plate.

When humans lived in tribes long ago, and the only food available was the wild animals they hunted, eating meat was a necessity and caused no harm to others or the environment. But in this day and age, in nations of economic power with a large affluent population like the United States, with supermarkets all about us stocked with every kind of food, we no longer actually need to eat meat. And raising mass livestock for the consumer's appetite causes much harm, health wise, ecologically and economically. HALF the earth's landmass is grazed by livestock, and sixty-four percent of the cropland in the United States produces livestock feed. Hogs raised for human consumption in stockyards and ranches outnumber people and cause extreme ecological damage, as do chickens. There are 600 million chickens in Delaware and Maryland alone, contributing to the production of 2 trillion pounds of manure a year, causing waste seepage into lakes and rivers which has killed millions of fish. To produce a pound of beef requires two hundred times more fresh water than to produce a pound of tomatoes. Hundreds of thousands starve to death every year while tons of grain fit for human consumption are fed to livestock. Raising livestock consumes one third of the grain produced on earth and is a major cause of world hunger. Most of the Amazon rain forest has been destroyed to create pasture for cattle. Six square yards of forest are destroyed to produce one fast-food hamburger. If you add all this up, it could be said that for every seven pounds of meat you eat, somewhere a human being dies of starvation. This is outlandish. Approximately eleven million children starve to death each year. It has been calculated that during a period of one year the average U.S. citizen eats a whole cow. How many deaths from starvation in Third World nations does that add up to? Despite the haywire rationalizations and justifications of gourmet food magazine editors, chefs, and just about every meat eater, when you consider all the damage done to the environment and the harm caused to human beings just because of civilization's craving for meat, we can understand why most intelligent people with a comprehensive grasp of our ecological situation become vegetarians. The diet of your average citizen is 90% controlled by taste buds, conformism, and commercial manipulation, having little to do with intelligent choice and adequate nutrition. The United States is in the throes of an epidemic of obesity. To develop a high quality vegetarian diet within a meat eating culture is a test of will power over the influence of engrained acculturation and commercial manipulation. This is the kind of important choice each person must struggle with to rise above the common impulses of lower appetites. "You are what you eat," has significant implications in regards to will power, inner integrity, and thus self-knowledge.

None of us had any choice concerning the weighty matters of where and when we were born, who our parents were, what language we first learned to speak, our first concept of God, and so on. The question is, since you did not have any choice in these matters, shouldn't you now begin, if you haven't already, to make "REAL" choices as to who you are and what you believe, according to your own decisions about how truthful different versions of such beliefs are? "Brought up according to custom" has nothing to do with learning for yourself what is right and wrong. Acculturation is thinking that has been done for you. When undertaking the quest for self-knowledge, you have to decide which customs and acculturated beliefs you want to keep and which ones should be tossed aside. You must become introspectively thorough enough to discover the influences stemming from what you were taught as a child, surrounded by parents and neighbors, teachers and peers, all with very similar beliefs, not only about food, but about God and patriotism and sports, and just about everything else. As growing children, we are strongly swayed to believe what our parents, family, society, believe about significant aspects of reality, yet as adults we are confident our opinions are based on choices we have made as individuals. It is clear the comprehension of reality of a vast majority of the human race is essentially an acculturated construct. Neither fame nor riches can overcome acculturation. Only hard won self-knowledge and the cultivation of willful inner choice can free an individual of soul-stifling traditional conventions.

An individual's true uncompromised being, his or her essence, lies beyond the instilled social programming of everyday mass consciousness. And yet the majority of human beings become sealed inside an egoic bubble within a collective nationalistic experience of the world, and interpret reality from an extensively biased position, never questioning their acculturated beliefs any more than they question what they eat. After a century of technological dominance entailing the burgeoning of secularism and the influence of stultified religion merged with the politicized idea of progress, the multitudes of Western civilization have become alienated from the guidance of authentic mythical and spiritual truths. Very few ever question let alone thoroughly contemplate these things. Ensconced within a mass layer of conformism, they perceive only the affinities of their engrained beliefs steadfastly held by almost everyone around them. Thus they blind themselves to anything challenging their limited view of existence.

Each individual is fully responsible in undertaking the task of breaking free of mind chains he or she feels detrimental to authentic development. This includes scrutiny of significant concepts that shape our everyday lives and influence our attitude and perception. Such scrutiny enables an individual to envision what lies beyond the gateway we have been unknowingly standing at the threshold of. There can be no faith in the potential for a greater, more genuine spiritual life influencing our civilization if a large segment of humanity does not come to realize itself to be but a prelude to something more. Human alienation from genuine spiritual vibrancy will end only when a large segment of the population finds the strength to stop being dupes of acculturated patterns of thought. Humans in great numbers must transcend being pawns in the play of existence. Though things happen to us through contingency, we are, potentially, much more than inert pawns, for we can choose to act amid the play of existential/spiritual forces.

One has to commit to an attentive effort in order to unfold the potential which lies like a dormant seed beneath the influence of biological fixation and acculturation. In this effort freewill is an essential tool. How we use our freewill is a moral choice imbued with significant meaning. Freewill is a subject mucho debated within varied fields of knowledge, with some thinkers even arguing it is non existent, claiming our lives are completely determined by genetic, social, and psychological forces beyond our control. Those who champion such determinism never realize that though there is a significant element of truth to this view, like most materialists and behaviorists they overlook the reality of both the trans-emergent quality of ego consciousness, which gives "will" space to act over instincts, and the inner dimensions of our soul, which, as clarified, is the very potential in human beings to overcome all deterministic factors. Danah Zohar writes of the indeterminate quality of freewill,[30] which she relates to the self-reflective quantum nature of focused thought. As to the empirical validation that free will exists, the book *Physics of Consciousness*,[31] by Professor Evan Harris Walker, sufficiently accomplishes this with precise data and equations. Even a number of staunch materialists have recognized a significant element of free choice within the human organism.

In a book called *Why We Feel*, bio-psychologist Victor S. Johnson observes that,

> *We are a creative species. Creativity is an inherent part of the evolutionary process and of the selection-based learning and reasoning mechanisms... The success of these procedures lies in their ability to conserve past gains and at the same time generate new creative hypotheses centered on this stored knowledge... Evolution, learning, and reasoning can all be viewed as creative problem-solving procedures that are inherently non-deterministic in nature. Working together, they allow living creatures to adapt and refine their functional interactions with an enormous variety of environmental events that exhibit inherently different rates of change... Learning permits adaptive modifications to more rapid but consistent change, and reasoning provides a creative mechanism for adapting to future but predictable variations in the environment. For "Homo sapiens sapiens," the source of their double wisdom depends upon making reasoned decisions, based upon learned environmental rela-*

tionships, that can anticipate environmental outcomes before they occur. Such creative mechanisms endow the human mind with the nondeterministic ability to discover highly original solutions to the many survival problems encountered in a complex changing world.[32]

Of the creative "mechanisms" capable of overcoming modern survival problems, we can consider the development of self-knowledge to be one of the most vital. This entails gaining flexible self-control of impulses and passions which run rampant through the common mind. And by common I mean every social class, working to ruling, barber or President, convict or member of the "beau monde." In addition, an in-depth discipline is required which demands a conscious harmonizing of the power of will with the humility of accepting one's insignificance amid cosmic-spiritual immensities. This is the essential condition of the Siddha, the Zen butterfly monk, the shaman, and any genuinely self-evolved spiritually awakened human being. Without this harmonization, liberation from acculturation may incite Faustian-Satanic hubris instead of genuine heart chakra awareness. Ironically, though such hubris ignites a vaunting condescension toward the hordes of humanity, it succumbs to the lowest ego-schemes to attain power and wealth, and is thus still tied to common desires, envies, machinations of jealousy, deceit, petty ambitions, and vengeance. This is not true freedom. The more power one has over others, the less power one has over oneself. Authentic freedom is to be free of all cravings for power, prestige, fortune.

Though we are expendable as individuals in the cosmic-spiritual immensity, once we have cultivated authentic freewill, we are capable of making inner choices that bring about the unfolding of infinite Being into the realm of finite being. Such inner choices require a high quality of reasoning as well as disciplined intention, or as Ortega y Gasset put it,[29] challenging one's circumstances. Actually, freewill is the most profound blossom of the plant of spiritual discipline, the quality of which depends on depth and scope of self-knowledge. As a species, humans have a psychic-energy niche in the cosmic/spiritual unfolding of existence, which can only be fulfilled if a significant number of individuals transcend their acculturated helplessness by living a life committed to the quest of awakening. No other goal, no matter how socially idolized, has such vital meaning. No external social activity or profession has substantial meaning in the great play of existence unless it is an extension of spiritual development.

13 – Cherished Convictions

And be not conformed to this world:
but be ye transformed
by the renewing of your mind.
—Romans 12:2

Anthropomorphism is the rudimentary tendency to project human qualities onto non-human phenomena. We are subconsciously subject to this on a daily basis—seeing a face in the clouds, on a rock formation, in a stain on the wall, or the gnarl of tree bark, or projecting human traits onto cats and dogs and other domestic pets. Mickey Mouse, Donald Duck, Bambi, and recent cartoon films about dinosaurs, are popular examples of how embedded such projection is in our relation to the natural world. Since ancient times humans have been prone to seeing wild creatures as imbued with human traits, when in actuality what we perceive in such things as caring for the young, mating rituals, etc, are our own animal traits. Anthropomorphism was definitely active in the primal human mind's tendency to see gods everywhere, amplifying and projecting human ambitions, desires, likes and dislikes, upon them. For instance, the archaic idea that a storm is God's wrath, or thunder is the noise of the gods clanging their swords, or an erupting volcano is an angered god. In fact, the Hebrew Yahweh was associated in ancient times with the awe inspiring mystery of volcanic activity. This has gone on unabated down through the ages, slowed down somewhat with the rise of science, until rejuvenated in the West with such New Age projections as "Mother Earth" and "Moon Goddess." In this regard, the New Age is ageless, for its adherents are relating to all of nature as early Native Americans did, which of course was similar to ancient Europeans with their wind gods, sun gods, sea gods, forest spirits, etc. In other words, it is a universal tendency of the primitive psyche which is still active within us.

Sages of the past, including certain prominent figures of the Bible, warned against capitulating to anthropomorphism. Isaiah staunchly criticized all attempts at humanizing God. The Greek philosopher Xenophanes stated that cats would probably conceive a catlike God—catmorphism! He assailed both Homer and Hesiod, authors of what can be considered the bibles of ancient Greece, for projecting too many human attributes onto the gods. Plato studied the works of Xenophanes as a youth, and came to agree with him on this issue. Two thousand two hundred and some years later, in 1840, Feuerbach clarified that religion was a process to tailor a greater non-human consciousness to fit reality based on human experience, answering the need for authoritarian/parental guidance and reciprocation of worship.

Like most people, I was caught up in religious ritual and imagery at an early age. I was raised a Baptist, and besides attending church in the Los Angeles area, various relatives took me to huge religious gatherings in halls, gigantic tent meetings, and occasions at "Holy Roller" churches where people spoke in tongues and rolled on the floor in ecstatic trance. I had been taught to pray as a child, and when my mother came down with cancer I prayed for her healing every night for quite some time. When she died just before my ninth birthday, it occurred to me that God was indifferent to the prayers of children. I have heard over the years that even when their most heartfelt prayers are not answered, eighty-five percent of adult Christians retain their trust in God. But when my mother died after suffering for so long, even as a child I had intuited something different was going on than what I had learned in Sunday School. By the time I was thirteen I had lost faith in the God I was taught to believe in. I stopped praying and began looking attentively at the world around me, gradually concluding as a maturing teenager that a supreme being, if it existed at all, had no special concern for the trials and tribulations of human beings. The only things I felt worth pursuing were adventure and knowledge. Twenty years would pass from the day of my mother's death before I confronted the numinous spiritual sphere of the living mysterium tremendum. Yet those years of worldly experience, of testing myself in varied environments that challenged both physical and mental abilities without any recourse to higher powers, prepared me for later spiritual visions and psychic insights of an intensity and scope I have seen drive some mad. I now approach religion with a well honed versatile perspective, balancing respect and reproachfulness, openness and skepticism.

The belief that religion is the truest way of interpreting the spiritual dimension of reality is where religion differs from philosophy. Religion is a cultural structure enclosed in its own biased certainty of essential spiritual truths, which it seeks to impose, while philosophy is open-ended. Underlined by the pursuit of revealing truth as far as possible concerning the most significant aspects of existence, philosophy doesn't claim to already contain any all-encompassing truth, and thus has no need for fabrication concerning the "hows and whys" of a God or gods. Yet philosophy does merge with the spiritual quest, gleaning from varied religions only what resonates with truth, thus releasing the seeker from the delusions and illusions religion is inundated with. Judeo-Christianity evolved as a religious-conceptual system conducive to reducing God for the comprehension of the multitudes, eventually claiming to have a monopoly on truth gleaned from the highest spiritual authority—the "God of gods" himself. Of course, such a claim leads to an inevitable clash when various religions with different Gods each claim the other Gods as lesser than theirs, if not invalid altogether. Thus I believe we must cultivate a spiritual perspective founded on impeccable eclecticism, culling from the narratives of each religion that which is imbued with the quality of truth and integrating it into our own spiritual radius of comprehension, tossing away falsehoods and fabrications. This approach prevents the hindering elements of tradition from intruding in a way that is detrimental to genuine spiritual growth.

If, we might ask, religious tradition is detrimental to an individual's spiritual quest, and if there is such a great diversity of individual subjective experiences of the numinous, how is it hundreds of millions are followers of a single religion? This has to do with several factors: the tremendous power of the collective, the dominant sway of conformism, the fear of isolation, the adhesiveness of instinctual grouping impulses, and the underlying archetypal force buried beneath traditional interpretation. Consider a recent poll showing up to ninety percent of Americans claim to believe in the Christian concept of God. Ninety percent. Can we even begin to question such an extensive belief system? Yes, and we must, if we are striving to reveal truth. Truth is not validated by belief, nor by numerosity of believers. Because an asylum inmate believes he is Napoleon, does not make him Napoleon. If millions of people believed the asylum inmate to be Napoleon, it still would not make it so. Because all the Nazis in Germany believed they were superior to the Jews, and thus thought they were justified in destroying them, did not make their belief true. We must conclude that just because a great number of people accept and give revered homage to the same religious imagery, this does not validate their belief. Nearly two billion people on earth believe in the basic tenets of Christianity. Though this certainly makes it a formidable belief system, it does not validate its truth concerning how "God" interacts with humanity. There are four billion people on earth who believe in other religions, and other gods.

Though the religious impulse comes from within, its manifestations are socially shaped through symbols and practices maintained and revised by generations of stultified leaders holding positions of authority. This is elucidated by Wade Clark Roof in his book, *The Spiritual Marketplace*.[1] Nonetheless, Aurobindo and the Dalai Lama both spoke of religion as being a stabilizing stage in humanity's spiritual evolution, a necessary encapsulation of the light needed to guide humanity toward greater light. Some spiritual leaders have spoken of religion as that which keeps the beast within humanity at bay. And this is probably so. The problem is, overly organized religion also keeps the genuine spiritual potential in humans at bay also, and has all too often released the beast, as verified by the Inquisition, the Crusades, the subjugation of Blacks, the genocide of Native Americans, and much else. The collective entrancement of religious tradition permeates the socialized mind, and though common belief catches some resonance from the essential archetypical-mythical force imbuing religious imagery, especially potent Christ-Solar/death-rebirth symbolism, such powers hardly ever significantly penetrate the psychic ambit of the ordinary believer. Though crowds of faithful aroused by a skilled preacher can become overwhelmed with a fervent sense of spirit, and the experience is real, moving the personality deeply, it is of an emotional-psychological nature with only traces of higher frequencies of numinous power coming through. Still, we must acknowledge, when delving into the perplexities and complexities of the paradigm of religion, we can never dismiss it as completely invalid just because we recognize its basic fallacies, delusions and fabrications.

Religion is a keynote principle of human consciousness, with a very extensive and varied belief spectrum, running from simple fundamentalist concepts to mystic levels of interpretation. The essential purpose of all major religions, suppressed behind the external elaboration of imagery and basic codes of conduct, is the resolve to generate the believer's impulse for transcendent endeavor, to activate the esoteric directive to move "inward" toward immersion into the spiritual essence of our very being. We can consider exoteric religious dogma as excessively organized metaphysical truths which have become distorted and petrified within the cultural ambit, and therefore must be dissolved and transformed, creating a more extensive comprehension of our existential spiritual predicament. Cultivating this "more extensive comprehension" is a significant component of the spiritual pilgrim's endeavor. To do this we must step back for a more objective overview of the religion we have adapted to and obediently followed for years, difficult as this may be.

One of religion's significant drawbacks is its overbearing function as moral overseer, relieving a person of the burden of making fateful decisions, which should be a uniquely individual experience. But many people, when confronted with in-depth psychological conflict or crisis, are programmed to automatically turn to the priest, pastor, minister, guru. They are thus relieved of their own inner struggle, usually being informed that God wants them to go this way, do this, not do that. This type of religious orientation can all too easily become a system of authoritarian dictates detracting from a person's inner impulse to grow and enhance his/her experience of life.

Christianity can be seen as a hybrid of myth and historical fact relating to the spiritual dimensions of existence, more or less an extensive hypothesis sufficiently embedded in the cultural psyche to be taken not merely as theory but as unquestionable validated truth. Yet Judeo-Christian religion is a structure of theoretical concepts based upon historical assumptions that have little evidence other than blind faith to substantiate their validity, which is no substantiation at all. Where religion differs from science is, when its beliefs are proven highly questionable, even reeking of falsehood and fabrication, instead of being put aside they are clung to all the more fiercely, which can be witnessed on a national scale in the Christian revival movement. This is because of the depth of psychological dependency religion produces in the believer. One of the reasons for such intense psychological dependency is, beyond the fabrications, religious belief is rooted in mytho-legendary interpretations of actual archetypal powers dwelling within our collective unconscious depths. This enthralling need to transform bewildering archetypal elements of existence into tolerable explanations and comprehensible imagery, can be traced back to early hominid ritual.

From the accumulated evidence of various fields of research — paleontology, anthropology, history of religious ideas, archeology, etc. — we can confidently, though cautiously, reflect upon our religious roots. How far back these roots go, we may never know. But they are deeper than we think. We can trace Judeo-Christian-Islamic concepts of God back through the growth of civilization, back through village and wandering tribe, to the earliest stages of human evolution, entailing primitive childlike anthropomorphic projections, embellished visionary intimation, and shamanistic experiences which breached archetypal dimensions of Being, releasing them into the ambit of human consciousness. Though some scholars claim what science weaves from such evidence is a highly questionable narrative, I believe we can glean enough from what we know to get a glimpse of our origins and the rising of the religious impulse, sufficient for the seeker of truth to envision her/his place in the great flow of human longing for spiritual validation.

As clarified in Chapter Five, primate fossils have been dated to over fifty million years ago. We know that twenty-two million years ago at least a hundred species of apes roamed over half the earth. We have evolved as a unique branch of primates from one of those species. The remains of a more recently evolved species of ape dating back 16.5 million years, which scientists have named Griphopithecus, were found in both Germany and Turkey. The research of Harvard professor Donald Griffin has shown that the minds of animals, especially primates, have conscious perceptive abilities completely ignored by behavioristically oriented science during the twentieth century.[2] Though a seedling form of egoic awareness most likely did not come about until possibly 250,000 years ago within the Neanderthal era, and quite likely with Cro-Magnon, who roamed the land circa 150,000 BC, would not early hominids of 7 million BC, with fifty million years of primate development behind their unique differentiation, have certainly developed a form of acute embodied consciousness? A hominid skull recently found in Chad, Africa, dating seven millions years ago, was inspiring for those who believe the first proto-humans may eventually be traced to as far back as ten million years. But nothing has been established for sure.

We do know that primal proto-humans, like their primate for-bears, were definitely intensely social within their immediate bands. And we know from Jane Goodall's work that chimpanzees, our closest primate relatives, have distinct individual traits of personality, with ways of expressing various moods by a language of gestures, facial expressions, grunts, snarls. Other research involving the sign language which the deaf use to express highly abstract ideas, verifies hand movements, gestures, facial expression, can communicate much more than was once thought. Two year old humans have a fair degree of self awareness and are capable of symbolic interplay with their environment and communication with parents. Would not an adult Homo habilis of two million years ago, far more mentally ad-vanced than a common primate, have had a much more developed mental capacity than a modern two year old human? Would they not have developed a language of gesture, facial expression, vocal noise code, far more sophisticated than chimpanzees? Our cave dwelling ancestors most likely had a quality of awareness they have not been given credit for.

We also know that Homo habilis had the creative intelligence to use stones to chip other stones into diverse shapes, for hide scrap-ing, chopping meat, hunting, etc. A creature that can make a knife or spear out of stones has a creative intelligence not to be overlooked. Surely with the daily venture of hunting huge prehistoric beasts, with the constant danger of being killed, with fellow hunters bleed-ing, dying, decaying, such hominids must have had an acute sense of their environment and the reality of death. Since, as Joseph Chilton Pierce demonstrated, all learning arises through transforming the concrete into the abstract, such constant bewilderment in confronting the daily struggle for survival in the face of death must have insti-gated rudimentary pondering of the unknown, especially when we realize that for millions, that's MILLIONS, of years before the domes-tication of fire, hominids spent each long night huddled together in dark shelters, not certain if the sun would rise again, surrounded by an endless night of prowling predators. Such intimate primal ambi-ence certainly stimulated communicative potential to an intensified degree.

Though modern humans have a brain volume of 1350 cubic centimeters, whereas that of Homo habilis was only 600 to 750 cc's, we know brain size does not make much difference as to intelligence. There are people who have had half their brains removed and go about living their lives with little noticeable difference from your normal citizen. That would mean they function quite well with 700 or less cubic centimeters of brain matter; just about equal to Homo habilis. The cerebellum, which is a necessary and important part of the brain for speech to be possible, was well developed in Homo habilis. Though its vocal chords may not have been capable of full use, sign language bolstered by well articulated sounds, grunts, clicks of the tongue, gave all the ingredients needed for substantial communication. Perhaps our sapience came about far earlier than scientific speculation has assumed.

600,000 years or so following Homo habilis, Homo erectus, with a brain volume at about 850 to 900 cc's, came onto the stage of evolution and roamed the land a million and a half years ago. Erectus is speculated to be the first hominid to discover how to put wildfire, possibly ignited by a lightning bolt, to domesticated use—an act which requires creative association on the pragmatic level, and acute intention. This meant no longer being huddled together through long dark fearful nights, but instead gathered about the blazing magic brightness of the captured power of fire. The communicative exchange that occurred during long leisure clockless hours of moon, stars, fire, was of an intimacy we cannot even imagine. We will never know just what occurred in those primal caves, during those long nights around that enchanted blaze. From what was elucidated in our discussion of language, concerning the art of gesture, facial expression, of signifying grunt and squeal, the rolling of eyes, which together can reach a highly complex level of communication, is it too much to assume that tales, fables, myths, religious inclinations, were born in those magical flame-cast caverns? Should we not question our impressions now concerning the religious inclinations of proto-humans? Perhaps that couple of hominids who left their fossilized footprints on the Latoli Plains of Africa 3½ million years ago were headed to or from some kind of religious ceremony.

In Chapter Five we saw how primal hominids as far back as 400,000 years ago were hunting with sophisticated throwing spears, and most likely participating in hunting rituals, thus rudimentary intimations of animistic presence. Neanderthal held ritual burials around 140,000 BC. Those primal hominids, who some say fully qualify as homo sapiens, most likely made attempts to alleviate their stark fearful awe as they blunderingly awakened to the mystery of existence and death. Such alleviation implies seeking succor of greater powers, which is one of the basic elements of every religion. Goodall has shown clearly that chimpanzees are not only puzzled by the inert body of a dead member of their group but they clearly seem to demonstrate a sense of mourning. Would not Neanderthal, separated from primate ancestry by over eight to ten million years as upright walking creatures, with almost one and a half million years of evolving beyond Homo habilis, have developed a more acute consciousness than we have given them credit for? Science was definitely wrong in its first 19th century impressions about Neanderthal, which carried over through most of the 20th century. One thing is certain, it is very likely the earliest proto-humans had more than brute club-carrying caveman intelligence.

As primitive homo sapiens evolved, as group became tribe, as caves gave way to village, attuned to their immediate territory, they had no idea of the vastness of the terrestrial world surrounding them, let alone any inkling of our planetary situation within an immense and expanding cosmos. Thus they developed an overwhelming sense of immediate environment as the totality of existence. Their desperate need to kill daily to survive and the ever present possibility of being killed, gave an intensity of apprehension and fearful awe to their entire existence. The constant demand for strategies to survive induced continually expanding inklings of self-reflective thought, thus a growing impulse to grasp for something more, something beyond the wild unhindered predator and prey flurry of their everyday situation. A keen awareness of dreams, barely separated from everyday consciousness, merged with the long nights of firelight and shadows, creating an intense imagination unhindered by reason. From this turbulent psychic brew merging with the primal mind's intuitive openness to numinous depths, an unbridled mytho-animism was born, igniting a colorful array of projections onto the unknown unnamed phenomena surrounding them. Everything was alive. Every life form thriving in the savage wilderness of primitive existence was imbued with the projection of dream-like spirits, animated with the emotional impulses of the primitive mind. And what a wild, fascinating, terrifying, seemingly unbounded reality it must have been.

Primal ritual was rooted in the urgent need to appease the strange and powerful forces swirling throughout the entire primeval wilderness. Such ritual was the matrix of religion, a ceremony of succor toward the bewildering immensity primal hominids found themselves thrown into. This sensitivity to the otherness of things was the first glimmering of spiritual awareness that over hundreds of thousands of years steadily increased in depth and luminosity. Somewhere along the way, as the constant feedback self-reflection loop we spoke of in earlier chapters intensified, they awakened to the first inklings of egoic separateness of their own embodied presence amid the lawless wonder of it all. Such semi-egoic awareness was constantly amplified by the terror of their "eat and be eaten" reality. Those first hints of dim self-awareness, burgeoning forth from the innate participational experience of their primeval world, stimulated an Eden like witnessing of thriving terrestrial fecundity, of nature's all-engulfing presence, of the mysterious depths of the night sky, the dazzling brilliancy of solar glory, merged with the bewilderment of the constant intrusion of death, flavored with the "realness" of astounding dreams, all intertwining in flourishing plasticity to shape the basic conceptual structure of the seedling egoic embodied mind.

Amid this fervent brew of psychic experience, within close-knit tribal ambits, the first elements of a beyond-the-pale individuality came forth in the practice of shamanism. The shaman was a unique tribal member — one who saw deeper, who was deemed capable of influencing to an impressive extent the discarnate inhuman powers primitives perceived all about them. It is possible dominant leaders of the first small groupings, whether male or female, were also the first practitioners of shamanistic arts — individuals who, as those in contact with and representative of greater spirits, gods, mysterious forces, received the first expressions of worshipful adoration by tribal members. When such a prominent tribal figure died, and occasionally reappeared in vivid dreams of those left behind, the dreamer could only grasp the experience as a glimpse into the world beyond death, a realm where chiefs and shamans and revered ancestors dwelt, all deserving of worship. Since such dreams merged with unhindered primitive imagination, the powers and activities of the dead were quite likely to have been amplified and elaborated extensively, transforming deceased chief/shamans into godlike proportions. Each newly chosen shaman, more culturally emboldened than those of previous generations, often through the use of plant and fungi, brought about states of ritualized trance which amplified their mind frequencies toward a resonance with deeper archetypal realms.

We have dealt enough with frequencies, meta-frequencies, hierarchal octaves, to know that psychic resonance betwixt the embodied mind and greater depths of reality cannot be ignored and shrugged off. In Thomas Mann's *Doctor Faustus*, the character Zeitbloom spoke of *"that tone which vibrates in the silence, which is no longer there, to which only the spirit hearkens."*[3] Like the frequency of a dog whistle attracting the ear of a wild wolf, the shaman's intensified consciousness attracts greater dimensions of consciousness, igniting a spiritual magnetism between lower and higher frequencies on the helicoid spectrum of Being. Such experiences were communicated from shaman and priestess to the tribal unit through ritual, song, dance, stimulating collective self-reflection toward a more expansive level of human awakening. Thus the sprouting of the soul-contact point between the egoic matrix and mysterium tremendum depths.

It is quite possible, since early primal hominid groupings were primarily matriarchal, those first ones attaining shamanistic powers were females. Artifacts representing awareness of a great Mother Goddess of life and death date back to Neanderthal tribal life of 200,000 BC. Whatever occurred within that primal-psychic-archetypal turbulence, the first crude anthropomorphic naming and ranking of spiritual beings was projected onto the realm of nature as goddesses of caves, canyons, trees, lakes, animals, wind, sea. After hundreds of thousands of years dominated by worship of Mother Goddess imagery, encompassing cultures across the planet, within the last 15,000 years such matriarchal influence gradually diminished due to patriarchal pressure generated by the evolving of the masculine ego. Within certain cultures, as ever more sophisticated mental abstraction burgeoned forth, masculine gods of awe inspiring power arose, intermingling with preexisting gods and goddesses. Thus a hierarchal polytheism reigned, with its medley of gods and goddesses, all subject to anthropomorphic projection of human urges—benevolent ones, lustful ones, tricksters, tyrants. Gradually, widespread but diminishing worship of Mother Goddess as an ultra-birthing Being possessing procreative-generative powers gave way to aloof masculine creator activity. But it would be thousands of years of the subjection of matriarchal influence before an isolated monotheistic supreme being—a one and only majestic God of gods—

was conceived. And Yahweh-Jehovah of Judeo-Christianity was not the first.

The endeavor of deeply delving into the history of religious ideas is to clear away still functioning archaic beliefs which have become obstacles to a more expansive existential-spiritual radius of comprehension. If we delve deep enough into traditional religious beliefs, through all the theological mish mash, objectively reviewing all we have been inundated with, we will usually discover that our religion has no more reason to qualify as the one true way than any other religion or belief system humans have constructed over the past ten thousand years. But I want to make it clear I am not saying because orthodox religion is a flawed structure of conceptual imagery rooted in fear, ignorance, and psychological projection, it is worthless and irredeemable in the context of our spiritual aspirations. I have already clarified that religion, despite its horrendous history and misdirective tendencies, because it is rooted in the impulse of spiritual awakening, retains beneficial aspects which are significant to keeping the human race on a fairly even keel as the process of evolving consciousness proceeds. And we must remember, as our best theologians, psychologists, and historians have validated, large portions of the dramatic stories within biblical text are mytho-symbolic attempts to describe the human relationship with archetypal forces dwelling within the mind's ultra-conscious depths. What we are after is to discover the spiritual pearl that can only be found during the deepest dives into the hidden recesses of our beliefs. This book is not for those content with common interpretations of their religion, where the Bible is used merely as God's guidebook to a secure stable life. It is for those who seek authentic spiritual growth unhampered by unnecessary and useless "religious" trappings which are based on all the fabrications and distortions we have exposed.

Judaism and Christianity are two of the five major organized expressions of humanity's religious impulse. The first has extended over four millennia, and the latter, connected in its roots to the first, from circa 20 AD to this day. The entire story of the Judeo-Christian God and His works has come down the ages to us through the written word gathered in what is known as the Old and New Testaments of the Bible — a book of such profound impact upon Western civilization that seekers of truth must thoroughly probe its ramifications to assess its influence on both their own psyche and that of the multitudes. This ancient book consists of two basic sections called "Testaments," the Old being Judaic, used by both Jews and Christians, the New solely Christian. In this chapter we'll address the development of the Old Testament.

Most stories, parables, psalms, that were eventually incorporated into the book we know as the Bible, began possibly ten thousand years ago in the era of oral transmission, where narrative was dependent upon the memory of each teller of the tale. Such tales were told century after century, mostly by highly revered bard-sages, until finally being impressed on clay tablets in cuneiform script, and after more centuries, inscribed upon scrolls of parchment and copper. The word "bible" comes from the world "biblia," which means "scrolls." Hermeneutic research reveals that contrary to all traditional perspectives no one can say for sure who wrote the various books that make up the Bible. We do know that it is more than its parts, and as a whole it has become a powerful moral force throughout the Western world. But the Bible was not a first, not unique as a written expression of humankind's relationship to transcendent numinous realms. It only seems so to Christians and Jews, as the *Mahabarata* seems like the book of books to the people of Hindu cultures, the *Prajnaparamita* literature to followers of Buddhism, the works of Lao Tzu to the Chinese, and the *Koran* to Muslims. Yet most religious folk of Western civilization believe the Bible to be the ultimate book of books concerning humanity's spiritual situation, supposedly having come forth from "God's" direct involvement with an ancient "chosen" tribe.

There is still debate among scholars concerning when the Old Testament came together. Some say it was at least partially formed in the ninth century BC, but that was an era of cultural turmoil when the two kingdoms of Judah and Israel had divided geographically and theologically, which does not seem like a time for scribes to organize their tribe's guiding scriptures. According to scholar Norman Galb, Jews of the first and second century BC wouldn't have had any idea of an Old Testament Hebrew "Bible," because, he claims, it did not exist as a complete religious work even then, but was still in its formative stages.

Many great spiritual and philosophical writings had been completed far before the various writings of the Old Testament were even in seedling form. Approximately nine thousand years before Christ, seven thousand six hundred years before Moses was born, six thousand five hundred years before Abraham, agricultural villages in the upper rainfall regions of Mesopotamia had established a culture rich in mytho-religious oral expression, embellished with music and dance. And from this cultural matrix, Sumerian civilization rose beneath the numinous radiance of the Mediterranean sun. Sumerians created cuneiform writing approximately 3500-3000 BC, inscribing clay tablets in and around Mesopotamia, at the same time that Egyptians were developing a kind of proto-hieroglyphics, also inscribed in clay tablets. During the 20th century, broken and scattered tablets were found inscribed with the famous epic of *Gilgamesh*, dating to the third millennium BC. The earliest forms of literature in the Mediterranean area consisting of lamentations about existence have been dated to 2500 BC. A library discovered in Syria consisting of 20,000 clay tablets of cuneiform writing was active in 2,000 BC. Hammurabi reunited and became king of the Semitic state of Babylon, circa 1750 BC, writing a great book of laws and codes to guide his people centuries before a single page of the Hebrew *Tanakh* (the Old Testament) was written. Somewhere around 1500-1200 BC, the great holy book of Hinduism, the *Rig Veda*, was being formed in India. During this era, as Moses supposedly came down from Mount Sinai after receiving the vision of the Burning Bush, the *Egyptian Book of the Dead* was being completed. In Egypt, circa 1350 BC, when the Hebrews were enslaved there, the Pharaoh Ikhnaton wrote his monotheistic *Hymn to Aton*, which was hundreds of years prior to the first writings being organized to form the Old Testament. Approximately 1000 BC, the first dictionary was put together in China. The Assyrian library of Ashur-bani-pal, created by the emperor Toglath-Pileser I, operated between 1115 and 1077 BC., containing fifty thousand cuneiform tablets. It is known that near Mt. Helikon in Greece, 700 BC, as scattered text of what would become the *Torah* ("the Law") were still being gathered from oral Hebrew tales and legends, Hesiod, a Greek poet peasant, wrote his epic *Works and Days*, which consisted of a collection of theological and moral songs composed by Boeotian bards. Hesiod's work was looked upon by the Greeks as the Christians look upon the Bible. Hesiod's epic was filled with writings concerning principles and values—always speak the truth, keep promises, obey laws, might does not make right, etc. Hesiod created an occasional god or goddess for his tales of a once "golden age" of humanity, and this was reflected centuries later in important works written around 40 BC, such as *The Ecologues* of Virgil, and Ovid's *Metamorphoses*. He wrote of humanity dwelling in a fallen state, from what had been a blissful existence, and this fall had been brought about by a woman's curiosity. Homer, possibly a contemporary of Hesiod's, wrote the Iliad, which also had the stature the Bible now has. Thus, since Greco-Roman influence was widespread wherever the nomad Hebrews roamed, it is most likely the patriarch scribes gathering tales and tribal codes and transcribing the first books of the Old Testament were aware of such works, and most biblical scholars agree that the pervasive influence of Platoism and Stoicism can be found throughout Judaic teachings. Around 400 BC, Plato had already become the student of Socrates, and had begun his philosophical works, prior to the *Five Books of Moses* (Pentateuch) reaching their final form. We now know these were not actually the work of Moses, but of four different unknown writers, whom scholars have dubbed "J," "E," "P," and "D," each having different styles of writing.

During the period the Old Testament was being woven together, the brilliant Greek poets and playwrights Euripides, Aeschylus, Sophocles, and Aristophanes, had already completed some of their greatest creative works, many containing tales of gods and other sorts of fantastic beings. There were no constraints or concerns as to verifying the "reality" of such things in those ancient days. It is quite likely the Hebrew priests gathering the material to be arranged into the Old Testament, or *Tanakh*, were influenced by writings and religions of varied cultures their tribe interacted with. Striving for their own uniqueness as the "chosen people," tribal patriarchs would not have hesitated writing imaginatively of attributes of gods taken from religions of other cultures and tailoring them to fit their own Hebraic interpretation of history.

We can contemplate the Old Testament as a hybrid of historical tribal events merged with mytho-religious legend and subtle esoteric symbolism, condensed in literary format—an eclectic collection sorted from numerous others that had been lingering in oral tales for centuries. For instance, Exodus supposedly occurred circa 1200 BC, but was not dramatized in written text until a thousand years later. Do you think for a moment what was written closely resembles what occurred an entire millennium before, if it occurred at all, which many scholars doubt. *Genesis*, a collection of writings with no chronological order, strongly echoes Babylonian and Mesopotamian area myths the Israelites picked up when Abraham's tribe passed through these territories on several occasions, under entirely different conditions—as conquerers, as vanquished, as slaves. Flood myths from various cultures were numerous. As recent archeological-geological research has verified, great flooding did occur in that area circa 5000 BC. So such a catastrophe would certainly find a place in the legends of those living there. In the most ancient tale of *Gilgamesh* (2500 BC), a character named Ut-Napishtim, the only survivor of a great deluge, had been told to build a huge boat and take a sample of each living creature on board. As the flood subsided, he sent forth a dove to find land. There is the tale from Hellenistic mythology circa 2000 to 3000 BC, of how the ancient Greek god Zeus, who resided on Mt. Olympus, in his anger destroyed humanity with a great flood, which Deucalian, son of Prometheus, escaped with his wife Pyrrha in a huge ark. Hindu sages wandered all about the ancient Mideast, telling of how their God Vishnu turned into a fish to inform the faithful Manu to build a huge boat which could hold two of every creature to save from the coming flood. There are tales (660 BC) concerning Zoroaster, who went to the top of Mt. Sadalan to receive the laws of God, just as in the story of Moses climbing Mt. Sinai. We could continue, for there were many moral tales and legends carried around by ancient traders, travelers, nomad seers, written down centuries before any biblical text came about. When all of this and much more that is known is analyzed and pondered by the intelligent open mind, to take the Bible literally as a pure and straight forward explanation passed down directly to human beings by the Creator of the universe, would be an insult to the powers of both analytical reasoning and intuitive comprehension.

As scholar James Henry Breasted clarified in 1933, (and with over 70 years of accumulated evidence since then, we are even more sure of now),

> In the history of morals the New Past suddenly discloses to us the long unsuspected fact that Hebrew civilization, with its important and profoundly influential records of religious and moral experience, is one of the latest, outgoing stages of human development, which was preceded by ages of productive and creative social and moral experience along the Nile and the Euphrates. We must therefore adjust our minds to the fact that the moral heritage of modern civilized society originated in a time far earlier than the Hebrew settlement in Palestine, and has de-

scended to us from a period when the Hebrew literature now preserved in the Old Testament did not yet exist.[4]

Geoffrey Ashe states,

An entity called Israel appears first in an Egyptian inscription dated about 1224 to 1214 B.C., in the reign of the pharaoh Merneptah. This tale is a paean naming various minor nations as cowed into submission by Egyptian victories. One line says, 'Israel is laid waste, his seed is not.' The inscription is imprecise as to Israel's whereabouts.[5]

Other than that, there is no valid evidence in any Egyptian re-cordings of Israelite captivity, or of Moses being raised by Pharoahs, and, despite popular magazine front page articles stating otherwise, there is little if nil archeological evidence to substantiate the epic drama of the Israelite tribe. Though much historical evidence is lack-ing to verify the specifics of the journey of the Israelites, upon which biblical legends of victories, defeats, enslavement are based, such tales of war and captivity do clarify that their travels brought them into reciprocal cultural contact with many and varied religions and gods, which became the mulch from which Judaism and thus the Old Testament blossomed. We should also keep in mind David M. Rohl's remarkable book, *Pharaohs and Kings*,[6] which clearly shows how intimately the biblical legend of the Israelites and that of the great dynasties of Egypt are historically related.

The extent of the known earth Abraham (circa 1700 BC) and Moses (circa 1300 BC) would have been aware of encompassed no more than a five hundred mile radius, Egypt to Persia, the Caspian Sea to the Libyan desert, the Black Sea to Aswan. Of course, a thou-sand years after Moses, following centuries of accumulating teach-ings of their beliefs, ancient Hebrew scribes, who began approxi-mately 500 to 100 BC to finally organize the first written drafts of the Old Testament, would have known about geographic explorations undertaken by the Roman Empire, whose armies were then making varied forays into the primitive unknown lands of what we now call Europe. They also knew of Greece and India and varied areas of primitive Africa. It was such patriarchal scribe-priests of Judaism who were possibly the only persons in their culture with any geo-graphical comprehension of distant lands, but even that was probably little and distorted. The ordinary population of the Israelite nation, like most people of that era, were mostly illiterate, knowing far less about the world than the average ten year old does today. Such culturally imploded multitudes, with a deep sense of "participation mystique" with their tribe, left little room for individuality and comparative reasoning. Thus each and every tribal member embedded in intimate blood relationship with their cultural unit, completely accepted the highly biased belief system of their tribe with unquestioning zeal. From such a limited, tightly acculturated mytho-archetypal alchemy came the Old Testament monotheistic concept of God.

Though we cannot clearly envision what it was really like for the peoples of the ancient Mediterranean-Levant, we can surmise from the way desert people in countries such as Ethiopia and Afghanistan live today that an almost unendurably harsh environment induced passionate unquestioning faith in a religion that promised succor to all in the belief of being among the chosen elite. We must consider this basic legend of the Israelites becoming the "chosen people," and place all of it within the proper context of the constant rise and fall of great empires, of conquests and defeats of tribal warfare over the course of centuries. Leaving out overblown Hollywood Ten Commandment images, and taking as objective a stance as possible, it is quite clear this Judeo-Christian saga came forth as just one among many tribal cultural epics occurring here and there around the Mediterranean area during those fervent times.

Unbiased biblical scholarship, with its substantially reliable methods and techniques for investigating various aspects of "holy" scripture, has come to the conclusion the Old Testament Bible is a work of greatness and banality, truths and distortions, a piecemeal construction involving centuries of textual manipulations and mistranslations by tribal patriarchs, ancient Jewish bards, early church theologians, priest scribes, extensively elaborating and fabricating to suit the intentions of the presiding religious authorities. One thing for certain, what we have as the Old Testament Bible now is not what it was in its earliest stage of compilation, which was in the form called *Targum Onkelos*, written in ancient Aramaic, a language adopted by the Hebrews when they left Babylon. During the captivity of the Jews in Babylonia circa 587 - 539 BC, Hebrew oral teachings, ancient tribal legends, morality tales, all heavily influenced by the various religions of the Mesopotamian area, plus streams of thought from Greek and Roman civilizations, were to various degrees being integrated into accumulating writings which were formed into the Babylonian *Talmud*, which was to become the Old Testament of Judaism. Centuries after being organized into final form, it was translated into Greek, and over the following centuries into Latin, then again into the languages of Europe, and thus English, a language which by itself has gone through tremendous transformations over the past five centuries. When St. Augustine arrived in Britain in 597 AD, over five hundred years after Rome had conquered the Isle, the English language did not exist. And for over seven hundred years no British King would speak what came to be called English. Most educated English speaking persons today can hardly read the English of Chaucer's original writings (circa 1370), due to the gradual and consistent changes it has undergone, which eventually transformed it into an almost entirely different language than it was centuries before. This is true of all contemporary languages. Language is a flexible, plastic, mutable, ever-changing phenomenon. And translation is a precarious project — the change of just one word can transform the meaning of a paragraph. In his work, *The Quest for the Origins of Language*,[7] Jurij Moskvitin brilliantly elucidates varied astounding semantic transformations which occur in even the most skillful translation of one language into another.

Laurence Binyon writes how problematic it is to translate medieval English into modern English, to render poetry created by a poet ensconced within one cultural criteria into language subject to entirely different criteria. We are dealing here with more than just the meaning of a word, but the fact that, grammatically speaking, nouns, verbs, subordinate clauses, etc., are all put to different use in each language. Consider: the English title of Freud's *Civilization and its Discontents* came from an earlier translation of the German title, *The Unease in Culture*. Similar in meaning, perhaps, yet not the same. Further translation from English into Russian or Egyptian, would shift the meaning even more. And several more translations into different languages over the coming centuries will only amplify the shift of meaning.

Significantly, with the languages the Bible has passed through over centuries — Aramaic, Hebrew, Greek, Latin to early English — certain basic elements of grammar in one language don't even exist in another. In his scholarly work, *The Greek Experience*, C. M. Bowra wrote,

*One of the main difficulties in translating Greek is that there are
often no single English equivalents for words which are perfectly
clear in Greek. For instance, the words which we conventionally
translate by 'good,' 'beautiful,' 'just,' and 'virtue,' all have
meanings which do not coincide with their English versions.*[8]

The brilliant writer Vladimir Nabokov wrote of the interpretative impact Kafka's earliest translators had made by turning the character from *The Metamorphosis*, Gregory Samsa, into a lowly cockroach, when in actuality Kafka had Gregory metamorphosed into a magnificently domed scarab beetle.[9] The implications here are profound when we contemplate Kafka's intense intimacy with the figure of Christ, and his knowledge of ancient cultures and art. Kafka was obviously aware that Albrecht Düer associated the symbolic aspect of the stag beetle with Christ. Some biblical linguists have written of the Aramaic word "scarab" being mistranslated as "worm," in Psalm 22:6, *"But I am a worm, not a man."* Certain imminent alchemists considered the scarab to be a symbol for The Great Work of transformation. In ancient Egyptian alchemy the scarab beetle's activity of making its nest out of dung for eggs to hatch from, symbolized the process of creating disciplines and procedures to bring forth spirit from flesh. The scarab is also associated in both Egyptian and Greek text with the solar aspects of the divine.

Thus we catch a glimpse here of how profound a "butterfly effect" the mistranslation of just a word can bring about. And during centuries of translation and re-translation of biblical text, it is most likely quite a number of mis-translations occurred. As biblical scholar and accomplished translator Robert Alter stated, *"There is something seriously wrong with all the familiar English translations, traditional and recent, of the Hebresw Bible."* This failing, along with the tendency to reduce and limit mytho-symbolism to an unyielding literal interpretation, has had far-reaching effects. For example, the esoteric interpretation of the Red Sea by ancient Gnostics symbolized spiritual poison for those who are unawakened, but simultaneously the very waters of rebirth for those awakening. Symbolically, the opening of the sea meant awakening, whereas the closing in upon meant being drowned in common somnambulistic unconsciousness. We must realize the earliest translators of the Greek Bible into varied European languages were church scribes watched over by exceedingly biased monks, who had not only no knowledge modern professional translators have at their disposal concerning this delicate process, but were bereft of any knowledge concerning esoteric symbolism. The subtle yet profound shifts of meaning occurring during centuries of continuing translations increasingly oriented toward literalism, have yet to be thoroughly recognized.

Robin Lane Fox demonstrates how the God of Judaism was not as unique as was thought up to the twentieth century, when discoveries in the fields of archeology, anthropology, paleontology, and hermeneutics, opened up a treasure of insights into our religious past.[10] Half the earth away from Yahweh's Levant ambit, during the same era the Hebrews were roaming about, P'an Ku, the Chinese creator of the universe, was just as valid a god to those who worshipped him. The same validity of belief could be said of the Egyptian Osiris, 3,500 BC, and of Brahman-Atman of Hinduism 5,000 BC, not to mention the cosmic and terrestrial goddesses who ruled previous to all masculine gods. It has been so with people and their gods all over the earth, and definitely of those many gods of the varied nations the Hebrews intimately interacted with for several thousand years.

Even to the Hebrews of early Judaism, Yahweh was just another god among a variety of gods and goddesses, until evolving over centuries of cultural change from a god of volcanic mountain heights to the prominent status of their one and only God. In the prehistory and history of the various and abundant gods of humanity, Yahweh-Jehovah is one of the more recent gods. As Monica Sjöö and Barbara Mor clarify in their book *The Great Cosmic Mother*, the historically recent male god as Yahweh-Jehovah came forth...

...in reaction to the original Goddess religion, which dominated human thought and feeling for at least 300,000 years. By contrast, God has been conceptualized as a complete male for only about three to four thousand years. For this reason, patriarchal religions must begin by denying evolution; for, if that long stretch of human growth time was acknowledged, it would have to be credited as the evolutionarily creative time of the Great Mother. To avoid this the Father Gods just somehow appear, as it were, by spontaneous generation, and human life just suddenly appears with them, fully formed, sprung arbitrarily from the forehead of the He-God, sometime around 2000 BC.[11]

When it comes to springtime fertility archetypes and rebirth rituals, all the metaphors used relate to the feminine, woman, who is birth vessel, the nourisher of the infant (spring), the daughter of Mother Nature. Symbols of dying and rebirth always lead back to matriarchal transformation mysteries. Through significant scholarship it is clear goddess images worshipped across the planet since the dawn of consciousness represent a diffusional process spreading outward like petals from the divine feminine procreative core of Mother Earth. As Elinor W. Gandon verifies in her work, *The Once and Future Goddess*, the first anthropomorphic images of God were feminine, and archeological evidence now affirms goddess religions occurring over 30,000 years ago, from the late Paleolithic on.[12] And yet, with what we now know of Neanderthal artifacts relating to awareness of the numinous, Sjöö's and Mor's speculation entailing hundreds of thousands of years seems a valid possibility, because chthonic-goddess religions were of the earth, of nature, partaking of the primal feminine element immanent within all terrestrial life. And knowing Neanderthal was probably a creature with a quality of spiritual awareness we have underestimated since the beginning of paleoanthropology, who's to say when such awareness began?

It should also be clearly and significantly recognized that feminine goddess imagery is not confined to the Earth (Gaia). In the writings of Xenocrates we find the idea that beyond the masculine gods of the heavens is the realm of the soul of the universe in which the <u>mother</u> of all gods dwells, whose nature is both destructive (Kali) and creative/procreative (Isis/Shakti). Geoffrey Ashe writes of a shamanistic deity known as Mistress of the Universe. As Ken Wilber so thoroughly elucidates, within the spiral surge of evolving consciousness, the feminine goddesses of the sky dwell on a higher level than the feminine earth goddesses. The Mistress of the Universe was a magnificent goddess figure representing the feminine aspect of the transcendent impulse also imbued within the rise of the egoic from the instinctual. As goddess of the universe, she has full independence from the chthonic. Through the perceptive works of various scholars it is clear how this widespread matriarchal spiritual paradigm was overwhelmed by patriarchal powers over the past ten thousand years. We can trace this from various directions through different religio-myths, such as Marduk defeating Tiamat the great dragoness, Zeus overcoming the great serpent Typhon, Yahweh conquering Leviathan, Uranus overshadowing Eros, Apollo as destroyer of serpent forces and chthonic dragons. Serpent and dragon figures related to earth goddesses of chthonic pre-egoic millenniums were gradually pushed into a demonic background by gods conducive to patriarchal rule. Western culture capitulated to this masculine domination of numinous archetypes. Consider men we perceive as imbued with wisdom, such as Aristotle, who glaringly manifested this patriarchal influence when he wrote of the force of life coming from the male sperm only, with the female no more than an incubator. Of course, this attitude was shaped by centuries of war, the brief and brutish life of humans during Hellenistic strife and the clashes between Sparta and Athens, plague wiping out one third of Athens, invasions from Persia, decades ruled by mad tyrants, plus more war and rumors of war, so that peace became no more than an interruption of war—thus physical strength and power, archaically related to the masculine, became the highest achievement.

As clarified, Judaism was influenced by Greco-Roman cultures, and the Greek philosophers. Greek concepts of the gods, especially Zeus and Apollo, had a significant monotheistic quality. And Aristotle, circa 344 BC, clarified the monotheistic concept of the First Cause. Zeus was seen to have an affinity with Jehovah in the writings of Antiochus IV Epiphanes, circa 170 BC. Thus it is not farfetched to posit the resonant influence of the masculine war/warrior schema of Sparta and Athens within the Hebrew religious matrix. Yahweh was a god of war, and the Israelites had no qualms of destroying their neighbors.

The majority of masculine gods of religions both East and West were, indeed still are, enthusiastic if not blatant instigators and lovers of war. Though the Hebrew Yahweh could be merciful and benevolent to those who pleased him, he was definitely passionate about war, and a fanatic about ethnic cleansing of any tribe other than his "chosen" Israelites. At least this was what the Israelites believed. The ancient Greek philosopher Theosophus said Yahweh was, for the Israelites, nothing but a powerful demon who commanded his people to attack even unoffending nations out of jealousy of their gods, slaughtering men, women and children without qualm. And yet, as to the omnipotent-omniscient protective powers of this tribal god which the Hebrews claimed as unique, we must keep in mind that Yahweh's chosen people lost as many battles as they won, and were conquered and enslaved more than once. It seems quite clear, as the work of Phyllis Boswell Moore has pointed out,13 this war mongering tyrannical biblical god does not qualify as a "God" that could have created the universe, or even the earth. He is a culturally created commander god, whose extensive reign through the Judeo-Christian conduit for three thousand years is equal to the reign of certain Egyptian gods who were around for at least as long, and Yahweh's reign will probably be less extensive than that of Hindu gods who have reigned for 5,000 years.

The Hebrews were ensconced within moral and spiritual certainties as stark and vivid as the landscape about them, whose confined beliefs locked out all the shades and finer distinctions of any greater truths. When an archetype is filtered through the primitive psyche of such an ancient people, to whom warfare is not an aberration of the cultural structure but an integral aspect, a war god is what you get. Thus, because a radical ethnocentric territorial imperative ruled, and expansion and conquering of territory was a way of life, the blatantly war-like god Yahweh came to be the all consuming conqueror god.

Absolute power to reward and punish does not make the Judeo-Christian "God" any more superior to other gods, nor any more deserving of reverence, obedience, worship, than a tyrannical emperor or dictator. As Euripides stated, "*If the gods do ought what is shameful, they are not gods.*"14 Yahweh-Jehovah being conceived as a supreme, all-powerful "person," thus a comprehensible god related more to the phenomenal world than the numinous depths, is just another superhuman, similar to the gods of the ancient Greek pantheon, or the gods of Viking sagas. Thus the biblical Yahweh, like the Greek Zeus and the Babylonian Marduk, is often ungodlike, in fact, often not even sage-like. Tribal scribe-priests, ambitious for power and territory, inspired by their visionaries who were believed to directly speak for "God," produced chapter after chapter in the Bible containing descriptions of what they believed to be manifestations of Yahweh's personality, his moods of anger, jealousy, concern, intrigue — all of which confirms this isn't a god, but an anthropomorphic projection imbued with every negative human trait, a confined cultural distortion of an archetypal force. Yahweh-Jehovah is a being with a "tribal sultan" mentality, a creation of the primitive mind rather than a creator of the universe and humanity.

Consider that our wisest sages, who we see as representing the highest development of humanity — Aurobindo, Jung, Krishnamurti, Schweitzer, Gandhi, and other lesser known sages — all overcame to a significant degree such negative traits as jealousy, greed, envy, hatred, and all emotions that boil up within ordinary undisciplined minds through lack of self-knowledge. Thus each of these spiritual sages—indeed, even ordinary people possessing sufficient self-knowledge and inner strength to manifest restraint of negative impulses—reveal a wisdom superior to that of the Old Testament Yahweh. Across the various continents of this planet, within every town and city, thousands of intelligent disciplined individuals have overcome these lower-mind negative traits. Therefore any authentic "superhuman" god-being certainly should have overcome them. Any supposedly godlike being spewing forth such negative traits is less disciplined, less mature, less intelligent than countless humans, and thus an inferior "god" of lower spiritual domains who does not qualify as the God of all gods and of all creation.

The seeker of spiritual authenticity soon comes to recognize that only an extremely defensive enclosed mind would deny the dozens of significant flaws concerning the concept of the God upon which both Judaism and Christianity are built. No supreme Being from which this fantastic mind boggling universe is an emanation could be anything close to the emotionally unstable egoic biblical God.

For "God" to literally create such an immense universe containing billions of galaxies, with trillions of planets and suns, black holes and supernovas, just so humans could undertake their salvational sojourn on this comparatively microscopic planet, is like building the Superdome just to house a flea circus. And what about God creating the universe, the solar system, the Earth, all in seven days? What God would be concerned with days? Calendars, names of days and months, even the linear concept of time, are inventions of the human mind that did not exist until civilization was well in progress. And why seven days instead of seven minutes, if omnipotent? Why would a creator god of this universe, supposedly omniscient, able to see into the future, who would command "be fruitful and multiply," have placed Adam and Eve on a small planet that was two-thirds ocean, eventually creating the problem of overpopulation? Consider Saturn, which is as much larger than the earth as a basketball is to a golf ball. Why did this all powerful god not create Eden on a planet as large as Saturn? This supposedly highly intelligent "creator" Yahweh, chooses this tiny globe of mostly water for creatures who need to live on land. Would an all-foreseeing God create a population of humans he would later look upon as a mistake to be destroyed in a flood? Why did he not foresee the mistake? And this God is definitely prone to mistakes. Over ninety percent of all species that have come into existence on earth have gone extinct. Over 90%. What kind of workshop is this planet? How could "intelligent design" be so wasteful and rife with mistakes. How could an omniscient God "intelligently" plan and design creatures that would fail to succeed, or be destroyed by unforeseen catastrophes? This would be "Imbecilic Design," or at least "Unintelligent Bumbling Design." If an omniscient God could foresee such disasters and still go ahead with his creative activity, what does that tell us? What does the fact that he let five thousand species of tapeworm survive tell us? Not to mention myriad other pernicious parasites. Even with his supposed plans involving special concern for humans, He did not hesitate to heartlessly drown everyone but Noah and his family without coming up with a compassionate alternative. Such slaughter is neither intelligently creative nor innovative, and lacks a concerned ingenuity that any truly omniscient caring Godlike being would surely have.

For most people dwelling beneath the sway of Judeo-Christian religious orientation, the word "God" connotes an awe-inspiring omnipotent being, Yahweh-Jehovah, who supposedly, with bizarre mind boggling creative diversity, brought forth everything that exists. They base their conceptual structure upon the belief that their God created the entire cosmos and all terrestrial life specially for humans to live and praise their creator. And the first humans required to do this were Adam and Eve. We all know the story. Eve is tempted by the serpent to entice Adam to eat the fruit of the tree of good and evil, which God forbade. Cast out of Eden, Adam, Eve, and all humans coming after them, must work out their salvation, because all of us are born tainted with the sin of the first couple's disobedience. Interestingly, there is a Gnostic version of the Garden of Eden myth that is very intriguing, which we touched on in Chapter One, in which Eve, as the daughter of Sophia (wisdom), takes the forbidden fruit from the serpent, who represents not evil but the awakening process. From this perspective, Eve's rebellious act is an attempt to transcend the sphere of Yahweh, who is not the God of the absolute ground of being but a demiurge of the instinctual semi-conscious world of primal sleep = Eden, from which Adam and Eve, now conscious to having risen beyond nature and attained the power of choice concerning good or evil, are "cast out" = rudely awakened. This version of the Eden story, with Yahweh symbolizing the instinctual, and the feminine symbolizing evolving consciousness, gives the biblical version a different flavor altogether.

In order to cohesively integrate and grasp the genuine actuality of our existential-spiritual situation, the seeker must have a certain acute intuitive perceptiveness blended with being sufficiently informed. Over the past century and a half, research from various fields, when organized and laid out clearly, verifies that unquestioning, unbending belief in the Yahweh-Jehovah God of Judeo-Christianity is not only highly questionable but mentally defective. The majority of those who believe in this God have accepted the religious premises of their belief without ever thoroughly examining them. They claim this is faith, but it is only assumption.

I could go on and on, taking the literal interpretation of biblical myth to its logical conclusions mired in absurdity—such as Yahweh just waiting as various civilizations rose all about the Mediterranean area, Sumer, Egypt, Babylon, Persia, Greece, to finally pick his "chosen" nomadic folk from among dozens of desert tribes. And why from the Mediterranean area? Why not China, or India, or Africa? Really, think about it. What kind of God would fill the earth with such varied races of people as the Eskimo and Bedouins, the Amazon Indian and the Finlander, the African Bushman and the Celt, and yet out of this flourishing variety of hundreds of cultures pick one particular tribe in the Mideast to make a covenant with? Why the bias? Why the extreme favoritism among his varied children? Why five thousand years ago instead of six thousand? Ten? Twenty? Why Abraham and Moses and not one of a thousand other tribal leaders at that time roaming the earth or ruling in established villages and towns? Why not a pharaoh, or Socrates, or Plato, or … ? We have here a God caught up in some kind of ridiculous ethnic favoritism. And what about the fact that the Bible, which tells the tale of this favoritism, was put together by those very favorite chosen folk? Hmmm.

The concept of God as encountered in the Old and New Testaments of the Bible, has been dealt with by some of the most brilliant minds of Western civilization—philosophers, scholars, theologians. It is well established that no logical argument can prove or disprove the existence this "God," or the gods of any religion. And yet a century of accumulated research from varied psychological fields, as well as mythology, can practically be said to have proven all anthropomorphized gods to be conceptual fabrications abstracted from dimensions beyond our limited sphere of egoic consciousness, where dwell archetypal "god" quality configurations which undeniably exist. Sound reasoning of an intelligence enriched with an expansive radius of comprehension will accept this.

From what I have written in prior chapters about archetypes, etc., it should be clear I am in no way involved with nominalism when I expose the reductive traits of anthropomorphism, personification, and projection. James Hillman believes nominalism drains the soul of what he sees as meaningful psychological attributes of the above three traits, which he feels can create an intimate spiritual link between an individual and the numinous depths. I agree with Hillman to an extensive degree on this matter, and what I am attempting is not to drain or detract from, but to purify and adjust, thereby deepening such a connection. To expose the reductive shallowness and distortion of archetypal imagery which anthropomorphism and personification are highly prone to, is to rid a believer of any delusive conceptual husk surrounding manifestations of the mysterium tremendum, thus possibly igniting a revelation of deeper experience of the "holy other." The less spiritual images are shaped and reduced by anthropomorphic and personified projections, the closer we approach the bewildering radiance of the true tremendum of such powers. And the closer we willingly approach the unexpected and unknown, the more open we become to this eternal magnetism within our depths, having intimate affinity to that which unfolds the rose that knows no why, calls the birds north in the Spring, excites the chick to peck its way out of the shell, and brings the salmon up great turbulent rivers. Such instinctual, natural heralding is the explicate manifestation of a deeper implicate numinous magnetism which flows through our chakras as the root source of chi and the essence of the silently pulsing Kundalini. At this very moment it abides within each of us, lying dormant, waiting for the individual, who, with exquisite reverence, dares to awaken it.

Though the human race may, as certain sages have clarified, have a necessary place in cosmic/spiritual evolution, and an individual committed to inner growth may contact an element of the mysterium tremendum, in the final analysis the idea of divine concerned control of the human situation is a joke. Consider the random chaos of natural destruction: earthquakes, tsunamis, hurricanes, tornadoes, floods. And then we have biological epidemics. Over the past 1000 years there has been the black plague, small pox, flu, Ebola, malaria, cholera, AIDS, etc, etc, etc. If these have been brought about by divine intention, just so we don't get too comfy, to orient us toward spiritual growth, well, this just doesn't work for the majority who are too beaten down to look up. A truly omnipotent all-knowing God, with any sense of goodness and compassion at all, who supposedly understood our situation to the extent of knowing whenever a sparrow falls, or a hair is missing from an individual's head, who truly had a grasp of human suffering, would not have added so much horror and terror to his design. As things are, humans have good reason to doubt and despair. To alleviate this doubt, why would not this Judaic-Christian God, who can supposedly intervene into human history, perform a few amazing miracles even the most cynical atheist couldn't deny? Would not a "caring" God who could flood the Earth to destroy humanity be compelled to perform as great a feat, but of a more positive kind, to assure the bewildered multitudes, so that billions would not have to resort to delusion and fabrication and self-deceit in order to believe? Why is God so freely offhand with cataclysms, but like a miser with world awakening miracles? But of course, such fantastic miracles do not occur because this anthropomorphic Judaic-Christian God of Western civilization never even performed those astounding biblical miracles of the past—either beneficial, such as parting the Red Sea, or catastrophic, such as the Flood. Such tales came forth from ancient legend makers prone to Pecos Bill tall tale elaborations.

A truly compassionate God-being would realize there should be limits to how much humans have to suffer, even for some "divine" reason. Yes, like C. S. Lewis, and most Christian theologians, one can come up with exquisite rationalizations, such as the apologist idea that suffering is not only necessary but beneficial for spiritual growth. Considering all the suffering that has occurred and occurs everyday across the earth, we should all be well on our way to enlightenment. Of course, suffering can be beneficial in relation to one's spiritual journey, but that is a highly individual matter, and could never work as a general rule of any kind. Individual suffering that benefits awakening is dependent on many factors, not the least of which is the perspective from which one's suffering is understood. But to look upon the horrendous catastrophes of nature that befall humanity, plus all the man-made destructivity of war, economic deprivation, etc., that devastate the lives of millions, as necessary for spiritual growth, is extreme rationalization produced by self-deluded religiosity. We only need to gaze at the thousands of photographs taken of those suffering from war, famine, disease, all around the earth, to realize such suffering destroys body and mind far more than it induces spiritual growth.

And what of the idea that all these horrors are caused by Satan, with evil as a necessary ingredient to God's plan? Well, to accept this idea, we have to reject the belief that Satan was an angel that rebelled against God. For if he were part of God's plan, he was only doing his duty obediently. Let me just say that evil does exist, but narratives of the Big Five religions never essentially explain why without relying on oversimplified fables. As Tim Callahan and other scholars have demonstrated, Satan is a fabricated mytho-religious figure created out of biblical mistranslation, distortion of image, manipulation of ancient text, and anthropomorphic projection.

It would seem basic intellectual curiosity would lead one to question all these things, just as a natural aspect of maturing. But with the confirmed believer enwrapped in self-justified ignorance, acculturated convention and conformism, this isn't so. Thus we have hundreds of millions of Christians who believe their God not only has quite understandable reasons for creating catastrophes of all sorts, but indeed, reasons for everything that happens. According to their explanations there are no accidents, and their "Intelligently Designed" cosmic plan justifies the most insidious horrors which have ever occurred. There's something frighteningly deranged about such a belief, which so easily shrugs off much of the evil that goes on in the world because they believe God somehow had a reason to bring it about. This is one area of belief in which the self-deception inundating both the New Age movement and traditional religion merge in affinity of delusion. Both are constructed from fear of the unexplainable, the mysterious, the unknown. Yet the unexplainable, the mysterious, the unknown, are of the very realm where any Being qualifying as "God" would dwell.

In the realm of myth and symbol, of legend and religious narrative, uncertainty lurks, with the interpretation depending on era, place in history, bias, and much else. One must become adept at deciphering symbol and metaphor, both of which can be expounded upon with profoundly revealing depth, as demonstrated in such books as *Ego and Archetype*, by Edward F. Edinger,[15] and *The Tao of*

Symbols, by James N. Powell.[16] Such writings serve as a kind of anti-dote to literal biblical interpretation prone to excessive confidence, as evidenced in too many volumes of theological scholarship. We must keep in mind that though scholarly and scientific research over the past one hundred and fifty years has given us an overview of the exaltingly immense and astounding journey of humanity, it is only a peek at what tremendous shaping forces, what brew of beliefs, what play of cultural ways, means and momentum, ignited and impelled the burgeoning of egoic consciousness during those magnificent pre-historic millenniums. Though the reliable evidence we do have re-veals a fantastic tale of humanity's rise from the primal world to high civilization, it also reveals how very much more we have yet to learn, and how much we may never know. Our hominid past entails the immensity of millions of years, timeless, void of calendar or clock, with each morning an awe-filled awakening to the rising from the horizon of the great golden radiant spheric being who spread light and warmth across the land and then sank into the dark un-known each night, many of those nights storm clouded, dark and cold, others clear and brilliant with the light of the haunting queen of darkness, the moon, and diamond stars scattered in puzzling patches, to be pondered with desperate longing, groping toward ex-planation. The human mind and its blossoms — myth, religion, cul-ture — arose from intimate cave dwelling firelight tale and an intense sense of mystery. Thus we must be aware of the bewildering dream-fantasy state from which primal imaginal awakening came about, grasping that myth is much more than mere fictionalized fable. As de Santillana and von Dechend put it, "Myth is neither irresponsible fantasy nor the object of weighty psychology, or any such thing. It is 'wholly other' and requires to be looked at with open eyes."[17]

Although those seeking truth should not let themselves be mindlessly captured by any particular myth or religious belief, they should also be skeptical of a skepticism which sees religion <u>only</u> as a belief system rooted in delusion and superstition. Religious belief comes from more than just the "sleep of reason," or naïve credulity. Despite its flaws, religion possesses symbolic content that resonates with much deeper, numinous forces. Any open-minded person should have no problem accepting that the conceptual images of the gods of all ancient cultures are manifestations of the living arche-typal depths filtered and interpreted through different levels of the acculturated psyche to suit specific cultural needs. The problem comes from a tendency toward entrenchment. The war mongering jealous and predominantly masculine god Yahweh definitely influenced the laws and ambitions of the tribal culture from which He came forth, thus culture and God shaped each other in reciprocal play. But, that much of Judaism, Christianity, and Islam, in this very day and age, still worship a powerful remnant of this religio-mythical concept, elucidates just how entrenched acculturated traditional dogma can become with its pervasive influence over the multitudes. Though the ordinary educated media-drenched person's awareness of astronomy, psychology, history, etc., today, is substantially broader in scope and depth than the more confined primitive tribal awareness of our ancestors, from which Judeo-Christianity bloomed, very few modern Jews or Christians have integrated such data into their worldview so that it might throw light onto the falsehoods and fabrications of their beliefs. Thus they have not spiritually transcended the religious tribal schema established five thousand years ago in the Mediterranean-Levant area.

Within the cultural matrix from which a mytho-religious belief system is woven, each individual's awakening to horizons extending beyond the collective ambit can come about only if she/he is able to discern the true from the false. Only the person willing to question and research the roots and development of religion is capable of grasping that many religious beliefs are, to a significant degree, psychological mirages. Like a mirage of a cool oasis brought about by the dehydration of a person lost in the burning desert, religious illusions and delusions are produced and sustained by the "dehydration" brought about by insufficient spiritual substance within the cultural ambit under the sway of modernism/materialism. The thirstier a person is, the more seemingly real the mirage. The more desperate one is for religious explanations, the more zealous the belief. Conceptualization and perception are shaped by what the ego craves in its need to alleviate psychological duress. This syndrome is well validated

Consider the story of the battleship Indianapolis, torpedoed in the South Pacific just as the Second World War was ending in 1945. Of the twelve hundred sailors on board, three hundred went down with the ship, leaving nine hundred adrift on the ocean with just a few life-rafts. No call for help had gone out over their radio system, so no one in the entire world knew these hundreds of sailors were out there. They were adrift in shark infested waters. When help finally arrived five days after the ship sank there were only three hundred and fifty survivors. Five hundred and fifty had drowned or were eaten by sharks. That's an average of one hundred a day, four to five an hour, one sailor being eaten or drowning every twelve minutes. The stories of the men who were rescued made it very clear that most of those who drowned did so because they became entranced by mirages. Time and again a sailor would hallucinate a floating restaurant, or an island of beautiful women, and dive into the sea to reach these places of comfort and security. His fevered enthusiasm would resonate in the dazed minds of his comrades, thus a dozen men would swim away from the rafts to follow him, and they would all drown. Going mad from thirst and stress, the sailors would perceive and believe anything promising relief, follow anyone who had a vision of paradisiacal islands within swimming distance, or exotic cities below them at the bottom of the sea.

Perhaps this may seem a harsh analogy, but the Indianapolis story clarifies how powerful the mirage inducing tendency of the mind is. And this tendency contributes to the persuasive power unquestioned religious beliefs have over the multitudes, who are so intensely thirsty in this secularized-materialistic age of spiritual dehydration. Again, I am not denying that religion partakes to various degrees of numinous truths. Even while subject to delusion and illusion, elements of genuine spiritual wisdom do come through. But for increasing numbers of people, a religion given over to such high levels of obsolescent fabrication is simply not enough anymore.

The concept of truth, the way of truth, the pursuit of truth in all significant issues, can attain an ascendant psychic frequency which magnetizes higher dimensions of consciousness, drawing them into the sphere of one's life. Thus one can partake of a kind of "knowing" relationship with the wholly other mysterium tremendum of Being. It is written in the Sacramentum Mundi, *"God is held to be knowable, but incomprehensible."* This know-ability has nothing to do with theological-religious delusions of knowing God's "personality," what He is, what He wants, etc. We must leave such reductive spiritually immature imagery behind if we ever hope to rise to an authentic relationship with the Wholly Other source of Being.

Today's main religions came about over a developmental process of hundreds of thousands of years, from ancient firelight rituals to the pomp and ceremony of the Vatican, to the stadium crowds surrounding famous evangelists, to those multitudes of worshippers sitting in pews of churches and temples of every size across this planet—with every prayer and hymn essentially a ritualized expression of the human intimation of numinous spiritual powers. With such a potent combination of ancient and innate influences, it is not hard to see why religion still generates such powerful personal convictions. Even with many highly educated persons who do not belong to any specific church, the religious impulse, based on a deep intuitive apprehension of the reality of the mysterium tremendum, can be subtly enriching, helping to give foundational meaning to their lives. Though religion began as primitive fearful propitiation to appease higher mysterious powers and humble oneself before potentially dangerous forces in hope of avoiding harm, or of receiving blessing, or at least acknowledgement, it has endured because it is imbued with the potential to create what sages from both East and West have clarified as the individual's matrix of contact with the essence of Being. To realize this potential, believers must rid themselves of outmoded imagery mired in primitive superstition, without casting away metaphoric symbolism which resonates with fecund archetypal depths.

Many a god has been vanquished along the way, and religions have come and gone, been transformed, mutated, but the impulse beneath them all, despite secularism, humanism, materialism, demystification, etc., will never fade, though it can certainly lose connection with the truth of its spiritual essence. Today, with the widespread educational systems of the developed nations, plus the advancement of mass media all across the globe—television, movies, internet, newspapers, books and magazines—most people have some sense of how science has undermined religious concepts based on limited comprehension of the world. This has led to a prevailing presentiment of the bewildering predicament of humanity within the flow of evolution. Many beginning to grasp this predicament close their minds and seek refuge by staunchly clinging to their religiously oriented system of belief which gives them a sense of comfort and foundation amid the astonishing immensity they have glimpsed. Others will flee to extreme fundamentalist interpretations of biblical text which distorts established scientific truths based upon stringently validated facts, such as the Creationist denial of the entire process of evolution. Others, seeing enemies everywhere, will convert their religion to a coalition of political force, hoping to annihilate the threat of paradigmatic change. Flight to evade the truth of our actual existential-spiritual situation is pandemic. That there are tens of millions of people with normal intelligence who let their religious beliefs blind them to the vast amount of converging evidence validating the process of evolution, shows us clearly the vulnerability of the human mind to avoid any truth which may threaten their well constructed psychological comfort zone.

We could say the Big Five traditional religions—Judaism, Christianity, Hinduism, Buddhism, Islam—are cultural elaborations of humanity's primal relationship to ultimate spiritual powers. But the problem with these major religions becomes, how do we separate the wheat of deeper esoteric truth from the exoteric chaff of indoctrinated belief, illusions, falsehoods, fabrications, distortions? This is a very significant question, and we will explore it as well as we possibly can, for when it comes down to extensive final ground answers between the seeker and his/her religious orientation, it is up to each individual's sincerity and their "negative capability" to continue until they have found what fits the puzzle of their own unique journey. This calls for deciphering exoteric mytho-religious dogma as metaphoric significations of esoteric truths.

The human longing for reciprocal interchange with mysterious spiritual depths, hopefully with an empathic all-knowing Being, is a potent fundamental impulse, rooted in the need to have our brief bewildering existence acknowledged by some higher caring numinous authority. This impulse is an intuitive intimation of the potential resonance that can actually occur between human consciousness and transcendent/deeper dimensions of Being.

When we consider the knowledge accumulated from a century of extensive research encompassing both mysticism and anthropological studies of shamanism and religious ritual, plus abundant contemporary psychological evidence of human experience of archetypal powers, including those induced by psychedelics, our only reasonable conclusion is that the reality of living spiritual forces abiding in deeper dimensions is beyond doubt. Such numinous forces actually exist within the vast depths of our unconscious mind, and it is only logical such realities, including "godlike" configurations, should not be denied. It is exceedingly important for the wary atheistic skeptic to realize that though religious imagery constructed of the linguistic complexities of symbol and metaphor do not prove the objective existence of enigmatic spiritual forces, such images are undoubtedly abstract manifestations of the living forces pervading the human ambit. But to worship the stove of traditional religious structure is to miss the mystifying magnificence of the archetypal fire burning within. To a person opening to such archetypal imagery as a living visionary experience, the proof of such deeper spiritual powers is in the head-on confrontation. And yet we must remember, archetypal visions come forth through a subconscious process vulnerable to the unhindered imaginal impulses from which hallucinations also arise. The confrontational experience is real, but discerning what is genuine vision from what is aberrant hallucination is another matter.

The quantum/psychological border between what is objective and what is subjective is strangely ambiguous territory, and, apart from the everyday appearance of things, internal/implicate and external/explicate levels of reality are incredibly intermeshed. This is vitally necessary for the seeker to grasp when dealing with depth psychology and mystical dimensions, where confrontation with numinous archetypal powers, which certainly qualify as gods and goddesses, can occur. This borderland territory where mystics, shamans, profound poets, an occasional philosopher, many psychedelic trippers, and all too many madmen, pass to and fro, must be contemplated, grasped as far as possible, without attempting to map it, as religion unwisely does. If need be, to awaken one's soul from the somnambulism of the multitudes, this territory must be ventured into by anyone seeking further verification of the spiritual nature of existence.

It has been written that all religions are like colorful stained glass windows which are illuminated by the numinous light of Being. But over the past centuries, this "stained glass" has become encrusted with the thick dust of rigid dogma, obsolete doctrines, and ethical and moral tedium. Such a darkening has made Christianity but a deteriorating fortification against the spiritually degrading influence of scientific materialism, philosophic nihilism, and secularization. Of course, this deterioration does not imply lack of staunch faith, which can be found in abundance among believers of every religion. That televangelists can arouse the emotional fervor of an entire auditorium of many thousands, only confirms the emotive intensity of crowd mentality, not the veracity of the preachings. Some televangelists have tapped into certain psychic powers and succumb to the delusion that they have been given a gift by God. Others are just self-deceived showmen with a certain megalomaniac flair. But all of them can get thousands ecstatically enraptured, clapping, singing, shouting praise. The trouble is, such displays have no more authentic spiritual substance than what can be found in an excited crowd during a World Series home-run play, or a Super Bowl touchdown. No matter how ecstatic most religious people may become, the soul = the potential for genuine awakening, remains enchained to the sphere of lower egoic needs.

Although historically religion, as with science, has been subject to transformation, to evolving, both religion and science have always had a tendency to protect the status quo "belief grid" from sudden expansive change. Time and again, over centuries, established science refused to recognize new discoveries which would demand significant change of concept and procedure. Even Einstein was vulnerable to this syndrome. While he was working on mathematical problems relating to his theory of relativity, he came up with an algebraic formulation that was inconsistent with the prevailing belief that the universe was unchanging in time. Einstein altered his equation to fit traditional belief, adding in a "cosmological constant" which would allow for a static universe. Later, when Edwin Hubble, through his skill in astronomy, proved the universe was expanding, Einstein withdrew his "constant," calling it his greatest blunder. Such defense of the status quo in science has a tenacious history, with scientists of the seventeenth century refusing to accept the factual evidence of William Harvey and Thomas Willis, clinging instead to the outmoded writings of Aristotle and Galen concerning the flow of blood and the form of the brain. Then there were those who opposed the discoveries of Pasteur and Semmelweis in the nineteenth century. And as late as 1976, chemical engineer Dr. Langer was scoffed at when he presented his discoveries concerning polymer plastics in relation to reconstructive surgery. Many prominent scientists today wallow in fortified materialistic belief systems to protect themselves against the insights coming forth from research into the paranormal, psychedelic experiences, depth-psychology, and mystical wisdoms. It is the same with religious tradition, which is like an exceedingly heavy anchor attached to a schooner with its sails full of wind, giving the impression of moving while remaining at a standstill. Various well known Christian theologian apologists, and hundreds of lesser ones, including uncounted evangelists, pastors, ministers, priests, are as mired in protecting the status quo of religious faith as were the skeptical scientists in the above examples. Whether scientist or clergyman, it is unconscionable to let established traditional beliefs stand in the way of more expansive truth.

With the exception of Buddhism, the major religions, with their many sects and denominations, are all rooted in the concept that there is a supreme omnipotent-omniscient being, who is involved with and concerned about human fate, evoking a worshipful response from the believer, which includes obedience to divinely established laws. Even in Buddhism the concept of a Supreme Being is projected by most Buddhists onto Buddha, who is worshipped by the masses in a manner similar to the way Christ is worshipped among Christians. Lacking active disciplined commitment to follow the way of truth, they remain on a superficial exoteric level of spirituality.

A foundational adhesive of religion is a given sense of cosmic purpose, implying intrinsic meaning. Creation myths play a vital role in the unfolding of this cosmic purpose, originating from primal intimation, prior to even the most ancient conceptions of a supreme being's purposeful intention encompassing all existence. As essential elements of ancient cultures, such myths become the fundamental symbolic narratives of all religions concerning a starting point, a beginning for all that has been brought forth from nothing. They are clearly metaphoric, and it was Judeo-Christianity's momentous failing to have ever taken its myths literally. This is a fault line that must be healed in order for higher spiritual frequencies to resonate within the stultified realm of collective religion.

It is well known in psychological research that schizophrenics are very prone to literalism because their minds cannot properly deal with symbol and metaphor coherently. Such is why one should observe fundamentalists closely. Nearly two thousand years ago the ancient Greek philosopher Philo (30 AD) said no one should consider taking the biblical creation myth literally. Yet one thousand nine hundred seventy-five years after Philo, we have contemporary scientific creationists who take the Bible literally with desperate passion. If we sincerely, with open minds, contemplate all we have explored concerning the Bible, what do we have? We have a handful of genuine jewels tossed in a large basket filled with synthetic gems, beads, stones, bangles. It is an exquisite merging of mythology, legend, questionable Judaic tribal history, eclectically chosen moral writings from various cultures, and clarifications and delusions of prophets and visionaries. But is it the "Book of Books" containing the direct word of the creator of the universe? Definitely not. And yet, if we use esoteric interpretations of religious symbolism within biblical text as P. D. Ouspensky and Maurice Nicoll elucidated, we can catch sparks from deeper realms of the mysterium tremendum burning within its pages, golden flaming needles of Sophianic wisdom within the immense haystack of ancient Hebrew writings. There is an archetypal power resonating through biblical symbolism, along with those of the great books of Hinduism and Buddhism, which, if deciphered rightly, can become conduits of communicative interplay with higher realms of being. But this is rarely accomplished within the zone of orthodox religious belief.

Transcending religious literalism in order to reveal deeper symbolic meanings is hardly an easy transition. As we have pointed out, literal interpretations of religious belief systems are of such a foundational stability for human beings to base the meaning of their lives upon that they will both consciously and subconsciously build barriers against any truths which may threaten that foundation. There are religious organizations in operation that refuse to accept the most validated research and even proven facts. Scholars at Technion University in Israel, (better known as Bias U), have convinced themselves that extremely questionable conclusions from computer research prove that Moses was God's sole authorized instrument in the writings of the biblical books of Moses. This is a clear example of how people who strongly believe in something will not only deny irrefutable evidence which threatens their belief, but will shape the very research they are involved with to fit their needs. Such scholars, like all zealous believers, have no idea what the concept of open-mindedness means. Any intelligent person open to truth, no matter how disturbing it is, will find substantial enough information to realize the Bible is not an infallible book produced by divine intervention, but the work of spiritual inspiration and human creativeness permeated and distorted to a large extent from centuries of ethnocentric and political manipulation by Church authorities. And though, once again, the Bible does have significant elements of Sophianic wisdom flowing through various narratives, and certain scholars have shown that biblical text can be read as philosophy to a rewarding extent, it is so weighted with centuries of literal interpretation that, for some, to separate jewels of esoteric wisdom from dogma and delusion may not be worth the expenditure of energy — an expenditure that could be put more rewardingly into reading the works of our sages, such as Jung, Aurobindo, or D. T. Suzuki, or others who tap into the deeper Sophianic wisdom stream of "satya," without the obstacles biblical text is prone to.

We would be foolish not to admit our major religions as they are conceived today will be looked upon 7000 years from now as we look upon religions of 5000 BC. If we were to condense the time spectrum of five billion years of life evolving on earth into a twenty-four hour scale, humanity, from the first hominid to now, has only existed for the last two minutes—and civilization, beginning with the Sumerians 4500 BC, through Greece and the Roman Empire, to this very day, has only existed for the last couple of seconds. According to this scale, humans will probably exist at least ten more minutes, maybe an hour at the most, before the sun burns out. The religious concepts of modern humans are still in the very early stages of what they will become. The Big Five religions of today have come from millenniums of bowing to mountains and sacrificing to clay idols up through the magnificent fervency of ancient Egyptian rituals, to the pomp and ceremonious ordination of Popes and Dali Lamas—all this within only three seconds on our time scale. Surely then, we must recognize religion as an evolving psychological edifice that has not yet reached its stage of completion, if it ever does.

Every Christian, Jew, Muslim, Hindu, has to pause and ask, *"What good is my faith, if, as with all other religions, it consists to an extensive degree of a delusive mirage shaped by ignorance of both the world at large and elaborated fabrications of what we actually are as spiritual beings?"* The potential to transcend and transform is the "good" of religious faith. The ability to transform blind unquestioning and therefore superficial belief into a deeper transcendent quality of faith, removes the exoteric husk from established religion, exposing esoteric kernels of truth. And let no one doubt—those kernels are there. Orthodox religious tradition at this point in time is similar to a beautiful garden as the first signs of winter appear. Plants once past their peak of blossoming are drying up, becoming inundated with weeds. The seeker must be a spiritual gardener, alone with the seeds of spiritual intuition, preparing the ground in which to plant them by disciplined commitment to various yoga techniques, and, if need be, careful ritualized shamanistic exploration.

We may now ask, is the belief in the biblical story of Yahweh/Jehovah as the supreme creator and sustainer of all existence, a justified belief? From all converging evidence gathered from every pertinent field of scientific exploration and centuries of clarifications from philosophy and mysticism, the answer is a resounding NO. Nor can any other religion justify this claim for their God. To be rid of archaic religious imagery lingering in the human mind, we must clear the slate with one satori sweep of intuitive intelligence and thus free ourselves to set out for symbols and metaphors that transcend the established Big Five religions, while eclectically integrating their unquestionable truths, leaving all the frills and fabrications behind.

Only the person who is open to questioning her/his existence from within is open to authentic truth. And such truth permeates all dimensions. Thus again we speak of "sat," or "satya," the truth force. Nicolas Berdyaev expressed it this way:

> *Truth is spiritual, it is in the spirit, it is the victory of spirit over the non-spiritual objectivity of the world, the world of things. Spirit is not an epiphenomenon of anything; everything is the epiphenomenon of spirit. Truth is the awakening of the spirit in man; it is communion with spirit.*[18]

All who are truly involved with spiritual individuation will eventually leave both traditional and New Age religious trappings behind and immerse themselves in the esoteric meanings of knowledges they glean in various ways from their daily surroundings—people and books eclectically chosen, disciplines consistently performed, perhaps even rituals and explorations boldly ventured through the use of plants and fungi personally grown and harvested. Though one may at first feel isolated, cut off from the warmth of the starry eyed gatherings around "spiritual" leaders, this shall be replaced by moments of exquisite ecstasy awaiting those who work alone yet shoulder to shoulder with known and unknown companions of the past and present, who have traveled the pathless way. The traveler will come to understand enlightenment and endarkenment have a reciprocal yin and yang harmony within the swirl of existence. It is only those who have struggled through the lonely "dark night of the soul," experienced the fear and trembling of confrontation with deep doubt, with evil and the demonic, who will realize what Nikolas Berdyaev called the "terrifying radiance" of spiritual reality, and feel deeply graced.

14 – Esoteric Resurrection

*To me, Christ remains a
significant and problematical entity.*
—Goethe

*Come and eat my bread
Drink the wine I have prepared!*
—Prov. 9:5

After pondering the Yahweh dominated aspects of the Old Testament, let us consider its stepchild, the New Testament, thus Christianity. Though still intimately connected with Judaism at the root level, Christianity is a narrative extension, a branching off, a birthing of a unique blossom, which, after 2000 years, is in need of deep transformation, renovation, innovation, founded on far more expansive knowledge.

Just as we have photos of the earth taken far out in space giving us a view of our planet that was much harder to grasp prior to the first moon landing, from accumulated research throughout the 20th century we now have an overview of the time, place and culture from which Christianity came forth, revealing far more than all the theologians, Popes, preachers, prophets, scholars, of previous centuries had any inkling of. Plus there is all that has been brought to light through scholarly research relating to translation, textual interpretation, and religious history, which we explored in the last chapter. When we consider the enormous body of such criticism and discovery, which essentially undermines the so-called infallibility of biblical narrative, it seems astounding that hundreds of millions of Christians all across the earth unquestioningly take the biblical story of creation, of God, of Christ, as their guide of faith. Approximately 60% of Americans actually believe the story of Adam and Eve is factually true. This should not surprise anyone familiar with the psychological knowledge the previous chapters have covered. Once we understand the condition of the collective consciousness of the masses, the power of acculturation and conformism, and the craving for simple explanations, we must accept that such widespread self-imposed ignorance in relation to religious belief is practically an innate aspect of the human condition. Such reductive faith in the exoteric literal interpretation of the New Testament severs it from its esoteric roots, thus becoming subject to distortion and politicized misuse. Let us attempt to overcome this, which, rather than undermining the truth of Christ, is like clearing centuries of muck off a great work of art, revealing its essential beauty and meaning.

Our attempt to deepen our knowledge of Christianity by probing into mytho-religious symbolism is underscored by the Sophianic wisdom which clarifies that the quality of an opinion is dependent on the depth and scope of worldly and spiritual knowledge it is rooted in. Deep firm roots are what separate genuine knowledge from mere opinion. In order to support myself along the way, I have done all sorts of work, from the hardest labor to various business ventures, always living a very frugal lifestyle—low rent and basic nourishing foods—thus less work and more time for quality creative pursuits. I once put together a small janitorial business where I was custodian to almost a dozen Christian churches. Although I usually worked late at night, avoiding their hours of activity, over a period of months I came to know various ministers and pastors, each representing a different denomination. It soon became quite clear their opinions of who and what Jesus Christ was all about had very shallow roots, confined strictly to Bible College indoctrination and reading matter strictly limited to Christian book store publications of the most fundamentalistic sort, or just a few degrees broader. In fact, though each of their offices had large full bookshelves, some containing a few works of significant theologians, it was clear such authors were hardly ever read, especially those of any depth, such as Hans Küng or Paul Tillich. This has been confirmed by various astute researchers, verifying the mental myopia of the majority of Christian pastors, priests, ministers, exposing them as people possessing little knowledge of significant theological, psychological, philosophical, or scientific writing. The intensity of the faith of many clergymen seems to be inversely proportional to their knowledge of themselves and the world around them. For anyone who can see deeper than the antics and pretenses of the personality, our dapper televangelists are blatant examples of significant ignorance hiding behind a mask of knowing certitude. I once listened to Dr. Bob Jones on television, President of (wouldn't you know it) Bob Jones University. He palpably validated this "confident ignorance" syndrome. And Jones is representative of all too many Christian spokespersons, such as John Hagee, John MacArthur, Larry Huch, every one of them avid at seeing the mote of "unChristian" behavior in the eyes of all who in any way criticize their faith, while remaining blind to the huge log of spiritual shallowness, vanity and hypocrisy in their own.

Writing of such radio and television evangelists, Charles Davis, in his insightful book, *Temptations of Religion*, states,

> *In listening occasionally to these programs...I feel repulsion, mixed with fascination. The overwhelming certitude has an almost physical effect on me. The convictions are expressed fluently and skillfully, but with the onward rush of a one-track mind. The emotional strength of the certitude reveals the pressure of repressed doubt.*[1]

Though profound spiritual contemplators, such as C. G. Jung, Sri Aurobindo, and the Dalai Lama, have recognized that, for a society at large, a religious orientation to traditional images is a necessary and stabilizing element, such stabilization, as most Christians demonstrate, all too often becomes a collective deadening of spirit. To discern what is needed for a religious quality of psychological stability which doesn't lead to politicized religion and spiritual petrifaction, is an individual responsibility. Let us accept this responsibility in exploring what we should definitely be aware of.

Among Christian theologians there have been two significant perceptions concerning the Jesus of history and/or the Christ of faith: (a) Jesus as fully human but exquisitely imbued with the spirit of God, attaining the power of resurrection; (b) the messianic Christ as God descending into human form, known as the Homoousia = God and Christ as one. These two essential perceptions of the Jesus-Christ figure have been wrangled about for centuries. There is another, more esoteric perspective, which we can approach by considering the Jungian living Christ archetype of spiritual soul-essence abiding in everyone. When thoroughly contemplated we see these three perspectives essentially intertwine through the mythoform-essence of the Christian belief system. Jacques Derrida's idea of "undecidability," which demonstrates certain realities cannot be fixed and confined to a binary "either this or that," is helpful here. It is as we saw with the wave-particle phenomenon, which surpasses the bounds of "either/or." Thus I will not make any strict attempt at segregation when it comes to the spiritual phenomenon of Jesus-Christ, but will flow with the subject matter to an extent sufficient for the purpose of this book, and for the individual striving to awaken to a greater "radius of comprehension"—and by that I do not mean a more extensive certitude of the traditional narrative of the Jesus figure, which has contributed to the shallowing of the teachings of Christ. Certitude within the religious matrix of belief usually denotes biased rigidity and lack of genuine comprehension of anything other than dogmatized versions of faith. We must strive to separate the fool's gold of socialized religious illusion and delusion from the true gold of mytho-symbolic alchemy. Again, keep in mind we are dealing with living mythological-archetypal realities, not just interesting fables, folk tales, religious legends. Mythopsychic tales of creation, the death and rebirth of gods and goddesses, the egoic awakening from the chthonic night, give us glimpses of the seething mulch of forces and powers from which our very minds—unconscious, subconscious, conscious—have come forth. Christian sects within Western culture have become like bubbles of foam in a great storm tossed ocean, blind to everything beyond their tiny secure sphere of exoteric belief, blind to the fact of being intimately, intrinsically a portion of that very ocean's turbulent immensity.

In order to rid ourselves of antiquated dogma and fabrication without unnecessary diminishment of the numinous quality of myth, we have to move beyond common theological considerations of what faith is. If the New Testament has any meaningful numinous quality, this can only be perceived when it is read as a mytho-mysterium narrative rich in esoteric symbolism. The historical aspects of the Christ/death-rebirth narrative reduced to exoteric literalism is a spiritual deterioration of the mytho-esoteric truth the life of Christ is imbued with.

Following fifteen hundred years of almost total rule, Christianity in its institutionalized form of the Catholic Church began to be undermined as the be-all/end-all of belief between 1500 and 1700, during the era of sweeping changes, including the Renaissance, the

Reformation, the discovery of the New World, the French Revolution, and all those subtle expansive changes which lie below the limited revelations of recorded history. Such changes propagated widespread awakening to broader considerations of what the human situation is all about. The expanding knowledge instigated by men of scientific curiosity and early global explorers, as well as the fragmentation that occurred within the Church due to the actions of Martin Luther, displaced the Vatican as a centered source of religious authority dispensing its power of psychological domination. And yet this fragmentation did not abate anti-science vindictiveness perpetrated by significant Church figures down through history who were zealously opposed to scientific study of the universe, sometimes imprisoning and even burning alive various prominent thinkers. Even Luther, agreeing with the Vatican, spewed righteous wrath upon the scientific contemplations of Copernicus, calling him an upstart astrologer and fool. Despite such religious defensiveness, over the following centuries, with the amplification of science and technological sophistication during the 1800's, criticism of religion expanded. The coming of Darwin, Freud, Einstein, as 1900 approached, plus the growth of knowledge in anthropology, archeology, paleontology, geology, etc., ignited the strongest wave of doubt concerning religious belief that civilization had ever known. As a result, varied scholars began investigating the validity of the historical Jesus.

Although countless books about the life of Jesus have been published, we really know very little about him. Hugh Anderson, Professor of New Testament language and theology at the University of Edinburgh, put it this way,

> *The fact is that we know nothing or next to nothing of Jesus' history for the first thirty years of his life. The materials are insufficient for anything like a biography of Jesus, either in regard to the inward development of his personality or to the outward course of events in chronological sequence. Pious, and sometimes not so pious, imagination has, to be sure, often tried to fill in the gaps, but the impressionistic pictures painted by imagination are no substitute for genuine historical reconstruction.*[2]

The shards of historical documentation by several Roman recorders mention Jesus as just another religious figure of no real account. Some scholars have even claimed the existence of Jesus of the Gospel is doubtful. Yet we know Pontius Pilate was Governor of Judea 27 AD through 36 AD, and early commentators such as Tacitus wrote of a person called Jesus being handed over to Pilate. The Roman historian Suetonius wrote about riots inspired by a person called "Chreestus." It is a sure thing that Christians did exist, and they had come together as followers of a person they called Christ. Concerning the subject of Jesus Christ, and the New Testament as a whole, I will strive to stay with what tangible scientific and scholarly research has revealed, while remaining open to the numinous quality of myth and its intriguing relationship to creative imagination and archetypal realities.

The New Testament did not come forth from quite as extensive and tumultuous a journey as the Old Testament, which evolved through at least a thousand years of the rise and fall of empires, incorporating myriad butterfly-effect changes in oral narrative, some surviving, some not surviving century upon century of nomadic wandering, war, conquering, defeat, settlement, dispersion. Still, the Gospels in the form we have them today went through their own significant transitions and alterations. The gradual gathering of tale and text occurred during tremendously fervent cultural transitions ranging from approximately 20 to 170 AD, until the 27 books which form the New Testament were finally chosen over 300 years after the Crucifixion of Jesus. Myriad sayings attributed to Jesus that were set aside for various reasons were designated as the Agrapha.

During this era Jerusalem had already been conquered and the Israelites cast into final dispersion in 73 AD. Within this cultural turmoil the stories, tales, legends, concerning Jesus had come forth from many directions and influences. One of the popular myths of the Mediterranean-Levant area during those times had to do with Dionysus, who was the son of the all powerful Greek god Zeus. Dionysus had been born as a result of a mortal woman, a virgin, being impregnated by Zeus. The scholar Arthur Evans wrote about the considerable impact the myth of Dionysus, worshipped for centuries prior to Jesus, had on early Christian ideas.[3] This was also true of the sun god Mithra, seen as beneficent and good. Influence from the Roman army, which controlled all the area the early Christians inhabited, was substantial, for many soldiers as well as civilians worshipped Mithra. As the Encarta Encyclopedia states:

Mithraism was similar to Christianity in many respects, for ex-

ample, in the ideals of humility and brotherly love, baptism, the rite of communion, the use of holy water, the adoration of the shepherds at Mithra's birth, the adoption of Sundays and of December 25 (Mithra's birthday) as holy days, and the belief in the immortality of the soul, the last judgment, and the resurrection.

Changes in the hand copied writings which were to become the New Testament "Holy Scriptures" occurred again and again over the first three centuries AD—what we could call editorial adjustments controlled by early church officials, plus minute changes, some with significant import, instigated by zealot reformers, perhaps even accidental mishaps and mistranslations by weary scribes. All of this was affected by the sway of intrigues among those first organizers of the Gospels, as well as the varying psychic disposition of the multitudes. Even when the Gospels were finally organized to suit the church's desired narrative of Jesus Christ, they were not immune to conflicting viewpoints eventually arising over the centuries from both within and outside the established church hierarchy, which resulted in such modifications and "corrections" as those ordered by the Emperor Anastasius in 506 AD, because he believed Mark, Matthew, Luke, and John were undependable and unqualified. And, of course, there were Luther's intrepid changes in text in 1522. Even with text not changed, through eras of great crusades, inquisitions, plagues, religious wars, powerful theological figures such as the French theologian Abelard in the Middle Ages, Archbishop Anselm circa 1100 AD, and John Calvin in the 16th century, to name just a few, influenced how the text would be interpreted. So we see the New Testament did not come forth untainted. It is the work of fallible humans with biased intentions. This is why most biblical scholars today agree with Tim Callahan, author of Secret Origins of the Bible, who clarifies why there are significant drawbacks to accepting the Gospels as written by reliable witnesses.[4]

What we do have relating to a powerful spiritual teacher circa 6 BC to 36 AD, is significantly intriguing. Scholars researching the Dead Sea Scrolls became aware that a person known as the "Teacher of Righteousness" existed during the era in which Jesus lived, who most likely had intimate contact with what was known as the Essene community—a brotherhood of ascetics living a very strict and extremely righteous monastic life. The Essenes seem to have been much too condescending and judgmental toward sinners to have produced the Jesus of the Gospels. Then again, maybe that is why a person like Jesus would eventually have left after having spent some time there. We just don't know. Actually, we don't even have any substantial knowledge of the exact date when Jesus was born. It certainly wasn't December 25. In those ancient times various emperors were prone to change the calendar to suit their vanity, such as having months named after them—August for Caesar Augustus, July for Julius Caesar— and certain calendars in those ancient times had August as the first month of the year and July as the last. The church most likely adopted the pagan solstice holiday for Mithra celebrated on December 25, as the day Christ was born, to make it more appealing to the collective mentality. The church was skilled in transforming sacred pagan ceremonial grounds into Christian church sites.

We do know the state of Galilee, where it is said Jesus was born in the village of Nazareth, was located near the bustling coastal crossroads of trade between Greece, Rome and Egypt. The warrior king Alexander the Great had conquered the area encompassing Jerusalem in 330 BC, and the Roman Empire conquered all Judea in 67 BC. Thus Greco-Roman influence suffused the cultural atmosphere when Jesus was born. In Greece, this was a period still heavily influenced by Hellenism, a time of fervent movements in trade and marketing, innovation in engineering, discovery in science, astronomy, mathematics, and the building of great libraries. Writings from the Upanishads, Buddhist text, dialogues of Socrates, Plato, Confucius, Zoroaster, and plays of Euripides and Aristophanes, enhanced the intellectual atmosphere. Nomad scholars came and went from India and Greece, many passing through Palestine, which had a population close to 600,000 circa 10 BC to 30 AD. The city of Stepphoris, three miles from Nazareth, was abundant with the arts and theatre. This fervency of cultural discourse and blossoming of new knowledges was the environment surrounding the boy Jesus, as well as many of those that were to eventually be involved in writing the New Testament.

Herod, the governor of Galilee circa 47 BC, had been a friend of Julius Caesar and a cousin of Mark Antony, and also had a comradely relationship with Augustus Caesar, who was emperor of Rome during the era of Jesus' birth. Cleopatra, history's famous female Egyptian ruler, had conceived a child by Julius Caesar in 46 BC. Years later, after Caesar was assassinated and her lover Mark Antony, by whom she had three children, was defeated, both Cleopatra and Mark Antony committed suicide, which was followed by the murder of Caesar's child, though her other three children were spared. Such were the politics and passions of power in those days.

Because of the Greco-Roman influence, many Galileans spoke Greek. Within a few days travel from Nazareth, one could come upon shrines for gods and goddesses of Greek, Persian, Roman and Egyptian belief systems. Archeologists have identified over eighty temples from that era. Many were vegetation gods who followed a perennial death and rebirth process with the seasons, such as Osiris, Tammuz, Adonis, Attis, Dionysus. The myth of Prometheus, who had been "crucified" as a consequence of bringing the gift of fire to humanity, had been folk lore for 2000 years when Jesus was a child. Various tribal people from Northern Europe made their way to Rome as traders or slaves, with tales of Odin who had been hung upon an ancient ash tree and wounded with a spear. They also told of the god Balder, who died each autumn of the year, to be reborn as spring came over the harsh winter landscape. Such tales would most likely have reached the busy crossroads of Judea.

Ascetics from as far away as India wandered the land, mystery cults and miracle workers were everywhere. There were numerous tales in circulation of those who could raise the dead and cast out evil spirits. Apollonius of Tyana was said to have such ability. In the pagan world where Jesus as a young man roamed ensconced in his Hebraic faith, various gods disguised as people were said to be everywhere, as silent invisible observers and potential exposers of human wrong doing, like undercover agents of morality. Such gods knew when you were sleeping, knew when you were awake, they knew when you'd been bad or good, so every citizen had better be good for goodness sake. In his work *Satyricon*, the ancient Greek author Petronius said many people thought there were more gods than humans walking about.[5] This could be called a kind of polytheistic omniscience. Thus we see here validation of the innate human need for moral conscience, preferably overwatched by a guiding authority of a superior nature. This was most certainly an aspect of the craving for a Messiah sent by the highest God to straighten everything out, right all wrongs, and guide humanity forever after in some earthly paradise.

Myth and legend throughout the entire Greco-Roman empire told of gods impregnating women who gave birth to godlike men. The very gods who were the mytho-historical founders of Rome—

Romulus and Remus—were born from their mother Rea Silvia, who was a virgin impregnated by Mars, the God of war. Thus, at the time the tale of the birth of Jesus came forth, to be a godlike being born of a woman impregnated by a god was nothing new or outstanding for most of the pagan world. Such legends were intrinsically enmeshed in Near East cultural myth, such as the story of Isis and Osiris, which William Irwin Thompson calls an overture to the Mary and Jesus narrative.

Biblical researchers thoroughly delving into the earliest gospel writings relating to Jesus Christ noticed certain elements which stood out in quality, which they organized into what was to become known as the "Lost Gospel," or the "Book of Q," which are the sayings of a person called Jesus—"lord-savior"—written not only prior to the orthodox New Testament, into which portions were later inserted, but prior to the date of the Crucifixion. In ancient text the title of "savior" didn't necessarily mean being the biblical Messiah. The Jesus of "Q" and the Jesus of the New Testament are related by the fact that most of the New Testament writings attributed to Jesus are derived from Q text. Yet followers of the Jesus written of in Q did not consider themselves Christians, for no one called the "Christ" had yet been spoken of. But even here there is more discrimination to be made, for, just like the canonical Gospels, only a fraction of sayings attributed to Jesus in Q can actually be connected to him. Add all this together with other research and it is indisputable that the Gospels of the New Testament have proven to be a very questionable source as to what actually occurred concerning the life and death of Jesus, and what he actually said.

The gospel narrative most Christians believe to be the story of Jesus is a collection of meager historical facts skillfully merged with elements derived from mythological-religious beliefs of both Judaic tradition and various cultures of the Mediterranean-Levant area, igniting a tale that evolved through elaboration of various writers for decades following the Crucifixion of Jesus. After over a century of wrangling, those chosen for the authorized version, called the "synoptic Gospels," were said to have been first written down by Mark, to be followed by the stories of other questionable authors— Mathew, Luke and John, whose names are the result of second century guess work. Whatever their names actually were, the writers of the four authorized canonical Gospels were not scholars or historians striving to record facts with rigorous accuracy. All four writers were dedicated believers attempting to persuade others about the glory and wonders of their faith, and like all such undoubting believers down through the ages, did not shy away from stretching and even fabricating the facts. During the first one hundred and fifty years following the Crucifixion, much of the writing concerning the activities of Jesus was found by even early church authorities to be fraudulent. Some of these were claimed to be letters written by Jesus himself, or the Virgin Mary.

As various biblical scholars have clearly shown, whoever the writer using the name of Mark was, he clearly copied from the Old Testament and book of Q, fitting what was needed into his own narrative purpose. Along came Matthew who then used Mark and the Gospel of Q to suit his own theological intentions, to be followed by Luke and John in a similar manner. So what we have are not four separate Gospels by four separate "witnesses," but somewhat plagiaristic copies of copies with variations and additions. Recent research verifies a large portion of the New Testament to be a hodgepodge of Old Testament paraphrases, and many statements attributed to Jesus are quotes from the lost Q Gospel. As to letters attributed to St. Paul, they have only a thirty percent possibility of being his—all the others were created by unknown writers with their own theological agendas. Biblical scholars state that only fifteen percent of the words attributed to the historical Jesus (who ever he was) could actually be his. Those who wrote the other 85% may have been newly converted rabbis, or any of the early Christians with scribal abilities. We don't know.

Like most intelligent people of that turbulent age of interactive multi-cultural influence circa 20 – 90 AD, Gospel biographers of Jesus were apparently aware of the ancient Hellenistic mystery cults, with their dying and rebirthing gods, and they probably had inklings of the works of Aristotle, Plato, and a variety of teachings from India. Whoever they were, they had a fair understanding of how an enlightened being of overwhelming compassion and wisdom would act and speak, and even possibly may have had acquaintance with such beings themselves, such as wandering Siddhas, sage rabbis, priests of Mithra and Dionysus, and/or they had the talent of a writer of fiction reinforced by the enthusiasm of inventive theologians concentrating on perpetrating their belief system.

As the insightful work by Bart D. Ehrman, *Lost Scriptures*, clearly verifies,₆ before the New Testament was organized into a cohesive form, there were dozens upon dozens of gospels going around during the first century and a half following the Crucifixion, many even written after the canon Gospels were gathered together.₈ Most were of course highly embellished, with an almost Pecos Bill "tall tale" quality amplifying the powers and miracles of Jesus, which the church leaders, who eclectically chose the canon synoptic Gospels, were usually wise enough to put aside.

Whatever or however, putting the New Testament together was undoubtedly a highly eclectic process, accomplished by early church authorities choosing ancient wisdom sources from an array of writings concerning Jesus which were circulated for the first two centuries following the Crucifixion. Still, there comes a point in anyone's sincere research into the New Testament Gospels when it can no longer be denied that the "gospel truth" is neither the whole truth, nor what literally occurred. And yet the narrative of Jesus Christ does resonate with archetypal power, partaking of relevant mythospiritual truths of an esoteric quality, which we can grasp if we decipher the symbolism rightly.

Unfortunately, most theological speculation does not rise to the level of "deciphering the symbolism rightly." Consider, for example, the theological "theories" of spiritual victories concerning the Crucifixion of Christ:

1. The Ransom theory = Christ's Crucifixion ransomed us from evil.

Ransomed who? Who is us? Just Christians? That's prejudice imbued with Christian bias and condescension toward other religions, whose followers make up two-thirds of the population of the earth. If we just consider the Christians of the world, more have been snared and entangled in the meshes of evil over the past 2000 years than prior to the Crucifixion; enough to make any ransom paid to be as futile as parents paying a kidnapper and still having their child murdered.

2. The Victory Theory = Christ's Crucifixion vanquished evil.

This is even more erroneous than theory number one. The past two hundred years alone have shown that evil is not only not vanquished, but has wreaked more havoc and suffering than all prior centuries, and continues to do so.

3. The theory that the Crucifixion satisfied God's desire for the punishment of Adam's sin.

Here we have to consider the vengeful Calvinistic concept of a punishment freak Jehovah, who righteously casts any of His creation that bumble His codes of conduct into Hell — not only punishing the first bumbler, but the poor bumbler's children and their children, and their children's children, unendingly. Considering the failure of theories one and two, apparently, despite the Crucifixion, old Jehovah isn't satisfied yet.

By any clear minded standards, these "victories" are indeed Pyrrhic.

The bias of such theological theorizing prevents the staunch traditional believer from ever gleaning insight from open dialogue or debate. Those of faith who do occasionally let their intellect roam a bit in the fields of knowledge, often come to the same conclusion as that of a priest who wrote to me,

I have dealt with doubt over the years, believe me, which I have always overcome, because some of the greatest thinkers in history such as Augustine and Aquinas, have acknowledged the validity of Christian belief, and this has given me the confidence that my faith is based on more than just my own meager opinion.

We must consider those he calls great thinkers of history. Whose history? Obviously, the history of the conquering religion, and thus the organized church—Christian civilization's "history of choice." Augustine and Aquinas were brilliant in many ways within their sphere of belief, occasionally tapping into the Sophianic wisdom stream of thought, but they were not enlightened sages. Both succumbed at times to anti-Semitism and anti-feminism, and were justifiers of holy wars. Their works helped sow of the seeds of the Inquisition. Both were as vengeful as Calvin in their righteous condemnation of their fellow man. All three revealed their repressed shadow as they gleefully damned so called sinners to torture in hell, believing those saved could enjoy looking down at the suffering of the sinners. Augustine's own fantasies shaped his concepts of humanity's relationship with God, divine judgment, predestination, heaven, and much else. He was a zealous theologian in a powerful position, which would influence the way Christians think about their beliefs to this day. His grand illusion of the "City of God" was his own passionate dream, having little to do with biblical text. At least Aquinas realized just before he died that the religious concepts elucidated in his voluminous work, *Summa Theologica*, were but vain particles of dust in the immense numinous wind, when he cried out, "It is all rubbish!... Everything I've written seems like empty straw..."7 If such "great" religious thinkers were so fallible to delusion and prejudice, why should their writings give anyone confidence of faith? And what of the myopic weltanschauung of the typical theologian or evangelist today? Their opinions are even less dependable. They skillfully articulate the argument that Christ is literally the exclusive son of God, if not God himself, which has been clearly demonstrated to be exceedingly questionable and insufficiently dependable as truth. Such theological theorizing is shallow in knowledge of myth, history, archeology, and religious ideas, and more. What the priest should have used to test his faith are the works of Christian mystics and sages, such as Meister Eckhart, Jacob Boehme, and Carl Jung, which take us beyond the exoteric box of tradition.

We've got thousands of theologians mired in literalism and bias, spouting their limited interpretations of God and the Bible to crowds just as gullible as those Voltaire called the "credulous rabble" three hundred years ago. Not that the other four of the Big Five religions don't have their mouthpieces to convince everyone their way is THE way. Judaism, Islam, Buddhism, Hinduism, Chistianity, together create an immense hermeneutic absurdity of vast scope, a chaotic mind collage of abstract concepts, delusions, distortions and embellishment mixed with genuine vision and meaningful myth. The only saving grace, and I cannot stress this too often, is the stream of Sophianic wisdom, clear and pure, flowing through the flotsam and jetsam of it all, which, if we are careful, attentive, sincere, meticulously eclectic and persevering, we can partake of. But first we must put aside what mires us on the superficial plane of orthodox traditional imagery and explanation.

Tim Callahan writes of the name "Jesus" being the Latinized version of "Jeshua," which means "Yahweh is salvation."8 Another variation is that the name "Jesus" came from the Aramaic word "Yeshua," meaning "the Lord saves," or "savior." Perhaps the use of "Lord Savior" was the result of the early writers of the Gospels naming their protagonist metaphorically, with the name "Jesus-Christ" being used the way the poet Dante used the names of his characters as personified abstractions, such as "Love" and "Fate." John Bunyan used this technique in Pilgrim's Progress, naming his characters "Charity," and "Hope," etc.9

It is known that Jesus would have spoken in the language of a Western Galilean vernacular of Aramaic, with inflections of certain words used in a different way than the Aramaic spoken in the Southern and Northern areas of Palestine. In other words, there were idiomatic phrases and expressions of Aramaic spoken in a certain geographical area which would have meant entirely something else in another area. Thus for various dialects of ancient Aramaic to be translated through Hebrew and then Greek was a task indeed, not to mention later translations into Latin and finally over centuries into medieval English, then later into the King's English, of which modern English is a derivative. Considering what we have dealt with concerning the precarious art of translation, it should be clear there is a high chance for fallibility when it comes to what any "original" narrative of the life of Jesus could have actually meant. We do know words from the Old Testament said to have been spoken by Christ while he was crucified are clearly later insertions into the New Testament. Of course, some would claim Christ was reciting Psalm 22 in his agony, but it's more complex. Consider Mark 15:34, *"And at the ninth hour Jesus cried with a loud voice, saying, Eloi, Eloi, lama sabachthani?"* —which is being interpreted as *"My God, my God, why hast thou forsaken me?"* But modern scholars interpreting these Aramaic words get, *"O Sustainer! O Sustainer! For this I have been kept!"* — which is quite different from an expression of being forsaken. And this is just one example of many which have profound implications

Though religion has a strong tendency to crystallize mythos, which has led to distortion and spiritual stultification, mythos has a way of finding conduits of release into the collective psyche. Consider the vibrancy of the religio-mythology of ancient Mithraism. Mithra was a beneficent god-being of light and wisdom in whose honor a sacrificial bull was slain between symbols of polarity, with no dependence on resurrection of a physical nature, creating a significant resonance within a spiritual center beyond the sway of opposites. When pondering the Christian mytho-religious narrative of

Jesus being crucified between two thieves, one supposedly saved and the other not, we must free ourselves from the warped crystallization of literalized tradition, opening ourselves to broader perspectives and approaches. The mytho-religious symbol of Christ is, both psychologically and spiritually, deeper than biblical history reveals.

The word "Christ" itself is a Greek translation of the Hebrew word "Messiah," which means "the anointed one." The Teacher of Righteousness, possibly being a religious leader of the Essene community of ascetics, thus an anointed one, could have been addressed as Jesus Christ. And later, after departing from the Essene community as a self-reliant Siddha-rabbi missionary, a few over enthused followers could have begun looking upon this Jesus person as the prophesized Messiah of Hebrew scripture. Who knows—even the best of scholars differ on these matters. The thing is, in those ancient times of extreme religious ferment, there were numerous tales of resurrections, Messiahs, gurus, avatars, all about the Mediterranean-Levant area, from Alexandria to the Caspian Sea, from Rome to the Red Sea, and surrounding terrirory.

In the Bible, Acts 11.26, we read, *"It was in Antioch that the pupils were first called Christians."* For the first seventy years following the Crucifixion the not yet named "Christians" had attended synagogues to worship within the fold of the Hebrew faith just as their parents and forefathers had. It was not until the Romans set out to destroy Judea, and the Jews revolted, that the unmilitant Jewish sect who believed Christ was the Hebrew Messiah refused to partake in the violence against Roman soldiers, and from then on the Jews saw them as no longer a part of their religion.

Early Jewish converts to Christianity did not give up Judaism, for they thought Christ was the Messiah of their own Judaic tradition, whose voluntary crucifixion was a show of sacrificial concern for the faithful, which their fellow Jews simply could not recognize. There was, as with most new movements, an exciting freshness among the early followers of Christ, which had a lot to do with seeking new pasture for religious needs which traditional Judaism could not fulfill—sort of like young Christians today going off to New Age groups, or ashrams in India, or Zen temples, or joining Hari Krishna chanters, or any cults that have a certain uniqueness about them. With those first early Christians there was most likely an openness of lifestyle and communal interrelationship and challenge, thus a sense of joyful camaraderie younger Jews felt their somewhat inbred law-ridden Judaic faith lacked. As for the gentiles of Judea who became converts to the Christian faith, most had been raised within pagan religions offering traditional mythic interpretations of gods who harbored little concern for the actualities of the real world. But with Christianity, here was a manifestation of God who had walked among them quite recently as a figure related to their cultural milieu, not lost in the passionate entanglements involving dozens of gods of ancient Greek and Roman fable and legend, who were for the most part indifferent, even scornful, of the human situation.

Following their being cast out by the Jewish community, early Hebrew Christians (followers of Christ) began to seriously put together their own New Testament, of which the four Gospels were not the first. They went about this without separating their belief from the Old Testament. When gentiles were converted into this early Judaic-Christian sect, they bought into the entire Judaic Old Testament traditional belief system. It was during Paul's evangelical journeys when proclamations about Christians being given a special covenant with God came about, along with the significant inspiration of Christ's teachings concerning being loved and given eternal life. Even when members of this odd sect came to openly call themselves Christians, and were gradually seen as completely separate from their Judaic brethren, they kept and merged Old Testament faith with their accumulating New Testament narratives, staunchly believing Christ was the Messiah spoken of by Old Testament prophets. And so their belief retained the exoteric power of historic Hebraic roots, but weakened the esoteric mytho-power of the essential message of Christ. As decades passed, Christians came to convince themselves that their growing flock was the truly "chosen one" of the covenant.

How the Christians first attached the New Testament to the Old is elucidated in Burton L. Mack's book, *The Lost Gospel: the Book of Q*:

> *The Christian claim to novelty could only be forceful if its recent origin could be seen as the perfection of ancient ideas. But, of course, the Hebrew scriptures belonged to the Jews, not to the Christians. Thus the Christian appropriation of the epic of Israel became an issue of fundamental significance for the church. It has to be read as a story that somehow anticipated the Christ, and it had to be arranged to interlock with the New Testament*

302

... Christians reversed the order of the prophets and their writings in order to end with Malachi. Eureka! One reads the Hebrew epic to the end, reads about the messenger to come, turns the page, and hears the voice of John (or Jesus) saying that Malachi's prophecy is coming to pass. What a neat connection between the "Old Testament" and the "New Testament.[10]

From the simmering alembic of the archetypal depths of the universal collective psyche, each culture creates its own complex religious brew of mytho-religious symbols, bringing forth the "God" that suits its circumstances. Consider how Ursa Major, the most observable constellation almost everywhere on earth, was worshipped by varied cultures in very diverse ways, demonstrating how time, place, environment shape the acculturated mind's interpretations of the archetypal forces pulsing up from the unconscious. Such external diversity of interpretation does not detract from the archetypal power imbued with universal affinity of meaning. The religious paradigm of Christ is rooted in archetypal crucifixion-resurrection imagery deeply intertwined with pre-historical myths of matriarchal goddess-vegetation deities, as well as the transformative death-rebirth process of ego giving way to higher spiritual realization. As Phillip Wheelwright states concerning such mythic alchemical magnetism,

On the surface a myth is a tale, a narrative, either about events believed to have occurred at some significant moment in history (e.g., the virgin birth of Jesus, his crucifixion and resurrection), or about prehistoric events (e.g., the creation of Adam, the Hesiodic Golden Age), or about events regarded as taking place outside of human time altogether (e.g., Athena's birth from the head of Zeus, Lucifer's revolt and expulsion from Heaven). But so far as these events are truly mythic their narrative accounts are not important in themselves but only in their reference to their tenor, which is something perhaps vague but yet of vast importance for the interpretation of human experience. The truly mythic, in short, has archetypal implications. Nevertheless the mythic is something more than the archetypal which it implicitly embodies. For the mythic involves not only archetypal ideas, but more characteristically archetypally significant events and situations.[11]

Because the numinous potential burgeoning forth from the mysterium tremendum within an individual's experience is subconsciously filtered and replaced by conditioned acculturated religious imagery. Thus we must strive to understand our cognitive perceptual filtering of both external and internal realities as far as possible. There is much resistance to this, and not without reason. If ordinarily unconscious knowledge and archetypal images igniting this potential happen to bypass the acculturated filtering process, a mental crisis usually comes about, which can precipitate either psychological chaos or meaningful awakening, or perhaps both. Genuine spiritual rebirth often requires the chaotic destruction (crucifixion) of preconceived belief systems constructed strictly from unquestioning acceptance of traditional imagery. Thus the seeker must prepare him/herself by delving into the deeper symbolic/esoteric interpretations of our religious beliefs. Probing the esoteric element of any religion isn't just a process of intellectual analyzation, of stripping away the exoteric husk layer by layer. It is more like opening the curtains covering a window so we can view further horizons. Religious dogma is entrancement with the exquisite patterns of the closed curtains.

It takes real courage to contemplate the possibility that your entire faith could be based on highly questionable, even unlikely premises. If you really probe, really dig deep enough through the theological mishmash, through the history of religious ideas, past the programs of conforming belief all clergymen are handed during their youthful seminary years, past all you have been taught in your church, you will discover your religion has no more reason to qualify as the 'one true way' than any other religion humans have constructed over the ages since the dawn of consciousness. Thus you are free to open yourself to the full mysterium tremendum which transcends all religious concepts that confine the soul's need of blossoming, trusting that such opening creates a deeper mytho-oriented faith which is nourished by the mulch of newly found wonder and awe.

But, as indicated, there is much that stands in the way of such open-minded contemplations. Psychological research has revealed that behind people's front of certainty and confidence in their religious belief, lies bewilderment and fear they are completely unaware of, because the unconscious mind, the very source of intuition, has its own way of detecting falsehoods contrived by the ego. This intuitive knowingness gnawing at the threshold of consciousness kindles the heat of desperation, which the ego skillfully represses with the weight of false confidence. The more intense the unconscious doubt, the more zealous the claim of the believer. Such a belief system will be defended at all costs, inciting both politically and religiously justified wars. Only through the activity of fervent willful self-analyzation, perhaps assisted by weeks of fasting and yoga, will that which is submerged in the shadows of the subconscious emerge to be seen for what it is. It is then that doubt fully blooms, casting its shadow over a person's faith. And within this "dark night of the soul," with patience, the true light of spiritual truth blazes forth, and the bewildered individual's essence is opened to the cultivation of a much deeper faith, not dependent on any questionable religious belief system.

It is important to remember in this context that the historical person we know as Jesus arrived within a certain cultural setting of religious and political turmoil, amid an array of other miracle workers, healers, prophets, seers and sages. To have only his life, out of all these diverse figures, transformed and amplified into a religion that would shape two thousand years of civilization, is surely a remarkable occurrence—but not necessarily "God" ordained. The over-sweeping of Western civilization by Christianity does not necessarily mean God's intervention into history, any more than Islam's reconquering of land taken by Christians during the Crusades implies Allah intervened into the history of the Mideast, or that the Aryan conquest of India implies Brahman controlled the history of India. What such momentous movements of religious belief verify is, when culturally dominating elements coincide with a certain idea imbued with archetypal resonance, history is shaped accordingly.

Let us return to the period from which Christianity arose, and consider two historical figures we have sufficient factual evidence about, who played key roles in this epic phenomenon of religious expansion. The first is Paul of Tarsus, a Jewish citizen of Helenized Rome and a persecutor of Christians, who became a reborn Christian after a dramatic conversion. Paul was the premier expositor of the resurrection of the body, thus the promise of immortality for all followers of Christ. The second is the Emperor Constantine, 306-371 AD, who became a significant lever in the geographic diffusion and mass acceptance of Christianity. The oral and written stories relating to the life of Jesus, of which there were hundreds in circulation circa

40 AD, were eclectically picked through by Paul, who then, we could say, became their marketing executive and traveling salesman "par excellence" for approximately thirty years. He not only expounded upon these tales but amplified and elaborated to such an extent that some modern theologians claim his evangelical teachings were adverse to the simple yet wise expositions of truth and love Christ taught. Nietzsche even claimed Paul perverted the parable/koan teachings of Jesus into doctrinal dogma. Pre-Pauline Christianity was of a more mythic-mystery quality, whereas over the centuries it became rationalistic dogma to uphold clearly defined moral standards. Much of modern Christianity abides beneath the influence of both the Old Testament and Paul's teachings, more so than the essence and truth of Christ. It was Paul's teachings that were given priority by Christian authorities as the Church rose to power. Though Paul was thoroughly Jewish and saw his endeavors as enriching traditional Judaism, because he believed Jesus to be the Messiah prophesized in the Old Testament, theologians have called him the prime founder of Christianity. His fervor of belief and genius of rhetoric made him an evangelist of powerful persuasion, a charismatic Billy Graham of his era. Because of his preachings, the small bands of Jews who believed in Christ began mingling with growing numbers of converted Gentiles, and for three hundred years after Paul's death, despite the constant persecution by various Roman emperors, Christianity experienced steady growth throughout the Roman Empire.

In 312 AD, during the Battle at Milvian Bridge, the emperor and military leader known as Constantine prayed to Christ for victory, and because he was victorious and had experienced a vision of the cross during the battle, he became the first Roman emperor to declare himself a Christian. His religious zeal mixed with political ambition eventually lead to Christianity becoming the state religion of the Roman Empire, which at that time had power and influence over most of the known world. Constantine was a more than enthusiastic believer, to say the least. The influence of his Christian conversion amplified his already semi-godlike stature as emperor, inspiring him to occasionally claim he was the thirteenth apostle, and therefore a special representative of the Christian God on earth. In this we realize that religious conversion does not automatically entail spiritual realization, thus the blood drenched history of Christianity's spread across half the earth. Constantine was closer in deed to the Old Testament Yahweh than the New Testament Christ. Like certain politicians today who claim to be Christians, Constantine was Machiavellian in the extreme concerning his political ambitions and fanatical religious enthusiasm—certain historical texts elucidate his deeds of cutting his own son's throat, strangling his wife and then murdering his father-in-law. He apparently liked things to go his way. He wasn't as gifted with rhetorical brilliance as Paul, but he was well studied in the theology of his time and could be very persuasive and quite eloquent, although occasionally when giving speeches concerning Christ, it is said he became incoherent. He was one of the first emperors to use "mass mailing" to disseminate his viewpoint all about his empire. In addition to placing his image on coins along with Christian symbols, he deliberately mistranslated the poet Virgil's work to suit his own ends, and even manipulated the sayings of the oracle at Delphi in a similar manner. His mother, Queen Helena, caught up in her son's fervor, was known to build a Christian church wherever local rumor said something significant concerning Jesus had occurred.

Constantine arranged to bring about the Edict of Milan in 313, guaranteeing tolerance and legal rights to all Christians after years of persecution, thus winning political position over one of his opponents and gaining a larger slice of the empire. When the nature of Christ's divinity became a controversial issue, Constantine called all the bishops across the empire to gather in council at Nicaea in 325 AD. Controlling the Council completely, his decision, and thus the Council's, to proclaim Jesus as one with the divine nature of God and therefore the Messiah, was possibly the most historically significant religious/political decision ever made. It could be said Constantine's position in the expansion of Christianity was equal to or even surpassed Paul's evangelism—Paul being the match and Constantine the fire. In making way for Christianity to become the ruling religion of the Roman Empire, and perhaps also an element of its collapse, Constantine, his own ambitions foremost in mind, helped bind church and state together. Thus when he moved the capitol of Rome to Byzantium, renaming it Constantinople, the beginning of the end of the empire (according to some scholars) gradually came about. But it would still be four hundred years before the political/governmental structure of the empire collapsed. Seventy years after Constantine's death, the Holy Roman Church had extensive reign, and would control what had once been the Roman empire for more than a thousand years. The warrior emperor Charlemagne was instrumental in the Church's envelopment of Western civilization. His military campaigning took over from what the Roman army had once accomplished, and he did it for the Church, for which he was amply rewarded.

Today's Christians should realize that prior to Constantine, non-Christian pagan religions believed to a large degree in letting others worship what they may, and the early Christians followed suit. Unfortunately, following Constantine, the un-Christlike behavior of those who called themselves Christians, now holding positions of political and religious power, began a blood drenched annihilation of those opposing their faith all across the known world. When the Church became all-powerful after the fall of Rome and the subsequent coronation of Charlemagne, practically all pagan religions and even Christian sects that did not interpret the Bible and the story of Christ as orthodox authorities demanded, were considered heretical and, as far as possible, wiped out. For more than a thousand years, with the instigation of the all powerful Church through a reign of Machiavellian cunning and military might, multitudes were slaughtered, tortured, exiled, to create a unified system of Christian belief throughout Western civilization. Concerning the inner circle intrigues of those adorned in church finery — popes, bishops, cardinals, priests, counselors — it was as Octavio Paz wrote,

> *Hostility and jealousy were cloaked in appeals to high principle: respect for authority, obedience, devotion to religious duty. Thus the foreshadowing of political-corporate manipulation of the modern masses. The spiritual orientation of the Solar-Christ demanded for awakening was buried beneath political ambitions of the Church's endeavor to institutionalize the ineffable.[12]*

For over one thousand five hundred years throughout the Dark Ages and Middle Ages, the Holy Roman Catholic Church controlled every level of education, including the knowledge of time. The Church shaped the calendar and decided when religious holidays would be held. Even after Luther's Reformation and the rise of Protestantism, church authorities, both Catholic and Protestant, held significant positions of power over community life for another four hundred years. Up to 1860, most colleges in the United States were controlled by religious authority, including Harvard. As one writer put it, religion was politics with pomp and ceremony, bells and ritual. America's pride as a Christian nation is blind to the fact that its enduring stability of faith is an extended residue of totalitarian religious domination, which is once again becoming predominant in contemporary politics, especially the element influenced by the Christian Right.

Thus from the time of the first Pope, the impetus of religion kept up a consistent external momentum through the reign of chieftains, emperors, and kings, who became zealous believers, and strove by any means to reinforce all attributes of their faith that would help keep them in positions of power. Association with the power of the Church became a status symbol. Having a Bishop or Cardinal in the family was like having a CEO or governor as a son-in-law today. Fashion merged with going to church. During the Middle Ages in Europe, one tenth of the population were priests. Theological politics ruled, severing the human psyche from the numinous resonance of mytho-archetypal solar presence. Thus externalized religious belief, bereft of essential contact with the authentic meaning of Christ, began its rule.

Opposition between Protestant church authorities and the Vatican increased. Protestants believed the Pope to be the anti-Christ. Besides the blood letting between Protestant and Catholic, various Protestant sects warred with each other for varied absurd reasons. The modern Religious Right in America today should take heed that religious power in control of government does not bring about peace and understanding among humans anymore than when the state (à la Stalin) rules without church involvement. Religious control of the state, bereft of genuine spiritual awareness, has proven to be the cause of as much or even more enthusiastic blood letting and tyranny than godless communism. What was forty-five years of Soviet communism compared to centuries of terror by the Inquisition?

It should be clear from just the last few pages, not to mention volumes on the same theme found in every library, that it was not the wisdom-teachings of Jesus or the spirit of Christ that spread Christianity over three quarters of the earth. It was the success of the Roman army, followed by battles and victories to be carried on for centuries by ambitious Christian rulers like Charlemagne, Otto I, Grand Prince Vladimir, and good King Olaf Trygvesson, who had anyone who refused to accept Christianity as their faith tortured to death. The deranged religious authorities of the Christian church who sanctioned all this, and also organized the Inquisition, were immersed totally in the certitude of their faith. They projected their dark derangement outwardly and saw it as perversion in others. Thus it should be clear that dogmatically oriented faith is certainly not a reliable test of whether or not a belief is grounded in truth. Those who are ensconced in a literal biblical faith in Christ become aggressively un-Christlike when their belief system is threatened from one direction or another. As clarified, their certitude is built of repressed doubt and fear, which produces an aggression that has been rationalized for centuries as an aspect of religious warfare against Antichrist forces. It was church leaders like Calvin who claimed all humanity was depraved and damned for eternity, although he and a few others were of the elect to be saved. (Sounds a bit like Reverend Dr. Bob Jones, or Pastor John Hagee, and others of their ilk). Calvin, like many modern day Christian leaders, not aware of his own shadow, was a dupe to his repressed tendencies, which spilled forth in his religious fervor. In his zealous derangement and staunch certitude, Calvin ordered people judged guilty of heresy to be burned at the stake with green wood, so they would suffer longer. How Christlike was that? Such figures of authority have always feared the truths of deeper knowledge, including philosophy. As early as 389 AD Christians burned down the great library of Alexandria, destroying hundreds of thousands of ancient scrolls. Such religious "terrorist" activity went on continually for centuries.

After Columbus discovered the "newfound" lands, men like Cortez and Pissaro and other conquistadors, sanctioned by Church authority, ravaged from Mexico through South America, and north through the American Southwest and California, all backed by the ambition for power and wealth of the Catholic church. This blood drenched march of Catholic Christian soldiers would be followed by the Protestant "Pilgrim's Progress." With the eventual help of the US Cavalry and "heroic" frontiersmen, puritanistic Christianity spread with predatory rapaciousness across the entire continent of North America. Early Christians with the finest intentions had the Bible translated into the language of the Massachusetts tribe, and within ninety years that very tribe was driven to extinction. Follow this basic line of historical facts further, we must once again conclude that Christianity spread across the earth not because everyone was learning to love their neighbor, but by military aggression and a ruling religious authority that threatened eternal damnation in hell for all who disobeyed. The religious zeal of most Christian missionaries of this day and age, though not always as blatant in their indoctrination techniques, and occasionally producing some good works of a pragmatic sort, still abides within the sphere of naiveté and arrogant self-ignorance of the shadow, in which the "conversion of others" impulse is rooted. The foundation belief is still, "believe as I do or you are damned." If it was up to certain politically far-right fundamentalists, the "necessary" God-ordained blood-letting would once again rule their missionary activities. Dozens of Christian spokespersons over the last few years have appeared on TV talk shows as advocates to justify the invasion of Iraq, and are still at it.

The blood drenched history of Christianity perpetrated by power hungry Christian politicians and clergymen, clearly demonstrates how the egoic mind, caught up in worldly pursuits, can distort and pervert the greatest spiritual teachings rooted within esoteric spheres of knowledge. But keep in mind, although we must acknowledge the savagery that has occurred, and is still occurring beneath the banner of Christianity, we should in no way let it taint the mystical wonder and archetypal reality of true "Christ-consciousness," which ignites in the human realm the universal awareness of compassion for one's fellow beings. Of course, this compassion is not confined to the Christian religious ambit, but burgeons forth in any religion or teaching that opens the spiritual heart charka to the world at large. Beyond the tarnish of ignorance and defilement attached to religion, beyond mistranslation and manipulation, the discerning intelligence can still glean sufficient amounts of esoterically rooted truth from the teachings attributed to the biblical figure of Jesus. That those truths were ignored while the unChrist-like Christian scourge spread across the earth with ruthless violence and suppression, can be attributed to the interpretation of religious text by way of the cravings of the human ego, not the deeper mytho-symbolic meaning of Christ. To get at these deeper esoteric meanings, we must peel away the layers of traditional propaganda and distorted legend modern Christianity still clings to, no matter how dear to our sentimental longings and engrained beliefs.

Such thoughts will be disturbing to any Christian who has, astonishingly, read this far. But psychological disturbance is a necessary ingredient in the alchemical brew of genuine inner growth. Recall what was said about the quest of truth being imbued with perplexity and paradox. The history of the Christian church, its political intrigues, struggles for leadership, destruction of heretical sects, with the victors' interpretations of biblical text becoming established doctrine, is a complex aspect of what religious belief is today. In the Church's thrust to shape what the multitudes were to believe, and the turmoil of intrigue and bloodshed such manipulation entailed, it is clearly demonstrated the Christian religion has a dark labyrinthine history of human fallibility concerning the exoteric-societal interpretation of the foundation it is built upon.

The earlier followers of Jesus who believed in what they thought would be the soon to come apocalyptic "Second Coming," had hold of a very impressive idea, (or rather it had hold of them), amplified in force by the skillful merging of this messianic hope with manipulated aspects of Old Testament prophecy. Most of the early Christians, within the first seventy years of the Crucifixion, all believed thoroughly that Christ would return while they were alive. This has become a perennial delusion of expectation. St. Augustine greatly influenced this direction of Christian theological thought, one of his most influential postulations having to do with the concept of "end times," or "last days." Over the centuries, when it was obvious Christ wasn't coming as soon as everyone hoped, leading elements of the Christian movement began playing down the eschatological aspect of Jesus' teachings. Still, almost every fin de siecle since the Crucifixion, millions of Christians have become entranced with expectations that the Second Coming was about to occur. In 999 A.D., following a 1000 year Christian rule, Pope Sylvester II claimed the Lord would return at midnight. Hundreds of thousands waited expectantly. Almost every Christian prepared to meet their God as the millennium came to a close. They were clearly disappointed. The Middle Ages saw signs of the Last Judgment cataclysm everywhere. The Christian Crusades were seen as an "end time" manifestation. The Puritan Pilgrims brought their apocalyptic visions to the "new found land." In 1776 the King of England was seen by many colonists to be the Anti-Christ, who is supposed to come just prior to the End. In the 1840's, a Christian by the name of John Nelson Darby coined the term "The Rapture," referring to the day the best of the faithful would be swept up to heaven as the Lord returned within an Apocalyptic storm. This is preached by varied ministers and evangelists of today. Century after century Christians have interpreted passages in the Bible to claim their era as the time in which the Lord would return and bring an end to the world as we know it. They never learn. And some become desperate in their zeal to help bring it about. Extremist cults of today are just the tip of a large grassroots belief in "end times" — and the first decade of each millennium is the most passionate time for this belief to sweep through the Christian faithful, second only to the arousal brought about by the onset of war, which many Christians anxiously interpret as a sign that the "end" is near. This is an entrenched element of the Christian psyche.

Within this fin-de-siècle, 1999-2010, the common believer's credulity is wide open for any collective irrationality to inundate. I have a newspaper clipping here which has to do with the members of a cult of Christians from Denver, arrested in January 1999 in Israel. They had been planning to perform acts of violence as part of a process to bring Jesus back for the Second Coming. Their leader described himself as representative of a figure from the *Book of Revelation*. But again, most Christians do not learn from experience. Those who were disappointed the Messiah did not return in January of 2000 prepared for January of 2001. And though that show also flopped, they now see signs in the War on Terrorism, including the war on Iraq, as a possible first stage of Armageddon. The Christian author Peter Novak writes of the approaching Rapture and Final Judgment, in his book, *The Division of Consciousness*.13 He is a writer with lots of skill at weaving concepts together to fortify his fundamentalist beliefs, but he has little intellectual scope or genuine spiritual awareness, and no psychological depth. He is representative of most authors of such simplified Christian persuasion, à la Hal Lindsey, Tim LaHaye, and David Noebel, plus all those others lusting for certitude so fervorously that they will believe any mirage signifying the oasis they call the "Rapture" — all, of course, sure that they will be among the chosen few. This fervor concerning the return of the Messiah Jesus, the apocalyptic vision of "end days" for the world as we know it, is a river of belief that runs through most Christian sects and denominations to various degrees of zealotry, influencing many of our politicians.

According to certain Christian theologians, when Jesus walked the earth, many considered him a radical dreamer of dreams, the giver of signs and wonders spoken of in Deuteronomy, who needed to be put to death because the ways of the God he spoke of did not coincide with the God of their Judaic tradition. After this outspoken wandering rabbi-Siddha was crucified, most Jews still believed the Messiah had not yet arrived, for if the true Messiah had come, as they believed, it was to make everything right, with no Crucifixion required, no departing, no need to spend your life waiting for him to return. What Christians today look forward to in the Second Coming is what the Jews expect their Messiah to accomplish during his First Coming. Why else should a Messiah come, if not to settle things once and for all. What kind of true God-empowered Messiah would come forth just to be killed and be gone again within such a short period? To most Gentiles and Jews during those first centuries AD, the Christians who believed that Jesus was the Messiah had merely invented the Second Coming story to assuage their disappointment that the crucified Jesus had not fulfilled their Messianic expectations when he was among them—sort of like all those Christians who thought the year 2000, then 2001, would bring forth the Messiah, then quickly made up theological excuses when He did not show up. Yet it was only because of that gradually expanding group of fervently committed followers, deluded as they may have been, that the faith in Jesus as Messiah was kept intensely alive for forty years, until St. Paul latched on and did his thing, followed by Constantine.

But the authentic meaning of the mytho-legend of Jesus Christ is not restricted to deluded messianic expectations, or any other distortions of the Christian religion. When the biblical-historical figure known as Jesus, from whom a few sufficiently validated oracular statements have come down to us, said, "*I am the truth and the way,*" it is certain he did not mean Christianity was the way, for Christianity as a religion did not exist when Christ was alive. And as we have seen, Christianity 300 AD through 2005 AD, to a very large degree, has not been substantially conducive to the way of Christ, whose teachings transcended the entire cultural ambit of the war-god Yahweh. Adding up scraps of ancient writings, including both apocryphal and canonical text, it seems quite possible Jesus, legendary Rabbi-Siddha of the ancient Mideastern world, was very possibly a genuinely enlightened being totally inundated by higher metafrequencies of consciousness.

In the chapter on language and the precarious skill of translation, we saw how a word or a sentence can be easily changed to produce a significantly different meaning. The words above attributed to Jesus, "*I am the truth and the way,*" having come through centuries of translation from one language to the next, most likely have shifted away from their original meaning. In ancient Aramaic, which Jesus would actually have spoken, the meaning would possibly have been more like, "The truth is the way," or perhaps, "I represent the way of truth," or, more esoterically, "I am the symbol of truth." For essentially, throughout all esoteric teachings, the truth is always the way, and all paths of truth lead to spiritual realization. The philosopher Julián Marías, wrote,

> *Truth establishes, therefore, an essential connection between man and the whole of reality, and functions, in a word, as the form of authenticity of human life.*[14]

And, as Gandhi stated,

> *If it is possible for the human tongue to give the fullest description of God, I have come to the conclusion that ... God is Truth and Truth is God.*[15]

A weighty statement indeed, giving us a sense of the profundity of what the essence quality of truth means within the matrix of human existence.

Nicholas Berdyaev spoke of Christ, ("Truth is the Way"), as the symbolic representation of the eternal emission of Being penetrating the "now." The ego with its dependence on linear constructs is crucified when it is fully awakened to its true significance in the midst of eternity. The socially restricted persona dies as the authentic spiritual self is born.

Heidegger said sequential time is an illusion, and only the constant moment of decision is real—the decision to wake to the essential truth of your being. Such awakening is crucifixion because it entails what Gurdjieff called "intentional suffering" = willingly bearing the burden, facing our existential spiritual predicament head on. *"If not now, when? If not you, who? If not here, where?"*

As R. E. Friedman demonstrates in his book, *Who Wrote the Bible*, what came together over the centuries was a book rich with interpretive possibilities, a psychic-spiritual Rorschach literature deeply tinged by a ten thousand year old primal mytho-symbol, the ancient sun god Re.[16] This symbol, resonating behind the narrative of Jesus with psychic meta-frequencies of transcendent consciousness, became too tightly wrapped in misconstrued messianic expectations. Once we see through the excess mish mash of such exoteric interpretations, we can put spiritually limiting literalism aside and relate to the archetypal truths and alchemical symbolism, attempting to perceive what scholars refer to as the "essential intentionality" which dwells within all mythic narrative. As clarified, the power of biblical text resides in its mythic quality. Jacques Waardenburg points out:

> *The truth of myth is not in the details of a story, but in its deeper meanings – the mytho power is to use the ordinary to reveal the extraordinary, the real nature of forces beneath the appearance of the situations of the narrative.*[17]

That mythological symbolism was an essential element of ancient spiritual life is an historical fact. Christian groups living in Egypt during the first century AD adapted the pharaonic symbol of creation, the Tau, " T ," later merging it with the symbol of death, †, the cross of crucifixion upon which tens of thousands of Jews, revolutionaries, criminals, Christians, had died. Eventually this merger formed into the primary symbol of Christianity. In essence, the Christian cross is a symbol of death and resurrection, with solar-rebirth implications of the rising sun intimately entwined with the image of Christ rising from the tomb. Esoterically, the Jesus Christ narrative of "The Passion" is a mystical representation of the ego's death and rebirth, significantly imbued with both alchemical and pagan solar and nature goddess symbolism. And so we see, despite superficialization by way of literalistic misconceptions, esoteric wisdom can be derived through intuitive comprehension of the symbolism involved. This is what imbues Christianity with its salvational hope, its potential to rise above the historical tumult and confusion of the quotidian world, including orthodox religious confusion. Actually, the very concept of a Messiah is rooted in hope. From a depth psychology perspective, the Messiah is hope personified. But the seeker must give up hope for an externalized Messiah appearing in flesh and realize he/she can no longer wait for some Second Coming, but must act to empower an inner magnetism, which may attract higher transcendent powers. Seeking such wisdom sources calls for an individual to activate what could be called an "inner Messiah" narrative = the process of spiritual individuation, the crucifixion of egoic needs, desires, ambitions, vanities. Beckettean waiting for a Second coming Godot is no longer called for, only a moving toward, a going further into the numinous depths of one's being.

Having scrutinized the living archetypal "myth" of Christ in order to free it of all manner of delusory projections, one of the most meaningful aspects that remains is the connection to the solar-psychic magnificence of the Sun. To the ancients, the Sun was an intensely awe inspiring and majestic phenomenon, with a numinous radiance everyone could grasp immediately with no need for further explanation — it was just there in all its mysterious magnificence, indisputable and permanent. They had no idea the universe was filled with billions of other suns, most larger than theirs, thus to them the sun was a singular awesome god-being commanding the entire sky. Still, we must not think "ancient" implies an automatic ignorance of deeper sensitivities toward ultimate concerns. Though inundated by superstition, the ancient relationship to the numinous otherness of existence makes the nationalistic tainted Christianity of America seem a spiritually dehydrated phenomenon. Numerous "modern" Christians have lost a genuine mystical respect for the true spledor of significant things, which all we have discovered through science cannot revive. A mytho/mystic perspective is necessary. Both the intelligent skeptic and the devout believer in literalism must cultivate a flexible mentality open to broader horizons concerning the truth of things.

Aurobindo wrote:

It is then through something supraphysical in Nature and ourselves which we may call the soul, whatever the exact substance of soul may be, that we are likely to get that greater truth and subtler experience which will enlarge the narrow rigid circle traced by physical science and bring us nearer to the Reality. There is nothing now to bar the most rational mind — for true ra-

tionalism, real free thought need no longer be identified, as it was for some time too hastily and intolerantly, with a denial of the soul and a scouting of the truths of spiritual philosophy and religion — there is nothing to prevent us from proceeding firmly upon whatever certitudes of spiritual experience have become to us the soil of our inner growth or the pillars on our road to self-knowledge.[18]

The narrative of the life of Jesus is a "logos" expression consequentially underpinned with "mythos." Mythos continually entwines with logos throughout all ancient cultures, through profound poetry, art, tales of shamanistic journeying, and the alchemist's ponderings of his retort, all taking flight on the surge of imagination, and often involving intentional visualization. When Paracelsus said, *"Imagination is the star in man,"* and William Blake praised imagination as an avenue to freeing the mind, and Jung agreed with both, they were implying something more than ordinary fantasy, pretending, daydream, for they considered imagination to be the wings of myth and spiritual vision. And when I speak of visualization as linked with imagination, I mean something more than pragmatic planning, blueprints, intentional conceptualization of utilitarian end-goals. I am referring to the psychologically disciplined art of visualization found in Buddhist and Hindu meditation teachings.

In his marvelous book, *Coming Into Being*, William Irwin Thompson writes,

> *The imagination is an intermediate realm between the ego in its perceptual body of senses and the intuition of higher, multidimensional states of consciousness. Information moves in both directions. Some kinds of intuitions come down to the ego, and some kinds of peripheral perceptions are transformed by the imagination as they surface into awareness and become rendered into an imagistic narrative.*[19]

James Hillman states,

> *The act of soul-making is imagining, since images are the psyche, its stuff, and its perspective... Only when imagination is recognized as an engagement at the borders of the human and a*

*work in relation with mystic dominants can this articulation of
images be considered as psycho-poesis or soul-making.*[20]

William Blake spoke of time and space being like blinders to our
minds, poetically claiming that if we removed these blinders, the
world would be revealed as pure imagination. Thus, when we consider myth, imagination, soul, let us attempt to remove all blinders
of stultified logic and literalism.

William Irwin Thompson states:

> *Most scholars never pass from the sociological and anthropologi-
> cal levels of a mythic text to the cosmological level because it up-
> sets their whole notion of scientific progress. They see themselves
> at the top of history and at the top of society, looking down at the
> ignorant and precivilized worlds of myth and transforming these
> geological ores into the polished jewelry of scholarship that
> earns them their tenure in their universities. But myth is not
> raw matter waiting to be transformed into the precious metal of
> science; it is already a metal, a refined and complex technical
> language of an initiatic elite.*[21]

Even fewer scholars pass from the cosmological mythic text to the
transcendent archetypal level. Relating myth to archetype is not to
make it the object of weighty psychology, but rather to relate its
"wholly otherness" to fermentation within psychic depths frothing
forth into human comprehension through symbolic imagery. As
Mircea Eliade's work clarifies, IF approached with open attentiveness, myth can disrupt quotidian time and lift man from his everyday mentality, because in essence myth resonates with higher meta-
frequency levels within the helicoid dance of consciousness. Unfortunately, as religious tradition validates, everything of mytho-
spiritual significance is vulnerable to reductionism, as myth has been
subject to in the New Age self-help genre – "shopping with your
own myth in mind," "myth in the workplace," etc. People will always
reduce aspects of the mysterium tremendum to suit their un-
mysterious egoic needs, be they Pat Robertson or Mel Gibson. The
spectrum of evasion is quite lengthy.

Myth works on the principle of signification — the tale signifies
a reality of deeper substance. Metaphor is similar, describing some-

thing other by way of something familiar, a presenting of comprehensible imagery to communicate something beyond imagery. Of
course, there are various types and degrees of both metaphor and
myth, but we are dealing here with that which relates to the religio-
archetypal ambit of human experience. Colin M. Turbayne states,

> *An effective metaphor, invented by a genius and extended to*
> *make an entire theory, tends to pass into another stage: from*
> *conscious metaphor into unconscious myth, from make-believe*
> *into belief.*[22]

The world of the New Testament is essentially a religious
tributary of a mythological matrix, and as such we must consider it
neither as a mythologist or demythologist, but as a seeker of arche-
typal/psychological truths. As Karl Jaspers said, *"The real task, therefore, is not to demythologize, but to recover mythical thought in its original
purity"*[23]

Even before the first Egyptian dynasty, circa 4000 BC, the
Sumerians worshipped the solar oriented Anu, the "God of Heaven,"
also known as "The One." Thus a kind of monotheism relating to a
God above all gods, strongly identified with the Sun, had deep and
extensive roots within the religious zeitgeist from which Judeo-
Christian religious concepts eventually came forth. Following
Sumerian civilization, the Egyptians worshipped the sun for century
upon century of dynasties beginning around 3000 BC. Every Egyptian pharaoh was hailed as the son of the sun god Aman, or Atum-
Re. This quasi-monotheistic deity of creation, having been worshipped for several millennia, encompassing the Egyptian enslavement of the Israelites, must have certainly influenced Abraham circa
1700 BC, and thus surely contributed to the readiness for the Hebrew
concept of the monotheistic god Yahweh. A contemporary of Moses,
the young pharaoh Akhenaten, circa 1365 – 1340 BC, elevated the
ancient Atum-Re from the god above all gods to the status of the one
and only true God—Aten—with Akhenaten as the son of this absolute God. This "son of the absolute God" system of belief was functioning one thousand three hundred years prior to Jesus being seen
as the son of the Hebrew God of gods. In certain ancient apocryphal
text Christ was referred to as the son of the sun, which, considering
the esoteric aspect of solar symbolism, is subject matter entailing
profound psychological-spiritual implications. It is also known that

Akhenaten equated solar power with the source of truth. Thus we see the intrinsic relation of Christ/Sun/Truth = spiritual light/enlightenment. *"I am the Truth and the Way."*

The sun has been representative of the divine for many cultures, and certainly imbued various mytho-poetic aspects of the Judaic-Christian narrative. Though many modern humans are impressed by the fiery splendor of the sun, and it is recognized as the sole energy provider sustaining all life on earth, the excessively rational secularized mentality of our civilization no longer considers implications of the sun's majestic numinous symbolism. Even the religious oriented mind of the average Christian is heavily influenced by the hegemony of materialism- secularism, and hardly ever relates the run-of-the-mill Bible version of Jesus with a mystic relationship to the symbolism of solar myth. This is because most suburbanized Christians lack spiritually oriented imagination regarding the innate symbolism of their own belief system. As Ouspensky said, *"Symbolism cannot be learned as one learns to build bridges or speak a foreign language ... For the interpretation of symbols a special cast of mind is necessary."*[24] And as Anthony Storr has written, *"Symbolism belongs with the higher reaches of human mental activity."*[25]

To the scientifically sanitized mind, the sun is just another cosmic marvel of phenomenal existence, a huge ball of thermonuclear fury, just one magnificent sun among many suns, and a small one at that—certainly no more a sign of any Higher Being's existence than those billions of other suns we see as sparkling stars in the night sky. Such a view is certainly understandable, and justified to a significant extent. But it should be clear by now, once we delve into metaphysical and mystical levels of existence, ordinary inflexible logic and static reasoning are not substantially reliable. Despite secularization, we should be open to mytho-mystic interpretation, for as Eugene Pascal stated, *"Human psyches are metaphysical by their very nature."*[26] Being open to the mystical doesn't imply vulnerability to credulity, or capitulation to the irrational. Even the most skeptical inquirer into such matters must admit what we perceive of reality is only representational appearances abstracted from a much greater dimension of existence. Things are much more than they seem.

During the last half of the twentieth century science discovered immense solar flares which burst 90,000 miles into space from the sun's surface. In 1959 a gigantic solar flare caused an electricity outage covering large areas of the United States and Canada. Such flares send out gigantic waves of energy that engulf the entire atmosphere of the earth everyday, inducing ionic disturbances of radio waves, affecting the weather and the growth of all plant life. To visualize the winds of solar energy sweeping over the earth, consider our planet to be the size of a green pea being engulfed by a cloud of energy six feet long and three feet wide. The acceleration of the growth of trees has been scientifically established to correlate with the frequency of sunspot maxima. If the growth of giant redwood trees and immense electrical blackouts are caused by solar activity, what then is the effect upon the electrical-chemical system of human beings? What is the unconscious effect upon each of us as condensed tornados of metapsychic frequencies? What is the effect upon the complex alchemy of our brains, our minds, our souls? The brilliant spheroid thermonuclear fury we so placidly perceive during the day is something much deeper and greater than we can comprehend.

Rodney Collin wrote: *"When we face the sun we address ourselves toward the center and source of creative energy within the solar system."*[27] All life on earth is dependent on light frequencies from the sun. Even those life forms deep in the sea dependent on geothermal vent energy, and those deep deep in the mantle not dependent on sunlight frequencies, would cease to exist if the sun died out. Surely, from what we know of the brain/consciousness conundrum, such extensive influence of the sun's cosmic radiation and the myriad frequencies of energy it stimulates throughout the solar system could have a numinous effect upon the delicate psychic spectrum of human consciousness — that most mysterious phenomenon of existence which empirical science, despite mucho premature claims, has no firm cohesive grasp of. One of the things we have explored about consciousness is how it functions within a spectrum of meta-frequencies which have a magnetized resonance with measurable brain frequencies. As clarified earlier concerning visual perception, the brain interprets the stimuli of light rays pouring through the retina, igniting cognitive activity which abstracts from "greater reality" to form our idea of what we are seeing. We must admit, and science has extensively validated this, everything is much more than appearances inform us. Everything is what we perceive it is, yet "something more" — cells, molecules, atoms, electrons, quarks, ...? Thus the great blazing brightness we call the sun is that brightenss, yet "something more" — much more. As Collin puts it:

The matter of the Sun, or electronic matter, is <u>beyond</u> <u>form</u> <u>and</u> <u>beyond</u> <u>time</u>. It is <u>even</u> <u>beyond</u> <u>the</u> <u>recurrence</u> <u>of form</u> <u>and</u> <u>the</u> <u>repetition</u> <u>of time</u>. [28]

In his brilliant book, *Essays on the Origin of Thought*, Jurij Moskvitin wrote:

There are many processes in the universe where a sudden drop of entropy is inseparable from some kind of radiative influence – the most important example being the connection between the development of living organisms and the influence of the light of the sun. The building of the improbable structure – the living organism – takes place on a horizontal level. The radiation from the sun takes place on the vertical level, to be understood of course, in the sense that this influence lies on the levels of the photons, the non-plus-ultra level of the quantum. The dominant importance of the sunlight in the building up of structures that are able to perform the photosynthetic process is well known, although <u>we</u> <u>do</u> <u>not</u> <u>yet</u> <u>know</u> <u>the</u> <u>exact</u> <u>nature</u> of the activity that first permitted the synthesis and interactions of the organic molecules that permitted the emergence of the first living organisms. The evolution of life is inexplicable without referring to a gradual perfection of the photosynthetic process – which means that the proto-organisms have evolved by perfecting their ability to absorb the radiative energy from the sun – which again corresponds to what I called the structure developing by means of deeper and more profound reflections. Apart from this, the drop of entropy during the growth of some organisms directly or indirectly dependent on radiation from the sun is <u>too</u> <u>great</u> <u>to</u> <u>be</u> <u>explained</u> simply in terms of energetic transference from the sun, which, comparatively speaking is limited. In other words a transmission of information is taking place. The evolution of life is then inseparable from the transmission of information from the sun and deriving from the quantum level. [29]

Within the richly fertile Sumerian Egyptian Greek Mediterranean-Levant matrix at the dawn of Christianity, the sun had potent numinous identification with each culture's God, which certainly contributed to the religious concepts of the Christian paradigm. Certainly the deep intimacy of Solar-God relationship in those ancient cultures had roots in the primal "participation mystique" of the earliest hominids' bewildering experience of the sun's majestic place in their harsh existence. The gradual expansion of primitive humans' perception of the sky, the moon, and primarily, the sun, flowing in correlation with and in some way stimulating evolving consciousness, (thus more sophisticated religious imagery), has a profound relationship to the solar-mind-God nexus. Gurdjieff spoke of the sun representing the highest point of spiritual ascendancy for human consciousness within the great helicoid spectrum of frequencies he called the "ray of creation." He spoke of Jesus and Buddha being in direct contact with this esoteric quality of the sun, referred to as the "sun beyond the sun." Humans on the planet Earth, being in direct physical and psychic relation to solar frequencies, can open themselves to such higher influences beyond the confines of the material world.

It has been established that Egyptian priests who worshipped the Sun as God ingested psychedelic mushrooms during certain rituals. When a person takes a psychedelic substance and gazes into the sun, it can become what "hippies" in the '60's called "God's Eye," a rainbow diamond of light frequencies that penetrates and dissolves the ego capable of willfully surrendering. As Arthur Zajonc clarifies in his book, *Catching the Light*, the sun was considered the divine eye of varied gods, east and west.[30] In Egyptian mythology humanity emerged from the sun god Ra's tears. I am reminded here of the little known fact that in South America there's a moth that feeds on the teardrops of larger creatures. Could it be our essence receives nourishment in this way from the tears of "God?" That may sound a bit romantic, but such a poetic twist of mytho-symbolism may reveal deeper truths than any rationalized literal interpretations can ever come close to doing.

By now, dear reader, it should be clear that things become hauntingly numinous once you see beyond the fishbowl confinement of ordinary science and religion. Seeing beyond demands transformation. Consider this: on two islands of Indonesia, scientists studying a single species of bat discovered the bats of one on these islands were evolving into a separate species with more highly refined sound-wave receptors, while those on the other island were not evolving at all. Listen closely when I say that only "ears" attuned to the numinous will "hear" the depth of what this book is attempting to communicate about the evolution of human consciousness. I am not playing semantic games, or indulging in condescension of an elite stance. If you hear a group of oriental musicians playing a melody from a 16th century Chinese dynasty, unless you are essentially attuned to that genre of music, you will most likely not understand how anyone could enjoy it. But with cultivation of knowledge and refinement of a taste for music outside your ordinary cultural milieu, you would have an entirely different attitude and experience. It is the same with the esoteric element of these writings. You must be willing to patiently open yourself. I'm not asking you to dispense with the necessary discernment which keeps one from falling into the absurdities of New Age theosophical-occult systems which skillfully weave ounces of spiritual truths into pounds of conceptual aberrations. To open yourself doesn't require loss of alert skepticism. It does demand relinquishing inflexible over-rationalized intellectuality. Let intelligently honed intuition guide you while traversing the realm of mytho-symbolism. The Encyclopedia Britannica states,

The symbol (religious and other) is intended primarily for the circle of the initiated and involves the acknowledgement of the experience that it expresses. The symbol is not, however, kept hidden in meaning; to some extent, it even has a revelatory character (i.e., it goes beyond the obvious meaning for those who contemplate its depths). It indicates the need for communication and yet conceals the details and innermost aspects of its contents.

Before the sand storms of centuries had blasted them away, the pyramids of Egypt had been painted brilliant white. The high priest believed their reflection of sunlight produced a ceremonious reciprocal response to the sun god Re. Yes, there is a lot of New Age tripe about pyramids. But much seemingly banal occult lore is similar to overused clichés — a definite insight or meaning lies at its origin. A clarity can be found beyond the hazy reductivism of naïve perception and superstition. It can be said that a pyramid is made from four equilateral triangles placed together, leaning inward to touch at their peaks. If an observer in a helicopter were to hover above an Egyptian pyramid, and look straight down at the peak, she/he would see the shape of a tetrad. In his book, *Mind Tools*, Rudy Rucker shows Jung's psychological tetrad, Plato's "quadrivium," and a math tetrad.[31]

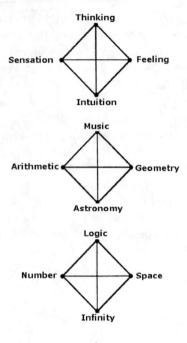

He also diagrams an ascending series of dialectic triads elucidating connective relationships of space, infinity, truth, randomness, information, logic, intelligence, and more.

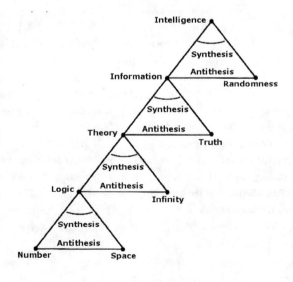

Rucker clarifies the archetypal quality of triads and tetrads as ancient and recurrent forms in human thought, thus archetypes. So when we concentrate and visualize a magnificently immense brilliant white pyramid sitting majestically amid vast sand dunes, the power it once radiated outwardly, as well as its unconscious symbolic resonance within the soul, may possibly be grasped.

The triangle is an element of profound spiritual symbolism found within most religious and alchemical text. The Star of David, though tainted by religious limitations, including sixty plus years of nationalistic fervor on the material-political plane, possesses deeper connotations. The star is a hexagram made of an ascending triangle passing through a descending triangle, representing the potential merging of quotidian consciousness with transcendent levels. This symbol, also known as the Seal of Solomon, is found in the alchemy of Paracelsus, the writings of Jacob Boehme, the Jewish Kabbalah, Sufism, Islamic mysticism, and esoteric Buddhism and Hinduism, where it is the symbol for the Anahata (heart) chakra. It is also the "double triadic" symbol of God in Christian mysticism.

In the words of Remo Roth,

> *The Seal of Solomon is the 'unifying symbol, and it is without exception assigned to the human heart, the place where the mystical relationship of man with God takes place.*32

As James N. Powell demonstrates in *The Tao of Symbols*, a gradation of these hexagrams, when collapsed into a two-dimensional diagram, creates the Shri Yantra, one of the most powerful symbols for spiritual meditation.33

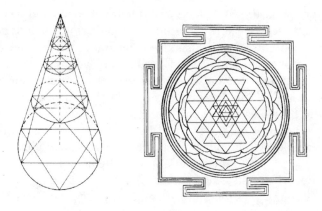

The legend of Christ arose in a land of pyramids and hexagramic symbolism, creating a ripeness for a religious linking of sun worship with a more personal god of omniscient caring intelligence that was concerned about humanity. The expectation of a death/rebirth imbued Messiah, tacitly associated with solar myths from various cultures, was connected to Jesus-Christ among his earliest followers. In fact, in various early Christian writings Jesus is referred to as the Sun of Righteousness.

During the rule of Augustus Caesar, Jesus, a wandering Siddha-Rabbi-sage in his adulthood, could easily have been acknowledged as the representative Son of the Sun. Pagan Romans could not only relate quite easily to sun gods, and sons of sun gods, but were very responsive to recognizing the affinity of the crucifixion tale of death and resurrection with legends of the death and rebirth of heroes going back to the dawn of the first agricultural communities, where myths were essentially rooted in the rhythms of nature, such as the decay of winter and the renewal of spring. Far before the Roman Empire, the Sumerians had worshipped a Christlike figure called Tammuz, which means "son of deep water," who was mourned every year when winter brought him death, and celebrated when he arose in spring. In dreams and myth, deep water symbolizes the mysterious unconscious depths of the mind. Sumerian priests were hardly alien to esoteric symbolism. Their teachings heavily influenced the Egyptians, who saw the sun sinking into the sea each evening as dying into the "deep water" of the unknown. In certain arcane text the sinking sun represents the somnambulistic state of ordinary consciousness, and sunrise as awakening to a greater radius of illumined comprehension. We can look upon the dying of the traditional literal interpretation of the New Testament as a prelude to a much richer esoteric realization.

Deciphering such spiritual-alchemical symbolism is to cross a bridge between exoteric religious tradition and esoteric attributes of individuation. Esoteric is not to be equated with occult, though there are junctures where they intermingle. Esoteric knowledge is accessible to those who seek it out and there is no secretive cultish quality about it. However, though accessible, the esoteric-mystical has always lain in the shadows behind the exoteric trappings of every religion. Where the exoteric radius of comprehension for the priest ended, the expanding radius of the spiritually oriented alchemist and lover of wisdom began. But make no mistake, such esoteric-mystical wisdom takes stringent devotion to acquire, and a life commitment to sustain.

In the seventeenth century text of the scholar of alchemy, Elias Ashmole, it is written, "*For they being lovers of wisdom more than worldly wealth, drove at higher and more excellent operations.*"[34] "Excellent operations" is what the quest is all about. All the known sages of history, one way or another, partook of such activities. For Socrates, philosophy was the cultivation of wisdom, a view his student Plato attempted to carry on, but failed in significant ways, which would leave his work vulnerable to limited interpretations on the level of social discourse. Aristotle believed the pursuit of Sophia was the highest quest humans could undertake, but he seemed to fail at relating this to his pupil Alexander the Great, who pursued such goals as ambition for power, glory, treasure, which Sophianic wisdom scorns. Centuries later Spinoza wrote that the supreme good was the love of wisdom. Despite streams of wisdom found in the works of these and other significant philosophers, we should always keep in mind that most of them were not spiritually awakened men and were even foolish in certain aspects of their personal lives, often blatantly wrong concerning some of the subjects they expounded upon. Their lack of being imbued with the fullness of true wisdom clearly verifies it is a state of awareness not easily come by. As I have stressed before, eclectically choosing what to keep and what to leave behind from the works of great minds is a skill the committed seeker must cultivate.

The fascinating figure of Sophia is an intriguing mytho-religious goddess figure representing higher wisdom. We find her showing up in various male and female forms in cultures across the earth — in the Mideast as Isis, Ceres, Diana, Dionysus, Mithra, Jesus. The mytho-symbolism and logos power of Jesus-Christ is rooted within the millennium upon millennium flow of Sophianic wisdom reaching back prior to the dawn of civilization. The English word "wisdom" as found in the New Testament is a translation of the Greek word "sophia," and it relates not only to the Judaic Shekinah and sapientia, but also the feminine vision insight of gnosis. As we explored in Chapter 13, within the esoteric Christian matrix of Western civilization, ancient text tells of Sophia as the mother of Eve, manifesting intriguingly as the serpent, who sent her daughter to inspire Adam to rebel against the tyranny of Yahweh, who is actually only a demi-urge. When we consider the righteous war mongering diatribe many televangelists spew out against Islam, spouting the name of their unChristlike war god to justify violence unto others they most assuredly would not want done unto themselves, it certainly seems they are worshipping a lower god lacking any resonance with Christ. Thus we can see how, from a deeper Gnostic perspective, the serpent in Eden symbolizes the impulse to know, to doubt, to question given knowledge, to probe that which is forbidden by ruling authority intent on protecting the reign of the demi-urge. Questioning is indispensable to the spiritual quest.

When probing the mythology of the serpent, one of the most intriguing symbols of Sophianic wisdom, or the awakening to deeper knowledge, the seeker must put aside centuries of biased religious denigration. Though the serpent has been seen as a trickster in some ancient legends, such as the epic of Gilgamesh, where the snake steals the plant of immortality from the hero, in most myths and fables from cultures across the earth the serpent represents a giver of knowledge that awakens us to spiritual wisdoms. On the head dress of ancient Egyptian pharaohs, a golden serpent was located at the third-eye chakra. An eleventh century Cambodian sculpture of Buddha has a halo of serpents, as do statues of various spiritually awakened ones of Hinduism and Buddhism. The Aztecs saw their god of light and compassion, Quetzalcoatl, as a plumed dragon in winged form. The Hindu Kundalini is a spiritual energy "serpent" representing the potential of transcendence, coiled in spiral form at the base of the spine chakra, ready to rise in helicoid surge, upward to the Third Eye of enlightenment. Prior to first Old Testament writings, Hebrews of the early Iron Age, 1000 BC, had worshipped the serpent for prehistoric centuries. Only when the Garden of Eden tale was written down by tribal patriarchs as a moral warning did the serpent become a symbol of evil and an enticer of negative influence. This is possibly due to early patriarchal Zoroastrianism, which had a strong influence on the Israelites, and taught that a dragon represented evil. Judaic-Christian biblical text tends to disparage nature and many of its creatures, sometimes perceiving even harmless animals as abominable. In Isaiah it is said that not only are serpents creatures of hell but even owls and ostriches are loathsome to Yahweh. As Narby elucidates in his work *The Cosmic Serpent*, this abuse of symbolism which equates nature's creatures with evil is due to matriarchal influence being undermined by patriarchal authority, which first began having effect during later Iron Age Hebrew rule.35 Even today, theologians, and certain depth psychologists, all too easily project a patriarchal coloration onto this symbolic serpent-Sophia relationship, mistakenly equating the Luciferian illumination aspect of Sophia with endarkening powers of Satan. The Christian narrative of Satan's arrogant rebellion grounded on craving for power has distorted and tainted the mytho-metaphoric rebellion of the Promethean/Luciferian spirit against tyrannical social-psychological repression. Etymologically, Lucifer is related to light, as in *lucency, lucidity, luciferous* (bringing light and insight) — whereas Satan relates to adversity and obstruction by way of deceit, ambition, cruelty, darkness. Equating the Luciferian spirit to that of Satan is a significant theological blunder.

Despite all outward design of separation within the Western religious tradition between feminine and masculine, matriarchal and patriarchal, their entwining activity dances its yin and yang harmony throughout our unconscious depths, unperturbed by external distorted unbalance. The inner depth activity of these polarized mytho-powers has had an extremely significant effect. Behind the predominance of Yahweh-Jehovah dwell perennially powerful gylanic manifestations, such as the highly consecrated Babylonian Ishtar, the Canaanite Anut, Sumerian Inana, Egyptian Isis, Greek Aphrodite, to name but a few who were held in reverent awe by various cultures the Israelites interacted with. In the shadows of the Hebrew patriarchal Old Testament milieu, the Shekinah equation perpetually simmers with the Sophia-goddess influence. We can find definite traceable connections from Isis suckling Horus to the New Testament Madonna and Christ Child, which are both imbued at the core with the spiritual-psychic octave frequency of Sophia. Sophianic influence branches throughout the ancient world, with connections to the Egyptian god Thoth and the Greek god Hermes, who is related to the planet Mercury, the very planet which in India is named Buddha. Trace the word 'Buddha' to its roots and, just as with the names 'Jesus' and 'Christ,' you pass through Endo-Euro-Aryan words all meaning either "anointed" or "wisdom." Carry it further and you can catch rivulets flowing within Scandinavian culture where Odin was a sort of primitive god of wisdom.

Jung writes of the "hieros gamos" of Christianity, a sacred marriage of God and Sophia by way of the Holy Spirit. We can find elements of this numinous marriage throughout teachings in the Q Gospel in certain statements attributed to Christ. This is also true of other Coptic-Gnostic text, plus the Gospels of Thomas. All such writings are intimately connected to what is known as "wisdom literature," which were streams of thought traced back to writings found throughout ancient civilization across the entire Mediterranean-Levant areas, as well as the empires of Greece and Rome. Sophia-wisdom literature existed in every culture the early Israelites interacted with or settled near. Biblical scholars researching Judaic Old Testament text have found a heavenly Sophia-wisdom figure at the side of God, acting as mediator in the process of creation. So what we are dealing with here is a living universal mytho-archetype connecting every person on this planet through the deeper flow of all existence to an impulse toward higher spiritual knowing. As scholar Michael Gelven elucidates, the essence of wisdom is a deep reverence for truth. This is esoterically related to the Christ narrative — *"The truth is the way"* — entailing dying and rebirth, renewal after the "crucifixion" of psychic crisis, living as a spiritual vehicle, surrendering persona to essence. The potential to ignite this salvational process of spiritual awakening lies within everyone.

Ancient alchemical text contains images of a serpent coiling around a crucifixion-cross. This represents the Sophianic stream of wisdom which infuses the story of Christ, dovetailing with Judaism to enhance and strengthen the feminine Shekinah, thus tempering the overwhelming aggressive masculinity of the Old Testament God Yahweh. The wandering rabbi-avatar, whose life is recounted to us through the legend of Jesus Christ, represents the epitome of Sophianic wisdom. Everyone, even intelligent atheists, acknowledge that the gospel Jesus-Christ figure can be looked upon as a teacher of significant wisdoms, especially compassion within the sphere of human relationships. But this figure, as the reader should by now perceive, has greater depth than the Gospels reveal. We speak here not of institutionalized narrative, but of living inner depth.

Certain text clarifies that a form of esoteric "Christianity" was being taught in ancient Egypt centuries before Jesus was born, practiced by certain spiritually purified persons who had attained an awakened state entailing compassionate empathy = love transcending common emotions and passions. This state of higher awakening had been experienced and witnessed within the ambit of early civilization for perhaps several thousand years BC, within the Persian-Sumerian-Egyptian mytho-religious ambit of human development. Yes, there has been and is now more going on across this planet, in the spiritual depths behind our daily comings and goings, than we ever learned in Sunday School, or from our history books. There most assuredly have been, and are, rare human beings, shamans, alchemists, Siddhas, yogis, capable of becoming an extraordinary or meta-ordinary type of being of the highest moral-psychic quality. These are the exceedingly rare anointed ones, and it is quite possible the obscure historical figure who we have come to know as Jesus was one of them.

As Sri Aurobindo, perhaps the only truly anointed one of the past two centuries, clarified in his work, *The Mind of Light*, the ascending frequencies of the deeply committed seeker of spiritual truth will resonate with descending meta-frequencies of the "supermind," permeating and imbuing the seeker's purified psyche.

> *He will become one with cosmic being and universal Nature: He will contain the world in himself, in his own cosmic consciousness and feel himself one with all beings; he will see himself in all and all in himself, become united and identified with the Self that has become all existences ... The descent of the Supermind will bring to one who receives it and is fulfilled in the Truth-Consciousness all the possibilities of the divine life ...This and all else that the spiritual consciousness can bring to him the divine life will give him when it reaches its utmost completeness and perfection and the supramental Truth-Consciousness is fulfilled in all himself; but even before that he can attain to something of it all, grow in it, live in it, once the Supermind has descended upon him and has the direction of his existence. All rela-*

*tions with the divine will be his: the trinity of God-knowledge,
divine works, and devotion to God will open within him and
move toward an utter self-giving and surrender of his whole being and nature.*[36]

Two thousand years of yoga in India has been essentially involved in such endeavor. Jesus, having possibly reached one of the
highest states of samadhi, would have attained substantial siddhi
powers, along with knowledge of shamanistic healing techniques
emerging from his early experiences with sorcery, as certain ancient
apocryphal text elucidate. Such a combination of abilities would present us with a truly powerful spiritual being. Yes, I know, we are
entering a New Age landscape of occult theosophical speculations
where delusion, fabrication, distortion of truth, as well as outright
mental aberration, lurk behind every tree and boulder of belief and
perception. But that's part of the obstacle course of separating the
wheat from the chaff the seeker must face and deal with. It is the
same when dealing with traditional orthodox religion. I have approached this mind-field as carefully as possible. But skepticism concerning the paranormal aspects of such things must be exceedingly
flexible. It should be clear by now that any interpretation of our existential-spiritual situation from an atheistic/physicalist perspective,
would be far too shallow, if not outright ludicrous.

From what is now known by all the attempts of various scientists to study the paranormal, plus the scholarly research of dozens
of highly intelligent men and women concerning alternate "higher"
states of consciousness, we can say there is a possibility that, after
years of unique training inducing spiritual awakening, Jesus, (as a
few other sages before and since have done), vanquished the subject-
object illusion between ego and wholly other essence, between appearance and archetypal-quantum depths. This entails a process of
matter/energy unfolding in a fused translucency of psychic opening,
the neuronic activity of the brain becoming altered to its most intense frequency capability. The purified embodied mind of Jesus,
merging with disembodied meta-frequencies of consciousness on the
highest (samadhi) level of the spiritual spiral of Being, ignited meta-
spiritual transformation—thus the mysterium tremendum became
enfleshed in "material" form. Perhaps this person we know as Jesus,
who according to apocryphal legend was a sorcerer in his youth, did
not experience his full power of anointment until he was "baptized"

by John the Baptist, in a ritual of a much more empowering quality than ordinary baptismal rituals going on in churches across this nation today. What most likely went on between Jesus and John is what is known in India as 'shaktipat' — one-on-one transference of spiritual energy from a powerful Siddha to a specially gifted devotee. Symbolically, the river John baptized Jesus in is the telepathic resonance of higher meta-frequency mind waves washing through the highly prepared and purified mind of Jesus. We are talking of possibilities here, of what may have occurred, possibilities overlooked and distorted by those who put the Gospels together during the first century AD.

We have touched on the relationship of the myth of Christ to solar symbolism, as well as the inner Self as Christ within. How does all this relate to the Resurrection, a concept the entire edifice of Christianity is founded upon? Let us consider what we have knowledge of. From Eskimo culture to the Maya, from the Siddhas of India and yogis of Tibet, from the practice of shamanism and sorcery in cultures all across the earth, and much else, we have occult and spiritual tales and legends of amazing psychic-spiritual capabilities humans can attain. From modern laboratories of psychological and psychedelic research, we have reams of scientific documents informing us about contemporary humans experiencing various dimensions of fantastic consciousness, entailing awareness of a second nonmaterial body, the astral body, the etheric body, which is usually invisible, but occasionally has been claimed to be visible. This disembodied form has been described as a state of cohesion just beyond quantum level activity. Considering what we know of the actual electro-chemical-quantum nature of our being and the perplexing paradoxical nature of reality, including plausible scientific theories of hyper-dimensions, superstrings, dark energy inundating the immense "emptiness" of the universe, the mind boggling strangeness of our concepts of time and space, parallel universes, supersymmetric particles, particles with no mass — is it not possible that there is valid truth to such an extensively expounded upon universal phenomenon as an energy component of our "material" body having the potential to manifest in form beyond the constraints of our flesh? To paraphrase J. B. S. Haldane, the universe is not only as wondrous and strange as we imagine, it is even more wondrous, even stranger, than we CAN imagine. If Siberian shamans, Tibetan yogis, and others of varied cultures have claimed to anthropologists for over a century to have the ability to manifest such a second body for astral travel, why not a mid Eastern rabbi-siddha? If Jesus was a truly powerful spiritual being, could he not have been capable of astral body manifestation? Even if it were a brief manifestation to a few witnesses soon after the Crucifixion, such an incident would have been sufficient to induce the strength of belief from which the first Christians formed their faith. Yes, I am tiptoeing along the edge of New Age credulity here, but not quite. Considering all we have dealt with over the last thirteen chapters, there is certainly room here for logic and reason to maneuver, if intelligently flexible. The skeptical materialistically oriented intellect must first face and ingest all the data available from empirical science which validates how undeniably fantastic and bewildering this marvelous phenomenon we call reality is, where logic and reasoning, though they need not be put aside, must give room for possibilities which go beyond their culturally imposed limitations. When that is sincerely faced, breathing space for a more extensive comprehension of who and what we are becomes available. Bottom line, don't automatically slam the door shut on the possibility of what at first may seem an impossibility.

What we are seeking in all this is the awareness that Sophianic wisdom is a reality accessible to any who undergo the endeavor to open themselves to their deeper essence. There are always a few such authentically awakened humans among us, seeking neither recognition nor acknowledgment, for they know the possible consequences, as Socrates and Jesus demonstrate. It is quite possible Christ was aware of and accepted the consequences of coming forth among humankind at his moment in history. As for finding a truly wisdom-imbued sage among us today who claims the status of spokesperson of God, whether theologian or guru, well-honed discernment will tell false from true.

But here we should pause. To equate the Sophia/Christ archetype with the historical figure of the person we know as Jesus, no matter how powerful or paranormal his abilities may have been, is to miss a most important insight into the workings of the mysterium tremendum within the realm of human existence. What we're really dealing with here is the universal spiritual phenomenon known throughout all religious belief systems as rebirth of common consciousness to higher spiritual awakening, with religious figures from every culture symbolizing such accomplishment. On the level of esoteric meaning, in relation to human psychology, the mytho-historical polysemous narrative of the New Testament can be seen as a rendering of the potential fulfillment of individual spiritual rebirth through the Calvary-quest/Crucifixion of the socially fabricated ego. The essence of the Christ myth = to die to your ordinary form of life in order to rise to another, is a call to each person to renounce the socially oriented Christianity of almost every denomination existing, and strive to give up all worldly concerns rooted in vanity and the self-centeredness of ego enhancement, security, prestige—a complete giving over of all goals which detract from authentic spiritual orientation. As Jesus stated, *"All who want to follow me must deny themselves..."*37 Such demands can be seen as rites of sacrifice in this life, undertaken in order to be truly reborn to a state of awakening beyond the egoically limited Christian religious "born again" experience.

Standardized religion, inducing a somewhat necessary but all too narrow moral sense of conscience, while comforting believers on the personal-emotional level, has proven to be essentially fallible, not capable of fully accomplishing the daunting task of developing mind and soul. As we have demonstrated, socialized religion has fallen beneath the sway of collective materialistic influences, entailing conformistic patriotism and addictive consumerism, with flags flying in every church and a new car in every driveway, making modern church going Christians very similar to the Pharisees and Philistines who bowed to Rome during the time of Jesus. Consider that 90% of German citizens who belonged to the Nazi Party circa 1930-45, were devout church going Christians. As writer Bill McKibben elucidated,

> *At the moment, the idea of Jesus has been hijacked by people with a series of causes that do not reflect his teachings... They undercut Jesus, muffle his hard words, deaden his call, and in the end silence him.*38

Even though specific aspects of traditional organized Christianity have kept a small but steady flame of unconditional love and compassion alive within the arena of human relationships, it is a precarious flame indeed, easily dimmed and even snuffed out by manipulation of secularized social forces. The seeker must avoid letting the realm of Caesar darken the realm of spiritual development.

On the stage of history a hundred years is just a blip, and it has only been a little over a hundred years since Nietzsche and Darwin set pen to paper, even less since the discoveries of Freud, Einstein, Hubble, upset the human conception of our cosmic-terrestrial situation which had been dominated by a religious conceptual orientation for nineteen hundred years. Ruling hand-in-hand with "royalty," the overwhelming influence of both Catholic and Protestant Church authority upon the economic-military-political powers of most of the nations of Western civilization did not begin to decline significantly until around 1912 to 1920, when revolution and war caused a significant lessening of royalty's influence across Europe and Russia. The effects of those significant cultural shifts are still being played out. Orthodox Christianity circa 2006 is like a large sand castle increasingly surrounded by the incoming tide of ever expanding knowledge from areas of science, mysticism, philosophy, which demand change, transformation, deepening of traditional belief systems mired in obsolete imagery. Theologian apologists, evangelists, preachers, Christian scholars, priests, pastors, with persuasive arguments that con the desperately needful masses, staunchly continue building futile dikes against this unstoppable tide. Thus we have the fundamentalist backlash, a surge of last-ditch-stand pseudo-Christianity, entailing the political stance of the Religious Right, which, like the ancient all-powerful Church in its paranoid Inquisitional zealousness, intensely opposes everyone who is a part of the cultural inundation of greater more expansive, essentially spiritual truths, whether they come by way of science or not.

As things are now, beneath the sway of such powerful religious-political forces, the average Christian puts as much emotive fervor into nationalistic pride (the realm of Caesar) as in their faith in Christ, short-circuiting any genuine interchange betwixt egoic mind frequencies and spiritual meta-frequencies. Authentic meta-baptism in the river of higher frequencies can only occur when the peerlessly oriented seeker of truth, who has partaken thoroughly of the Sophianic wisdom stream of alchemical-yogic knowledge, is no longer attached to acculturated patterns of religious or socially induced beliefs or ego-enhancing materialistic goals. When it comes to genuine spiritual commitment, the well manicured, excessively affluent, coiffured televangelist, the career-secure pastor and minister, all want to remain safely standing on the sidelines, praising Jesus and mouthing his teachings without ever really considering stepping away from the security of the collective, as Simon of Cyrene symbolized, to truly take up the cross and bear the weight of authentic individual awakening. It should be clear that the substantially verified reality of archetypal-mythological forces relating to the figure of Christ have been significantly devitalized within the mind of the believer heavily influenced by institutionalized religion. The hypnotic collective power traditional religion holds over the common ego has developed over millenniums of converting what is intolerable and incomprehensible about spiritual existence into what is tolerably comprehensible for millions of faithful. The past two hundred years has merged such religious faith with the American Dream of garnering worldly possessions. The multitudes cling so stringently to their simple comforting religious imagery because it offers such an effective evasion of genuine spiritual struggle.

As elucidated in the last chapter, if we place the entire four to five billion year process of evolution within a twenty-four hour scale, with humans evolving from primates during the last two minutes of that twenty-four hours, then ten thousand years of civilization would only be the last couple of seconds. Thus, as we stand on the threshold of the third millennium AD, the last nano-second on the scale, humanity seems to be in the infancy of some fascinating process of unfolding spiritual consciousness. The writings of some of our great spiritual sages and profound thinkers clarify this is so. The problem is, self-destructive anti-spiritual forces have arisen within the ambit of civilization beneath the guise of religion. Thus it is urgent we learn to mature by standing and facing existence for what it is, and then make that fateful choice either to meet the challenge of the spiritual quest we have spoken of since page one, or slip into the comfortable slippers of collective conformism and seek fulfillment on the egoic-social level of existence, which all in-depth spiritual sages have warned is a futile dreaming. Amid the ancient Old Testament proverbs, Sophia-wisdom has it that *"Those who diligently seek me will find me."*39 In the New Testament the ever fascinating mytholegendary figure of Jesus states, *"Seek and ye shall find."* At one time, chiseled in the granite over the portal of Apollo's temple at Delphi, were the words *"Know Thyself."* Each of these three quotes imply willful striving. Seeking is a conscious intentful act. Grace is being awakened to the opportunity to act.

Though there have been those among us who, upon experiencing the great awakening, saw all their striving as unnecessary and even foolish, that is hindsight. Surprisingly, and ironically, they never seem to grasp that the so-called unnecessary striving was an essential aspect of their own awakening, as was the case with Siddhartha's extended periods of fasting, Bodhidharma's nine years in a cave, and Jesus' years as a wandering ascetic before meeting John the Baptist. No one awakens without effort. Any seemingly serene ones who claim otherwise should arouse skepticism. Wisdom, the doorway to the highest state of human consciousness, is not easily attained. Sophia is a demanding goddess. To move toward this inner light of greater truth, to activate this inner ascendance, we should keep in mind the words of Sri Aurobindo, "The divine descends from pure existence through the play of consciousness...as we ascend from matter through a developing of life, soul, mind."[40] This "developing" is what the quest is all about.

How does the esoteric quality of the "wisdom stream of knowledge," once tapped into, activate an ascending frequency within the seeker's daily life? Robert Nozick writes of the conscious state of wisdom as "giving all and everything its due," which I grasp as recognizing the ephemeral wonder of every person, place, thing, animal, vegetable, which "strikes our attention" while momentarily passing through our life, simultaneously giving homage to whatever resonates within our own inner depths. This giving things which come within our aesthetic attentiveness their spiritual due has affinity to Zen Buddhist teachings on how to see the world clearly, as it is, unblemished by delusion and distortion, each moment a haiku quality perception, a dance of knowing the psychological snares and spiritual qualities involved in each human interaction.

The word "prajna" is Sanskrit for wisdom, which the Hindu sages clarify implies depth of understanding, comprising well honed discernment and psychological centeredness in the acts of perception and discourse, imbued by diligent study of significant fields of knowledge and spiritual development. As such cultivated understanding comes about, everything expands in richness, in light and darkness, enhancing and spurring consciousness to an ascending frequency which ignites an echoing response from descending meta-frequencies of the mysterium tremendum. When seeking becomes your "calling," you will be "called" in return.

And so, we may wonder, just what is this mysterious force that creates such a magnetic calling toward some numinous ascendant flow imbuing the entire phenomenal universe with its power of accelerating expansion, imbuing the entire primal ocean's myriad creatures, ferocious and predatory, with the impulse to survive,

adapt, selectively expand, imbuing wild creatures with homing instinct, imbuing the seedling as it bursts the soil, the caterpillar as it
creates the cocoon, imbuing all existence with its splendorous be-
yond-reason magnetism, carrying us toward an unknown even our
most profound mytho-religious imaginal ability has yet to grasp.
From all that can be gleaned about the concept of the transpersonal
evolution of human consciousness by eclectically delving into art,
literature, poetry, mythology, psychology, philosophy, music, theology, yoga, we can surmise that in our physical-egoic form within the
flow of terrestrial-cosmic evolution, we exist within the wild foam-
ing crest of an immense spiritual tsunami. Its sweep across the ex-
panse of time over the shoreline of history reveals the cascading ep-
och of our moment of consciousness. Within this maelstrom, the individual's impulse to awaken to it all ignites a resonance within the
very soul of existence—Being beyond being. To willfully strive to
comprehend the unfathomable mystery surrounding and permeating us, to derive meaning rooted in numinous truth, to partake of the
spiritual resonance of Being, is the pursuit we are involved in here—
the pursuit of Sophia, archetype of wisdom, which is the psychic-
spirit essence in which Christ was anointed.

What is known in Jungian psychology as the "Self" is a radiant
dimension of our being which can become the alembic where our
ascending intention merges with descending meta-mind frequencies,
creating what in esoteric circles is known as "Christ consciousness"—the inner sun of Being, the solar center, the soul-our center,
the center everywhere, the circumference radiating outward into
everywhere-nowhere, a living mandala resonance of the "holy
other." This is the still-point of zazen. As the great wheel turns
round this still-point axis, as the tornado swirls round the stillness of
its center, as the spiral of Being whirls its gyration of frequencies, we
are here, now, amid the wild awesome wonder of it all.

Recall what we dealt with concerning mytho-religious symbolism relating to the primal will's semi-egoic (patriarchal) impulse to
free itself from the confinement of the pre-egoic (matriarchal) instinctual response to reality. Judeo-Christian religion has seen this process as a fall, as being cast out of Eden. An interpretation free of religious fabrication would speak of this ego birthing as being activated
through the medium of primal cognitive expansion, the seedling ego
rising from the womb of nature toward some dim unknown light of
more extensive awakening, like a creature of the great sea depths

rising toward the surface as it senses the light of the sun. As to our distant ancestors, once partially awakened, the intensity of the primal hominid's will to survive ignited a self-reflective feedback loop, creating a frequency of semi-egoic activity, bringing about an exceedingly gradual resonance with higher frequencies of Being. We cannot pinpoint when and how all this bewildering activity of awakening from proto-hominid to self-reflective hominid came about. We have touched on how artifacts of crafted weaponry have been dated back several million years, and domesticated use of fire to 750,000 years ago. What we know is that we who are alive now, without any evasive ideas of personal past lives, are related in intrinsic intimacy with all those that have come before us and all they have experienced in the depths of their being. And all this pre-historical and historical psychological-spiritual mulch we have contemplated is an aspect of the journey each person awakening to her/his inner potential becomes part of. Thus here we stand, perplexed, surrounded by paradox and mystery, with most of our fellow beings ensnared by ignorance of significant knowledge, addicted to political and religious illusions which comfort them. Yet there are many of us, having seen through the delusions and illusions of our era, who long for a greater light, a genuine awakening, an unfolding of a truer acknowledgment and comprehension of our existential-spiritual situation.

The human impulse for intimate contact with the source of creation, the longing to experience a magnetic merging toward wholeness with the very core of the mysterium tremendum, abides "in potentia" within every human being. This is what evangelist St. Paul meant by all men having Christ within—"Christ" symbolizing our potential to cultivate genuine spiritual realization. This "potentia" is what Aurobindo called the very soul of an individual. This mythos/logos power to ignite an individual's inner magnetism is imbued within the holy books of all religions, whether the Upanishads, the Bible, the Bhagavad Gita, the Koran, the Torah, or the doctrines attributed to Buddha. It is in pursuit of such esoteric streams of wisdom at the root of embellished fable, parable, legend, that the seeker of authentic self-knowledge approaches such works. But, as should be quite clear, it is not an easy task to pluck the wisdom of guidance from amid such an impressive array of centuries of intentional and unintentional biased slanting of fact, literalization and fabrication, even outright fraud. To even consider opening the Bible as a book of spiritual guidance, one must cultivate the ability to perceive, as John McManners puts it, "*the bright inner core of a vast confusion.*" In other words, sifting for ounces of "quito gold" amid tons of fool's gold, ruling out all that does not hold up in the light of unbiased research and intense analysis. First we must understand that the religiously oriented person projects their individual needs, desires and longings upon such text, perceiving and interpreting every word in ways most fulfilling for his/her personal commitment. Being aware of this, one strives to read with as much objective discernment as possible, without succumbing to either sterile intellectual analysis or gullible subjective need. With such an approach, if consistent, the esoteric meanings pertinent to the seeker's fate, over a period of time, during the trials and triumphs of individuation, will be revealed.

All religions have a stream of wisdom which teaches compassionate empathy, and Christianity has no monopoly on such teachings. There are over six billion humans on the planet Earth, of which at least four billion are non-Christian: Buddhists, Hindus, Jews, Muslims, who all bow to a greater spiritual reality. They pray, they care, they love, they comfort, but they do not believe in Christ as God come to earth as the one and only Messianic savior of humankind, though many regard him quite highly, even as a kind of avatar, or a great sage, and rightly so. Most religions have a god or goddess of equal compassion in their belief system. The Chinese goddess Kuanyin is a Christlike bestower of mercy. In Tibet, Maitreya, known as the spiritual "Being of Love," is a messiah figure expected to come in some future era as the last Buddha. Yet even without the assistance of mytho-religious images of compassionate gods and goddesses, the human heart chakra will still manifest compassion. The Bushmen of Africa have no book of guidance, not even a page, yet sincerely and spontaneously care for and comfort each other. It is the same with the natives deep in the Amazon forest, and the Australian aborigine, and other primitive peoples who have never heard of Christ. As the sage Maimonides states, "*Forms without matter not visible to the eye, are known by the eye of the heart.*"[41]

The people of every civilization and tribe that existed for many thousands of years before Christ was born, had spiritual belief systems, moral standards, ethics, myths, tales, philosophies, which taught them care and concern for one another. The teachings of Christ concerning a basic moral attitude toward one's fellow humans are not exceedingly unique as far as religious or philosophical teachings go. The uniqueness of the Christ-Calvary narrative for Western civilization is its esoteric symbolism relating to the spiritual transformation of the ego—Christ being a symbolic representative of divinity immanent within the human dimension of existence, requiring of us to step away from the realm of Caesar, of empire, of external desires and ambitions, and take up an authentic participation in the quest for genuine awakening.

Satprem, in his book about Aurobindo, wrote:

*What we take to be the ultimate Truth is very often only a partial experience of the truth – and undoubtedly the totality of the Experience does not exist anywhere in time or space, in no place, in no being however luminous, for the Truth is infinite, it always goes ahead.*42

He then goes on to quote the Mother, Aurobindo's spiritual mate, a fitting quote to end this long and challenging chapter:

'But always man takes upon his shoulders the interminable burden... He does not want to drop anything of the past and he stoops more and more under the weight of a useless accumulation. You have a guide for a part of the way, but when you have traveled this bit, leave the road and the guide and go farther. This is a thing men do with difficulty; when they get hold of something which helps them, they cling to it, they do not want to budge from there. Those who have progressed with the help of Christianity do not want to give it up and they carry it upon their shoulders; those who have progressed with the help of Buddhism do not want to leave it and they carry it upon their shoulders, and the journey is clogged and you are indefinitely delayed. Once you have passed the stage let it drop, let it go! Go farther.'

15 – Concept of God

And if the soul were to ask,
'How much farther?'
You must answer:
'On the other side of the river;
not this one before us,
the one just beyond.
— Alejandra Pizarnik

The tweedledum tweedledee tug-of-war between biased theologians, church officials and committed believers versus mystics and philosophers, over whether God is a caring supreme personality comprehended through rational faith or the ineffable incomprehensible seemingly indifferent Being beyond being, has been going on for many centuries and continues today. A good portion of this book, unavoidably and of necessity, and somewhat helplessly, has apparently become a third millennium participant in this perennial controversy. So be it. As Wittgenstein stressed, it is only in dialogue that we can begin to cultivate a more expansive comprehension of God. In pursing this I do not pretend to have any final answers to ultimate questions. As I lay out what I have discovered in half a century of worldly and alchemical adventures, plus trolling through archives, antiquated bookstores, libraries great and small, for knowledge of genuine substance, which I diligently studied, scrupulously pondered, meticulously analyzed, it is to offer what the individual attempting to live an authentic existence based on truth should at the very least be fully aware of.

Repudiation of the anthropomorphic concept of God as a parental overseer in the sky did not just come forth over the twentieth century. Teachings of classical Judaism highlight a firm belief that the nature of God is unknowable. The ancient Judaic tribal sages, conveying their religious message orally, would allow no one to speak the word which referred to their God. Only certain priests during special ceremonies would be allowed to speak the holy word. Buddha said that all names for God are in vain, that the nameless can only be acknowledged in silence. But today's theologians, televangelists, pastors, priests, have ignored such reverent submissiveness toward the mystery of the sacred. They have no qualms over speaking or writing of what God says to them, what God wants of us, what God thinks about this and that. Even New Age mystics and semi-mystics speak of God in this manner.

It should be quite clear that depth of commitment in probing for the flaws and truths of your own religious concepts is essential if you seek to become more than an acculturated puppet, free to live an authentic existence, free of self-deceit. The Big Five religious belief systems are formed from and dependent upon acculturated dogma. A Catholic priest, a Buddhist priest, a Jewish rabbi, a Muslim imam, are all quite confident their view is "THE VIEW" of what our spiritual situation is all about. This is why a good rule of thumb is, never feel sure about your religious perspective until you have made an extensive unbiased effort to know all you can about your religion's origin and development, and why you feel it is THE religion to believe, instead of another. As you become more knowledgeable, stimulating a more all-encompassing perception of existence, your perspective becomes more holistic, thus more reliable as to how things really are. Almost everything in the universe has a multidimensional aspect to it, and there isn't anything that can be entirely grasped from a single, thus limited, viewpoint. Take a very simple example. Consider a prizefighter. His fans, who only see him box in the ring, know him as a tough and intense fighter; his children know him as a gentle and easygoing daddy; his wife knows him as both of these, as well as a provider, lover, and friend. To see him more completely, you have to take in all of these viewpoints, plus, if possible, get to know him yourself. The more you know about someone or something, the more holistically balanced your understanding, and the closer you are to the truth of whoever, or whatever, is involved. A reciprocal psychological rippling is activated as truth expands consciousness. Knowledge actually broadens perception, and this widening of perception opens you to more knowledge of what is being perceived—thus the growth of an individual's radius of comprehension becomes a dance of expanding perception and knowledge amplifying each other, stimulating an ascending helicoid frequency of consciousness.

Unfortunately, this rippling also works in the opposite direction. The more defensive people are about their provincial religious or political belief system, the more limited their potential for growth becomes, the more imploded their radius of comprehension. This is clearly seen in fundamentalist evangelical Christians, who can become desperately aggressive in defense of the belief that their religion is the one and only validated by God through the Bible. We have seen how absurd and mentally deficient such a belief is. How can so many people be so duped? The most pompous vain televangelist can bring forth drops of spiritual truth by tapping into the river of Sophianic wisdom flowing through biblical text, thus producing the false image of being a speaker of wisdom when he/she is actually only a skilled mouthpiece. Multitudes of believers susceptible to skillfully constructed image and hypnotized by charisma and oratorical skill, will see the most ridiculous fools as great religious teachers. It is the same with many outside the traditional religious milieu, such as those who believed Castaneda was an all-wise *nagual,* or those who see popular yoga instructors as enlightened beings. In this era, the majority have become spiritually parched while staggering through the secular desert of a materialistic consumer society, and they will lap up even polluted water, filling themselves with childlike zeal, with no regard for mature questioning of possible illusions or delusions.

Most human beings form a self-satisfied perception of scientific, religious, political, racial and moral systems between twenty and twenty-five, and very few, despite any mid-life crisis, change essentially over the following fifty or more years. In my own extensive research I have found that materialistic scientists, political conservatives, theologians and scientific creationists, who have written books, reveal in their bibliographies never to have read anything significant that is counter to their view of the way things are, and thus are clearly subject to confirmation/oversight bias. The rigid certitude of people's biased belief systems is directly proportional to their ignorance of the very truths that would prove them wrong. Such people will never make even the slightest effort to question their cherished convictions, because they believe they already know the whole truth and are confidently content. But repressed intuitive knowledge constantly simmers beneath their consciousness, producing fearful intimations that they are wrong. They develop a righteous defensiveness which breeds aggressiveness and can even become dangerous, ready to destroy any opposition to their belief — atheists, communists, Muslims, liberals, anyone who sees things other than how they see them. Since the all too limited image of the Christian God is being undermined from many directions, staunch believers crave for Armageddon, to have the whole world immolated rather than see themselves as wrong. They rationalize this suicidal ploy to escape truth by believing such immolation will be their moment of rapture.

Those beneath the sway of their culture's traditional religious misinterpretations are not aware their faith is in any way tainted by darker spiritual influences. There are organizations so ensconced in their fundamentalist illusions and delusions, they seek to convince millions to remain faithful to falsehoods they staunchly believe are truths. Organizations like PsychHeresy Ministries of California, which strives to protect Christians from the "psychologizing of faith," or the Creation Research Society of "scientists" who passionately strive to defend Creationism in a manner similar to White Supremacists and KKK members defending the Old South. There are numerous books similar to Tim LaHaye's and David Noebel's, *Mind Siege: The Battle For Truth in the New Millennium*,[2] a typical fundamentalistic defense of pseudo-truth against authentic truth, sort of like orthodox scientists who fought against Pasteur's idea of the existence of germs, because what the heck, nobody could see them! Just the title of their book reveals how fervently these people will delude themselves that falsehoods are truths, when they are actually battling against the truth. Millions of Christians are prey to arguments which zealously defend their deluded religious conceptions, because, as has been clearly validated through both scholarly work and scientific research, most people cannot handle too much reality, and only a simplistic anthropomorphic God with His comforting divine plan will make them feel at ease.

Influenced since childhood by grandparents, parents, community, and bolstered by the force of collective belief rooted in a stringent conforming to religious tradition, few Christian faithful, secure in their church pews, have ever felt the inner magnetism of the call to spiritual growth, to seek, to find something deeper, truer. And their faith is kept strong by an offer they can't refuse — the enticement of a future peace, of bliss, in a place called Heaven, which most describe as a sort of immense Norman Rockwell suburb of the American dream fulfilled for all the faithful. The deep craving for immortality of the ego/persona is one of the driving forces behind the major religions, and their ideas of afterlife. But it is not my intention to try to destroy all aspects of theism. I am basically trying to clarify that, at this point of human existence on earth, within the threshold of the third millennium AD, our era is in as much turmoil of spiritual uncertainty as were the cultures surrounding the Mediterranean-Euro-Levant area circa 500 BC to 500 AD. Whether the reader may become a committed seeker or not, anyone concerned at all with comprehending the truth of the human situation must recognize, as that noteworthy contemplator of our religious situation, John MacQuarrie, put it, *"the need to guard ourselves against uncritical acceptance of false or inadequate views of the world."*

Let us not forget, as I have repeatedly emphasized in the last chapters, that religion possesses significant meanings that need to be brought to light. Only a materialist lost in the sterile halls of the analytical intellect, cut off from significant intuitive knowledge of the depths of things, would deny that something substantial must surely be present within the compelling numinous impulse upon which all religions have been built. There has never been a culture anywhere on earth without ritual and worship relating to a higher spiritual power. No matter how vulnerable to delusion, illusion and anthropomorphic projection the Big Five religions have been subject to, they have certainly been signal flares in the immense psychic-cosmic night that engulfs this tiny planet on which humanity struts and frets its bewildered history—flares signifying something other, entirely other, wholly other, existing within the depths, obscure, paradoxical, astonishing, yet there. But, once again, what the nature of this "something other" is, we have no idea. The ways and means of the Absolute Infinite—whether you call it God or not—will forever remain beyond the grasp of human comprehension, despite all the theological volumes which claim otherwise. That an individual can, through persistent spiritual discipline, personally have epiphanic contact with emanations of the Absolute Infinite, does not imply comprehension. In the pages of the theological encyclopedia, the Sacramentum Mundi, we find the phrase, *"God is held knowable, but incomprehensible."* Maybe our incapability for total comprehension could be a kind of grace given. As Friedrich Schlegel stated, *"Truly, it would frighten you if the entire world became comprehensible."*

It is challenging indeed to realize that an indispensable element of an individual's relationship to the mystery of the Absolute Infinite is to abandon all conceptual images of God. Even Gregory of Nyssa, a profound figure of the early Church circa 370 AD, wrote, *"All concepts of God are facades."*[3] The brilliant scholar Joseph Campbell spoke of the varied "masks of God" which manifest in different cultures across the earth. Such conceptual facades are endless when it comes to the human mind's cognitive interpretation of the ultimate core-consciousness of all existence. Even among the millions who belong to the same religion and speak the same language, the image of their God, because it is such an extremely subjective concept, varies almost as much as each person's physical features do. Billy Graham, Sun Myung Moon, the Christian leader of the Klu Klux Klan, the Pope, St. Francis, Savanarola, Calvin, Martin Luther King, David Koresh, Jerry Falwell, Benny Hinn—they all have claimed to believe in the same God, but if you observe how each of these men have interpreted their God's word concerning values, principles, moral guidelines, and then contemplate how each of these men have lived, it would seem they each had a different God in mind.

Let us move toward contemplation of a relationship to "God" that is free from any traditional religious trappings. Of course, that may be nearly impossible, considering how entwined the roots of religion are within the archetypal dimensions of the psyche. We are immersed in imagery developed over hundreds of generations, instilled in childhood, merging with primal group tendencies to conform to collective traditional belief. There are myriad reams of research clearly verifying the entrenched hypnotic magnetism within each of us to conform to the religious and political belief systems of our culture. The research of Solomon Asch on the insidious power of conformism,[1] shows how a person will claim a lie to be the truth if a group of peers all believe the lie to be true. The larger the group which agrees to a blatant distortion of truth, the more likely an individual will give up his/her own validated and reasoned out knowledge of what is true, just to conform. Michael Talbot deals with this in his book, *Mysticism and the New Physics*:

> *This belief is dramatically demonstrated in experiments undertaken at Harvard concerning the effect of social pressure upon*

350

perceptual judgments. When asked to correctly match the length of a line with that of one of three lines presented, participants made the 'wrong' choice less than one percent of the time. However, in a group where the majority was coached beforehand to unanimously choose the 'wrong' line, the decision of the unknowing participants was measurably affected. Under group pressure minority subjects agreed with the majority's 'wrong' judgments 36.8 percent of the time even when the length of the two allegedly equal lines differed by as much as seven inches.[4]

Seven inches is a very obvious difference, and yet these people still gave up their genuine perceptual grasp of reality in order to conform. As Theodore Adorno stated, *"For the individual, life is made easier through capitulation to the collective with which he identifies."* Thus we can see why, once a person becomes a member of an organization, whether religious, political, military, corporate, etc., the pressure to give up individual choice in favor of group decision is overwhelming.

The individual who breaks away from acculturated conformism in order to cultivate the ability to seek deeper intimate contact with the mysterium tremendum of Being—God—is a rare person indeed. Most people of fair intelligence caught up in the pursuit of a career, relationships, building a home life, saving money, pursuing entertainment or hobbies, may enjoy reading certain magazines and an occasional novel, but they find contemplating books concerning ultimate things an unnecessary mental challenge. Others have a way of intellectually delving into and assimilating the heaviest knowledges without it effecting their lives to any meaningful extent. I have met professors of philosophy, physicists, psychologists, who might as well have been store clerks. I'm not implying that pondering ultimate things need be a weighty obligation, or call for a stringent asceticism depriving a person of joy, enthusiasm, or companionship. Once sincerely involved in the quest for spiritual growth, an inner intensity which blooms from the urge to awaken to the truth of one's existence transcends any sense of tediousness. But of course, an individual's attentiveness to such subject matter depends on the ripeness of time, place, circumstances, producing a readiness to give priority to what is most beneficial for her/his psychological-spiritual enrichment.

There is no denying the majority of people in the United States live ensconced in conformism to traditional religious and political belief systems, remaining superficially content with what they know. Even worse, they assume they know far more than they actually do. Lawrence Krauss, in his interesting little book, *Fear of Physics*,[5] tells about the period when he was teaching at Yale, one of our most prestigious universities, where, most of us assume, the students are all well informed. Krauss discovered, to his understandable amazement, that 35% of his Yale students thought the population of the United States, which is around three hundred million, was somewhere between one and ten million, which, Krauss pointed out, is less than the population of New York City. After reading this, one day in the local college hangout I personally asked more than a dozen college students about the population. Most guessed between twenty and forty million, three said at least a hundred million. Yet all these students were content with their ignorance, assuming they were sufficiently knowledgeable. This self-contentment with such little knowledge of the world is what both Socrates and Chuang Tzu said was the root of the vanity and ignorance which permeates the collective psyche.

Pea-sized radius of comprehension concerning what the world is about is pandemic. The late night TV show host, Jay Leno, has a segment where he goes out into the streets and asks different people questions you would think every person of average intelligence would know, such as being able to at least identify the famous painting of George Washington crossing the Delaware during the American Revolution, which some said was Columbus and others Napoleon. Even very well dressed young people looking like aspiring executives did not know what the letters IBM stand for, or NATO. Of course, there are a number of people Leno questions who have obviously been raised in educationally deprived circumstances, though Leno, another run-of-the-mill multi-millionaire celebrity with no idea how myopic his own intelligence is, seems completely oblivious to this, having them on his show only to give his audience a laugh. Still, most of the people on the street Leno interviews are of average intelligence, who obviously completed high school. Yet many of these were stumped with questions such as: *"What foreign country borders California?"* and *"What nation bombed Pearl Harbor in 1941?"* Easy questions having to do with geographical locations or important historical incidents were beyond the range of knowledge of even students he interviewed on college campuses. A poll taken during the 1999 Bush-Gore Presidential campaign revealed many people did not recognize photographs of Lieberman, Cheney, Janet Reno, whose highly profiled faces had been splashed throughout the media daily. Some did not even recognize Gore, who had been Vice President for eight years! Though the majority of citizens of the USA are probably a bit more informed about historical and current events than those Leno chooses to spotlight, they know very little of significant things relating to the very meaning of their existence on planet earth. It is a sure bet that very few of them have any substantial knowledge concerning how they formed their concept of God. And yet they believe they know all they need to know. It is the same with many Christian priests, ministers, televangelists, with their conformist belief systems, who typically reveal a very limited radius of comprehension as to significant knowledges.

Dostoyevsky wrote that centuries of human longing for spiritual succor must be substantiated somewhere, sometime. I believe it is only substantiated in the fate of an individual who is courageously committed to the quest for truth, whatever the cost to the desires of the ego. Jesus is said to have stated, *"The truth is the way."* Thus Christians seeking truth beyond Sunday sermons should be willing to face the actuality that the anthropomorphized biblical concept of God, created thousands of years ago by humans who conceived the world to be tremendously different than what we now know it to be, is a reduction of the mysterium tremendum. Such reduction of the Wholly Other into some sort of all-knowing grandfatherly ethereal overseer should cease. Where is the numinous mystery in this biblical God that manicured televangelists and seminary programmed theologians speak of as if they knew everything there was to know about him? If you can speak so confidently of the whys and wherefores of such a God, where is the true awe? If Christians could realize humans have no idea what a real God at the source of such a fantastic creation as ours would be like, they might learn how to truly bow down. And they would surely have a deeper understanding of what the Crucifixion/death-rebirth narrative of Christ is about.

When I contemplate such things, the urge comes over me, (as it has on several occasions over the many months I have worked on this manuscript), to just grab my backpack, jump in my van and head fifty miles to the city, to my favorite funky little bar to drink pale ale, smoke a joint and wait for the band to start. When I reach a fine existential buzz, I pay no heed to the younger folk wondering about the old guy doing a weird tai-chi boogie in the strobe light dazzle, and just lose myself in the brilliant flickering. After weeks of research and writing, with Mozart, Phillip Glass, Yo Yo Ma, Bach, playing in the background, a live rock or reggae band brings about a certain relief of tension, an invigoration, a renewal, which I need. Then again, more often, instead of going to town I hike up river through the forest, the rapids becoming more turbulent and wild as the river widens, wending higher into the mountains. Swimming nude in a wilderness pool, and hours sitting on a huge boulder in the middle of the river, has astounding powers of rejuvenation. Thus I pass my days, and continue with this writing I've committed myself to. Still, with God as the subject, I can occasionally envy those who are at ease never pondering one single question concerning ultimate things. And it's not like the world won't evolve without this book. I've read multi-dozens of books dealing one way or another to varied degrees with all the issues we've touched on, some shallowly done, some in depth. All that can be said about such things is scattered through the shelves of most libraries. One book more or less won't be noticed. In 1976, on a deserted midnight beach, I burnt a thousand page manuscript, knowing, as the sparkling cinders rose into the night sky, I was free of such obligations, and that if I ever put pen to paper again it would be after a certain deeper ripening of my own quest had come about. And so here I be, nearly thirty years since that bonfire blaze – the ripening coming with a cost entailing significant personal tragedy, several confrontations with death, failure in various aspects of my life, and moments of triumph. Thus if you hold this book in your hands, you have verification that whatever else occurred, I continued returning to this oval oak table to toil at the wordcraft of communication, to honor the blessing of this Jana yoga project, this writing as self-exploration, closely reviewing my own convictions, looking for flaws, weaknesses, chaff, as I attempt to impart what comes forth from the alchemical brew of my thought.

Because the concept of God is an abstraction, it is worth having some grasp of how language and concept relate. We have dealt with this in past chapters, but let's explore it a little further. A word is a symbol that is never the thing or concept it symbolizes. The word "dog" does not bark; even the word "bark" is not a sound, though it can be vocalized to mimic the sound a dog makes. You cannot drive the word "car" to the store. You cannot cut yourself with the word "knife." You cannot eat the word "apple." If I yell the word "apple" to a crowd, an apple does not fly out of my mouth, and no one in the crowd sees anything to grab and eat. Likewise, if I yell the word "God," you won't see or feel God, though it may trigger your own image of God to appear in your mind. Realize that there are hundreds of languages, with different alphabets. The word "God" is made up of three letters from the English alphabet aligned to form a symbolic metaphor that triggers a conceptual image only in the minds of English speaking people. Turn the letters around, and you get the word "dog," (which can't bark). The letters have no intrinsic meaning when isolated. What does "G" mean? "O"? "D"? Only when placing them in a specified grammatical order do they linguistically radiate the symbolic power to trigger a mental image.

Just as the map of a geographical area is not anything like the reality of that area, the conceptual image the word "God" triggers cannot in any way capture the actual reality of a supposedly omnipresent ultra-conscious being. This naming, this "God-ing" process, this labeling of the mysterium tremendum, is in itself a powerful act of psychological reductionism. By such naming we reduce the infinite to a finite magnitude which the human mind can shape to fit its needs. The word "God" itself is a shot-glass sized ontological metaphor dipped from the immense ungraspable sea of the mysterium tremendum.

The giving of a name to an intangible ineffable reality, essentially unnamable, has been the greatest flaw of religion. The noun "God" objectifies that which is non-objectifiable, inviting psychological projections conducive to cultural needs. Metaphoric expression imposes boundaries, giving form to the formless, creating an entity out of an abstraction. Take, for example, the abstract concept of "inflation," often used in the following way: inflation is hurting our economic situation, thus we must struggle against inflation because it threatens our well being. But what exactly is this "inflation" we are prepared to fight as if it were a physical entity threatening us with bodily harm? Clearly, inflation is not a physical entity one can shoot or imprison. It's an abstraction that attempts to convey a complex economic situation. It is nothing we can get a hold of, or push and shove, or hit with a hammer.

We must understand how the mind automatically puts a boundary around that which has no bounds, including itself. Here are three abstract ontological metaphors denoting non-physical entities which are often misused in this way:

1. Mind – *the concept of mind all too often is conceived as a contained entity;*
2. Soul – *the concept of soul triggers a sense of a bounded ethereal entity;*
3. God – *God is conceived as an immense specteral living entity.*

The word "entity" means something with a complete separate and contained existence. But containment implies bounded finiteness. Since the conscious mind, which we might consider "contained" within ego parameters, disperses and merges with the subconscious at an elusive enigmatic "boundary line," and the subconscious merges into the unconscious transcendent realms of existence which are infinite, then actually even conscious egoic mind cannot be considered completely, if at all, contained. It is the same with our concept of the soul. And God is supposedly infinite. Thus neither mind, soul, nor God, can be considered as bounded entities. Anyone who deems to use the word "God" should always recognize that it partakes of a numinous sense of boundlessness = endlessness = infinity, thus compensating for the fact that the sort of imagery the word "God" triggers off in a person's mind is most often a specifically finite acculturated experience. There is an insightful esoteric saying, "A God whose ways can be comprehended is no God at all." Incomprehensibility denotes the very substance that imbues the mysterium tremendum with genuine God quality.

Whether we are dealing with concepts of God confined to traditional religious images or those that have supposedly broken free of such restrictions, a kind of religious immaturity is rampant in our civilization. A TV show concerning the after effects of 9/11 validated this in interview after interview, where people were making statements like, *"Why did God let this happen,"* *"I'm angry with God for letting this happen,"* *"How could He have taken my loved one,"* *"Why would God allow such evil?"* It was quite clear most of these people had never thought so intensely about their God, apparently having been content with comforting Sunday sermons, and overly confident nightly prayers. Tragedy and horror had been occurring all across the earth everyday of their lives, broadcast across the nation by way of newspapers, TV, magazines, radio—and yet such worldwide catastrophe had not caused a ripple of doubt in their minds concerning "God's ways." But once catastrophe strikes close to home, and their little bubble of belief is significantly disturbed, oh my, oh my, questions came from every direction. Christians of the United States, never having suffered war ravaging their country, have cultivated a naïve sophomoric attitude toward "God." This is a hindrance to the seeker of spiritual truth.

Though Muslims are taught not to attempt to visualize Allah, and certain sects and denominations of Jewish and Christian faith today claim they do not think of God with any particular image, if questioned you will find these same people believe unhesitatingly that their "imageless" God is concerned not only with the human situation but with their own personal fate, their everyday thoughts, acts and prayers. What we have here is the ubiquitous ingenuity of the believer's mind, which, even while attempting to avoid anthropomorphic imagery, still projects personalized human tendencies onto a basically non-representational numinosity. Many New Agers feel they are beyond anthropomorphic tendencies, with their blending of Hindu and Buddhist belief systems positing a supreme spiritual being, a transcendent ultimate consciousness beyond comprehension. However, if you pay close attention to conversations of their religious/theosophical perspectives, you can usually detect their "God," like ordinary traditional believers, is very aware of them as individuals, aware not only of the thoughts and actions of their egoic life from birth to death, but even of "previous" births and deaths, to a degree which entails karmic records of their good and bad deeds, all implying an intimate acquaintance with how they are doing on their great multi-life spiritual journey.

Our minds would be far more spiritually clear if we could rid ourselves of all anthropomorphic contamination as we ponder this "something wholly other" we attempt to corral and tame to be our God. Once clear, what then are we to make of this *mysterium tremendum et fascinans*, this numinous presence transcendent and immanent within all and everything? Since we cannot know its essence-nature, how should we relate to it, how do we communicate to it, if at all possible? Do we have to define "Being beyond being" to fit some conceptual imboundedness which we find comforting, in order to experience contact? Must we even attempt to define this "Being beyond being" at all? Would not attempting definition be futile?

Arthur Koestler said it is impossible for the rational mind to define the absolute. Various spiritual sages have made similar statements clarifying how we cannot comprehend the infinite consciousness which encompasses us, because the absolute is not reducible to affinities with ordinary conscious experience, nor does it have any of the human personality traits of the finite ego. The term "Being beyond being" is closer to the idea of the "spiritually infinite." As David Hilbert has stated, *"The infinite! No other question has ever moved so profoundly the spirit of man; no other idea has so fruitfully stimulated his intellect."*[6] Rudy Rucker clarified, *"The world is, in each of its parts, infinite."*[7] And Aurobindo speaks of an indwelling infinity within the finite, *"Each finite is that deep infinity."* These expressions have a definite connection to the hologrammic concept of the universe—each of us radiant with infinity at the core of our being, each an innate intimate aspect of not only all that is known of the micro-macro universe but of the significant mystical dimensions of the unknown. Thus to free us from ingrained imagery, instead of "God," let us consider the metaphor "Absolute Infinite"—a spiritually oriented abstraction transcending common ideas of a supreme deity.

Ordinary consciousness enwrapped in religious imagery can have no idea what an enigmatic "infinite consciousness-tremendum" could be like, or be up to, or be concerned with. Thus all theological speculation, rhetoric, conjecture, rumination about the ways, whys, means of a creation deity, is vanity and starkly absurd. The Bible tries to say this in Job 38:4, *"Where was thou when I laid the foundation of the earth?"* But oddly, the entire story of Job describes a very knowable, human-like, thus unGodlike god, zealously claiming his unknowability. Having a God resembling a stern father speaking to you about His own unknowability contradicts what He is speaking about. Scripture comes closer to what we are dealing with in Isaiah 46:5, when God supposedly declares, *"To whom will you liken me? Who is my equal? With whom can you compare me? Where is my like?"* Thus it would seem that even the Judeo-Christian God agrees, when it comes to infinite numinous presence of Being, we can only stand mystified in wonder. Meister Eckhart, the profound Christian mystic, created a sort of semantic-conceptual koan when he stated, *"It is God's nature to be without a nature."*

To even begin to ponder the true nature of an incomprehensible omnipresent ultra-Being, we must first accept that we do not know what the true nature of reality is. What science does know of gravity, electricity, space, time, dark matter, subnuclear energy, etc., is rife with paradox, perplexity, and uncertainty. And, with the exception of shallow minded materialists overconfident they have it all down pat, the deeper broader complexities of human nature completely bewilder our brilliant scholars and researchers. So, does it not seem futile to contemplate the nature of some awesome "God Being?" I can only answer, "What can we lose by doing so?" We've come this far, and can only enhance our conceptual capabilities through any attempt to discern, rather than define the nature of this Absolute Infinite. This means not only expanding and enhancing our own conceptual graspings, but ridding ourselves of any self deceiving imagery we may be clinging to.

A few significant thinkers of the past injudiciously claimed the intelligence and intentions of God could be intuited by the contemplation of nature. Spinoza said *"No God but nature."* Emerson's praise of the divine force imbuing all of nature was inspired by his study of Hinduism and the immanent play of Shakti, tending to overlook the destructive Shiva-Kali aspects of nature. Shakespeare, on the other hand, consistently expressed both nature's beauty and dark predatory impulses. In King Lear, the maliciously cunning Edmund worships nature as his goddess. This is a far cry from the contemporary Disneyfication of nature, exemplified by such things as cartoon predators portrayed as gentle Bambi-like creatures, which is further validation of the human urge, especially in affluent Western nations, to suburbanize all disturbing aspects of existence.

If the fantastic myriad life forms of nature reveal God's "intelligent design," what kind of intelligence is involved? Nature is a vast complex extravagant array of beautiful and preposterous predator and prey activity, from amoeba to killer whale. The vast extinctions of an immeasurable number of nature's creatures, entailing the ravages of disease, earthquake, hurricane, tsunami, meteor, indicates nature's indifference to its own manifestations of life, including human. When we consider the abundance of prehistoric monstrosities which roamed the earth, and the rapacious world within the ocean's depths, plus the vast activity of parasite and virus that thrive on this planet, then the belief that Nature represents God opens up a Gnostic-like conception of an indifferent careless demiurge creator of life on earth. Of course, terrestrial existence does have its enchanting splendor, as well as creatures of gentle disposition, to be sure. But such gentle creatures are often another creature's prey, and the most beautiful landscape can suddenly erupt in volcanic violence, or collapse as the earth quakes, or be inundated by flooding river or raging sea, or torn apart by hurricane and tornado. If we are going to contemplate nature in relation to God, let us look at everything as it is, not through rose colored glasses.

To transcend the terrestrial "eat and be eaten" perspective is to realize the natural world is undeniably a manifestation of a deeper numinous source. If, as the Sufi mystics say, the entire known universe is but a string of jewels on the hem of God's majestic robe, then it certainly doesn't represent the nature of the Being who wears such a robe. When we speak of God or gods, perplexity and paradox are always near at hand. We know that all phenomena of terrestrial existence through which nature manifests its creative force, the extensive array of forms within the enormous panorama of myriad environments—swamp, mountain peak, desert, arctic ice floe, jungle, city—all emerge from the congealing of subnuclear energies and quantum pulsations, essentially a phantomish root source, an existential enigma. And it is an enigma that cannot be dealt with by way of empirical methodology. Perhaps it is within this phantomish enigmatic dimension, in the deep stark silent "beyond nature" magnitudes of meta-frequency activity, that the "nullity" of the Absolute Infinite may be glimpsed.

As clarified, beyond our limited sphere of sensory egoic awareness, we are electro-magnetic beings made of fantastic quantum stuff which merges and is part of the entire surge of the universe, which itself is an emanation of the Absolute Infinite, beyond any imagery of the Big Five religions, beyond any imagery at all. Thus when humans, one way or another, break through the egoic sphere into transcendent levels of consciousness, they have actualized their potential to personally contact what we are always unconsciously in contact with—the dynamic void of Ultimate Being. It is this potential for resonant human contact with the ineffable Presence unfolding in the life of individuals opening themselves, that is the core of the spiritual quest.

The existence of some supreme infinite meta-consciousness encompassing the finite consciousness of human reality is no longer to be doubted. What needs to be not only doubted but cast aside, are these limiting images of God. This also goes for Hinduism, Islam, Judaism. The discarding of all masks of God opens us to the true infinite vastness of "Being beyond being." In other words, no level of transcendent consciousness can be experienced until one is capable of abandoning the level upon which their ego has established a secure, stable belief system. Paradoxically, at the esoteric core of every one of the Big Five religions lies the potential to transform all known God images in the direction of mystical realization.

I believe I have made it clear that in my attempt to highlight the extensive fallibility of orthodox religious belief systems, I have in no way meant to imply the Absolute Infinite, which can never be ensnared by the conceptual imagery confined to any institutionalized religion, is not openly available to human contact, no matter how incomprehensible such a God-quality configuration of greater consciousness may be. That is why I have referred to various writings of direct personal experience of spiritual realities that transcend the egoic sphere of consciousness. The realms of consciousness possible for us to experience are infinite in depth and scope. We have evolved as creatures of the finite knowable quotidian world, yet we are infinite in essence. The entire 5000 year history of yoga-mysticism concerns striving toward unique personal contact with transcendent spiritual levels of consciousness. However, the Absolute Infinite should never be reduced to metaphoric imagery bounded by human ideas of a divine personality. The truly Absolute Infinite would not in any way partake of human-like attributes, nor would such an unimaginable meta-consciousness have any significant human-like concern for human beings seeking contact. And yet, paradoxically, perplexedly, by way of various mystical teachings, God/Presence does have an interdependent reciprocal relationship with humanity. Various conduits of mystical thought expound something similar to the statement of Angelus Silesius, *"I know God cannot live one instant without me; were I to become nothing, He would give up the ghost."* Gurdjieff spoke of life as a cosmic necessity, for without life the universe as we perceive it to be would not exist. Jung spoke of God being in some way as dependent upon humanity as humanity is upon God. The Kabala clarifies the need God has of humanity to fulfill "His" own enigmatic existence. Such claims cannot be judged from the perspective of ordinary reality, but only from that of deep visionary experience beyond the level of appearances. Grasping this relation to "God" in an ordinary way is why most religions cultivate a misconstrued sense of being the "chosen ones" = the acculturated ego's interpretation, for its own aggrandizement, of a deeper dimensional relationship.

These things we speak of are exceedingly perplexing because so much of existence, comprehended by way of our sensory nature, contradicts any idea of a need for either life or humanity within the immense processes of the universe. All anthropic considerations and concepts of intelligent design with humans in mind, when thoroughly analyzed, collapse into the trash heap of human delusions, fabrications, and manipulated biased interpretations of facts and theories. Yet, according to esoteric teachings, the universe, on the level of frequencies and meta-frequencies, does have an intimate relationship to life, including the life-energy resonance of the human race—but it is not dependent on individuals. It's like a bee-keeper who is dependent on many thousands of bees to produce his honey—if the bees all die, no more honey. But one bee, or even a hundred bees, means nothing. Thus, for a single individual to make a meaningful connection with higher realms demands a kind of self-sacrifice, or perhaps we should say ego-sacrifice, where no reciprocation of any kind is expected.

And yet, from accumulated knowledge gathered from cultures across the earth concerning human contact with numinous dimensions, there seems to be emanations of consciousness unfolding from the higher core of Being, that exude a growing sense of concern as they "descend" toward our reality, igniting compassion within the awakening soul of the spiritual seeker. Sufi scholar Henri Corbin considered such emanations to be "angelic" configurations of consciousness issuing from archetypal depths into our lives. Most of our great sages would agree. Though this whole area of angels, allies and higher masters of a meta-spiritual sort, is rife with theosophical and religious distortion, and prone to delusion, hallucination, and egoic aggrandizement, something definitely wondrous and spiritual is going on.

The skeptic humanist is going to start hyper-ventilating here, and justifiably so, considering all the simple minded crap about angels that has flourished in both the New Age and traditional Christian ambits, not to mention Hollywood's contribution of the past decades. And yet, by now the reader should know no doors can be slammed shut when it comes to paranormal-spiritual realities. Let us recall that the universe and the numinous dimensions of the human mind are not only as strange as we have seen, they are most likely stranger than we are capable of seeing.

As William Irwin Thompson and other scholars and sages have clarified, the average intellectual of a skeptical atheist/agnostic sort considers such beings as angels and gods as absolutely imaginary, belonging to a pre-scientific primitive age, no more real than Santa Claus or the Easter Bunny. But volumes on the reality of archetypes, volumes concerning yogic states of consciousness, volumes of psychedelic research, should inform anyone with a halfway open mind that something is going on encompassing the human situation that is of a spiritual-mystical quality we dare not just smugly push aside. Over the past 150 years experts in the fields of archeology and language have discovered various religious texts, as well as the writings of mystic visionaries, which speak of an angelic hierarchy — angels, archangels, Archai, Exusiai, Kyriotetes, etc., up through a number of levels, varying according to religious/spiritual orientation. Once beyond the Archai level we are dealing with "configurations of consciousness" the ancient civilizations of Egypt, Greece, Rome, India, Persia, and other cultures would have considered gods. Such configurations of higher levels of being are filtered through the unconscious/subconscious matrix and thus tailored to an individual's religio-cultural orientation. Though the appearance of angels and gods of higher spiritual frequencies are anthropomorphically shaped by the mind when entering the human ambit of existence, they are not just subjective creations. As Aurobindo clarifies, such beings existed within their dimensions long before human consciousness arose, and are beyond all labels.

Robert Romanyshyn has written,

A metaphor is not essentially a way of seeing how one reality is <u>*like*</u> *another. It is a way of seeing one reality* <u>*through*</u> *another. Its resemblance, if we should call it that, is the resemblance which a reflection bears to the reality of which it is a reflection.*[8]

And, as Hans-Georg Gadamer succinctly states,

The concept of symbol has a metaphysical background that is entirely lacking in the rhetorical use of the allegory. It is possible to be led beyond the sensible to the divine. For the world of the senses is not mere nothingness and darkness but the outflowing and the reflection of truth.[9]

Perhaps here we can see the relationship of symbolic imagery of higher beings such as "angels" to the helicoid ascending and descending levels of consciousness spoken of earlier as the great spectrum of Being. It is by way of opening to higher more expansive levels of consciousness that one contacts emanations from meta-levels closer to the source of the Absolute Infinite, a source not to be contemplated lightly or identified with any religious concept of God.

We are attempting here to distinguish clear spiritual perspective from religious distortion. Consider the often quoted tale attributed to the Persian mystic poet Sana'i (1120 AD), of five blindmen who were asked to describe an elephant. One grabbed its tail and said it must be like a tree branch; another grabbed its ear and said it must be like a large mat; another grabbed its leg and said it must be like a temple pillar; another grabbed its trunk and said it was like a python; another touched its huge belly and said it was like a whale. Each blindman provides only one perspective. If the blindmen had repeatedly changed places, until they had all held every part of the elephant, they would have at least caught an inkling of something greater than they first thought. But they would never change places, any more than a Christian fundamentalist would live in a Buddhist monastery. Each blindman found a hold, and each clung to his own image, refusing to let go. This has been the perennial cause of religious wars. In a religious war the victor shapes the religious history and belief system of the culture which is conquered and ruled. Such is how Judaism, Christianity, Islam and Hinduism became all powerful within their religio-geographic ambit. The tale of the five blindmen is an apt analogy for the way not only major religions but their various sects and denominations create their own ideas about the ways and means of God. Just as the elephant is something entirely different than each blindman conceives it to be, God is wholly other than the diverse conceptions of the varied religions. Only the blind person who suddenly regains his sight would be able to comprehend the elephant for what it is. Only the awakening individual will attain the potential of visionary perception which integrates all differing exoteric viewpoints within an esoteric comprehension—thus mystical awareness. All genuine mystics have a foundational holistic affinity of universal trans-egoic vision, merging with the eternal Presence beyond all religious belief systems. As the Rig-Veda states, *"It is one, though men call it by many names."*

Discerning the validity of higher powers one believes one is in contact with is subject to curious complications. It seems egoic subjective interpretation (the blind man syndrome) will always interfere with purity of vision in those who are not truly "yogically" prepared. Researchers attached sensitive instruments to the vocal chords of mental patients who claimed God talked to them. As the patients sat silent, their mouths closed, their lips not moving, they would signal the researcher that God was now talking to them. Though the patients uttered not even a whisper, their vocal chords began to move. They were like ventriloquists, subconsciously speaking to themselves, believing the words they were perceiving were from God. This reduction of the tremendous mystery of Being to fit the individual psyche is not only a syndrome of the starkly mad, but quite widespread among the religious "sane" of our world.

I have not written the preceding fourteen chapters, nor am I writing the following, for scholars of linguistics or symbolism, or what have you, but to highlight certain elements of the quest for laymen/seekers to deal with and integrate how they may. This attempt is to carefully clarify, hopefully without detrimental reductive effect, our existential-spiritual situation and the potentials and possibilities within it from which an individual can glean substantial authentic meaning. Any clearly defined anthropomorphic image of God is an abstraction from the unknowable, an attempt to contain the uncontainable, like dipping a cup of water from a stormy sea, taking it home and placing it on the mantle to be worshipped as if it were the sea. Religion comes about when the mantle becomes a shrine, and as generations pass, the cup of sea water is worshipped with little regard to the reality from which it came forth.

Now that we have pondered the significance of concepts that shape our lives and all too often limit or stunt genuine spiritual growth, we can begin to push the gate open just a bit more and catch a glimpse of the depths we have partially pondered. Since the simple can occasionally be a key to approaching the profound, let us indulge. If you walk by a wooden fence and see a hole in the wood, you would have to admit the hole exists. Just what is the hole made of? Nothing? But it is there, right in front of you. Standing near the fence, the hole is a simple obvious fact that no one can deny — a small circle of nothing. Is the hole an object? The dictionary clarifies "object" as something physical or mental, toward which one's attention or action is directed. Mortimer Adler writes of how any subject attentively pondered can be considered a "mental object." Thus during the moment of attentiveness the hole in the fence is a perceived object. If we burn down the fence, the hole disappears. Yet a memory trace of the hole lingers. Is the mental image less real than the actual hole was before we burnt the fence down? Where does the hole go when the fence is burned down? It doesn't go anywhere. Then, does it remain? No, it neither goes nor remains — the hole in the fence doesn't become nothing, because it was nothing to begin with. Such ponderings may seem like a simple mental game, a playing with words, (which in some ways it is) — sort of like 'how do corn and beans and barely grow?' Actually, if you try to give as complete an answer as possible to that proverbial question, entailing the planting of seed, the process of sprouting, of photosynthesis, of pollination, the life of bees, of agriculture, of farming, plowing, irrigation, rain, weather, we realize "simple" is always imbued with the potential of transformation into ever extending complexity.

Now think of a white buffalo. Some people can close their eyes and a fairly clear image will hover before them. Others cannot do this. Yet when I say "white buffalo," they know what I mean, because a certain mental stimulation occurs — a vague impression of a white buffalo is there, but without any definite image. If a neurobiologist says your image of a white buffalo is a kind of hologram created by neuronic activity, what does that mean? We could call it a trans-emission, or a meta-emergent property of the brain, which would mean exactly what? Definitely we are dealing here with intangible phenomena no more substantial than a hole in a fence. Now think about when you have a vivid dream. Does the white buffalo you have just visualized come from the same place as the images which appear in your dream? When you wake up, do dreams go where the hole in the fence went after the fence burned down?

Is not a dream of making love, a memory of making love, and a fantasy of making love, all composed of the same enigmatic element? We are dealing here with more than just semantic mind games. We are dealing here with the elusive quality of human consciousness and language, of who and what we think we are, of what "God" is, of the very stuff from which any significant meaning can be derived. When speaking of the hole in the fence, the white buffalo, and the dream of making love, no matter what neurologists and biopsychologists say of such things, we are speaking of puzzling eidolonic phenomena. If you pause right now and slowly say the words, "airplane," "ocean," "kite," "kitten," "baboon," "rain," your mind will produce a kind of spectral image of each thing as you say it, but nothing really clear. If you close your eyes and concentrate on one of these subjects, with patience an image will gradually become fairly well defined. With practice, a clear visual image can be created. With concentrated imagination we can create vivid images in our minds. What are they essentially made of? Though brain activity is definitely instrumental to your "imaging," the images aren't restricted to this. They are more than the product of synapse-dendrite sparklings, and definitely transcend neuronic activity. To speak of the spectral quality of our mental imagery is in no way farfetched.

Now consider what mystics, shamans and sages, as well as creative artists and others, call visions. What do they mean by spiritual visions? What separates spiritual vision from imagination and dreams? You can close your eyes and imagine the white buffalo, and then open your eyes and be just your ordinary every day self. You can have a remarkably vivid dream and wake up amazed, but soon the dream fades and you are basically unchanged. Every day our consciousness is inundated with an abundance of fantasy, and our nights with dreams, yet with nary an iota of effect on our lives. But genuine spiritual vision is an experience that overwhelms a person's entire reality and sense of self, and dramatically and permanently changes that person's life because he or she has glimpsed into the very depths of Being.

Descriptions such as "depths of being," "absolute infinite," "infinite depths," "groundlessness of being," "dynamic void," "emptiness," "nothingness," "abyss," all have an underlying relationship to any concept of a supreme God. But religious people of Western civilization find it much more difficult relating their image of deity to such words than people of the East do. The West has created a fear of nothingness as oblivion. Karl Barth equated the void with death. Barthean theology even equates nothingness with evil, claiming God strives to overcome nothingness—the void—by way of creation activity. Judeo-Christian thought sees creation as rescued from the abyss, whereas essential teachings of Buddhism see creation as an illusion. Of course, over the centuries, to please the multitudes, Buddhist heavens have come about, and of course the concept of reincarnation, both of which escape the void which to Buddha is Nirvana, the bliss of dissolving into dynamic nothingness, which isn't nothing at all, but is ….? To quote Hans Waldenfels, who paraphrases the Zen sage Kitaro Nishida, *"This nothingness is not simply another denial, but simultaneously an absolute affirmation."*

If we rid ourselves of all anthropomorphic projection and imagery concerning God, we must confront the radiant abyss. Joseph Chilton Pearce notes,

> *The atomic proposal that the most energy arises from the smallest bit of substance was a logical offense, but QUANTUM physics held even bigger offenses in store. Truly BIG energy, the evidence from quantum mechanics suggested, comes from no matter at all, but from the empty spaces between the particles of matter. Break up an atom, our littlest item, and we get our biggest bang (to date). But within the spaces of an atom, or in spaces without atoms, quantum physicists said, lie far larger fields of energy. The most comes not from the least, but from nothing at all.*[10]

F. David Peat states,

> *Paradoxically, the nothingness of the ground state, out of which the universe is sustained, is both a vacuum and a plenum. It is a vacuum because, as in the everyday idea of empty space, matter is able to move through it without interruption. But it is also a plenum because it is infinitely full of energy. Indeed, the observable material universe is nothing more than the minor fluctuations upon this vast sea of energy.*[11]

And Geza Szamosi writes,

> *The universe indeed seems to have come from the vacuum; i.e., from nothing. In some sense the primordial vacuum is nothing; it may be defined as nothing: No matter, no space, no time. On the other hand, it is also a seemingly inexhaustible fountainhead and reservoir of everything which exists — just the opposite of nothing. It would perhaps be best to forget the word "nothing." It may be one of those many human symbols which once created, continues to haunt us. There may be no nothing at all.*[12]

The intuitive sense of Absolute Infinite unfolds from the implicate realm unfiltered by acculturation, which the concept of God is inundated with. Only the mind purified of such influence is open to sensing the Presence of Being, awakening to what we have always been, always are, immersed in and imbued with. This Presence can only be perceived, sensed, when the ego surrenders to that which is beyond the sphere of common sense rationality and emotive religious delusion. In Zen this can occur spontaneously to one who has become ripe through intentful seeking. It is known as Satori, which is somewhat of a merging of intuitive sensing and mystical insight — a moment of poetic epiphany which breaks the bonds of language enchaining us to the acculturated egoic sphere of reality. Ironically it is language, in which we are encaged, that is the very instrument which contains the potential to open the gate to such freedom. It is a 'fire to fight fire' maneuver, dependent on how you consciously use language, to speak, to think, to watch your own thought process as a soaring hawk watches the landscape for prey, catching any movement of useless fantasy, manipulative metaphors, collective beliefs, negative emotions.

Learning to purify egoic patterns of thought in order to create a mental clearing place for the unfolding of intuitive sensing and mystical insight, is the process which cultivates the *"royal ideas"* Aurobindo wrote about, and what Heidegger spoke of as *"unique thinking"* — an attempt to highlight and preserve essential truths within the flow of thought. Socrates said, *"I am the midwife of significant thought."* The ordinary person just lets thought come forth as it may, swirling hither and thither through ego awareness, only restrained by a mundane focusing necessary for daily survival, or at most, a limited involvement in such things as political concerns or religious rite. This is why most people who use psychedelics are captured by the unlimited play of makyo, the realm of endless dream and fantasy, the multi-dimension of the ten zillion things, amplified to where hallucination and beings of all shades and sorts manifest — amazons, elves, UFO's, and fantasies of past lives — an unremitting carnival of patterns, forms, and multidimensional adventures. The 5000 year tradition of yogic disciplines to overcome our helplessness amid such phenomena is not to be shrugged off with impunity. Without discipline, without sincerely striving to master quotidian consciousness, you cannot live with any authentic awareness of your own existence, nor can you expect genuine contact with greater realms of infinite Being.

The ability to think unhindered by the unnecessary intrusive commonplace babble which has been termed "roof brain chatter," is a bottom-line requirement. This demands acute introspective self-observation of your state of mind, simultaneously harmonized with vigilant awareness of your surrounding reality and quality of social and personal relationships. Such harmonious subjective-objective awareness, grounded on a sufficient knowledge of self and the world at large, facilitates the intuitive attunement of the ascending frequencies of the self-cultivating mind, which may then contact and resonate with descending higher spiritual frequencies. When this harmonious alignment occurs, it is what is known by genuine yogis as *jivan-mukti* = liberation from all vanities. It sets the stage for full illumination. William Barrett stated, *"Man is illuminated by letting Being reveal itself."* Your perception of reality deepens and expands as the infinite is seen shimmering within the finite, and all phenomena become numinous hieroglyphic script.

What we are getting at here is a cultivation of pellucid perception of all phenomena. The etymology of the Greek word "phenomenon" means "that which reveals itself." We dealt with how all phenomena are essentially made up of what science has labeled subnuclear energies, and how the enigmatic marvel of light is dispersed throughout all existence. Bishop Robert Grosseteste, circa 1240, wrote about how light was the first form of corporeity, *"Multiplying itself from a single point infinitely and equally on all sides, light formed a sphere — and from this all things came forth."* The immense diversified process of evolution we emerged from and into at birth does not gain its expansive ever-branching momentum from externally imposed stimuli. Its entire immense unfolding into explicate reality is empowered from an internal implicate force. Bohm speaks of an internal order from which "information" exudes/unfolds as external reality, blossoming out of the implicate flow of what we could call the basic life-force essence. According the A.H. Almaas, essence and existence are one — presence as palpable ontological essence.[13]

Implicate order has an hierarchical symmetry, one level encompassed within another, like spectral Chinese boxes. Recall the diagram in Chapter Fourteen of superimposed interlacing triangles. This has an affinity to Gurdjieff's concept of a helicoid ascending-descending spectrum of consciousness he refers to as the *"ray of creation."* Empirically, we know higher frequencies of light contain more energy than lower frequencies. Robert Nozick speaks of a scale of values exhibited throughout the natural world, connecting with the ancient concept of the *"great chain of Being."* According to Ken Wilber, both the *"great chain of Being"* and the concept of a holo-grammic universe have a close affinity to this spiritual reality of ever increasing ascending levels of consciousness. Both Aurobindo and Teilhard de Chardin relate this to the explicate evolution of con-sciousness. We can conceive the individual self-cultivating mind as an ever expanding radius of comprehension unfolding from within the great spiraling form of infinite Being. Spheres of consciousness within the tornadic swirl of greater Consciousness implies ex-change — information resonance. Light is a conveyer of information. Bohm speaks of the super-quantum potential of ever constructing information. We have physicists who expound on degrees of quan-tum consciousness as ultra complex skeins of creative information permeating all living systems. As physicist-philosopher Dana Zohar has clarified,

> There is recent evidence to suggest that biological evolution itself may be, in fact, <u>responsive</u> evolution. It may possibly be a quan-tum dialogue between the creature and its environment, a dia-logue that has the capacity to elicit and realize one of many <u>pos-sible</u> directions of evolution (mutations) latent in the DNA code. The likelihood of this is strengthened by recent evidence for quantum coherence within DNA itself.[14]

Jung revealed the inherent creative aspect of the human per-sonality and its impulse toward continual spiritual development to be an unfolding from within. We find this theme throughout the works of all the spiritual sages, philosophers and poets we have mentioned. How a person aligns his or her life to this theme of spiri-tual development depends on many things, not the least of which is chance. Chance plays an important role in the awakening of an indi-vidual to deeper realms of being. Those random quirks of destiny that come together in a definite gestalt which ignite an attentiveness toward awakening, are what Jung refers to as *"meaningful coinci-dences."* Of course, what an individual is ripe for and thus able to glean from such meaningful coincidences is another matter. There are no guarantees. The human existential-spiritual labyrinth of un-predestined fate consists of ever branching paths of alternate choices, opportunities, which, though open-ended, can be strewn with crip-

pling obstacles. It all depends on one's readiness, experience, ingenuity, and how the random roulette wheel of tragedy, of triumph, of
meaningful coincidence, spins your number about. The more concentrated your efforts, the less subject you are to random interference of obstacles that can undermine freewill.

Now at the end of this book, some will justifiably ask, "Is the
existential-spiritual endeavor this book is about worth the effort, the
commitment, the dramatic life changes, the uncertainty, the personal
challenges and upheavals, the possible dangers and hardships?"
Well, you are already involved when tossed by birth into this bewildering realm of conscious existence. The choice is whether you want
to wander the comfortable, secure, neatly trimmed but endarkened
and limited pathways of collective conformism, or daringly seek out
illuminated branchings that lead to a more expansive experience of
existence, including definite spiritual enrichment. All nature moves,
changes, transforms, apparently with no definite aim. Yet all creatures of sea and land and air are imbued with creative adaptability
which reveals an element of, if not specifically teleological purposiveness, then undeniable innate directionality toward novelty
and expansive growth. Human consciousness, the most flexible self-
aware form of consciousness on earth, resonates with the intentionally transcendent. Thus the human mind within the ambit of the personality is instilled with an impulse for greater development. But the
spiritual essence of this impulse is universally stifled because humanity has externalized the transcendent orientation and projected it
onto the idea of technological progress, the building of empires, of
individual success in the social arena—the poor man dreaming of
riches and the rich man dreaming of further financial conquests, everyone caught up in heroic political and pseudo-religious dreams of
accomplishment and glory on the social-egoic level. All this is but
the sublimation of the much deeper impulse to evolve.

Endeavors such as creating a fine work of art, or a profound
work of philosophical or scientific thought, or efforts to alleviate the
suffering of one's fellow beings, all partake of a higher spiritual quality than any common schemes of fame and fortune. But the highest
orientation humans are capable of is the individual journey toward
spiritual awakening. We are essentially beings of numinous light
imbued with the potential of eternal genesis, to constantly evolve, to
cultivate continual self-discovery. Humanity is not what it was fifty
thousand years ago, and in another fifty thousand years we will be

something other than what we are now. We do not know what this creature in transformation really is, or will finally become—if there is anything final. In such an immense creation of inherent and increasing change, finality would be an oddity. Perhaps there is only the completion of different stages of an enigmatic process, the blossom of a flowering plant, the tree's fruit, the butterfly from its cocoon. Each of us is a combination of ripening bud and gardener responsible for the care of our own blossoming. Each individual attuned to the inner quest is always at a spiritual crossroads. You must now ponder the decision which will carry you through dark nights of haunting illumination and exquisite subtle joys of awakening, taking full responsibility for your own spiritual fate. You could call it "grace given" to even find yourself aware of such a choice.

Endnotes/Sources

Pushing Ultimates introductory quote, *"Few push such ultimates..."* is from the poem "Notes to Go With a Compass," by Ann Stanford, from her book of poems, *Weathercock*, The Viking Press, 1966.

Preface

First introductory quote, *"I have been criticized for being a wayfarer..."* Paracelsus, from "Paracelsus the Physician" by C. G. Jung, in *The Spirit in Man, Art, and Literature*, Bollingen foundation: Pantheon Books, 1966.

Second introductory quote, *"Be not ignorant..."* the King James Bible, Ecclesiasticus, 5:15.

1. C. S. Lewis, letter to Sheldon Vanauken April 17, 1951.

2. C. G. Jung, CW 7 "Two Essays on Analytical Psychology," para.201, *On the Psychology of the Unconscious*, 1912.

3. May Sarton, from her story about a group of people that calls their house "The Ark."

4. G. K. Chesterton, quoted in *To Say What is Ours*, John Ahlbach and Vicki Benson (eds).

Chapter 1

Introductory quote, *"It is important for psychological maturation..."* C. Michael Smith, *Jung and Shamanism in Dialogue: Retrieving the Soul, Retrieving the Sacred*, Paulist Press, 1997.

1. Jean-Paul Sartre, *Truth and Existence*, original text established and annotated by Arlette Elkaïm-Sartre; translated by Adrian van den Hoven; edited and with an introduction by Ronald Aronson, University of Chicago Press, 1992.

2. R. D. Laing, *The Politics of Experience*, Ballantine Books 1967.

3. Carl Sagan, *The Demon-Haunted World: Science As A Candle In The Dark*, Ballantine Books March 1997.

4. *Psychological Reflections: an Anthology of the Writings of C. G. Jung,* Selected and edited by Jolande Jacobi, c.1953 by Bollingen Foundation, first Harper Torchbook edition published 1961.

5. Phillip Wheelwright, *The Burning Fountain,* Indiana University Press 1954.

6. Attributed to Socrates, as found in the *The Apology, Phaedo, and Crito of Plato,* translated by Benjamin Jowett, P. F. Collier, c. 1909.

7. Jeremy Narby, *The Cosmic Serpent: DNA and the Origins of Knowledge,* Putnam Publishing Group 1999.

8. Gnostic interpretation of Garden of Eden, *The Gnostic Gospels,* Elaine Pagels, Vintage Books 1979.

9. Anonymous, *Rosarium Philosophorum,* 1550.

10. Gina Cerminara, *Insights for the Age of Aquarius,* A Quest Book: The Theosophical Publishing House 1973.

11. E. F. Schumacher, *A Guide for the Perplexed,* Haroer Colophon Books 1977.

12. Kenneth T. Gallagher, *The Philosophy of Gabriel Marcel,* Fordham University Press, New York 1975 [c. 1962].

13. *Dhammapada,* from the Pali Tipitaka - Gandhari Edition.

Chapter 2

Introductory quote, *"Men must endure their going hence ..."* Shakespeare *King Lear, V: ii.*

1. David Tacey, *Jung and the New Age,* Brunner-Routledge 2001.

2. Eric Fromm, as quoted in the book *Affluenza: The All Consuming Epidemic,* by John DeGraff, David Wann, and Thomas Naylor.

3. Michael Novak, *The Experience of Nothingness,* Transactions Publishers 1998.

4. Hans-Georg Gadamer, *The Beginning of Philosophy,* 1998, tr. Rod Coltman, Continuum Publishing.

Chapter 3

First introductory quote, *"It is the singular person..."* Evan S. Connell, *The Aztec Treasure House*, Counterpoint Press 2001.

Second introductory quote, *"A sense of the mystical..."* Albert Einstein, *The World As I See It*, The Citadel Press 1999.

1. James Billington, quoted in an article by Jay Tolson, "A Meeting of the Minds, With A Nod to Yesterday" US News & World Report, June 28, 1999.

2. Mark Twain, quoted in *The Wit and Wisdom of Mark Twain*, by Alex Ayers.

3. Cornelis Verhoeven, *The Philosophy of Wonder*, Macmillan Company 1972, page 17.

4. "The Smartest Man in the World" about Chris Langan, filmed by Errol Morris.

5. *Descartes' Dream: the World According to Mathematics*, Philip J. Davis and Reuben Hersh, Harcourt Brace Jovanovich 1986.

6. Phillip Wheelwright, *The Burning Fountain*, Indiana University Press 1954.

7. "They know not what they do." Jesus Christ, Luke 23:34.

8. William Barrett, *Irrational Man*, Anchor Books: Doubelday 1958.

9. Martin Heidegger's essay "The Origin of the Work of Art" 1935.

10. "Morality and the Novel" by D. H. Lawrence, in *Ten Masters of the Modern Essay*, by Robert Gorham Davis, Harcourt, Brace and World 1966.

11. Albert Einstein, 1929, as quoted in an article by Jay Tolson for US News and World Report, "E=mc^2 Got That? Sure?" Dec. 18, 2000.

12. Edward Bulwer-Lytton, *Zanoni*, page 55.

13. Franz Kafka, as quoted by Gustav Janouch in *Conversations With Kafka*, Goronwy Rees translator.

14. Mortimer Adler, from *The Encyclopedia of Philosophy*, edited by Paul Edwards, MacMillan 1967.

Endnotes

Chapter 4

First introductory quote, *"We are as yet below..."* William Barrett, *Irrational Man: A Study in Existential Philosophy*, Anchor Books: Doubleday 1958 .

Second introductory quote, *"Let us go up!"* Vinicius de Morais, Brazilian poet and musician.

1. Michael Shermer, from an article in Skeptic magazine, "Proving the Holocaust: the Refutation of Revisionism and the Restoration of History" Skeptic Volume 2 Number 4, June 1994.

2. K. C. Cole, *First You build a Cloud: and Other Reflections on Physics as a Way of Life*, Harcourt Brace, 1999, originally published Sympathetic Vibrations, 1st ed. W. Morrow 1985.

3. Marc Bekoff, *Minding Animals: Awareness, Emotioins, and Heart*, forward by Jane Goodall, Oxford University Press 2002.

4. John McWhorter, *The Power of Babel: a Natural History of Change*, W. H. Freeman 2001.

5. Geza Szamosi, *The Twin Dimensions*, McGraw-Hill 1986.

6. Susan Langer, *Philosophy in a New Key; a Study in the Symbolism of Reason, Rite, and Art*, Harvard University Press 1957.

7. James N. Powell, *The Tao of Symbols: How to Transcend the Limits of Our Symbolism*, Quill 1982.

8. John D. Caputo, *The Mystical Element in Heidegger's Thought*, Ohio University Press 1978.

9. A. H. Almaas, *Essence / The Elixir of Enlightenment: The Diamond Approach to Inner Realization*, p.100-101, Samuel Weiser, 1998.

Chapter 5

Introductory quote, *"Get a man to see the mysterious depths..."* Austin Farrer, *The Glass of Vision*, Dacre Press, 1948.

1. Vincent Micelli, *The Gods of Atheism*, Arlington House 1971.

2. Patricia Churchland, *Philosophy*, 84, Oct. 1987, p. 548.

4. William Irwin Thompson, *Coming Into Being*, St. Martin's Press, 1996.

4. Joe Rosen, *The Capricious Cosmos: Universe Beyond Law*, Maxwell Macmillan International, c1991.

5. Edmund Husserl, *The Crisis of European Sciences and Transcendental Phenomenology: an Introduction to Phenomenological Philosophy*, translated with introduction by David Carr, Northwestern University Press 1970.

6. Alain Aspect, Jean Dalibard, Gerard Roger, Institute of Optics at the University of Paris, referred to in *The Holographic Universe*, Michael Talbot, 1991 HarperPerennial.

7. Francis Crick, *The Astonishing Hypothesis*, Scribner 1994.

8. Richard Dawkins, *The Blind Watchmaker*, W. W. Norton 1996.

9. Norman Packard, as quoted in *Complexity -- Life at the Edge of Chaos*, Roger Lewin, University of Chicago Press 2000.

10. Edward F. Edinger, *Ego and Archetype: Individuation and the Religious Function of the Psyche*, Shambhala 1992.

11. William Broad and Nicholas Wade, *Betrayers of Truth: Fraud and Deceit in the Halls of Science*, Simon and Schuster 1982.

12. Albert Einstein, 1930 "What I Believe" in Forum and Century 84.

13. Max Born, *My Life: Recollections of a Nobel Laureate / Max Born*, Scribner 1978.

14. Samuel Coleridge, "primary imagination" *Biographia Literaria*, from *Collected Works, volume 7, parts 1-2*, edited by James Engell and W. Jackson Bates, 2 volumes, 1983.

15. Rudy Rucker, *Mind Tools: the Five Levels of Mathematical Reality*, Houghton Mifflin 1987.

16. Robin Robertson, *Jungian Archetypes: Jung, Godel, and the History of Archetypes / Robin Robertson*, Nicolas-Hays, distributed to the trade by Samuel Weiser 1995.

17. Joseph Chilton Pearce, *The Crack in the Cosmic Egg*, Julian Press, 1988.

18. Paracelsus, quoted by Jung in his *Psychology and Alchemy*, tr. R. F. C. Hull, Princeton University Press 1968.

19. William Blake, "Imagination is eternity" from "Ghost of Abel" in *The Complete Poetry and Prose of William Blake*, edited by David V. Erdman, commentary by Harold Bloom, University of California Press 1982.

20. Johann Wolfgang von Goethe, *Faust: Parts I and II,* an abridged version, tr. Louis MacNiece, Oxford University Press 1952.

21. Bernard J. F. Lonergan, *Understanding and Being*, E. Mellen Press 1980.

22. Roger Shattuck, *Forbidden Knowledge: From Prometheus to Pornography,* 1996 St. Martin's Press.

23. F. David Peat, *Synchronicity*, page 115, Bantam Books 1987.

24. Joe Rosen, *The Capricious Cosmos*, Macmillan, 1991.

25. Danah Zohar, *Quantum Self: Human Nature and Consciousness Defined by the New Physics*, William Morrow 1990.

26. "Concerning Heidegger and Art," George Steiner's *Martin Heidegger,* 1978, University of Chicago Press.

27. Danah Zohar, *Quantum Self* (see 25).

28. Michael Novak, *The Experience of Nothingness*, Harper & Row 1970.

29. Oliver Sacks, "The Mind's Eye" New Yorker, July 28, 2003.

30. Kenneth T. Gallagher, *The Philosophy of Gabriel* Marcel, Forward by Gabriel Marcel, Fordham University Press 1975 [c1962].

31. Joe Rosen, *The Capricious Cosmos: Universe Beyond Law*, Maxwell Macmillan International, 1991.

32. Ken Wilber, *Eye to Eye: the Quest for the New Paradigm*, Anchor Books 1983.

33. Arthur Koestler, *The Roots of Coincidence*, Random House 1972.

34. Lawrence Leshan, *The Medium, the Mystic and the Physicist: Toward a General Theory of the Paranormal*, Viking 1974.

Chapter 6

First introductory quote, *"To what point must we enlarge our thought..."* Friedrich von Schelling.

Second introductory quote, *"For they being lovers of wisdom..."* Elias Ashmole, 1652, alchemical text.

1. Antonio R. Damasio, *Descartes' Error: Emotion, Reason, and the Human Brain*, G. P Putnam 1994.

2. Antonio Battro, *Half a Brain is Enough: The Story of Nico*, (Cambridge Series in Cognitive and Perceptual Development) Cambridge University Press 2001.

3. "Is Your Brain Really Necessary?" Roger Lewin, Science, December 1980, also "The Disposable Cortex" John Lorber, Psychology Today, April 1981.

4. Michael D. Gershon, *The Second Brain: the Scientific Basis of Gut Instinct and a Groundbreaking New Understanding of Nervous Disorders of the Stomach and Intestines*, HarperCollins 1998.

5. Sir John Maddox, "The Unexpected Science to Come" Scientific American, December 1999, 281(6): 62-67.

6. Steve Pinker, *How the Mind Works*, Norton 1997.

7. John Casti, *Searching For Certainty: What Scientists Can Know About the Future*, William Morrow 1991.

8. Amit Goswami, Institute of Theoretical Science, University of Oregon at Eugene; from his article "A Quantum Explanation of Sheldrake's Morphic Resonance" found on the *Science Within Consciousness* website.

9. Roger Penrose *The Emperor's New Mind: Concerning Computers, Minds, and the laws of Physics*, forward by Martin Gardener, Oxford University Press 1989.

10. Ellen Ullman, "Programming the Post-human: Computer Science Redefines Life" Harpers Magazine, October 2002, v305 i1829 p60(11).

11. Bruce Pandolfini, *Kasparov and Deep Blue: the Historic Chess Match Between Man and Machine*, Fireside 1997.

12. Albert Borgmann, *Holding On To Reality: the Nature of Information at the Turn of the Millennium*, University of Chicago Press 1999.

13. Sir James Jeans, *The Mysterious Universe*, The MacMillan Company, Cambridge, The University Press 1932.

14. Judith Hooper and Dick Teresi, *The Three-pound Universe*, Macmillan, 1986.

15. William Irwin Thompson, *Coming Into Being*, St. Martin's Press 1996.

16. Werner Heisenberg, as quoted by Arthur Koestler in his chapter "The Perversity of Physics," from *The Roots of Coincidence*, Hutchinson and Company 1972.

17. David Bohm, quoted by Ken Wilber in "Physics, Mysticism, and the New Holographic Paradigm" Chapter Five, *Eye to Eye: The Quest for the New Paradigm*, Shambhala 1996.

Chapter 7

First introductory quote, *"In the mountains of truth..."* Nietzsche, *Maxims*.

Second introductory quote, *"The limits of reason..."* E. Randall Floyd, *Great American Mysteries: Raining Snakes, Fabled Cities of Gold, Strange Disappearances, and Other Baffling Tales*, August House 1991.

1. Nick Herbert, *Elemental Mind: Human Consciousness and the New Physics*, E. P. Dutton 1993.

2. Hooper and Teresi, *The Three-pound Universe*, Macmillan 1986.

3. Bruce H. Hinrichs, "Never Mind?" The Humanist, January-February 2002, v62 i1 page 36(3).

4. John Hick, from the book *Immortality*, edited by Paul Edwards, Macmillan 1992.

5. Walter Penfield, *The Mysteries of the Mind*, Princeton University Press 1975.

6. Marie Louise von Franz, *Projection and Re-Collection in Jungian Psychology: Reflections of the Soul*, Open Court, 1978.

7. Oliver Sacks, *Awakenings*, Doubleday 1974.

8. Concerning Phineas Gage, in *Descartes' Error: Emotion, Reason, and the Human Brain*, by Antonio Damasio, G. P. Putnam 1994.

9. George Wald, "Life and Mind in the Universe" International Journal of Quantum Chemistry; Quantum Biology Symposium, 1984, pp 1-2.

10. Karl Pribram, quoted in *The Holographic Universe*, by Michael Talbot, HarperCollins 1991.

11. Steve Jones, *The Language of Genes: Solving the Mystery of our Genetic Past, Present, and Future*, Anchor Books/Doubleday 1995.

12. J. Narby, *The Cosmic Serpent: DNA and the Origins of Knowledge*, Putnam Publishing Group 1999.

13. Ralph Estling, in the article from Skeptical Inquirer, "Obscurantism, Tyranny, and the Fallacy of Either Black or White" Sept-Oct 2004.

14. Pat Duffy Hutcheon, *Leaving the Cave: Evolutionary Naturalism in Social-scientific Thought*, Wilfrid Laurier University Press 1996.

15. Gilbert Ryle, *The Concept of Mind*, Hutchinson's University Library 1949.

16. Renee Weber, *Dialogue With Scientists and Sages*, Routledge and Kegan Paul 1986.

17. Hooper and Teresi, *The Three-pound Universe*, Macmillan 1986.

18. Kenneth T. Gallagher, *The Philosophy of Gabriel Marcel*, forward by Gabriel Marcel, Fordham University Press 1975 [c. 1962].

19. Ibid.

20. Lao Tzu, *Tao Te Ching: The Way and Its Power*, tr. Waley.

Chapter 8

Introductory quote, *"The very maximum of what one human being..."* Soren Kierkegaard, *Concluding Unscientific Postscript*, page 346, Princeton University Press 1974.

1. *We've Had a Hundred Years of Psychotherapy – And the World's Getting Worse*, James Hillman and Michael Ventura, 1992 Harper Collins.

2. H. L. Mencken, as quoted in *Redneck Nation*, by Michael Graham, Warner Books 2003.

3. Theodore Roszak, *Unfinished Animal*, Harper and Row 1975.

4. David Tacey, *Jung and the New Age*, Brunner-Routledge 2001.

5. Amy Wallace, *Sorcerer's Apprentice: My Life With Carlos Castaneda*, Frog Ltd, 2003.

6. Bernie Glassman, Tricycle Magazine, Fall 1999, "Yasutani Roshi: The Hardest Koan" Brain Victoria, with responses from Robert Aitken, Bernie Glassman, Bodhin Kjolhede, Lawrence Shainberg.

7. Robert Nozick, *The Examined Life: Philosophical Meditations*, Touchstone 1989.

8. Deepak Chopra, Esquire Magazine, "Deepak Chopra has (sniff) a cold" by Chip Brown, October 1995.

9. William Patrick Patterson, *Eating the I: a Direct Account of the Fourth Way-- The Way of Transformation in Ordinary Life*, 1992 Arete Communications.

10. Miguel de Unamuno, *Tragic Sense of Life*, tr. J. E. Crawford Flitch, Dover Publications 1954.

Chapter 9

Introductory quote, *"From here through tunneled gloom..."* Walter de la Mare, "The Railway Junction," from *The Complete Poems of Walter de la Mare*, page 295.

1. Walt Whitman, "I Sing the Body Electric," from *Leaves of Grass*, page 79.

2. Gabriel Marcel, from *The Philosophy of Gabriel Marcel*, by Kenneth T. Gallagher, Fordham University Press 1975 [c.1962].

3. F. David Peat, *Synchronicity*, Bantam Books 1987.

4. Beatrix Murrell, "Cosmic Plenum," from the *Stoa del Sol* website.

5. Stuart Chase, *The Tyranny of Words*, Harcourt Brace 1938.

6. Arthur Zajonc, *Catching the Light: the Entwined History of Light and Mind*, Bantam Books 1993.

7. David Bohm, in *Dialogue with Scientists and Sages*, Renee Weber.

8. Robert S. Ellwood, *Mysticism and Religion*, Prentice-Hall 1980.

9. Sri Aurobindo Ghose, *The Life Divine*, Sri Aurobindo Ashram, Pondicherry, India.

10. George Leonard, *The Silent Pulse: a Search for the Perfect Rhythm that Exists in Each One of Us*, Dutton 1978.

11. Wayne Hu and Martin White, "The Cosmic Symphony," *Scientific American*, February 2004, v290 i2 p44(53).

12. Fred Alan Wolf, *Taking the Quantum Leap: the New Physics for Nonscientists*, Harper and Row 1981.

13. Stephen Jay Gould, from "Biology Rules," by Niles Elderidge and Stephen Jay Gould, *Civilization 5, Oct/Nov: 86-88*.

14. William Shakespeare, *Much Ado About Nothing, Act II, Scene III*.

15. Rodney Collin, *The Theory of Celestial Influence: Man, the Universe, and Cosmic Mystery*, Weiser 1973.

16. Joachim Jeremias, Professor Emeritus of the New Testament at the University of Gottingen, from his book *The Parables of Jesus*, tr. S. H. Hooke, Scribner 1972.

17. Geoffrey Ashe, *Dawn Behind the Dawn: a Search for the Earthly Paradise*, H. Holt 1992.

18. P. D. Ouspensky, *In Search of the Miraculous*, Harcourt Brace 1949.

19. Meister Eckhart, "divine abyss" from Evelyn Underhill's *Mysticism; a Study in the Nature and Development of Man's Spiritual Consciousness*, E. P. Dutton 1930.

20. Terry Eagleton, *Against the Grain: Essays 1975-1985/Terry Eagleton*, Verso 1986.

21. Maurice Nicoll, *Psychological Commentaries*, Samuel Weiser 1996, [c. 1980 Isobel Salole].

22. Robert S. Ellwood Jr, *Mysticism and Religion*, Prentice-Hall 1980.

23. "Quantitative Analysis of High-Frequency Oscillations (80-500 Hz) Recorded in Human Epileptic Hippocampus and Entorhinal Cortex" Richard J. Staba, Charles L. Wilson, Anatol Bragin, Itzhak Fried, and Jerome Engel, Jr. *Journal of Neurophysiology, October 2002*.

24. Shakespeare, *Macbeth*.

Chapter 10

First introductory quote, *"But what ear can catch the mysterious..."* Manuel Jose Othon, *Elegy*.

1. The biofeedback work of Michael Tansey, referred to in *A Symphony in the Brain: the Evolution of the New Brainwave Biofeedback* by Jim Robbins, Atlantic Monthly Press, 2000.

2. Tiziano Terzani, *A Fortune Teller Told Me: Earthbound Travels in the Far East*, Harmony Books 1997.

3. Brain Swimme, in an interview with Renee Lertzmann, "Brain Swimme on the Story of the Universe," *The Sun, May 2001*.

4. "Why beholdest the mote..." Matt 7:3.

5. "And he cometh unto the disciples..." Matt 26:40.

6. C. G. Jung, *CW 9i* page 160.

7. Thomas J. McFarlane, in an online article from the website www.integralscience.org, "Quantum Physics, Depth Psychology, and Beyond," June 21, 2000.

8. Phillip Wheelwright, *The Burning Fountain*, Indiana University Press 1954.

9. Ira Progoff, *Jung, Synchronicity, and Human Destiny*, Julian Press 1973.

10. F. David Peat, *Synchronicity*, Bantam Books 1987.

11. William Patrick Patterson, *Eating the I*, Arete Communications 1992.

12. Michael Talbot, *Mysticism and the New Physics*, Arkana 1992.

13. Mathew 6:25, 28, 29, 34. *King James Bible.*

14. Daisetz Teitaro Suzuki, *The Awakening of Zen*, edited by Christmas Humphreys, Shambhala 2000.

15. Edmund Burke, "An Appeal From the New to the Old Whigs, in Consequence of some Late Discussions in Parliament, Relative to the Reflections of the French Revolution," New York, 1791, from *Eighteenth Century Collections Online*, Gale Group, Document #CW3307693647.

16. William Butler Yeats, "Anima Hominis," from *Essays, New and Revised Edition*, Macmillan 1924.

Chapter 11

First introductory quote, *"As a man is, so he sees."* William Blake, in a letter to the Rev. Dr. Trusler.

1. John Horgan, *The End of Science: Facing the Limits of Knowledge in the Twilight of the Scientific Age*, Addison-Wesley 1996.

2. Etienne Gilson, *The Unity of Philosophical Experience*, C. Scribner's Sons 1937.

3. Carlos Castaneda quoting Don Juan in an interview with Sam Keen, "Seeing Castaneda, *Psychology Today*, 1972.

4. Robert Avens, *The New Gnosis: Heidegger, Hillman, and Angels*, Spring Publications 1984.

5. William Kluback, *Sri Aurobindo Ghose: the Dweller in the Land of Silence*, P. Lang 2001.

6. Martin Heidegger, *What is Philosophy?*, tr. with intro. By William Kluback and Jean T. Wilde, Twayne Publishing 1958.

7. Mortimer Adler, in *A Modern Introduction to Philosophy: Readings from Classical and Contemporary Sources*, edited by Paul Edwards and Arthur Pap, Free Press 1957.

8. *The Philosophy of Gabriel Marcel*, Kenneth Gallagher, Fordham University Press 1975 [c. 1962].

9. A. N. Whitehead, *Modes of Thought*.

10. Cornelius Verhoeven, *The Philosophy of Wonder*, Macmillan 1972.

11. Jose Ortega y Gasset, concerning perplexity, *Man and Crisis*, tr. Mildred Adams, Norton 1958.

12. David Bodanis, *The Secret House: 24 Hours in the Strange and Unexplained World in Which We Spend Our Nights and Days*, Simon and Schuster 1986.

13. William Blake, *The Marriage of Heaven and Hell*.

14. Hooper and Teresi, *The Three-pound Universe,* Macmillan 1986.

15. Jurij Moskvitin, *Essay on the Origin of Thought*, Ohio University Press 1974.

16. Lawrence LeShan and Henry Margenau, *Einstein's Space, Van Gogh's Sky*, Macmillan 1983.

17. Arthur Zajonc, *Catching the Light: the Entwined History of Light and Mind*, Bantam Books 1993.

18. *The Philosophy of Gabriel Marcel*, Kenneth Gallagher, Fordham University Press 1975 [1962].

Chapter 12

First introductory quote, *"Truth is the precious harvest..."* George Eliot, *Felix Holt the Radical.*

1. Nathan A. Scott Jr., *The Poetics of Belief: Studies in Coleridge, Arnold, Pater, Santayana, and Heidegger*, University of North Carolina Press 1985.

2. William Kluback, *Sri Aurobindo Ghose: the Dweller in the Land of Silence*, P. Lang 2001.

3. Aurobindo, *The Future Evolution of Man: The Divine Life Upon the Earth.*

4. Gregory Chaitin, "The Limits of Mathematics," July 23, 1994.

5. Ernst Behler, *Confrontations: Derrida/Heidegger/Nietzsche*, Stanford University Press 1991.

6. Alain de Botton, *The Consolations of Philosophy*, Pantheon Books 2000.

7. Stanley Fish, *The Stanley Fish Reader*, edited by H. Aram Veeser, Blackwell Publishers 1999.

8. William Barrett, *Irrational Man: A Study in Existential Philosophy*, Doubleday 1958.

9. William Barrett, *Irrational Man*, Chapter 9, "Heidegger."

10. Robert Avens, *The New Gnosis: Heidegger, Hillman, and Angels*, Spring Publications 1984.

11. Arthur Zajonc, *Catching the Light: the Entwined History of Light and Mind*, Bantam Books 1993.

12. Blaise Pascal, *Pensees, Section III*: "Of the Necessity of the Wager," 211.

13. Nicholas Berdyaev, *The Realm of Spirit and the Realm of Caesar*, tr. Donald A. Lowrie, Greenwood Press 1975.

14. William Barrett, *Irrational Man: A Study in Existential Philosophy*, Anchor Books: Doubleday 1958.

15. Albert Borgmann, *Holding on to Reality: the Nature of Information at the Turn of the Millennium*, University of Chicago Press 1999.

16. Ibid.

17. Martin Heidegger, "Building Dwelling Thinking," from *Poetry, Language, Thought*, tr. Albert Hofstadter, Harper Colophon 1971.

18. John McWhorther, *The Power of Babel: the Natural History of Language*, W. H. Freeman 2001.

19. Edward Said, *Reflections on Exile and Other Essays*, Harvard University Press 2000.

20. D. T. Suzuki, *An Introduction to Zen Buddhism*, Chapter 5, "Zen a Higher Affirmation," page 69, Grove Press 1964.

21. Philip Davis and Reuben Hersh, *Descartes' Dream: the World According to Mathematics*, Harcourt Brace Jovanovich 1986.

22. George Lakeoff and Mark Johnson, *Metaphors We Live By*, University of Chicago Press 1980.

23. Phillip Wheelwright, *The Burning Fountain*, Indiana University Press 1954.

24. Colin Turbayne, *Metaphors for the Mind: the Creative Mind and its Origins*, University of South Carolina Press 1991.

25. Lawrence LeShan and Henry Margenau, *Einstein's Space and Van Gogh's Sky: Physical Reality and Beyond*, Macmillan 1982.

26. Terry Eagleton, *The Idea of Culture*, Blackwell 2000.

27. Daniel M. Wegner, *White Bears and Other Unwanted Thoughts: Suppression, Obsession, and the Psychology of Mental Control*, Viking 1986.

28. C. G. Jung, "On Psychic Energy," (1928), *CW8: The Structure and Dynamics of the Psyche*, p.111.

29. Jose Ortega y Gasset, *Psychological Investigations*, tr. Jose Garcia-Gomez, Norton 1984.

30. Danah Zohar, *The Quantum Self*, Morrow 1990.

31. Evan Harris Walker, *Physics of Consciousness: Quantum Minds and the Meaning of Life*, Perseus Books 2000.

32. Victor S. Johnson, *Why We Feel: The Science of Human Emotions*, Perseus Books 1999.

Chapter 13

Introductory quote, Romans 12:2, King James Bible, World Publishing Company.

1. Wade Clark Roof, *The Spiritual Marketplace: Baby-boomers and the Remaking of American Religion*, Princeton University Press 1999.

2. Donald Griffin, *Animal Minds: Beyond Cognition to Consciousness*, University of Chicago Press 2001.

3. Thomas Mann, *Doctor Faustus*, tr. Helen Lowe-Porter, Everyman's Library 1992.

4. James Henry Breasted, *The Dawn of Conscience*, 1933, Scribner 1968.

5. Geoffrey Ashe, *Dawn Behind the Dawn: a Search for the Earthly Paradise*, H. Holt 1992.

6. David M. Rohl, *Pharaohs and Kings: A Biblical Quest*, Crown Publishers 1995.

7. Jurij Moskvitin, *The Quest for the Origins of Language,* as referred to by Gary Lachman in his book *The Secret History of Consciousness*, Lindisfarne Books 2003.

8. Cecil Maurice Bowra, *The Greek Experience*, World Publishing Company 1958.

9. "Nabakov on Kafka" from the original lectures by Vladimir Nabokov, interestingly rendered in the VHS *"Understanding the Metamorphosis: Nabokov on Kafka"* starring Christopher Plummer as Nabokov (1990 and 1999).

10. Robin Lane Fox, *Pagans and Christians,* Knopf 1988.

11. Monica Sjoo and Barbara Mor, *The Great Cosmic Mother: Rediscovering the Religion of the Earth*, Harper 1991.

12. Elinor W. Gandon, *The Once and Future Goddess: A Symbol for our Time*, Harper and Row 1989.

13. Phyllis Boswell Moore, *No Other Gods: An Interpretation of the Biblical Myth for a Transbiblical Age*, Chiron Publications 1992.

14. Euripides, from *Hippolytus*, 420 BC, tr. by E. P. Coleridge, *http://etext.library.adelaide.edu.au*, eBooks@Adelaide 2004.

15. Edward Edinger, *Ego and Archetype*, Shambhala, 1992.

16. James N. Powell, *The Tao of Symbols: How to Transcend the Limits of our Symbolism*, Quill 1982.

17. Giorgio de Santillana and Hertha von Dechend, *Hamlet's Mill: an Essay on Myth and the Frame of Time*, Gambit 1969.

18. Nicolas Berdyaev, *The Realm of Spirit and the Realm of Caesar,* tr. Donald A Lowrie, Greenwood Press 1975.

Chapter 14

1. Charles Davis, *Temptations of Religion*, Harper and Row 1974.

2. Hugh Anderson, *Jesus and Christian Origins; a Commentary on Modern Viewpoints*, Oxford University Press 1964.

3. Arthur Evans, *The God of Ecstasy: Sex Roles and the Madness of Dionysos*, St Martin's Press 1988.

4. Tim Callahan, *Secret Origins of the Bible*, Millennium Press 2002.

5. Petronius Arbiter, *The Satyricon*, tr. William Burnaby, "Project Gutenberg."

6. Bart D. Ehrman, *Lost Scriptures: Books That Did Not Make It Into the New Testament*, Oxford University Press 2003.

7. Thomas Aquinas, *Summa Theologica*, Benzinger Bros. Edition, 1947, tr. by 'The Fathers of the English Dominican Province."

8. Tim Callahan, *Secret Origins of the Bible*, Millennium Press 2002

9. John Bunyan, *The Pilgrim's Progress*, P. F. Collier and Son 1909.

10. Burton L. Mack, *The Lost Gospel: the Book of Q and Christian Origins*, Harper 1993.

11. Phillip Wheelwright, *The Burning Fountain*, Indiana University Press 1954.

12. Octavio Paz, *Children of the Mire*, tr. Rachel Phillips, Harvard University Press 1974.

13. Peter Novak, *The Division of Consciousness: the Secret Afterlife of the Human Psyche*, Hampton Roads 1997.

14. Julian Marias, from his book *Miguel de Unamuno*, tr, by Frances M. Lopez-Morillas, Harvard University Press 1966.

15. *"Gleanings from the writings of Mahatma Gandhi bearing on God, God-realization and the Godly Way,"* by M. K. Gandhi, compiled by R. K. Prabhu, Navajivan Publishing House 1955.

16. Richard Elliot Friedman, *Who Wrote the Bible*, Prentice-Hall 1987.

17. Jacques Waardenburg, from his chapter "Symbolic Aspects of Myth," in *Myth, Symbol, and Reality*, edited by Alan M. Olson, University of Notre Dame Press 1980.

18. Aurobindo, *The Life Divine*, Sri Aurobindo Ashram, Pondicherry, India.

19. William Irwin Thompson, *Coming Into Being*, St. Martin's Press 1996.

20. James Hillman, *Archetypal Psychology: A Brief Account*, "Part One, 7. Soul Making" Spring Publications 1983.

21. William Irwin Thompson, *Coming Into Being*, St. Martin's Press 1996.

22. Colin Turbayne, *Metaphors for the Mind: the Creative Mind and Its Origins*, University of South Carolina Press 1991.

23. Karl Jaspers, "Myth and Religion," from *Myth and Christianity: An Inquiry Into the Possibility of Religion Without Myth*, The Noonday Press 1958.

24. P. D. Ouspensky, *The Symbolism of the Tarot*, tr. A. L. Pogossky 1913.

25. Anthony Storr, *Churchill's Black Dog, Kafka's Mice, and Other Phenomena of the Human Mind*, Grove Press 1988.

26. Eugene Pascal, *Jung to Live By: A Guide to the Practical Application of Jungian Principles for Everyday Life*, Warner Books 1992.

27. Rodney Collin, *The Theory of Celestial Influence: Man, the Universe, and Cosmic Mystery*, Wieser 1973.

28. Ibid.

29. Jurij Moskvitin, *Essays on the Origins of Thought*, Ohio University Press 1974.

30. Arthur Zajonc, *Catching the Light: the Entwined History of Light and Mind*, Bantam Books 1993.

31. Rudy Rucker, *Mind Tools*, Houghton Mifflin 1987.

32. Remo Roth, *The Return of the World Soul: Wolfgang Pauli, Carl Jung and the Challenge of the Unified Psychophysical Reality*, Ch. 5 "The Seal of Solomon and the Unsolved Problem of Psyche's Complimentary Incarnation," from the website *www.psychovision.ch*.

33. James N. Powell, *The Tao of Symbols: How to Transcend the Limits of Our Symbolism*, Quill 1982.

34. *Theatrum Chemicum Britannicum* edited by Elias Ashmole, a reprint of the London edition 1652, with a new introduction by Allen G. Debus, Johnson Reprint Corporation 1967.

35. Jeremy Narby, *The Cosmic Serpent: DNA and the Origins of Knowledge*, Putnam Publishing Group 1999.

36. Aurobindo, *The Mind Of Light: the Supramental Manifestation Upon Earth*, Robert McDermott, National Book Network 2004.

37. *King James Bible*, Mark 8:34.

38. Bill McKibben, "The Christian Paradox" *Harper's*, August 2005.

39. *King James Bible*, Proverbs 8:17.

40. Aurobindo, *The Live Divine*, Sri Aurobindo Ashram, Pondicherry, India.

41. Maimonides, *The Laws and Basic Principles of the Torah,* tr. Immanuel M. O' Levy 1993.

42. Satprem, *Sri Aurobindo Or the Adventure of Consciousness*, tr, from the French by Tehmi, Harper and Row 1968.

Chapter 15

Introductory quote: *Alejandra Pizarnik: A Profile,* edited by Frank Graziano, tr. Suzanne Jill Levine, Logbridge-Rhodes, 1987.

1. *The Legacy of Solomon Asche: Essays in Cognition and Social Psychology,* edited by Irvin Rock, L. Erlbaum Associates 1990.

2. Tim LaHaye and David Noebel, *Mind Siege: The Battle for Truth in the New Millennium,* World Publications 2000.

3. Gregory of Nyssa, of the Cappadocian Fathers, Eastern Orthodox tradition.

4. Michael Talbot, *Mysticism and the New Physics,* Arkana 1992.

5. Lawrence M. Krauss, *Fear of Physics: a Guide for the Perplexed,* Basic Books 1993.

6. David Hilbert, (1862-1943), quoted in J. R. Newman's (ed) *The World of Mathematics,* Simon and Schuster 1956.

7. Rudy Rucker, *Infinity and the Mind,* Birkhäuser 1982.

8. Robert Romanyshyn, *Mirror and Metaphor: Images and Stories of Psychological Life,* Lightning Source 2001.

9. Hans-Georg Gadamer, *The Beginning of Philosophy,* 1998, tr. Rod Coltman, Continuum 1998.

10. Joseph Chilton Pearce, *Exploring the Crack in the Cosmic Egg: Split Minds and Meta Realities – An Investigation of Non Ordinary Reality,* Pocket Books 1974.

11. F. David Peat, *Einstein's Moon: Bell's Theorem and the Curious Quest for Quantum Reality,* Contemporary Books 1990.

12. Géza Szamosi, *The Twin Dimensions: Inventing Time and Space,* McGraw Hill Book Company 1986.

13. A. H. Almaas, *Essence with The Elixer of Enlightenment: the Diamond Approach to Inner Realization (two books in one volume),* Samuel Weiser 1986.

14. Danah Zohar, *Quantum Self: Human Nature and Consciousness Defined by the New Physics*, William Morrow and Company 1990.

To order a copy of this book,
go to www.PlumBell.com

Or, if you prefer, copy the
order form on the next page,
and mail it with your check
or money order.

ORDER FORM

I want _____ copies pf PUSHING ULTIMATES, price $21.50 plus $1.97 shipping = $23.47 each. Canadian orders are $5.00 more, and must be accompanied by a postal order in US funds.

My check or money order for _____ is enclosed.

Name _____

Organization _____

Address _____

*City/State/Zip*_____

Phone _____

Email _____

PlumBell Publishing
P.O. Box 640
Eureka, CA 95501

Please allow 10 days to two weeks
for delivery